# WHY BE MORAL?

## KAI NIELSEN

PROMETHEUS BOOKS • BUFFALO, NEW YORK

For Jocelyne Couture, again

Published 1989 by Prometheus Books
700 East Amherst Street, Buffalo, New York 14215

Copyright © 1989 by Kai Nielsen

Library of Congress Cataloging-in-Publication Data

NIELSEN, KAI, 1926–
    Why be moral? / by Kai Nielsen.
        p.      cm.
    ISBN 0-87975-519-9
    1. Ethics. I. Title.
BJ1012.N54      1989
170—dc 19                                                                89-3524
                                                                              CIP

Printed in the United States of America

# Contents

6   Contents

# Introduction

# Skepticism Over Morals

The sources of skepticism over morals are varied. There is skepticism rooted in epistemological considerations. But there is also ontological skepticism over the place of values in the world of fact and there is a nonepistemological and nonontological skepticism over morals: a skepticism rooted in moral reflection itself. It is important to recognize that this last skepticism is not rooted in epistemological or ontological skepticism or at least it is not directly and obviously (if at all) rooted in these forms of skepticism. It emerges from our very reflection about moral claims themselves, from various moral arguments and from the variety of, and the intractable conflict between, ethical theories themselves, rather than from some general epistemological theses or assumptions. It does not even emerge from ontological theses about the place of value in the world of fact.

Epistemological skepticism over morals is rooted in general philosophical theses concerning what can be the case and what it is possible to know or reasonably believe and in theses concerning what moral beliefs and conceptions really are. In a way it is *external* to morality rather than *internal* and it employs certain contestable models of what knowledge can be. It remains to be seen whether it or some other form of skepticism—perhaps the more direct "less philosophical" skepticism—is the more powerful form.

However, such considerations notwithstanding, I am going to focus here on epistemological skepticism over morals. I should, however, initially note that some philosophers believe that nonepistemological skepticism, if pushed hard, turns out to be dependent on such an epistemologically based skepticism. Perhaps that is enough to motivate focusing on it and putting aside non-epistemological and non-ontological skepticism for the nonce, though it is still my hunch that that is the most significant form.

First appeared in *Queen's Quarterly*, 88, no. 1. (Spring 1981): 109–114.

Epistemological skepticism over morals has its classic expression in David Hume (1711-1776) and Francis Hutcheson (1694-1746).[1] In trying to see what is at issue here, it is useful to compare and follow out the analogy between "moral qualities" and secondary qualities like that of color.

To say that a pencil is yellow is to say that it will cause an impression of yellow when light-rays from it stimulate a certain kind of sense organ. An animal with different sense organs might well see the pencil as having a different color or no color at all. Analogously, Hume and Hutcheson claim that to say something is good—say caring for a friend who is in a hopeless state of despair—is to say that such acts arouse in beings with certain predispositions an emotion of approval. The moral quality, like a secondary quality, is not something inherent in the act but in reality is simply a feeling in a person with a certain predisposition. We tend to think it is something more but in that we are here simply, though understandably, confused. And indeed it is natural enough to wish for moral qualities which are somehow just there to be discovered and accepted as part of the "furniture of universe." But belief in such an objectivity is belief in a myth. Moral qualities aren't like that. They are no more inherent in the object than are secondary qualities.

Moral judgments, as Hume puts it, do not ascribe a quality or relation to the thing so judged, but express a sentiment in the breast of the person so judging. In that way they are essentially a matter of feeling rather than of knowledge or some "dictate of reason." Philosophers, such as Hutcheson and Hume, who gave such an account of morality in terms of sentiments, were jointly referred to as the moral sense school. What they clearly give us to understand is that for a being with a different moral sense something quite different would be judged to be right or wrong, just as someone with a rather different sensory apparatus would not perceive the pencil to be yellow. And for a neutral observer of the actual—someone or something which thought and observed but had no affective predispositions at all and thus no moral sense (say a computer)—nothing would be felt or acknowledged by him or it to be right or wrong. Indeed such a being would have, and indeed could have, no understanding of right or wrong, though such a being could, of course, recognize in others various predispositions to approve or disapprove of different things. But, to such a being, nothing would or could appear to be right or wrong, good or bad, desirable or undesirable. Hume is not just making the claim that what is good and evil *depends* on what is approved of or disapproved of, but that that is all there is to it. So-called moral beliefs just are tendencies to approve or disapprove of certain things and actions.

Hume and Hutcheson, it is important to understand, thought that in a very general way all human beings had the same moral sense. Though they give it different cultural phrasings, all human beings, or at least all statistically normal humans in all cultures, agree in certain of their fundamental approvals and disapprovals. They could have been different in this respect, but, as a matter of fact, they are not. There is a sufficient *de facto* overlap in what people approve of or disapprove of to justify rejecting what philosophers have called *cultural relativism,* namely the sociological or anthropological thesis that even fundamental moral beliefs differ between cultures.

However, as John Balguy (1686-1748), a contemporary critic of Hutcheson and Hume, trenchantly observed, the falsity of cultural relativism still leaves the moral sense theorist with a not inconsiderable difficulty.[2] Indeed it poses a problem for anyone who reflects on the foundations of moral belief and is tempted to accept the underlying epistemological foundations of the classical empiricists. Let us suppose, Balguy remarks, that there is a God (Balguy's essential point doesn't require such an assumption but it makes the stating of this point less cumbersome). Balguy then asks moral sense theorists whether God had a reason for endowing human beings with the moral sense they have rather than endowing them instead with a moral sense which made them approve of cruelty and disapprove of kindness. If God had a *reason* for endowing us with the moral sense we have, then that reason is a reason quite apart from any human disposition to prefer kindness to cruelty.[3] After all, God sees things as they are. He couldn't, being God, not see things as they are. But, if even God has *no* reason, as moral sense theorists must believe, for preferring kindness to cruelty, then it would seem that moral beliefs can have no objective validity. It just *happens to be the case* that human beings approve or disapprove of certain things. If they came to approve and disapprove of quite different sorts of things, that could not constitute a mistake or error on their part or any failure in moral understanding. And if some lone iconoclast, some cultural rebel, such as Nietzsche or Stirner or Dostoevsky's undergroundling, came to approve or disapprove of still different things, that too could not constitute an error or a mistake on his part. They just have a different moral sense. And we could not, with any nonideological force, claim that they were mistaken.

If such an epistemological account of moral questions and the "ground" they give us for moral understanding is correct, this shows, Balguy claims, that then there can be no moral knowledge. Indeed it not only undermines the very possibility that moral beliefs could be "dictates of reason" or somehow have a "rational foundation," it in effect shows, as well, that the "moral sense school" cannot even establish that moral claims can have a reasonable rationale. This consequence Balguy took to be sufficient to show that moral sense theories must be inadequate in their very root conceptions. He took it as an evident *reductio* of such an account. But, as is frequently the case with such *reductio* arguments, they can be quite indecisive for others might think that a clear headed, thoroughly non-evasive person should just accept such consequences.

There are, however, a number of objections that have been made to such an epistemological skepticism over morals. Many of them also take the form of attempted *reductio* arguments of one form or another. Perhaps, in spite of what I said above about the indecisiveness of *reductio* arguments, taken together they have some reasonable force. We will look at some of these arguments and trace out some responses that skeptics can reasonably make to them.

If a human being or group of human beings came to exist who had a set of predispositions such that they did not at all disapprove of activities characteristic of the Roman Circus—the slaughter of thousands of animals simply for amusement and the feeding of people to the lions and the like— then, if we were moral sense theorists, while we would call such people cruel and they would, in turn, call us squeamish, there could be no objective or rational ground for saying that one view was right and the other wrong. But, it will be responded, that is monstrous and absurd, so such a view of morality must be mistaken. When we clearly see the implications of a moral sense view, we will come to recognize that it is absurd. And, plainly, we will also see that a moral skepticism based on such a mistaken moral epistemology must also be mistaken.

To this argument it is natural enough to respond that it begs the question. The emotive epithets "monstrous" and "absurd" merely show what such a skepticism would surely predict, namely that these are things about which people holding what we regard as the culturally standard moral views happen to have very strong feelings. That is, they are some of the things they happen to most deeply approve and disapprove of. Since moral views, on such an account, are simply such strong feelings, it is hardly surprising that they will be strongly felt.

If, alternatively, we say that the "moral view" of the proponent of cruelty is absurd and monstrous because it is *irrational,* then we need to be able to specify what mistake in reasoning our cruel man must have made. What inductive or deductive mistake must he have made? What faulty observations or what confused metaphysical beliefs must be his? It is a useful exercise to try to specify what mistakes of that sort he must have made. It does not appear, at least, to be the case that there must have been some. It is also the case that it is certainly possible that he could be *efficiently* cruel, taking the most efficient means to achieve his ends, and thus satisfying another mark of what, at least on the conventional view, it is to be a rational person. (On such a view, a rational person will take the most efficient means to achieve whatever ends he has, but there is no way of establishing the rationality or irrationality of the ends themselves.[4]) In short, our cruel man need make no intellectual mistake and he could very well be an efficient and prudent maximizer of his own ends. Claims of irrationality here may very well be little more than the utilizing of emotive language to try to discredit a position one cannot show to be mistaken.

It is important to recognize that such an epistemological skeptic is not saying that nothing is really right or wrong, good or bad. He is not repudiating his own moral commitments. (That is one of the reasons why he is perhaps better called a subjectivist than a skeptic.) Rather, he is giving a theoretical account, which he believes to be the best account, of what they are, namely distinctive feelings, and he is rejecting another theoretical view, namely the *objectivist* view that *nothing is really right* or *wrong unless it is objectively right or wrong*. When he encounters others who have different actual moral beliefs than his own, he, in accordance with his own theory, will take that to be a case of people having different deeply entrenched feelings. But, faced with such diversity of reaction, he need, no more than the objectivist, abandon or even at all discount his own moral convictions. He will of course realize that he is just pitting feelings against feelings. However, since for him talk of moral truth or objectivity is a piece of mythology, he need not at all try to discount his most deeply embedded feelings. He doesn't believe for one moment that if moral beliefs are discovered to be simply feelings and nothing more, they therefore should be discounted. Why should he repudiate what he deeply feels? For him to say "x is wrong" is to say "I disapprove of x and I want you to do so as well" and it is, as well, to give to understand that there is no other coherent sense of wrong which entitles people to say: "But in that case x cannot really be wrong." That is simply, without reason, to insist on the objectivist's account.

In returning to a defense of such a view in the first quarter of the twentieth century, Edward Westermarck clearly and rightly had a sense that he was sailing against the wind, that this skeptical view was the iconoclastic, challenging view of the scrutinizing moral consciousness, as he called it.[5] By now the dialectics of the Enlightenment have carried us to a different stage, or at least in a different direction, and something like this subjectivist view is, culturally speaking, the reigning orthodoxy among educated Westerners. (There is not, however, anything like such a reigning orthodoxy among philosophers, though subjectivism does have a strong representation.[6]) What surely needs to be done, if indeed it can be done, by the opponent of subjectivism is to show how it is that fundamental moral claims could be true and known to be true, how it is, if it is, that the subjectivist's rather standard account of rationality and reasons for action is mistaken and what it would be like, independently of pro-or-con attitudes, to show that there are some fundamental moral beliefs, such as the belief that all human beings should be treated with equal respect and concern, which could be shown to be such that any rational, properly informed human being must be committed to them. Subjectivists from Hume and Hutcheson to Westermarck and J. L. Mackie have denied that there can be such a justification of moral beliefs. Cultural posturing notwithstanding, do we know or have good grounds for believing they are mistaken?

## NOTES

1. David Hume, *Treatise of Human Nature* (London, 1739–40) and *Enquiry Concerning the Principles of Morals* (London, 1751); Francis Hutcheson, *An Inquiry into the Original of Our Ideas of Beauty and Virtue* (London, 1725) and *Essay on the Nature and Conduct of the Passions and Affections with Illustrations Upon the Moral Sense* (London, 1728).

2. John Balguy, *Foundation of Moral Goodness* (London, 1728-9).

3. Note the distinctive application here of an argument that goes back to Plato's *Euthyphro*.

4. I have raised questions about this conception of rationality in my "Distrusting Reason," *Ethics*, 86 (July, 1975) and in my "True Needs, Rationality and Emancipation," in *Human Needs and Politics*, Ross Fitzgerald (ed.), (London: Pergamon, 1977).

5. This comes out clearly in the very first chapter of his *Origin and Development of the Moral Ideas*, 2 vols. (London, 1906) as well as in his later *Ethical Relativity* (London, 1932). In former note particularly the following passages in the first volume: pp. 12, 98, 119-120, 122-124, 131, 160-161, 168, 182, 201-202, 214-235, 244, 247-248, 283-284, 300 and 312-313. In the second volume: pp. 178-79, 226-228, 738 and 741-746 deserve notice as do pp. 46-47, 76-77, 112, 160-162, 146-147, 200, 217 and 235 in *Ethical Relativity*.

6. D. H. Monro, *Empiricism and Ethics* (Cambridge, 1967); J. L. Mackie, *Ethics: Inventing Right and Wrong* (New York, 1977) and Gilbert Harman, *The Nature of Morality* (New York, 1977).

# 1

# Why There Is a Problem about Ethics
## Reflections on the Is and the Ought

I

Why should there be such extensive perplexity over morals? Why should so
many thoughtful people—including people with all the moral passion of a
Russell, Camus or Sartre—be so skeptical about the objectivity and rational
justifiability of morality? Why should so many people feel driven, in spite
of their very strong moral feelings, toward some form of ethical skepticism,
relativism, or subjectivism? Is it just that so many honest, informed, intelligent and reflective people suffer from some reasonably simple logical
confusions?

It seems to me thoroughly implausible to suggest that. Rather I think
the sources for skepticism over the objectivity of morals are very deep and
very natural and very much need to be carefully faced and non-evasively met—
if indeed they can be met at all. To do this we will first need carefully to
note what this challenge comes to when it is intelligent and informed. I will
try here to specify and bring out the force of one—but only one—very crucial
facet of this challenge and then show that it does not easily or perhaps even
at all collapse before the fashionable and in the main correct criticisms of
those popular forms of subjectivism which have been labelled non-cognitivism
and emotivism.

Let us begin by asking whether we have good grounds for believing that
there are objective and indeed sound procedures for justifying one moral code
as distinct from another or one set of moral judgments as distinct from an-

First published in *Danish Yearbook of Philosophy*, volume 15 (Copenhagen, 1978), pp. 69–96. Reprinted
by permission of the publisher.

other when there is a conflict between different moral codes or when they are incommensurable. There is in fact a vast array of methods used to rationalize moral claims. Why should we suppose that only one or some favored few or indeed any of them are correct? What reason have we to believe that there is or even can be such a correct method? It may well be the case that we are not in a position to claim that many or all of these procedures are equally sound or equally justified, for, after all, that would imply that such a claim could itself be made out and this itself would at least appear to imply just the kind of criteria for assessing moral reasoning and comparing its varieties that we seem at least not to have. Though we are in no position to assert that two moral codes are or even may be equally sound or equally justified, we are in no position to deny it either. We are left with the nagging feeling that—our wishes to the contrary notwithstanding—this or something rather like it may be so or at least, and perhaps more plainly, it may be so for many conflicting or incommensurable moral codes. So—if we are to avoid being evasive—we need to consider the plausibility of moral skepticism and some form of subjectivism in which that skepticism is rooted.

Ethical skeptics maintain that no one can ever say with any justification that something is good or bad, right or wrong. Some actions may indeed be right and others wrong but there is no way of knowing which they are. Subjectivism has taken many forms, some of which are easily refutable, but in its more sophisticated forms it is a very difficult customer indeed. A form which deserves careful attention can be succinctly stated as follows:

> There is no way of rationally resolving *fundamental* moral disputes, for *fundamental* moral judgments or *ultimate* moral principles cannot correctly be said to be true or false independently of the attitudes of at least some people.

If there is to be any way of rationally justifying the institution of morality, this variety of subjectivism needs to be squarely met and refuted. Is such a subjectivist claim justified? We find an assortment of contemporary philosophers with very different philosophical orientations accepting something very much like this. Westermarck and Hägerström in Scandinavia, Russell and Ayer in England, and—for all their fierce love of justice—Camus and Sartre in France, all accept—though often reluctantly and ambivalently—some such account of morality. What should be said about such a claim?

I think we can grasp something of the central rationale behind such a subjectivism if we will examine some of the claims of the Swedish philosopher Axel Hägerström. In his important inaugural lecture "On the Truth of Moral Propositions," Hägerström first points to some of the persuasive and deep *de facto* cultural variabilities and conflicts in ethical belief that exist between people placed differently in cultural and historical time and space.[1] Taken by themselves, as Hägerström was well aware, such considerations would not constitute a very serious threat to the claim that some moral beliefs are objective. But when the individual discovers that there are often such conflicts within contemporary society—indeed even between culturally homogeneous and reflective individuals—and when he further discovers such conflicts within himself and can find no means of resolving them, then he begins (if he is rational) to question the objectivity of moral beliefs.

Confronted with such conflicts in our actual moral valuations "we are led," Hägerström tells us, "unavoidably to the question, which is the right? What is the standard by which we may measure the correctness of different views?" Our moral *consciousness* is indeed close at hand, but its counsel is divided and often ambiguous, and we have made the horrible discovery, that persons, whom we have every reason to believe are equally conscientious, equally non-evasive, and equally honest, often have very different moral beliefs. In following their own conscience they are often guided in very different ways. We are led, Hägerström remarks, to the unwelcome suspicion that "our conceptions of right and wrong" may "actually be only mocking appearances."[2]

This, Hägerström reminds us, raises a question of truth or falsity. Is this so or isn't it? Are our moral conceptions subjective, in the way I have defined 'subjective', or are they not? This is not itself a *moral* matter but is a matter about what is the case. Hägerström remarks, in a manner that someone like Habermas or Horkheimer would surely regard as scientistic, "Naturally, a question of truth must be answered in a scientific way. Therefore all other interests than the desire for truth must be suppressed and any objective grounds must be adduced. It will not do to view such an assumption *a priori* as absurd, simply because it may not agree with certain interests, regardless of how significant they are."[3] We have, if we are humane, certain emancipatory interests which are such that a negative answer is required to serve those interests—interests which are very precious to us—but nonetheless what is at issue is a theoretical matter (albeit a theoretical matter which is most relevant to our practical interests) and the question is one of truth about what is and is not the case.

There are several ways that one might object to Hägerström's remarks here. One might object to his contention that all questions of truth are scientific questions. There are truths of logic and perhaps there are commonsensical truths, e.g., "Bored wives tend to have affairs." There could perhaps even be moral truths, e.g., "Smith ought to be deposed." Hägerström would, I think, cover truths of logic and what I have called commonsensical truths, under the notion of a scientific way of ascertaining something, e.g., by logical analysis and/or by careful observation either with or without theory construction. As for 'moral truth', he argues that there is no special sense of 'moral truth'. If his argument can be shown to be correct here, then his claim that "a question of truth must be answered in a scientific way" will be seen to be quite unexceptionable.

However, at this juncture there is another important objection to Häger-ström's account which should be aired. It could be argued that Hägerström here is in effect moralizing in a way that could only be warranted if some objective view of morality were true. He tells us that "all other interests than the desire for truth must be suppressed and only objective grounds must be adduced."[4] But how does this become a categorical imperative? Whence comes the objective moral force of those two 'musts' in that statement of Häger-ström's? His judgment is indeed itself a moral judgment and, it might be argued, a stern puritanical one at that. But why should one accept it if one doesn't want to? If our conceptions of right or wrong are "only mocking appearances," then I can have no more, and no less, reason for accepting it than any other moral view.

It is the *manner* here and not the *matter* that leads us into puzzlement. Hägerström suffers from ellipsis and from dramatizing a point rather than from inconsistency. His point put in an antiseptic manner is simply this: whether moral claims are objective or subjective is a question of fact. As such its truth is determinable only in a scientific way. Thus, if *we want* to know what is so here, i.e. whether subjectivism is true, we must suppress all other inter-ests except the desire to discover the truth and consider only the objective evidence for or against subjectivism. This is a modest hypothetical imper-ative and, if the first two premises are true—and it is at least reasonable to believe they are true—we have here what most certainly appears to be a sound argument. But sound or not, there is nothing at all invalid or even paradoxical about Hägerström's argument here.

At this point, Hägerström asks a question, which by now is well-known among analytic philosophers, but when he gave his lecture in 1911 it had never explicitly and self-consciously been asked before. What is involved is this: one might argue that while subjectivism (a *theory* about ethics) is true, no moral proposition itself is true or false or even capable of being true or false, anymore than is 'Close the door' or 'Would that it were snowing'. Moreover, if moral propositions can be neither true nor false, then they can-not serve as premises in arguments and thus it is logically impossible for there to be valid moral arguments or any genuine moral reasoning or any discovery or revealing or uncovering of moral truth at all.

There are, Hägerström points out, absurdities that no one will inquire into, if he has the slightest sense what he is asking, e.g., 'Is gold just or un-just?' or 'How high is up?' But, Hägerström argues, as Wittgenstein did later, the history of human thought—including philosophy—abounds with equally nonsensical questions only they are sometimes 'deep nonsense' because their nonsensicality is such that it is *hidden,* often for very good psychological rea-sons, in the way we use our language and in the way we are quite naturally inclined to reflectively view our language. Hägerström thinks just this is true about the question: can moral judgments be true or false?

This, Hägerström argues, is an ersatz question parading as a genuine question though it takes a keen understanding both of human psychology and the nature of moral discourse to come to see that this is so. Hägerström puts the general question he will ask concerning moral propositions as follows:

> Just as gold is neither just nor unjust, so it may be that obligation or moral right is of such character that one can say neither that it actually holds nor that it does not hold for a certain mode of acting. It may be, therefore, that when we conceive a certain action as objectively right and another as objectively wrong, we combine with rightness and wrongness a concept which is altogether foreign to them. In such a case the question of the truth of moral propositions would be absurd. If, regarded in and of themselves, they do not at all represent anything as true, nor say anything at all about this or that's actually being such or such, it would be meaningless to ask about their truth.[5]

But why should we assume that 'objective rightness' is a contradiction or meaningless and that 'an objectively true moral statement' is meaningless? (Note that if 'an objectively true moral statement' is meaningless so is 'an objectively false moral statement'.) Why should we believe that this is so? Hägerström (like Westermarck) answers that considering what it is that we have an obligation to do or what it is that we ought to do, we can find no objective, authoritative norm-establishing or norm-conferring reality. In trying to find an objective ground for moral beliefs we search for a *normative reality,* an authoritative *reality,* that would categorically bind us to act in a certain way, independently of the wishes or desire we in fact happen to have or indeed even would have on reflection. But we do not find such a reality. In fact we find the more we examine such matters that we do not even have an intelligible conception of what it could mean to assert that there is such a *normative reality* or that values or norms have cosmic, and thus objective, significance. In reality all we find are emotions, attitudes, conations, and/ or social demands resulting (for the most part) from social stimulation. We find no ought or goodness in the world. As Hägerström put it himself: "Existence and value signify something entirely different. Therefore value cannot be included within existence. A moral authority or norm, as a reality which is good in itself, is, objectively regarded, something absurd."[6] What we have are feelings—indeed powerful driving feelings—that we ought to do so and so or that such and such is right, but there is ascribable to actions or events themselves no objective property, rightness, in virtue of which we could establish quite independently of our affections, that so and so either is or isn't the right thing to do. Our emotional involvement with moral considerations—considerations crucial to our sense of being human beings—frequently masks this truth from us. But, as Hägerström puts it,

If we stand as cold observers before ourselves, that is, in reality interested not in what is observed but only in the investigation of what is observed, what can we discover? We recognize, in the midst of a manifold of other phenomena, a feeling of duty in connection with a judgment of value and a direct interest in a certain action. But all this yields nothing more than a certain kind of psychological event. That the action ought to be done is not at all a part of what we can discover. The keenest analysis of what is present reveals no such thing. Or in a similar way we investigate a certain action. We can establish that the action arouses the strongest appetite or the strongest desire or that it leads to my well-being or that of another. We can discover—let us feign the possibility—that it is commanded by a god or an unobservable being. But every attempt to draw out of the situation the conclusion that it is actually in the highest degree of value to undertake the action is doomed to failure. No obligation or supreme value can be discovered in such a way, for if we are standing indifferently before ourselves and our actions, only observing, we can only establish actual situations. But in the fact that something is, it can never be implied that it ought to be. That something is better than something else is meaningless for the indifferent observer. For him nothing is better or worse.[7]

## II

It might be thought that Hägerström's account is clearly faulted for it is tied in with and thus compromised by the vicissitudes of emotivism and non-cognitivism and it is by now no longer news that such accounts are radically mistaken. Moral terms, as distinct from plainly and paradigmatically emotive terms such as 'blasted', are not *necessarily* emotion or attitude expressing or evoking; moral utterances stand in relations of contradiction and entailment while expressions of emotion do not; by treating any *causally* effective reason as a good reason for doing something, emotive accounts collapse the distinction between *getting* someone to do something and *justifying* the doing of whatever it is that is being proposed. Moreover, we cannot—as the emotivists believe we can—clearly distinguish between the evaluative and descriptive uses of terms such that we can, either for terms or whole utterances, clearly distinguish the descriptive bit (component) and the evaluative bit (component) and claim that it is the evaluative component—the attitude expressing and evoking part—that is crucial in making a judgment a moral judgment; finally it is crucial to recognize that attitudes and beliefs are not so clearly distinguishable and separable as noncognitivists would have it, for an attitude, as something which can be adopted, chosen, abandoned, criticized or corrected, involves (and necessarily so) beliefs so that all attitudes are belief-laden. These and other considerations undermine emotivism and noncognitivism so that many will believe we have no good reasons for accepting Hägerström's 'no-truth-in-morals-thesis'.

No doubt the last word on these meta-ethical issues has not been uttered, but all that aside, the core of what I have elicited from Hägerström is not tied up with these vicissitudes of non-cognitivism. The no-truth-in-morals-thesis is indeed tied up with what broadly conceived should be called an empiricist epistemology and methodology and with the belief that value and existence belong to different categories and that one cannot in any interesting sense derive—that is deduce—an ought from an is. And here I think a good case can be made for a position bearing at least a family resemblance to Hägerström's and I should like here to go some of the way toward doing it.

The controversy over deriving an ought from an is is a very tangled one. Traditions emanating from Price, Hume and Kant have contended that no such derivation is possible; by contrast Hegelians, Marx and orthodox Marxists have thought such a derivation was possible as did the pragmatists strongly influenced by John Dewey.[9] When I first studied moral philosophy, Anglo-American analytical philosophers, powerfully under the influence of Moore and the non-cognitivists, gave us to understand that there was no greater virtue in a moral philosopher than not to commit the *naturalistic fallacy* and that, as Hare put it, any attempt to derive an ought from an is was a form of circle-squaring.[10] However, with the breaking up of old rigidities about how language functions, principally through the influence of Wittgenstein, but through the work of Austin as well, able philosophers, solidly in the analytical tradition, such as Foot, Melden, MacIntyre, Black, Mavrodes and Searle, have challenged what they took to be a non-naturalist dogma and sought to show that such a derivation can be carried out.[11] (I shall, therefore, sometimes refer to them as derivationists and to their non-naturalist opponents as non-derivationists.) Searle in particular made a determined effort, finally with the background argument of a full-fledged theory of language, to carry out such a derivation.[12] But criticism of his particular effort is stalemated. Similar things can be said of Foot's, Melden's and MacIntyre's efforts. Many would accept Foot's own re-appraisal that it has not been shown, as Hare believes, that such a project is in principle impossible but neither has Searle nor anyone else shown that we can derive an ought from an is.[13] Critics of Searle, for example, argue that he has not shown that unproblematic, normatively neutral statements of fact entail moral claims or moral judgments. He has not succeeded in providing us with any conjunction of purely factual and analytic premises which entail a moral conclusion. Critics, including such a sympathetic critic as Foot, have responded that his alleged analytic premiss 'One ought to fulfill one's obligations' is not in fact analytic but is rather itself a normative claim, that some of his allegedly purely factual premises are covertly evaluative, that even his conclusion—supposedly normative—is not actually normative and, that he has not achieved a logical connection as strong as that of an entailment.[14]

Yet, Searle, in spite of those and other criticisms, has held his ground and critical opinion is divided as to how much he has accomplished. However, it does seem safe to say that the institutional facts that Searle appeals to are not the normatively neutral facts which would enable one to bridge the fact-value gap, for they are already themselves in part evaluative. Thus, if we try to go from Jones promised to pay Smith five dollars to Jones ought, *ceteris paribus,* to pay Smith five dollars, we are forgetting that in the logic of the case it need not be true that everyone or even every rational person need so value the institution of promise-keeping. Jones, if he has a certain set of values, need not deny that he owed Smith five dollars, but, holding the institution of promise-keeping in lower esteem than most people do, he might consider it a humanly desirable task to weaken it and thus he could, without any inconsistency at all, not draw the conclusion that he ought to pay Smith the five dollars. If, in turn, it is responded that the *ceteris paribus* saves Searle in such a situation, then it should be responded that whether in such a context things are or are not equal is itself a substantive normative matter and cannot be resolved simply by knowing what the non-normative facts are.

Searle seeks to show that the so-called is/ought question is not the or even a fundamental question of moral philosophy in the way it has been taken to be. Instead, once it is properly understood, it will be seen to be a fairly trivial problem in the philosophy of language. Alison Jaggar in an important paper has powerfully argued that this is not so but that the resolution of the is/ought problem is tied in with the resolution of a cluster of central issues in moral philosophy and requires, as well, a careful consideration of the actual role of moral discourse in our lives.[15]

However, Searle is not alone in trying to defuse this issue by showing its triviality. Stephen Toulmin does the same thing with the Wittgensteinian sensitivity to context Jaggar recommends and Peter Singer, in an unfortunately neglected article, also tries, from a different perspective, to show the triviality of the dispute.[16] I shall in the next section examine Singer's article, for it seems to me that it unwittingly achieves just the opposite effect and, if its implications are thought through, it brings us back to Hägerström and his no-truth-no-derivation theses. To establish against someone like Hägerström that it can be determined over some fundamental issue what, through and through and everything considered, should be done simply by reference to some normatively neutral matters of fact, independently of the attitudes and commitments of the people involved, would indeed be a major breakthrough in moral theorizing. But it is just that—or so I shall argue—that has *not* been done and Singer's deflationary article in reality goes some of the way to showing why that is so and why no such derivation of an ought from an is is possible.

III

Singer, in a healthy and understandable desire to get on with normative ethical issues and normative ethical theorizing, wishes to exhibit the triviality of the debate over two issues that, until recently, have dominated moral philosophy, to wit the issue of the relation of the ought to the is and the definition of morality. The two questions are intimately related, for some definitions of morality allow us, in a certain way at least, though a way which I shall argue is misleading, to move from statements of fact to moral judgments and others do not. It is thus not unreasonable to believe that there is no resolving whether an ought can be derived from an is independently of deciding how morality and the moral point of view is properly to be characterized.

Given a spectrum of more or less plausible conceptions of morality, Singer characterizes two conceptions on either end of the spectrum and shows that while they take very different positions about the is and ought, nothing substantive and non-terminological turns on these differences. He then goes on to show that for some selected positions at other places on the spectrum the same thing obtains. The two "extremes" are stated in simplified form but bear a reasonable resemblance to the positions classically articulated, on the one hand, by D. H. Monro in his *Empiricism and Ethics* and, on the other, by Kurt Baier in his *The Moral Point of View*. The Monro-like account is labelled by Singer *neutralism* (form-and-content neutralism) and the Baier-like position, in deference to Hare, is called *descriptivism*. *Neutralism* does not build in *any content or form constraints*, such as a reference to interests or universalizability, in its characterization of what can count as a moral principle, claim or consideration. A moral claim or principle can have any content whatsoever. Moreover, on this neutralist account, as distinct from Kant's or Hare's, there are no formal requirements like being such as could be willed as a universal law or being acceptable to an impartial observer or being approved by a rational agent on reflection. For a neutralist, a person's moral principles are the principles, whatever they may be, which that person takes to be overriding. On this conception even egoism is not ruled out as a possible moral position, for, as long as the egoistic principle or maxim is overriding for the agent committed to it, it counts as his fundamental moral standard. And this, for the neutralist, is true of any principle or maxim no matter what its content. An anthropologist, if he held such a conception of morality, would find out what a tribe's moral principles are simply in finding out what principles are overriding for them.

On such a conception of morality, there is a very close logical connection between our moral principles and our actions. We cannot, on such an account, knowingly and rationally fail to act on our moral principles, for whatever is overriding for us is of necessity a key element in our morality.

Whatever their content a person's fundamental moral principles are those principles which are overriding for him. A failure to act in accordance with those overriding principles would on such an account be a rational failing on his part. For the neutralist, the question 'Why be moral?' plainly cannot arise, for there can be no gap between recognizing that something is in accord with one's moral principles and one's rational decision to do that action.[17] Yet, vis-à-vis the is/ought question, it is the case that *whatever* facts are pointed to in trying to convince someone holding such a position that he ought to do a certain thing, it remains the case that he can consistently always deny that moral conclusions follow from these facts. Even if it is pointed out to the neutralist at time T2 that at time T1 his overriding principles were XYZ, that fact does not logically entail that at time T2, or at any other time, he should act in accordance with them. It is plausible to claim that it is logically possible on such a conception of morality, that anything with any content or form could be his overriding principles and thus no factual statements, expressive of any determinant factual content, can *entail* that he should act in a certain way, for it is always at least logically possible for him to adopt overriding principles which do not follow from them and thus it is always possible for him to consistently accept the factual statements and assert moral principles that are incompatible with them. And this will be so no matter what the facts are. So while there is a close connection between moral principles and action on a neutralist account, there is no deriving these principles from facts. There is no discovery of what in truth we ought to do from discovering the facts. There seems on such an account of morality to be no way of establishing the truth of moral utterances and Hägerström's no-truth-thesis and no-derivability-thesis with its radical distinction between value and existence seems vindicated.[18]

Do things fare better on *descriptivist* accounts of morality? Superficially they do, but, appearances here are deceiving. For a descriptivist a principle can only be a moral principle if it satisfies certain criteria of both form and content.[19] To take one simplified brand of descriptivism as an illustration: a principle is only a moral principle when it, either directly or indirectly, serves to further human happiness and lessen human suffering. A principle which was unrelated to happiness and suffering could not be a moral principle. Another form of descriptivism would be the claim that a principle to be a moral principle must be related to or answer to human interests.

Now if we accept such an account of morality, including, of course, a more sophisticated account of the same sort, we can indeed derive certain moral conclusions from certain putative statements of fact. If it is a fact that X, Y, and Z will promote human happiness and reduce human suffering then it follows, given that account of morality, that *ceteris paribus* X, Y, and Z ought to be done. Moreover, we can establish the truth of certain moral conclusions, to wit that it is true that X ought to be done, if X, more than any alternative, brings about more happiness and less suffering. Or, on the other descriptivist account, it is true that X is good, if X answers to human interests and whether X answers to human interests is a verifiable factual statement. (If that isn't a pleonasm.)

However, as is usual in philosophy, there is a rub—indeed there are several rubs. I shall consider only two. The first rub, by now one frequently noted and frequently argued about, is occasioned by the problem, in effect noted by Moore and returned to by Stevenson and Hare, that such definitions persuasively define morality and, indeed, in these persuasive definitions evaluative notions are already incorporated into the definitions such that the definitions themselves are not normatively neutral so that (to take an example) we are not going from the neutral analytic premiss that to take the moral point of view is to be committed to doing XYZ, together with the statement of fact that XYZ obtains, to the moral conclusion that we should do XYZ.[20] We cannot make this move, for the so-called analytic premiss is not analytic at all, and, as Moore shows, by his open-question argument, wherever we characterize XYZ in terms of some purely factual or empirical content, we can always ask, without making any verbal mistake, whether XYZ is good. There is no verbal mistake in asking whether 'furthering human happiness is good or desirable'. It is not like asking whether 'furthering human happiness is furthering human happiness'. Similarly we can, without making any purely verbal mistake, ask whether 'what answers to interests is good' or whether 'we ought to do what answers to interests'. The short of this old point is, that it at least appears to be the case that such descriptivist definitions of morality are not evaluatively or normatively neutral; what they in reality do is to give voice to evaluative conceptions themselves. Thus we remain, after all, on the ought side of the is/ought gap.[21]

Even if there is some way around this, there is another rub—a rub noted by Singer—which, when duly noted, seems at least to dash any hope of ever being able to deduce what through and through we ought to do from a knowledge of the non-moral facts. We can unearth what is at issue in the following way. Unlike the *neutralist* account, the *descriptivist* account does not provide a logical tie between moral principles and action. Moral principles on such an account are not necessarily overriding. "We are not," as Singer well puts it, "free to form our own opinion about what is and what is not a moral principle; but we are free to refuse to concern ourselves about moral principles."[22] The why-be-moral-question, on such an account of morality, can be coherently raised and a man need not be acting irrationally if he fails to do what, on such a conception of morality, moral principles dictate. The man who is more interested in art and the development of culture than the furtherance of human happiness and the avoidance of human suffering need not be acting irrationally if he does not act in accordance with what even he takes to be the dictates of morality, for on his account, moral principles are not of conceptual necessity overriding principles. The same is true of the man who cares about nothing but himself. His egoism is not his morality but it doesn't follow from that that in living in accordance with such an egoistic lifepolicy, he must be acting irrationally. "The descriptivist cannot tie morality to action, as the neutralist did, because he has tied it to form and content. So morality may become irrelevant to the practical problem of what to do."[23] On the descriptivist account, there may no longer be an is/ought gap, but there still is something very like it—a something which made for Hume, Hägerström, Ayer and Hare, what they took to be the is/ought gap, a problem in the first place, namely a fact/action, reason/action, reason/commitment gap. That is, it will not be the case, that there are any moral non-neutral facts (cold facts) about some proposed course of action which are such that where these are the facts in the case, for any rational person, quite independently of what his sentiments may be, it entails that he or she try to carry out that action. Where fundamental principles of action and life policies are concerned, there is nothing, through and through, and everything considered, that the cold facts and human rationality (neutrally conceived) dictate that we must do such that if we do not, we will be acting irrationally and ignoring the truth, i.e., what the facts are in the case.[24] Recall that Hägerström contended that it is a mistake to believe that moral principles are principles of the type such that they are true or false in such a manner that any neutral observer, through and through rational, and acquainted with and non-evasive about the facts, must accept them or rightly be accused of irrationality or intellectual or factual error. There is no such impersonal truth to moral claims; and this—or so it seems—is but one way of saying that they are not principles which can in any proper sense be said to be true or even false at all. That is to say, the no-truth-thesis and the rationale behind it is grounded in the realization that fact and norm, existence and value and the is and the ought belong to different categories. People engaging in the activities they vaguely label are doing radically different things with thoroughly different rationales.

Values, Dewey to the contrary notwithstanding, are not a distinctive kind of empirical fact and, Moore to the contrary notwithstanding, they are also not a distinctive kind of 'non-natural fact'. It is this that Hägerström wanted to bring out and, as I read him, Hume as well, and it is this that is important behind the claim that one cannot derive an ought from an is. It leads us to see, against objectivists from Plato to Rawls, that reason and a thorough knowledge of the facts and of theory will not, by themselves, enable us to know what we are to do and what kind of life and styles of acting are required of us or are through and through, and everything considered, desirable. If we could derive an ought from an is in the way that Hume, Hägerström and Hare deny that we can, we would also be able to refute the no-truth-thesis and set out an objective foundation for morality. Singer's analysis is in effect one further argument to show that this cannot be done and that in essence Hume, Hägerström and Hare are right.

To come to such a conclusion is not, as Singer thought, to establish the triviality of the is/ought debate, but to show—or go some way toward showing—that the non-derivationists are right and that a gap exists between fact and action, reason and acting and reason and commitment, such that our picture of the foundations of morality is very different than it would be if this were not so.

A descriptivism with any other form and content would have the same type problems about the is/ought and reason/action gap. It would not help to combine neutralism and descriptivism and say that a principle is a moral principle only if it answers to interests and is overriding. For someone could still intelligibly ask, in a way comparable to asking 'Why be moral?' 'Why take as overriding those principles which answer to human interests?' He might not *care* about the interests of others. The fact that some principles answered to interests and would not be classified as moral principles unless they were also overriding would not rationally settle for him the question of this taking principles with such a content as overriding.

Things are not essentially changed if we turn to in-between positions on the spectrum of positions between neutralism and descriptivism. Hare's position, for example, is neutralist in *content* but committed, through his appeal to the universalizability principle, to a certain determinate *form*. On his account certain forms of egoism appear at least to be ruled out as possible moral positions, but, while this position, like neutralism, pure and simple, appears to preserve the tie between action and morality, it does not preserve the tie between fact and morality. For Hare moral principles by definition are prescriptive and universalizable; prescriptivity preserves the tie between commitment and action, but universalizability limits formally what principles can count as moral principles. So there are some principles, or at least conceptions, on which people might act which are not moral principles. We must, on Hare's account, be able to prescribe universally what we morally commit ourselves to or it will not count as a moral commitment. But this provides only a psychological barrier to certain acts, for *universalizability itself places no constraints* on what we can prescribe universally. If what Hare calls the fanatic is willing to universally prescribe things that will harm him, then he cannot, on Hare's own account, be shown to be mistaken if he consistently does this. Any generalizable principle can be prescribed and, as with neutralism, it is very unclear if anything at all, except perhaps certain forms of egoism, can be ruled out as wrong on those grounds.[25] That few people are willing to starve to death for an ideal does not prove that we can show that such an ideal is not universalizable or show that it follows that we have proved, from purely factual and analytic premises, that it is wrong.

Moreover, on Hare's account, even the tie between morality and action is not sustainable, as it is on a purely neutralist position. Suppose a man has as his overriding maxim or policy of action something which is non-universalizable. Hare can consistently say that such a person has no moral principles but that does not settle the issue about whether he is acting rationally or doing what, everything considered, he should do if he acts on such a non-universalizable maxim of action. (Suppose he is an individual egoist, and remember not all 'shoulds' are moral shoulds.) He might, on such an account, as on a descriptivist account, opt out of acting on moral principles and not be any the less rational for all of that.

It is not clear what other kind of 'middle' position we could give, but if it has *any content* at all built into its conception of what morality is, it seems that the question can be coherently raised: 'Why act on principles with such a content?' If it is just a fact that morality requires ABC, it always seems possible, as Moore in effect realized, where ABC is characterized in non-normative terms, to ask coherently why do ABC? If in turn A or B or C are themselves partially characterized in normative or evaluative terms, then we are not in fact going from fact to value. In either event, we have an is/ought gap. If, on the other hand, the position is still some contentless conception of morality, it remains totally unclear in what way it could cross the fact-value gap, for it never gets on the fact side of the matter in the first place. And again, like any Kantian ethic, it is compatible with any substantive position whatsoever.

No definition of morality can bridge the gap between facts and action. Suppose Searle manages to give us a paradigmatic promising case then, if such an institution is judged desirable, it does follow, under such circumstances, that one ought, *ceteris paribus,* to pay what one promised to pay. Even so, such a derivation does not commit one to any action. It does not give us a counterexample to the claims of Hume and Kant, and in our time of Hägerström, Moore, Ayer and Hare, that no statements, recording even the sum of value-neutral facts and their analytic auxiliaries, entail some categorical statement asserting what, everything considered, we are to do. It is that claim that defenders of the gap between the is and the ought were concerned to make and it is that claim, which seems to me still to be intact.

## IV

This could be accepted for those cases—perhaps fewer than we are wont to realize—where there is a clear distinction between fact and value and still it could be retorted that the picture of the Great Divide given by the non-derivationists is thoroughly unrealistic.[26] There are many concepts, centrally used in moral reasoning and reflection, and many utterances similarly so employed, which are hardly classifiable as 'purely factual' or 'purely normative' and concerning which we cannot by careful analysis break them up into their 'factual bit' and 'normative bit'. This general line of argumentation has been powerfully urged by Charles Taylor, Richard Norman and Bernard Williams.[27] I shall set out, and then comment on, something of Bernard Williams's way of conducting the case, for he succinctly makes the central points.

Williams argues that to stress that we cannot derive "evaluative principles with 'oughts' in them" from pure statements of fact "distracts attention from, regards as secondary, the enormous numbers of concepts which we ourselves use, and other societies use, and people in the past have always used, which have got an evaluative force of a certain kind—that is, their deployment has something to say for or against acting in certain ways, or suggests an attitude for or against certain courses of action and persons and so on."[28] These concepts are usually not culturally invariant and they are not divisible into 'ought' bits and 'is' bits or analyzable into descriptive and evaluative components. Williams's examples are owing someone some money, promising, being cowardly, being sentimental, being treacherous, it's one's job, saving face or losing face. These are concepts which, when used in normal linguistic environments, have evaluative implications and some of them, like losing face for the Japanese, have very strong evaluative implications. If we try to characterize or paraphrase terms expressive of these concepts in purely neutral descriptive and factual terms and then add that the terms we are characterizing are as well, but in a way that is independent of their connotation or cognitive meaning, pro and con attitude expressing terms or something of that sort, we leave out, as Williams puts it, the fact that without the human interests these concepts respond to, we wouldn't have these concepts at all: there wouldn't be such concepts to have any connotation. In that way these interests are partially, but still irreducibly and unavoidably, constitutive of these concepts. There is no capturing what these concepts are about in purely 'cold fact' terms and then saying that in addition such concepts usually have a certain evaluative force but that, while remaining about the same realities, they might come to have a quite different evaluative or normative force. Consider—to take just one example—'treacherous' in sentences such as 'He is very treacherous'. We have here the notion of someone who will betray a trust, who is traitorous or disloyal or perfidious, who is deceptive and who cannot be relied upon. Terms such as 'traitorous', 'disloyal', 'deceptive' or 'perfidious' have at least as strong an evaluative force as 'treacherous', but, particularly with such terms as 'deceptive' or 'betray a trust,' there are stretches of identifiable behavior which, if they occur, count as cases of 'betraying a trust' or 'deception', though it is another thing to say they are definitive of it or constitute it. In this way such terms and through them 'treacherous' come to have a factual content. Yet, the meaning of these terms is not characterizable just in terms of these bits of behavior or more of the same behavior plus a con-attitude on the part of the user of these terms.

To talk in these terms (e.g., of treachery and of betrayal of trust) is to see the world—in a 'seeing-as-sense'—in a certain way, a way people who do not have these concepts would not, and indeed could not, 'see the world'.[29] Nor could they simply 'read off' these concepts from noting that behavior. Without certain interests there would be no such concepts, though, reciprocally, without such concepts there would be no such interests. The concepts treacherous, being in debt and promising, as distinct from that of being poisonous, are concepts which pick out certain social or institutional facts, facts whose very reality or existence depends on the concepts in question. The facts involved are facts about social institutions which owe their very existence to certain pervasive human interests, institutions which notoriously, both affect and cause human desires. But it remains the case, Williams reminds us, "that a social fact is still a fact." But it is a special kind of fact, a fact constituted by certain concepts and human interests. And this is an important distinction to draw, for the point about concepts like saving face or one's job or property or stealing or a debt is that the development of these concepts is intimately bound up with an entire set of institutions. The proposal to get rid of the evaluative force of one or another of these concepts is not a proposal for a kind of logical reform about what words we use to describe the world, nor, merely, how we are to comment on what is the case. Rather this would be a proposal "to change our entire view of our social relations." Different types of social science—Marxist economics or sociology and bourgeois economics or sociology—will, with differing interests and different conceptions, have different paradigmatic conceptions as to what constitutes social reality and these conceptions are tied to different world-pictures.[30] This makes the problem of their assessment rather tricky for what will or will not count as a fact—an institutional fact—which in turn might be used in a normal evidential way, is, in part at least, a product of the relevant systematically embedded concepts and interests (valuations). But this, by a quantum leap, complicates the problem of establishing truth or testing theories in such domains. Moreover, while à la Searle, Foot, or Melden, certain ought statements may be derivable from statements of *institutional fact,* these statements of institutional fact are themselves not on the 'purely is' or 'purely factual' side of the at least putative is/ought gap, for they have an irreducible and non-isolatable normative component.[31] Moreover, it is not even clear that they ever entail moral claims—ought claims—of a sufficiently fundamental categorical nature to be genuine propositions clearly on the ought side.

We have a cluster of statements, importantly relevant to morality, which are not realistically classifiable as either purely factual statements—what W. D. Falk calls, statements of 'cold fact'—or purely moral propositions. (E.g., 'You ought to love your enemies', or 'You should treat people with more consideration'.)[32] Non-derivationists have neglected them and failed to see their importance in giving us a picture of the world in which we distinctively place 'cold facts' and so place as well—or indeed even have the possibility of coherently making—more explicit purely moral judgments. Nonetheless a recognition of this complexity does not refute non-derivationists, such as Hume, Hägerström and Hare, who argue that there is no deriving a categorical moral ought or a judgment of intrinsic value from purely factual ('cold fact') statements.

What needs to be recognized is that the line between where we have a factual disagreement and an evaluative disagreement is much less sharp than the traditional non-derivationist picture gave us to understand (Moore, Hägerström, Ayer and Hare are paradigms here), that many moral concepts (e.g. treacherous, class enemy) are not as distinctively moral as the concepts typically discussed in traditional moral theory (good, right, ought, duty) and that these less distinctly moral concepts are, as Williams puts it, "tied up with the sorts of concepts we use to describe human nature, the sorts of human characteristics we find interesting, important, significant." All this is worthy of note and a proper dwelling on it will provide additional support in our struggle to get out of the shadow of Moore and find significant new directions in moral philosophy and in our coming to understand that social science cannot be normatively neutral. Still there is nothing here to refute or even undermine the positions of Hume, Hägerström or Moore about the is and the ought. The considerations raised do not show us how it will be possible to derive an ought from an is—a fundamental categorical moral proposition from purely factual statements—or establish the truth or justifiability of fundamental moral propositions.

## V

We need, in seeing the force of a position like that of Hume's or Hägerström's, to see a little more fully what is being claimed. In talking about facts which do not entail value judgments, we are talking about those value-neutral characteristics of objects or situations which are true of the objects or situations and which hold, independently of the affective significance of those objects or of that situation, for us or indeed for anyone. In that way, as W. D. Falk has well put it, the facts may not be hard but they are cold, for they are that which is empirically or scientifically ascertainable and they are that which characterizes the object or situation short of its affective significance. We do, of course, say of certain situations or things that they are good or bad or that they ought or ought not to obtain. But what is said about these things or situations when such words are used does not further qualify the thing or situation in question: making still more determinate its factual specification. Instead it supervenes on it. If I say 'Southern Africa is beginning to revolt' and then add that 'That's as it should be', my 'That's as it should be', unlike my 'beginning to revolt', does not further specify what is happening in Southern Africa, but, in Hume's terms, expresses an entirely new relation or affirmation, to wit that by way of a correct view of what is happening there, it will occasion a favorable response in a human reviewer. (Query: what are the criteria for a correct view?) Reason, that is sense-observation and reasoning, enables us to ascertain the facts in the case: it "adds to our knowledge of the world, of objects, states of affairs, characters, actions."[33] But evaluating, grading, appraising, assessing, aesthetically and morally judging are very different activities than such knowledge or information yielding activities. Further, they are what is involved when in being confronted with things as they are, we, taking the objects or situation as known, respond to them. In such evaluative and appraising activities, we are concerned about "the dynamics between things as they are and ourselves."[34] We are concerned with their affective relevance or significance for us. Without an understanding of the facts in the case, we could not make such assessments, but such assessments are not further recordings or specifications of the factual situation. Coherently to make the claim that revolution in Southern Africa would be a good thing, we must know some plain, cold facts about Southern Africa. But its being a good thing is not just another fact about Southern Africa, but is, as Falk well puts it, "a supervenient and descriptively supernumerary conclusion from the cold facts in another order of discourse."[35] Evaluative concepts, as both Hume and Moore see, are fact-dependent and fact-supervenient concepts, and in being such they are quite distinct from factual concepts. But Hume, unlike Moore, saw that all judgments of value and all normative judgments rest on: a) an understanding of what the object or situation we are concerned with is like and b) on our *affective* responsiveness to such an understanding of what it is like. The value of something, though it holds by reason of the facts, is not provable by them or derivable from any description or further specification of the facts. We cannot, as both Hume and Hägerström stress, simply observe or demonstrate the value of something: rather value is discerned by critical and reflective *taste:* that is by reflecting on, taking to heart and patiently, intelligently, and dispassionately *responding* to, objects and situations, where we are in extensive possession of the facts concerning them.

For Hägerström, and perhaps for Hume, there is a gap between fact and norm, because moral judgments cannot be derived from reason, i.e., we cannot demonstrate their truth or verify their truth. But for all that, they need not be wanton, for, while not derivable from reason, they must be made, to count as justified moral or evaluative judgments, impartially and fully in the light of reason, i.e., with a full awareness of and a reflective reviewing of the facts in the case.

So when we fully take to heart and reflect on what evaluating and judging are—what kinds of activities they are—and how very different these activities are from the activities of describing, informing, or simply neutrally and indifferently characterizing, it is plain enough why it is impossible to derive an ought from an is or identify value and existence, but it should also be equally evident why matters of fact—considerations about what is the case—must always be essential for any due and reflective appraisal or judgment concerning what ought to be the case or ought to be done.


## VI


Someone might still respond—reviving the dialectic of the argument about the is and the ought once again—that if the above is a tolerably correct picture of the scope of reason in morals, it does not go far enough to meet our reflective expectations, for it remains the case that there might be agreement about the facts—the 'cold facts'—and disagreement about what to do even when the disputants involved are people who conscientiously and dispassionately and indeed without intellectual error reviewed the facts, and took them to heart, in the way morality requires. Reason, on such an account, does not have the *authority* to say to a reflective rational agent conversant with the facts that if such and such occurs or obtains or is the correct, purely factual characterization of the situation—if these are the cold facts—then, no matter what your affective response, such and such must be done. And supporting this, it could be further remarked, that we have, Hume and Falk to the contrary notwithstanding, no criteria for what is a correct or proper appreciation of the facts when we have gone without evasion through the procedures Hume and Falk recommend. The procedures of review could be carried out to the full and without evasion or any blinking from the facts and there still could be disagreement about what to do: the affective responses need not be the same. If this obtains, we do not have any way of knowing, at least on their account of knowing, who is making the correct or proper response. In fact, on such an account the very notion of a proper or correct response in such a situation seems at least to have no application. But then it is at least tempting to conclude that there is no essential advance here over a Stevensonian conception of a disagreement in attitude not rooted in disagreement in belief. Our expectations about the relationship between value and existence, norm and fact, have led us to hope that just the opposite obtains: that, even over the ends of life—over some of the most fundamental human choices—so our expectations mythologize, if the facts are such and such, there just are some things we must—categorically must—do on pain of irrationality.[36] But, if we follow out carefully the dialectic of the argument over morals, that understandable expectation or at least hope seems at least to be dashed. It appears to be a confused human reification.

    This claim is of such a vast scope and, if sensible, is at least so seemingly portentous in its implications that we should be careful and try at least to assure that we have followed out correctly the dialectic of the argument. Perhaps the Humean-Hägerströmian-Russellian ballast has somehow ill tilted us. Surely, it will be said, one of the things we have failed to do—concentrating on deducibility and entailment as we have—is to consider seriously the possibility of logically sound non-deductive arguments from purely factual premises to moral conclusions. In that way, as Toulmin and Edwards among others have amply shown, we do readily and easily pass from fact to value, from the is to the ought.[37] From the fact that the wires are high voltage we conclude that we ought to keep away, from the fact that the water is polluted we conclude that we ought not to drink it, from the fact that the knife is sharp we conclude that we ought to be careful and, more generally, from the fact that something will harm people we conclude that we ought not to do it. Perhaps, as Toulmin argues in *The Uses of Argument,* the analytical ideal of entailments is a spurious norm of cogent reasoning.[38]

Moving from the above recognition of how easily we do pass from the is to the ought, it might be argued that if people want to do anything at all (have particular aims and goals that they want to achieve) and they are capable of consistent thought and action, then there are certain things they must want, certain things they must value. It isn't that here we are going back on our Humean-Hägerströmian contentions about the non-derivability of categorical norms of statements of fact, but that we are recognizing the propriety of another pattern of reasoning. That is, when we make *hypothetical* value judgments, we can ascertain whether they are true or false by an appeal to the empirical facts. It is sometimes the case that if a certain factual situation obtains, then it follows that a certain hypothetical value judgment is true. It is perfectly correct to argue that if you want to do a certain thing and if you are going to be consistent and achieve your goal, then you must do whatever is indispensable to achieving that goal. If something is valued by us, then we ought to value, though not necessarily in the same way, whatever is indispensable to our achieving the thing we value. And what is or is not necessary to achieving what we value is an empirical question: something which will be determined by the cold facts. Rawls, for example, powerfully argues that there are certain things—certain primary natural and social goods as he calls them—that we must want if we want or value anything at all.[39] For, unless they are had, we could not achieve the other things we want. This is a question which is doubly factual: whether that is so (whether there are any such things) and what things, specifically, if any, are so necessary. But, it is tempting to argue, if both answers are yes—and whether they are or not is a factual issue—then, if certain facts obtain, it follows that certain things should be valued, *if anything is valued at all and people want to achieve what they value.* The primary social goods Rawls appeals to will illustrate this: they are rights and liberties, opportunities and powers, income and wealth (a share in the common stock of means), and self-respect. Putting aside self-respect, which is more complicated, and not confusing wealth with the desire to be wealthy but taking it simply as the desire to have some of the available stock of means, Rawls's claim is that, as a matter of fact, if you do not have these things in any measure at all, you will not be able to realize your plans (whatever they are). Without some liberty, we could hardly carry out any of our plans, get anything we want, so liberty must be a good for us. Similarly, without rights and powers our chances to gain what we value are considerably lessened, so these things must be goods for us. Rights are also similarly strategic. And people must have some of the stock of means to achieve the things they want—to realize their intentions—so those things too must be regarded as good by human beings, must be things they ought to have. In our culture this means having some income and wealth. These are conditions which are necessary for human beings to act.

Yet, tempting or not, it is a mistake to argue in this way, if it is thought that such argument will support derivationism. For it is not the case that the truth of any of these factual assertions will guarantee that anyone who understands them must assent to a certain normative conclusion. Hägerström's unmoved spectator of the actual would not have so to commit himself or indeed commit himself at all. But, if Rawls has identified, as he at least seems to, some of the conditions necessary (presumably factually necessary) for human beings with any aims or desires at all to act in the world, then Rawls will have identified some of the conditions any human being will have good reason to want if he (she) wants anything at all. If the facts are as Rawls describes them, it follows for such people—people with desires and people who can be and desire to be rational, i.e., desire to take the means necessary to achieve their ends—that they ought to desire the having of those goods Rawls calls the primary social goods *if what they desire for its own sake is indeed desirable*. But this last Moorean caveat is necessary and supports the non-derivationist.[40] We cannot identify what is desirable with what is desired for its own sake. Only on the assumption that what is so desired is desirable do certain factual statements entail certain normative commitments for people with certain natures who desire the continuance and stability of their natures. It is, of course, true that in fact people do have these natures and most likely, in the broad sense relevant to the issue to which we are speaking, they will want to remain basically as they are. But this does not show that we can get a categorical ought from an is, derive what is desirable from what is pervasively desired.

The non-derivationist will still respond: a) that these primary social goods are instrumental goods and not intrinsic goods or something we ought categorically to value and b) that there is nothing in logic or in the facts in the case that can require people to have such natures, and if people had different natures, very different wants or no wants at all, they would not have to conclude that such things are primary goods which they ought to—

indeed must—have for their human flourishing. If it turned out that certain people did not care if their wants were endlessly and pervasively frustrated, then it would have not been established that it is the case that they would have good reasons for desiring such primary goods.[41] Moreover, without knowing that these wants are things they ought to want or are desirable, they cannot conclude that they must, to be rational, regard such alleged primary goods to be the things they ought to have.

The derivationist could in turn respond that now the non-derivationist has taken him to a desert island. Certain facts would perhaps not establish certain values for Martians but for people anything recognizably like we know them they would. People could not be rational and not care about whether their desires were pervasively frustrated and that conceptual point aside, people are not like that, for they (generally speaking) do want to satisfy their desires and thus—a point the above non-derivationist argument neglects—they do need to have these primary goods to achieve whatever else they want. So, if they are rational and want anything at all, then they will want these primary goods. But again, it should be responded, their wanting x does not in itself make x desirable or something they ought to have, though it may make it, *ceteris paribus,* desirable.

The dialectic of the argument between the derivationist and non-derivationist seems to have landed us in the following position: the non-derivationist is right in claiming that there are no cold facts, including facts about human nature or about what people want, sufficient to force a consistent unmoved but through and through rational spectator of the actual to make any normative commitments or take any moral posture whatsoever, but for rational people—agents, not pure spectators—with a human nature recognizably like people as we know them and committed to trying to achieve what they most overridingly desire, certain facts do indeed require certain normative commitments. Meaning by 'rational' in 'rational person' a person who will take the means necessary to achieve his or her most prized ends, a rational person must (among other things)—the facts being what they are—desire liberty, opportunities and the possession of rights. So relative to our human nature and most fundamental commitments, certain facts—'cold facts' if you will—do determine values, but for some pure, affectless intelligence (if such there be) or for some being with totally different emotions this might not be so. So Hume and Hägerström are right *sans phrase:* no facts determine values. But, given the above background, such a conceptual point does not, after all, seem to be very important. There is, in a certain way and with the above qualification, the possibility of founding morality on the nature of man and *pace* Moore, the basis for establishing by analysis systematic connections between values and the nature of man and the world, while still preserving the insight common to Hume, Hägerström and Moore, that a) value and fact, norm and existence and the is and the ought are all distinct and b) the further insight that no categorical moral statements can be derived from the cold facts, including the facts of human nature or shown to be true or false in the way semantic theory can provide truth conditions for 'The cup is on the dish' or 'Most Swedes are Lutherans'.

NOTES

1. Axel Hägerström, *Philosophy and Religion*, translated by Robert T. Sandin (London: George Allen & Unwin Ltd., 1964). Hägerström's inaugural lecture discussed here was delivered in 1911. It is worth noting that this precedes by a good decade the statement of emotivism and non-cognitivism in the English speaking and German speaking countries.

2. Ibid., p. 82.

3. Ibid., p. 83.

4. Ibid.

5. Ibid.

6. Ibid., p. 87.

7. Ibid., pp. 88-89.

8. The following collect together some of the classical assessments of emotivism. E. Bedford, "The Emotive Theory of Ethics," *Proceedings of the Eleventh International Congress of Philosophy* X (1953); Richard Brandt, "The Emotive Theory of Ethics," *The Philosophical Review* (1950); W. D. Falk, "Goading and Guiding," *Mind* (1954); P. R. Foot, "The Philosopher's Defense of Morality," *Philosophy* (1952); Kai Nielsen, "On Looking Back at the Emotive Theory," *Methodos* (1958); Einer Tegen, "The Basic Problem in the Theory of Value, *Theoria* (1944); and Bernard Williams, *Problems of Self* (Cambridge, England: The University Press, 1973); pp. 207-229.

9. Probably the most useful discussion of the is/ought question in Marx and Marxist thought occurs in Lucien Goldmann's "Is There a Marxist Sociology?" *Radical Philosophy* I (January, 1972). I have discussed some of the issues vis-à-vis Marx in my "Class Conflict, Marxism and the Good-Reasons Approach," *Social Praxis* 2 (1974) [see chapter 6 of the present volume]. John Dewey's approach to such an issue is perhaps best exemplified in his *The Quest for Certainty* (1929). Sidney Hook, in his "The Desirable and Emotive in Dewey's Ethics," Sidney Hook, (ed.), *John Dewey: Philosopher of Science and Freedom* (New York: 1950), pp. 194-216, has made what is probably the most determined effort to meet the challenge of the non-derivationist from a Deweyan point of view. I have tried to assess such arguments in my "Dewey's Conception of Philosophy," *The Massachusetts Review* (Autumn, 1960): 110-134.

10. R. M. Hare, *The Language of Morals* (Oxford: Clarendon Press, 1952), pp. 79-93.

11. See the essays by MacIntyre, Searle, Foot, and Phillips reprinted in W. D. Hudson (ed.) *The Is/Ought Question* (London: Macmillan & Co. Ltd., 1969) and see A. I Melden, "Reasons for Action and Matters of Fact," *Proceedings and Addresses of The American Philosophical Association* (1961-1962): 45-60.

12. John R. Searle, *Speech Acts* (Cambridge: The University Press, 1969).

13. See Philippa Foot's introduction to her anthology *Theories of Ethics* (Oxford University Press, 1967), pp. 7-13.

14. Judith and James Thomson, "How not to Derive 'ought' from 'is'," W. D. Hudson (ed.), *The Is/Ought Question*, pp. 163-172.

15. Alison Jaggar, "It Does Not Matter Whether We Can Derive 'Ought' from 'Is'," *Canadian Journal of Philosophy* 3, no. 3 (March, 1974): 378-379.

16. Stephen Toulmin, *The Uses of Argument* (Cambridge: The University Press, 1958) and Peter Singer, "The Triviality of the Debate Over 'Is/Ought' and the Definition of 'Moral'," *American Philosophical Quarterly* 10, no. 1 (January, 1973):, 51-56.

17. Singer, op. cit., p. 52.

18. It might be argued that neutralism is actually not so independent of empirical challenge. Suppose a neutralist N claims that X, Y, and Z are his overriding principles and that in fact he does indeed honestly believe them to be so. But further suppose that a perceptive anthropologist or social psychologist shows N that, given N's actual behavior, he, N, is deluded in thinking X, Y, and Z are his overriding principles, for his behavior shows convincingly that, his verbalizations and conscious attitudes to the contrary notwithstanding, A, B, and C are his overriding principles. Surely this would show N that he was mistaken in his belief as to what were his overriding principles, but it would not enable him to derive what he ought to do from the empirical facts, for it would remain the case that in deciding what he ought to do, simply knowing the facts that the anthropologist or social scientist unearthed would not enable him to deduce what (after that awareness had sunk in) his overriding principles are or to deduce what are to be his overriding principles.

19. Singer, op. cit., p. 53.

20. G. E. Moore, *Principia Ethica* (Cambridge: The University Press, 1903) and C. L. Stevenson, *Ethics and Language* (New Haven, Connecticut: Yale University Press, 1944), chapter 6.

21. Kai Nielsen, "Covert and Overt Synonymity: Brandt and Moore and the 'Naturalistic Fallacy'," *Philosophical Studies* 25, no. 1 (January, 1974): 51-56.

22. Singer, op. cit., p. 53.

23. Ibid.

24. I am inclined to think that the absurdity of such a Humean conclusion gives us good grounds for not construing 'rationality' neutrally, as it typically is in the analytical tradition. If, alternatively, we enrich our conception of rationality, after the fashion of the Frankfurt school, we still will not have derived an ought from an is, for our enriched, and I would judge more adequate, conception of rationality is not normatively neutral. See Kai Nielsen, "Distrusting Reason," *Ethics* 87, no. 1 (October, 1976): 49-60 and "Can There Be an Emancipatory Rationality?" *Critica* 8, no. 24 (December, 1976): 79-102.

25. D. H. Monro, *Empiricism and Ethics* (Cambridge: The University Press, 1967), pp. 147-233.

26. Kurt Baier, "Decisions and Descriptions," *Mind* (1951).

27. Charles Taylor, "Interpretation and the Sciences of Man," *The Review of Metaphysics* 15, no. 1 (September, 1971); Charles Taylor. "Neutrality in Political Science," *Philosophy, Politics and Society*, Third Series Peter Laslett and W. C. Runciman (eds.) (Oxford: Blackwell, 1967); Kai Nielsen, "Social Science and American Foreign Policy," *Philosophy, Morality, and International Affairs*, Virginia Held, Sidney Morgenbesser and Thomas Nagel (eds.) (New York: Oxford University Press, 1974); Richard Norman, "On Seeing Things Differently," *Radical Philosophy* I (January, 1972); and Bernard Williams, "The Sad State of Moral Philosophy," *The Listener* 85, no. 2184 (February, 1971).

28. Williams, op. cit., p. 137.

29. See Norman's, Taylor's and Nielsen's essays cited in footnote 27.

30. Ludwig Wittgenstein, *On Certainty* (Oxford: Basil Blackwells Ltd., 1969) and G. H. von Wright, "Wittgenstein on Certainty," in G. H. von Wright (ed.), *Problems in the Theory of Knowledge* (The Hague: Martinus Nijhoff, 1972), pp. 47-60. Most particularly see pages 59-60 in von Wright's article.

31. Someone with a metaethical position like that of Hägerström, Ayer, or Hare might well respond by arguing that the claims made in the language of institutional facts can be transmogrified into a neutral, purely empirical language of 'cold facts'. But it is just this that cannot be done, as Williams, Norman, and Taylor have powerfully argued. A recognition that many of our key concepts—concepts linked with questions about our societal existence and the human sciences—are an inextricable fact/value mishmash a) does not resolve the is/ought deduction question and b) it might—and I believe would— suggest that the is/ought question is not as important as it has traditionally been thought to be, for there are all sorts of issues, involving normative arguments, where the derivation question does not naturally arise. It will, in turn, be responded, that there remain more fundamental and more abstract moral evaluations where there is no such mishmash and where there is no derivation of these moral conceptions from factual ones. To determine how important this observation is, and how trivial or non-trivial non-derivationist claims are, involves the tricky job of perspicuously displaying the connections between the abstract moral appraisals and the more specific appraisals involving concepts which are a fact/ value mishmash.

32. W. D. Falk, "Hume on Practical Reason," *Philosophical Studies* 26 (1975): 1-18 and W. D. Falk, "Hume on Is and Ought," *Canadian Journal of Philosophy* 6, no. 3 (September, 1976): 359-378.

33. W. D. Falk, "Hume on Is and Ought," *Canadian Journal of Philosophy* 6, no. 3 (September, 1976): 369.

34. Ibid.

35. Ibid., p. 370.

36. The subtle and sustained attempt by Philippa Foot to treat moral claims as a distinctive sort of hypothetical imperative is of importance in this context. Philippa Foot, "Morality as a System of Hypothetical Imperatives," *The Philosophical Review* 71, no. 5 (July, 1972): 305-316; Philippa Foot, "Morality and Art," *The Proceedings of the British Academy* 46 (1970): 3-16; Lawrence C. Becker. "The Finality of Moral Judgements: A Reply to Mrs. Foot," *The Philosophical Review* 72 no. 3 (July, 1973); Robert L. Holmes. "Is Morality a System of Hypothetical Imperatives?" *Analysis* 34 (1974); Philippa Foot, "Is Morality a System of Hypothetical Imperatives?', A Reply to Mr. Holmes," *Analysis* 35 (1974); W. K. Frankena, "Under What Net?" *Philosophy* 43 (1973); W. K. Frankena, "The Philosophers' Attack on Morality," *Philosophy,* 49 (1974); Philippa Foot, "Reply to Frankena," *Philosophy* 50 (1975); and D. Z. Phillips, "In Search of the Moral 'Must': Mrs. Foot's Fugitive Thought," *Philosophical Quarterly* (April, 1977).

37. Paul Edwards, *The Logic of Moral Discourse* (Glencoe, Ill.: The Free Press, 1955) and Stephen Toulmin. op. cit.

38. Stephen Toulmin. op. cit., pp. 161-177.

39. John Rawls, *A Theory of Justice* (Cambridge, Mass.: Harvard University Press, 1971), pp. 90-95 and 396, 433 and 447.

40. That it was mistakenly directed against Mill is beside the present point. See Everett W. Hall, *Categorical Analysis* (Chapel Hill, North Carolina: University of North Carolina Press, 1964), pp. 100-132 and Kai Nielsen, "Mill's Proof of Utility," *Bucknell Review* (1977).

41. It may be that this very supposition is incoherent, for if P did not care about X, then X could not be said to be something that P pervasively wanted. Yet I think there is a reading of the above sentence in which it is not incoherent. I would like to thank Arthur Caplan for his perceptive comments on an early version of this chapter.

# 2

# The Functions of Moral Discourse

I

Moral language is obviously a part of ordinary language. It is not a technical language like the language of physics or the language of art criticism. It is not a language for which we must have a special *expertise* in order to understand it, though indeed to talk *about* it and make generalizations about it does require a special *expertise*. Moral language is the language we use in verbalizing a choice or a decision; it is the language we use in appraising human conduct and in giving advice about courses of action; it is the language we use in ascribing or excusing responsibility; and finally, it is the language we use in committing ourselves to a principle of action.[1] Moral language is a *practical* kind of discourse that is concerned to answer the questions: "What should be done?" or "What attitude should be taken toward what has been done, is being done, or will be done?" Moral language is most particularly concerned with guiding choices as to what to do when we are faced with alternative courses of action.

As a form of practical discourse, morality functions to *guide* conduct and *alter* behavior or attitudes. As Hume, who was quite aware of this practical function of moral discourse remarks, moral language serves to "excite the passions."[2] Taking this remark from its eighteenth century idiom we might say that the language of morals serves to motivate action and to alter volitions.

There is, however, a crucial ambiguity in the above characterization. As Falk and Hare have made us aware, there is at least a *prima facie* distinction between *telling* someone what to do and *getting* him to do it. That is, there is a distinction between *guiding* action and *altering* behavior or "exciting the

---

From *Philosophical Quarterly* 7 (July, 1957): 236–248. Copyright © 1957 by Basil Blackwell Ltd. Reprinted by permission of the publisher.

passions." A person in the capacity of a moral adviser may tell someone what he ought to do. He may show him what is the best course of action to follow in a given circuumstance. But, he may do all these things and still *not* succeed in getting him to do the act.

Nonetheless, it is important to note the close *link* in practical discourse between *telling* and *getting* or between *guiding* and *goading*. If I, as a moral adviser, tell A this is the best course of action and A agrees that this is the best course of action then I need not ask A if he is going to *try* to do it or set himself to doing it. We can say that in a quite *ordinary* sense of 'implies',[3] A's saying that it is the best course of action implies that A will *try* to do it, everything else being equal. Principles of guidance or moral advice characteristically function to alter dispositions and to prod us to certain courses of action. A principle of guidance which never did this would be a very curious principle indeed.

Moral advice serves directly to guide action; that is, it serves to tell us which of several alternative courses of action we *should* choose. But principles which could not serve to alter behavior or redirect attitudes towards certain types of behavior could hardly count as 'principles of guidance'. (This is not just a practical matter but follows from the *use* of 'principles of guidance').

A somewhat stronger point can be made. Only those 'principles of guidance' that *generally* function to alter behavior are genuine principles of guidance. If a 'principle of guidance' never served to alter behavior or dispositions to action it would not be regarded as a 'principle of guidance' in the fullest sense but merely as a maxim which could serve, but did not in fact serve, as a principle of guidance. It is part of the role of moral discourse to alter behavior and alter dispositions to action. Any principles which do not do this, but only logically could do this, are not regarded as moral principles in the fullest sense of the word.

Without denying the distinction between *guiding* and *goading,* I shall say that the characteristic functions of morality are to guide conduct *and* to alter attitudes or dispositions to action.


II


This description of the characteristic functions of the language of morality is not sufficient. Let us further examine the functions of moral discourse. Not all practical discourse is moral discourse. Not all conduct is moral conduct and not all advice or appraisal of conduct is moral advice or moral appraisal. Nor are all attitudes or dispositions to action moral attitudes or moral dispositions to action. To say that moral discourse functions to guide conduct and alter behavior is very much like saying that swear words are used to express anger or that the language of cheerleading is designed to make people yell. Swear words do express anger and cheerleading language usually does prod people to yell, but these are hardly adequate descriptions of the functions of the language of swearing or the language of cheerleading. Similarly the above description of morality is hardly a sufficient description of the functions of morality.

In further describing the characteristic functions of the language of morality I am going to develop the descriptions of the function of morality given by Toulmin and Baier. While I am not in complete agreement with the way that either Toulmin or Baier have developed these notions, I believe their basic characterization of the functions of morality is correct. I shall state their basic characterization of the functions of morality and then try to explicate it by answering anticipated objections.

Toulmin and Baier speak boldly of the "function of morality." Some may be disturbed by this and think that Toulmin and Baier have shifted away from linguistic or conceptual analysis altogether and have started talking about the referent of the sign rather than about the sign itself. For many reasons, more or less irrelevant to my argument in this essay, I feel that making this semantic distinction in contexts of this sort is more confusing than enlightening. However, I have consistently, I trust, spoken of the 'language of morals' rather than of morals. Toulmin and Baier, however, speak quite directly of the function of morality. However, I believe they are 'getting at' the same considerations that I seek to explain by talking of the uses or meanings of the phrase 'the functions of moral discourse'. Keeping in mind the above-mentioned semantical distinction, I shall present Toulmin's and Baier's claims in their own mode and then, when returning to my own development of their argument, I shall speak of the uses or the functions of moral language.

I shall turn now, for a moment, to Toulmin's and Baier's own analyses.

In his *Examination of the Place of Reason in Ethics* Professor S. Toulmin makes several statements of the characteristic functions of morality or (as he calls it) of ethics.

1. The function of ethics (provisionally defined) is "to correlate our feelings and behavior in such a way as to make the fulfilment of everyone's aims and desires as far as possible, compatible." (p. 137)

2. Ethics is concerned with the harmonious satisfaction of desires and interests." (p. 223)

3. ". . . we can fairly characterize ethics as a part of the process whereby the desires and actions of the members of a community are harmonized." (p. 136)

4. "The function of ethics is to reconcile the independent aims and wills of a community of people. . . ."(p. 170)

5. "What makes us call a judgment 'ethical' is the fact that it is used to harmonize people's actions." (p. 145)

Kurt Baier, whose position is very like Toulmin's, also conceives of the functions of morality in the same general way. To take the moral point of view is to "regard the rules belonging to the morality of the group as designed to regulate the behavior of people all of whom are to be treated as equally important 'centers' of cravings, impulses, desires, needs, aims, and aspirations; as people with ends of their own, all of which are entitled, *prima facie,* to be attained."[4] A "genuine moral rule must be *for the good* of human beings."[5] But all our desires are to count alike and all "centers" of desire, excepting definitely recognized and *universalizable* exceptions, are to be treated alike.[6]

The primary reference of moral concepts is not some sort of mysterious, non-natural property; rather, while remaining gerundive concepts, they also refer to variable human dispositions, feelings, interests, desires and the like.[7] Moral discourse is concerned with altering feelings and with guiding actions so that people can live together in harmony. Like the mythical 'social contract' of the English and French philosophers of the seventeenth century, morals serve to bring man's independent desires and needs into some manageable 'peaceful coexistence'.

However, it must *not* be thought, from the above account, that Toulmin and Baier regard morality as an activity that seeks to attain social cohesion *at any price*. It is the characteristic function of morality to harmonize conflicting desires and interests in a *particular way*. Morality seeks to harmonize various interests in such a way that there will be no more suffering than is absolutely necessary for there to be social life. Moral rules are intended to allow as many people as possible to achieve as much as possible of whatever it is that they want. Morality adjudicates between these desires and interests only in the sense that it insists that we only seek to achieve those desires which are compatible with our other desires or with the desires of other people. Thus, morality is irreducibly *social*.[8] Toulmin contends that the concept of 'duty' "is straightforwardly intelligible only in communal life."[9] 'Duty', 'obligation', etc., in their basic uses, do a job only where we have a situation where a choice is involved that will affect the interests of another member of a community.

Toulmin's own development of the characteristic functions of morality leaves something to be desired. It *seems* to suggest that there could be no questions of international morality or any moral agreement between members of different communities.[10] I do not think that this is Toulmin's intent or a consequence of his analysis but I am not concerned with an exegesis of Toulmin here.[11] But *if* it is his point he is surely mistaken. In developing the above conception of the characteristic functions of morality I shall contend that the very meaning of the word 'morality' excludes the possibility of there being a Nazi morality or Hopi morality or American morality that is *just* an American, Hopi, or Nazi morality. By this I mean (for example) that if A is blameable for a given act, he would be blameable *whoever* he is, unless his being that particular person or a member of that particular group made some morally relevant difference. And, what is to count as a 'morally relevant difference' must in turn be universalizable. Moral utterances are objective in the sense that they do not apply exclusively to any given speaker or class of people but are meant to count for all people in like circumstances. Moral utterances are universalizable; they must be so if they are to count as 'moral utterances'. In their most characteristic forms, moral judgments are utterances in which the "rational element predominates"[12]; full-fledged moral judgments are to be contrasted, as are full-fledged judgments of perception, with an immediate report or an unconsidered exclamation.[13] Like Hume and Westermarck, Toulmin emphasizes that:

> In ethics, as in science, incorrigible but conflicting reports of personal experience (sensible or emotional) are replaced by judgments aiming at universality and impartiality—about the 'real value', the 'real color', 'the real shape' of an object, rather than the shape, color or value one would ascribe to it on the basis of immediate experience alone. (p. 125)

The above conception of the characteristic functions of morality might be stated rather generally, though pedantically, in the following manner. I shall refer to this general statement of the characteristic functions of morality, or moral discourse, as (W). It reads as follows:

(W) The characteristic functions of moral discourse are to guide conduct and alter behavior so as to achieve the harmonious satisfaction of as many independent desires and wants as possible.

It is important to note that this is a descriptive statement saying what sort of activity moral discourse is and what sort of functions it has. (However, it is crucial to note just what sort of descriptive statement it is. More on this in IV.) It is not intended to exhort anyone to be moral or to take the point of view of morality or anything of that nature. It is not prescriptive or normative at all. It only points out that moral discourse serves to guide conduct and alter behavior in the above fashion. Whether behavior *should* be altered in that fashion or conduct *ought* to be guided in that fashion is something which cannot be determined just by examining the functions of moral discourse. Because the word 'moral' occurs in it and because we normally assume that people ought to be moral, there is, of course, upon reading (W), a normal tendency to think that it is something we ought to do. But it is intended here as a completely non-normative statement. Fur-. ther, when I speak of the characteristic functions of moral discourse I mean to be using the words 'moral' and 'functions' quite descriptively and not also as *grading labels* that would suggest the functions of moral discourse are ends we ought to seek. This also applies to my use of 'harmonious' in (W).

## III

Let me now turn to some possible criticisms of (W). It is natural to suggest that with 'naturalistic' or egalitarian universalistic leanings I have *persuasively defined* 'moral discourse'. It might be said that such a conception of the functions of moral discourse may very well characterize the conception of the characteristic functions of moral discourse in secular 'internationally minded' Western circles, but it does not adequately characterize what some of our ancestors and what some of our Western neighbors regard as functions of moral discourse. And it certainly does not adequately characterize the conceptions of the functions of moral discourse in tribes radically different from our own.

This kind of criticism can be particularized and extended. It is *probably* true that the 'plain man' would be shocked, if not just amused, at being told that he uses moral discourse in the way I have said he uses it. He might even add: "This is monstrous. When I say something is moral, I mean it is the *right* thing to do. Morality pertains to *right conduct*. It's the activity that is concerned with advising and counselling us in what we *ought* to do and how we *ought* to live. It has nothing to do with all your fiddlefaddle about interests, harmonious satisfactions of desires and the like. Morality deals with what is *right*."

Such a reaction, though quite natural, misses my point about the characteristic functions of moral discourse. The following two considerations are crucial here.

*First,* 'morality' itself, like 'good', 'right', 'beautiful', 'nice', 'neat' and 'honest', is normally a *hurrah word*. Taking a moral point of view is the thing we *ought* to do; if something is moral it is commendatory, something that ought to be done. Thus, assuming the point about the *naturalistic fallacy* is well taken, we can never *define* 'morality', any more than any other evaluative term, in completely naturalistic or empirical terms. The plain man upon seeing our 'definitions' misses precisely the normative element or the dynamic element in them that he rightly associates with moral and valuational predicates. He then wants to say: "Morals does not harmonize people's actions; it tells them what they *ought* to do." But his objection is not to the point.

I am not trying to define 'morality' or 'morals' in the sense that R. B. Perry tries to define 'value'. Rather, I am concerned to characterize the functions of moral discourse. I am not trying to define what we mean by 'morality' in a "purified empiricist language" or any other so-called "ideal language." Rather, I am trying to describe or characterize what sort of roles moral discourse has in life. This is *not,* however, an empirical sociological description of the morals and manners of the human animal. Rather any such study would have to presuppose just the conception I am trying to get clear about. That is, it would have to presuppose we clearly understand what the functions of moral discourse are. Rather, I am asking: How does moral discourse fit in with the other forms of discourse? What sort of job or jobs does it do? Concerned with this task I can speak, in terms of satisfactions and social harmony and the like and, without the slightest inconsistency, admit that a term like 'morality' is not definable in wholly naturalistic terms.

Let us note a second consideration. Our plain man's 'definitions' are unenlightening. To be told that morals pertains to right conduct doesn't help us out at all in understanding the functions of morality, for we only ask, "But, what is right conduct?" I am trying to push aside that "surface grammar" in order to try to understand the style of functioning of moral utterances; that is, I am trying to come to understand how moral utterances really operate. I am concerned to give what Toulmin has called a "functional analysis" of moral discourse as an activity. Toulmin makes the same general point about a "functional analysis" very explicitly when he is discussing: "What is Science?"[14] But I believe it is readily applicable to his remarks and to my remarks about the functions of moral discourse. Toulmin remarks that, in describing the function of science, he does not wish so much to contradict or to compete with the man who says "Science is systematic and formulated knowledge" or the man who says "Science is organized common sense" as to *elucidate* such enlightening remarks by an analysis of the function of science.[15] I think that he would say the same thing of the man who said that "Morals is concerned with right conduct" or that "Morals is a practical science that gives us the rational basis for our actions." But these last characterizations of morality or moral discourse though correct are unenlightening. Having no explanation of the actual functions of moral discourse we remain philosophically puzzled. We ask: "What conduct is right conduct? And what do we mean by the rational basis for our actions?" My method (and Toulmin's method) is radically different. I am—as I have said—simply trying to describe the role moral discourse plays in our lives. Though my manner of speech may at first be shocking to the ordinary man, I see nothing about it, once what I am trying to do is understood, which would allow us to say that the above view of the characteristic functions of moral discourse is plainly wrong as an *explication* of what we in ordinary life mean by the characteristic functions of morality.

## IV

There is an additional problem for this kind of analysis. Let me bring this problem out by examining a question that might naturally be asked of me at this juncture. The question is the following: *"Is (W) empirical or analytic?"* This indeed is an embarrassing question. I candidly say "embarrassing question" because (1) I am troubled about just what to say about the rigidity and exclusiveness of the distinction between analytic and empirical statements, and (2) I do not want to say that (W) is either analytic or empirical in any straightforward sense. (But by this I certainly do not mean at all to suggest that I am worried about whether it might be a so-called synthetic *a priori*.) I feel uneasy about my analysis at this point, but I shall try to make clear why I do not feel that we can appropriately call (W) either analytic or synthetic. Note, by way of preliminary clarification the following two considerations.

First let me make clear why I do not want to take an 'out' that would allow me to skirt or avoid the whole problem. I could do this by pointing out that some of the constituent terms of (W), i.e., 'morality' and 'harmonious', have an irreducible emotive or expressive dimension and therefore (W) can not be called either empirical or analytic. But I have in my above treatment "emotively neutralized" 'morality' and 'harmonious satisfaction'. I have fastened exclusively on the criteriological aspects of (W). I can then (if I care to) add that the word 'moral' or 'morality' is a *commendatory* word or a pro-grading label. The word 'morality' could be applied to a completely different class of actions and still—at least for a time—remain a commendatory word. But grading labels are never just emotive or just commendatory. They always refer to a given class of actions, objects or attitudes. They are representative as well as expressive. *If* the word 'morality' were applied to a completely different class of actions from those we have been describing, then we would have to say that the same word has a new use or a new meaning and that, in a quite ordinary sense, we were not talking about the "same thing" at all. For the above reasons I think we can ignore the emotive or commendatory aspects of 'morals' and 'morality' in the *above context*.

Secondly, (W) could be made analytic by stipulative definition. But this would not help us, for what we want to know is whether in ordinary language (W) is analytic or not. Or, more precisely, when considering only the criteriological aspects in ordinary language, whether (W) is analytic or not.

With these two preliminary matters out of the way I can best bring out my reasons for not wishing to classify (W) as being either analytic or empirical. Note first that (W) *seems* at first glance to be a straightforward empirical statement. But then ask what would count as a disconfirmation of (W)?

I shall consider three characteristic functions of moral discourse that purport to be disconfirmation. I shall call them (S), (N), and (B). I shall seek to show that, depending on how they are understood, they are either improper descriptions of moral discourse or quite compatible with (W). I shall try to show that they are improper descriptions of moral discourse by showing that they fail at some point to make literal sense or that they violate our use of moral language. In making this last claim I am not simply appealing to (W) and thus begging the question at the outset. Rather I will appeal to the fact that we all know how to *operate* with moral language and can recognize bits of moral language when we hear it or see it written. Appealing to this ability of ours, I will try to show how (S), (N), and (B) violate, in one way or another, our language sense. Because of this they cannot serve as functions of moral discourse if the phrase 'functions of moral discourse' is to have its customary meaning. And in giving an analysis of 'the functions of moral discourse' this is all that is at stake. I am not trying to answer what would be the functions of moral discourse if the phrase 'the functions of moral discourse' were to have a different meaning from what it has.

Let us turn first to (S).

> (S) A characteristic function of moral discourse is to guide conduct and alter behavior so as to develop an integrated self.

Now, would we accept this as a disconfirmation of (W)? I think not. In justification of this, note the following line of reasoning. Some people might wish to contend that (S) too was a characteristic function of moral discourse. Since morality is an *open-textured* concept, it is quite possible that moral discourse could, *in some contexts,* function to develop an integrated self. However, to say that (S) is a function incompatible with *and* more basic than (W) would be to fail to understand that duty-words and obligation-words (paradigms of moral expressions) take their standard uses not from personal contexts but from inter-personal or social contexts.[16] Indeed we can speak of duties to ourselves, but this is a secondary use of 'duty' that is parasitic for its meaning on a standard use of 'duty'. This standard use of 'duty' is a use which functions to prescribe acts we must perform for other people quite apart from whether these acts would integrate our personalities or not. Thus anyone who offered the above function as a disconfirmation of (W) could be shown to be making a purely linguistic error; that is, he would *not* be using duty-words or obligation-words correctly.

Suppose someone offered as another disconfirmation of (W) the following conception of the characteristic functions of morality. Let us call it (N).

> (N) The characteristic functions of moral discourse are to guide conduct and alter behavior so as to develop a superior class of man for which the rest of mankind are to exist simply as a means. That is, the

rest of mankind are not to be regarded as moral agents with a worth of their own.

Traditional philosophical ethicists would probably claim that here we have a conflict between two basic conceptions of moral discourse and the moral life. (N) describes the function of moral discourse in a Nietzschian or quasi-Nietzschian morality of the "superman." I am making the more philosophically radical—though not, I trust, commonsensically radical—suggestion that (N) is not, and cannot be, a characteristic function of moral discourse at all. This is so because of the meaning we attach to the word 'man'. To be a man is to be *by definition* a moral agent. Even the Greek with his slaves and the Germans with their treatment of the Jews are not exceptions to this. It was necessary for them to give some universalizable reasons for slavery or Jew-persecution. It was necessary for the Germans, for example, to conceive of the Jews as a lower class of man—a class of "men" hardly human at all—in order to rationalize their treatment of them.

To be a man is to be just the sort of animal to whom, in specified situations and at a specified stage of development (beyond infanthood and before utter senility), moral blame and praise attach. It is true that in certain contexts certain human beings have moral priority over other human beings. But this moral priority is always based on certain specifiable and *universalizable* reasons. Thus in our culture we have, in certain reasonably definite contexts (the sinking of a ship, etc.), the rule: "Women and children first." We could readily envisage a culture with a morality in which *not* this moral rule but one incompatible with it obtained, but we cannot envisage a context—unless we change the use of 'moral consideration'—in which men were not treated as moral agents *at all*. Our Nietzschian with his (N) is asking us to do just that and because of that he is not describing a possible function of moral discourse at all. Again our arguments do not turn on any empirical considerations but merely on implicatory relations between standard uses of 'man' and 'moral'. And, in virtue of the uses of these words (N) could not possibly count as a disconfirmation of (W).

Let us consider another claim which might serve to disconfirm (W). Let us call it (B).

(B) The characteristic functions of moral discourse are to guide conduct and alter behavior so as to develop a superior class of men who do not seek the ordinary mundane desires of ordinary men but who attempt to "go beyond desire" altogether.

*Assuming* the validity of the rule that in morals " 'ought' implies 'can'," I wish to contend that (B) sets up a logically absurd "ideal" that cannot even *in theory* be obtained. It would only be possible for the "superior class of men" to *attempt* to go beyond desire; they could not *possibly* go "beyond desire." And, as I shall argue below, *if* the word 'attempt' has its usual logical force they cannot even *attempt* to go beyond desire. (B) is asking them to attempt to do something they cannot *in theory* do and it therefore violates the " 'ought' implies 'can' " restriction.

But to establish the above point clearly I must show *why* a man cannot possibly do what he is asked to do in (B) and why it could not possibly serve the function it purports to serve.

To see this point consider the following question. How could a morality based on (B) alter behavior? It is analytic that man only *does* what he is *motivated* to do.[17] Moral exhortations from any norm based on (B) could only take place on the absurd condition that men were men without desires. (Consider . . . could we call a being a *human* being if he were totally without desires? What would it be like for a *human* being or a sentient creature to be without desires?) But, if humans were without desires then exhortation could not possibly have any function. The word 'exhortation' could not have any meaning or use. If the conditions which (B)—on one interpretation— states were fulfillable; that is, if men could possibly become desireless then it would be nonsensical to speak of altering behavior, or, for that matter, of guiding conduct, for it is only possible to guide conduct if behavior *can be* altered. (B)—if taken literally—sets up conditions which make it theoretically (logically) impossible to alter conduct. This is so because a person can only do those acts that he is motivated to do. And a *"desireless person"* could not possibly have any motivation. When people state something like (B) they seem to mean to say that they *desire* to go beyond a certain *class* or range of desires which they desire not to desire. Their problem is of the same logical order as that of the drunk who desires not to desire alcohol. In other words we have a conflict of desires. But here we are clearly not attaching any *literal* sense to the phrase 'to go beyond desire altogether'. Men like Gandhi and Epictetus are recommending that we have as few desires as possible. Viewed soberly their requests amount to asking us to only want or desire a certain very limited group of activities. But they cannot be telling us to go beyond desire altogether.

There is still one further quite distinct consideration about (B). It might be claimed that I have in the above interpretations misread (B). (B)—the argument might continue—does not violate the " 'ought' implies 'can' " requirement. It does *not* say that a function of moral discourse is to guide conduct so that some superior men can go beyond desire but only that moral discourse functions to guide conduct so that these superior men will *attempt* to go beyond desire. If (B) stated a characteristic function of moral discourse, a person making a "moral appraisal" in accordance with it would be advocating *attempting* to go beyond desire and *not*—the impossible—going beyond desire. It might be said that again my analysis has indicated an egalitarian bias this time with a rather "Deweyite" twist. It would be claimed that I am simply *assuming* the *moral principle* that it is *wrong* to set for men goals which they cannot attain but which they can only attempt to attain.

But the above argument will hardly do for it does not make logical sense to ask someone to *attempt* what cannot *possibly* be attained. The word 'attempt' means to make an effort at, to try, to attack. But one cannot make an effort at or try to attain what is altogether impossible any more than one can find or even look for the color of heat. We do have a *secondary use* of language in which we say: "But you must try the impossible." But we don't mean this *literally,* we mean it *figuratively.* The secondary use is used characteristically in contexts in which we want, for some reason or another, to exhort a person to do something that is *very hard* and in which his chances of success are slim indeed. A coach might say this to his team when it was far, far behind, a soldier to his comrades when they were trying to make it back to their own lines, or a doctor to a patient. But if something is *logically* impossible, we cannot sensibly ask anyone to attempt the impossible. This would not be a genuine attempt but only a caricature of an attempt. The word 'attempt' could not have its standard meaning here. Thus (B) does stumble over the " 'ought' implies 'can' " requirement and thus stumbles into absurdity.

All these above examples seem to militate against treating (W) as an empirical claim. Any alleged disconfirming statements are ruled out on purely linguistic grounds. At this point it is entirely natural to ask of me: *"What would you take as a disconfirmation of (W)?"* My answer is that I cannot honestly conceive what would count as a disconfirmation of (W) or for that matter as a confirmation of it. This is why I do not want to call it an empirical statement. In other words I do not think its truth or falsity is an empirical issue in any usual sense of 'empirical issue'. But then it is natural to ask: "Is not (W) analytic?" And, I do not want to say that it is analytic either. Let me now give my reasons for not calling it analytic.

First, the contradictory of (W) does not seem to me self-contradictory though it does seem absurd and pointless. That is, I can not conceive of any possible application in morals for its contradictory.

Second, morality seems to be to be an *open-textured* concept. Like 'gold', 'man', 'game', etc., and unlike 'triangle', 'square', 'rhomboid', etc., 'morality' does *not* seem to have any defining conditions that are both necessary *and* sufficient. I can define a triangle as a three-sided figure and this definition will include all possible triangles. I cannot conceive how the term 'morality' or the phrase 'a moral consideration' could be so exhaustively defined apart from some linguistic stipulation on our part. Thus, as there are in ordinary discourse no necessary and sufficient conditions to define 'morality', we cannot treat (W) as analytic. I repeat we can *make* (W) analytic but it is not so in ordinary language.

As long as we try to fit everything in natural languages into the corset of analytic or empirical we are bound to be unsatisfied. But I see no need so to force our conceptual categories. (W) is just a statement descriptive of or characterizing the function of morality; it states the *characteristic* functions of the activity or form of life we call 'moral discourse'.

(On this level it *might* be called an empirical statement about the linguistic usage of the word 'morality' and the 'functions of moral discourse'. But this would have the paradoxical conclusion of reducing philosophy, or at least this kind of philosophy, to a bit of rather *a priori*—and therefore (by definition) bad—empirical linguistics. I was not trying to develop a generalization of the kind made in empirical linguistics. Further, (W) does not seem to me to be that kind of generalization. To use Ryle's way of putting it, I have sought to explicate the *use* and not just the *usage* of 'the functions of moral discourse'. But it is both difficult to *say* and difficult to *know* just when one is talking about usage and when one is talking about the uses of language. To get at the uses of language we must examine usage and it is hard to say or to know just when one has "got behind" the maze of usage to the *uses* of language or the style of functioning of our various areas of discourse. It is perhaps here that we can properly speak of "insight," though here this means nothing more mysterious than a cultivated sensitivity to the operations of language.[18])

V

Leaving the above puzzling aside and even leaving aside the question of whether it is analytic, empirical, or something else altogether, it still seems clear that (W) does not set the *limits of moral reasoning*. This much seems established no matter what is said about its logical status. On this point I am entirely in agreement with Toulmin's analysis.

However, the ground and the type of assent we need to give to (W) would vary depending on just what kind of a logical status it has. Thus the question asked in the preceding section is not without importance.

Lastly, it might be objected that I have not demonstrated the truth of (W). This is perfectly true. I must only remind you that all proof and all reasoning is not demonstration. I have attempted to give some *reasons* why it seems to me to be true. This reasoning does not amount to a demonstration and I do not see how, from the very nature of the case, a demonstration is possible. Yet I have given what seems to be conclusive reasons for its truth. I could, of course, attempt to examine more so-called disconfirming examples like (S), (N), and (B). But that would still not give us a demonstration. At this point the most reasonable procedure seems to me to be to turn to the *method of challenge* and ask: if these reasons are not conclusive what reasons would count as conclusive reasons in this context? If (W) is not a statement of the basic and characteristic functions of moral discourse, what is?

## NOTES

1. P. H. Nowell-Smith, *Ethics,* chapter 1. And Nowell-Smith, "Psycho-analysis and Moral Language," *The Rationalist Annual* (1954): 36.

2. David Hume, *Treatise,* Book III, Part I, Section 1.

3. See P. H. Nowell-Smith on "contextual implication" in his *Ethics,* chapter 6.

4. Kurt Baier, "The Point of View of Morality," *The Australasian Journal of Philosophy* (August, 1954): 123.

5. Ibid., p. 126.

6. Ibid., pp. 123–126.

7. Stephen Toulmin, *An Examination of the Place of Reason in Ethics.* (Cambridge, England: Cambridge University Press, 1956), pp. 125–129.

8. Ibid., chapter 10.

9. Ibid., p. 136.

10. Dykstra takes this to be Toulmin's point or a consequence of his theory. See V. H. Dykstra, "The Place of Reason in Ethics," *The Review of Metaphysics* (March, 1955): 458–467 and V. H. Dykstra, "An Examination of Stephen Toulmin's Theory of Morals," unpublished Ph.D. thesis (University of Wisconsin, 1953).

11. For my arguments here see my doctoral dissertation, chapters 9 and 10. See Kai E. Nielsen, "Justification and Morals," unpublished Ph.D. thesis (Duke University, 1955).

12. Toulmin, op. cit., p. 129.

13. Ibid., p. 123.

14. Ibid., p. 104.

15. Ibid., p. 103.

16. Nowell-Smith, *Ethics,* chapter 16.

17. This is true even when, in one sense, man does what he doesn't want to do, i.e., acts from a *sense* of duty; for, even then he acts so because the *sense* or *feeling* of duty *motivates* him to act in such a manner. And thus in *another* perfectly intelligible sense he does what he wants to do. This would, of course, only include what are ordinarily called voluntary acts (eating, going to the movies, buying a new hat, keeping a promise, etc., etc.) and not involuntary acts (breathing, seeing when one opens one's eyes, dying, being born, etc.).

18. G. Ryle, "Ordinary Language," *Philosophical Review* (April, 1953). See also Rossi-Landi's discussion of this in his introduction to Oxford philosophy prefacing his translation of *The Concept of Mind.* Ferruccio Rossi-Landi, *Lo spirito come Comportamento* (Turin, 1956).

# 3

# Justification and Moral Reasoning

## I

In moral philosophy, the justificatory problem is a crucial one. In ordinary, non-philosophical moments, we sometimes wonder how (if at all) a deeply felt moral conviction can be justified. And, in our philosophical moments, we sometimes wonder if *any* moral judgments *ever* are *in principle* justifiable. Surely, we can find all sorts of reasons for taking one course of action rather than another. We find reasons readily enough for the appraisals we make of types of action or attitudes. We frequently make judgments about the moral code of our own culture as well as those of other cultures. But how do we decide if the reasons we offer for these appraisals are good reasons? And, what is the *ground* for our decision that some reasons are good reasons and others are not? When (if at all) can we say that these grounds are sufficient grounds for our moral decisions?

Some have said that moral judgments express prejudices. We are told that we can only guide people to attain what they already desire, but that, apart from the moral habits of a given culture, there is no reasoning about the *ends* men seek. Reason, as Hume and Russell remark, not only is, but ought to be, the slave of the passions. But, others, of an equally analytical bent, have argued that certain facts are good reasons for a moral judgment quite apart from the desires, likes, wishes, or passions of the people involved. There are good reasons in morals. We can give logical grounds for these good reasons rather than merely give reasons which are "exciting reasons." The former conclusion has for some (though not for others) given rise to skeptical moral conclusions. These skeptical philosophers have seemed to believe that the "subjectivist way" leads to nihilism and despair over the rational grounds

Originally appeared in *Methodos* 9, nos. 33–34 (1957).

for our moral appraisals. The choice between "Nazi morality" and "democratic-liberal morality" is ultimately just a choice. The Joadians, alarmed by the alleged conclusions of this "subjectivist way" or "emotivist way," have sought, amidst a great wailing and gnashing of teeth, some more certain "metaphysical" or (in some instances) theological "moral ground" or "ground of life" to combat this "skepticism" over the justifiability of moral judgments. Without directly taking sides in this partisan conflict and without adding my voice to the hue and cry, I shall attempt to examine the *logic of moral reasoning*.

But this is a rather large task. I shall limit myself in the present essay to an explication of moral reasoning about individual acts and moral reasoning about the *prima facie* rules of conduct we sometimes use in justifying particular acts. In doing this I am going to begin by an examination of Stephen Toulmin's conception of the logic of moral reasoning. (Toulmin's central contentions on this subject are contained in chapter 11 of his *An Examination of the Place of Reason in Ethics*.) I do this because I regard Toulmin's approach via an examination of the function ethics plays in life to be the best point of departure in examining the logic of moral reasoning. Further, I believe that while this theory needs modifications in certain respects, both his distinction between two kinds of moral reasoning and his conception of the literal limits of justification in ethics are in the main correct. His theory, however, has been severely criticized. I shall go over the same grounds with these criticisms in mind and try to develop a more adequate account of moral reasoning.

Because of space, there are several matters I shall not consider in this essay. First, I shall not consider the question of whether it is sensible to ask for a justification to reason morally at all. I do not regard Toulmin's theory adequate here; I think such a question can sensibly arise though such a question cannot properly be called a *moral* question. Second, I shall not consider questions about the limits of the so-called "paradigm case method" or questions about whether Toulmin has committed the *naturalistic fallacy*. Toulmin does not commit the *naturalistic fallacy* in any obvious sense for he makes it perfectly plain that he does not identify the *meaning* or *use* of a moral judgment with the good reasons for a moral judgment.[1] But serious questions can arise about whether Toulmin commits the *naturalistic fallacy* in seeming to say that somehow—by noting the function of ethics and noting what, in terms of this function, are called good reasons—we can *derive* good reasons in ethics. I will here assert flatly that I regard it as logically impossible to *derive* good reasons in ethics from a description of the function of ethics. Toulmin's own theory is vague at this point. I believe, however, that if we are *committed* to the moral point of view his overall conceptions about the logic of moral reasoning follow. In what follows I want only to indicate the literal limits of moral reasoning, assuming that the reasoners are *committed* to the moral point of view. Such good reasons in ethics are not, however, logically coercive for Hägerström's "unmoved spectator of the actual." I would like to note, however, that what I call "the moral point of view" is not intended to be any particular moral point of view but a point of view general enough to cover any considerations that any group or tribe (including our own) might regard as moral considerations.

Moral reasoning, for Toulmin, is a unique and irreducible mode of reasoning. Rejecting an empiricist program of logical reconstruction, Toulmin and the "neo-Wittgensteinians" or Oxfordians emphasize that there are modes of reasoning other than the scientific or empirical, and that these modes of reasoning have their own implicit standards of precision and relevance. The philosophic job is to map the logic in the various language areas: morals, law, ritual, perception statements, etc. While assertive or indicative discourse is well mapped by formal logic, moral discourse is not. Toulmin, in trying to map the language of morals, is covering new territory. He is trying to map the unscheduled inferences of everyday moral expressions. Language is a many-leveled structure, each level having its own 'mode of reasoning'. Each mode of reasoning has its own fabric, its own formal motifs, criteria of truth, relevance, verification, and meaningfulness. Trouble or perplexity arises when the context is neglected, as it almost always is in philosophy, or at the fracture points of the modes of reasoning where the threads of the fabric of one mode or reasoning lead into another. We must give up, argues Toulmin, looking for universally applicable answers to 'What is goodness?' 'What is truth?' or 'Which reasons are good reasons?'; we must develop a contextualistic or functional analysis that will show that there is no need for despair or skepticism over this failure of philosophical theories to find universally applicable answers for the above "questions."

Toulmin argues that there are two kinds of moral reasoning, each with its own sphere of operation. The first is generally speaking deontological and the second utilitarian; the first is concerned with the justification of the moral rules themselves. Toulmin contends that if one wants to know if a particular act is right, in an unambiguous case where there is no conflict of duties, one appeals to the moral rule current in one's community. If, however, there is a conflict of *prima facie* duties among which one must make a choice, or if no rule applies at all, or if we are questioning the rule or even the whole moral code itself, teleological considerations come to the fore. We test the moral rule or rules *qua* rules (or the social practice as a social practice) by the negatively stated principle: 'Preventable suffering is to be avoided'.[2] Toulmin himself puts it very succinctly: we distinguish good reasons from bad "by applying to individual judgments the test of principle, and to principles the test of general fecundity."[3]

Almost all Toulmin's critics have agreed that his account of moral reasoning is oversimplified. But they have disagreed among themselves as to just *how* it is oversimplified. Rawls feels that Toulmin has treated moral rules too much like legal rules.[4] Moral reasoning, he argues, is not that rigid. Aiken agrees with Rawls that Toulmin's account is too rigid, but believes that moral reasoning is somewhat more rule-governed than Rawls would admit. We shall now examine some of these criticisms of Toulmin's account of the types of moral reasoning. We shall turn to criticisms of his *first type* of reasoning first, and, when we have critically examined questions arising about it, we shall then turn to his *second type* of moral reasoning.

## II

We are now considering objections to Toulmin's first type of moral reasoning. It has been argued that Toulmin is wrong in believing that a particular act clearly subsumable under a moral rule cannot be further justified by an appeal to utilitarian considerations. This criticism is applicable to Toulmin's discussion of the obligation to keep a promise. Toulmin first notes that questions about promise-keeping are in some respects significantly parallel to questions about whether or not something is straight. To see this, first note the questions we could ask about 'Is this really straight?' On the one hand, we could ask, 'Is this really straight?' in a context within which the usual Euclidian criterion of straightness is accepted. On the other hand, we could ask this same question meaningfully by making it a *test case* of the Euclidian criterion of straightness. Similarly, with 'Must I keep this promise to return x's book?' if it is asked within a context in which 'Promise-keeping is morally obligatory' is accepted as a moral rule, it is a *prima facie* obligation. And, if it does not conflict with any other *prima facie* obligations in the same moral system, the question is answered merely by citing the rule. In *this* context, no further justification is needed or, indeed, possible. One cites the rule of the road and that is the end of it; and, even if keeping *that* promise turns out to have bad consequences, it still is the right thing to do, just as it is right to drive (in America) on the right-hand side of the road even if someone whom we do not see, coming from the opposite direction, swings wide on a curve and hits us before we can get out of the way.[5] In contexts of this genre we would argue in the following fashion:

A: (Answering his own introspective question, "Must I keep *this* promise to return x's book?") "Yes, I feel that I ought to take this book and return it to x."

B: "But, ought you really to do so?"

A: "Yes, I promised him I would return the book today."

B: "But ought you really?"

A: "I ought to, because I promised to let him have it back."

B: "But, how, why ought you?"

A: "Because I ought to do whatever I promised him to do."

B: "Why?"

A: "Because it was a promise."[6]

Critics have questioned Toulmin's claim that with respect to the above kind of arguments about particular promises, in justifying such promises, we always appeal *in clear cases* to the *prima facie* obligation to keep promises. As Rawls claims, even in the unambiguous case, we do not go on appealing to the moral rule, for it is quickly realized that this appeal has already been made in the initial move. In going on, in rondo form as I did above, I have only made what was already known from the first defense painfully and pedantically explicit. But people, in justifying their acts, do not always appeal to "the thing done." Rawls says that it would be quite natural to reply to a further question about why it is a duty to return a book as promised: "He needs the book because he is lecturing on a chapter in it tomorrow." "He is studying for an examination tomorrow and this book contains the best account of the subject" and so on.[7] These are just samples of the many kinds of answers we do give. Further, these reasons seem to be offered in accordance with the principle of utility. Nor, Rawls argues, would it do for Toulmin to reply that these other justifications were really an effort to justify the rule rather than the particular obligation; for the reasons refer to the special circumstances of the particular obligation in question.[8]

Yet, I do not think that Rawls's criticism will do, initially plausible though it may seem. Its plausibility results from confusing the clear unambiguous case which Toulmin has in mind, when he speaks of justifying an action subsumed under the practice of promise-keeping, either with cases of deliberation about what to do when practices conflict or (more importantly *here*) with cases of deliberating about whether or not this action is one of the exceptions allowed by the practice. Actually, Rawls's considerations are usually used in trying to decide whether *this case* is or is not a legitimate exception allowed by the *practice*. Because this last question is so easy to confuse with Toulmin's clear case, we find Rawls's example convincing. But, *in a clear case*, we cannot further justify an act of promise-keeping by an appeal to utilitarian considerations. Indeed, it is of the utmost utility for the *practice* that we cannot make this utilitarian defense for an act clearly subsumed under it. The very *raison d'être* of such a practice is to make such an appeal unnecessary. Because it is a clear case of an act subsumable under the practice of promise-keeping, such a defense cannot be made.[9] This, indeed, is an analytic truth but it does not become for that reason trivial.

The difficult and interesting moral problems (from a practical point of view) are, of course, *not* these clear cases. Rather, they are cases in which we have conflicting rules or in which we are not sure of the application of the rule. In such instances we must weigh the various considerations and then decide what to do. In fact, clear cases are "trivial as *moral problems.*" Jones lends me a book and I say, "I'll bring it back Tuesday." Unless complicating circumstances arise, in which event the above case, by definition, is not a clear case, we know perfectly well what we ought to do and why we ought to do it.

There is a second objection to Toulmin's *first type* of moral reasoning. This objection has been made by Rawls, Peters, and Mackie. It is that moral reasoning is not as rule-governed as Toulmin takes it to be. Frequently, and not just when there is a conflict between rules, we appeal directly to utilitarian considerations to justify particular actions; or we appeal to a "vaguer" notion of equity or *universalizability;* or at times we simply appeal to what a reasonable man would do.

Now, this objection must be accepted. Moral reasoning about particular acts is much less rule-governed than Toulmin seems to imply. Note the following example: A law student is studying for a bar exam. About a week before the exam he receives an urgent long distance call from his sister asking him to drop everything and come to help her. Suppose that his sister is a chronic alcoholic and is likely to be in dire circumstances. Assume further that there is no one else to help her. But, suppose also that the law student's leaving school at this time might cause him to fail his exam. The moral decision which has to be made here is not a matter of doing something in accordance with a *prima facie* obligation. Yet, there is no clear conflict over *prima facie* duties. He has, indeed, a *prima facie* duty to help his sister. But there seems to be no conflicting *prima facie* duty that we could oppose to it. It is obvious enough, without analyzing the situation exhaustively, that considerations here do not so much turn upon a conflict of *prima facie* duties as upon considerations of *equity* and *utility.* The principle of least suffering directly weighs here for a particular moral decision. Is his *prima facie* duty to help his sister overbalanced by the personal suffering and hardship attendant on failing the bar exam? Questions of equity are definitely raised here. He must weigh these none-too-precise considerations and then decide what to do. But this is hardly a matter of a quasi-legal subsumption of a given act under a *prima facie* obligation in the fashion of Toulmin's paradigms of moral reasoning about specific acts.

These last criticisms of Toulmin are well taken. If Toulmin's theory is not amended here it is overly rigid and implicitly prescriptive. It is clear that, though we sometimes justify a moral act by showing that it is in accord with a *prima facie* obligation, we often justify a given act directly by an appeal to utilitarian considerations, or even, where the probably felicific consequences are not now discoverable, by an appeal to some vaguer notion of what a "reasonable man would do." Toulmin's theory would make it logically impossible to make these moves in moral discourse. But, in a *pre-analytic* sense of 'know', we know that we can make these moves in moral reasoning. Hence, Toulmin's theory cannot be right as an *explication* of ordinary moral reasoning.

However, I believe Toulmin's theory could be amended here without his needing to give up his basic contention that, in the first type of moral reasoning, we cannot further justify a moral *act* clearly subsumable under a moral rule by an appeal beyond the moral rule itself. One would have to go on to say only that there are different situations in which we appeal to utilitarian considerations or to what "a reasonable man would do" in justifying an act. One would have to specify these situations so that we could say in what general kinds of situations we must make one move rather than the other.

There are also the following considerations. People and cultures differ in the weight they give to rules and to utilitarian considerations. But the recognition of this difference still does not upset Toulmin's logical consideration that, when the rule is accepted by the person making a decision to act in a given fashion and the act is clearly subsumable under the rule, we cannot further justify this act by an appeal to utilitarian considerations. The above modification of Toulmin's theory does not indicate that there is something wrong with his bifurcation of moral reasoning into two kinds. Rather, it proves that the situations in which the first kind of reasoning applies are less typical than he implied. He should have gone on to talk about the "logic of" those moral acts which are not subsumed under moral rules. But such a consideration does not at all invalidate his remarks about the "logic of" moral acts clearly subsumable under moral rules. To amend Toulmin's theory so that it will account for the other situations requires no radical innovations, much less an abandonment of his distinction between two kinds of moral reasoning.

## III

We shall now turn to criticisms of Toulmin's *second kind* of moral reasoning. These criticisms, if correct, will have more serious implications for his approach as a whole.

Note the following criticism made of Toulmin's *second kind* of moral reasoning. Peters points out, against Toulmin's second type of moral reasoning, that conservative frequently appeal not to utilitarian consideration, but simply to tradition to justify *prima facie* obligations. We may debate morally, defending a normative utilitarianism, with the Catholic who appeals to the "Wisdom of the Holy Mother Church" or with Sir Edward Coke (or, in our time, with a Peter Viereck or a Russell Kirk) who advocate a return to tradition to amend the "moral chaos" of our "secularist culture"; but we can hardly accuse such people of uttering logical nonsense in their basic arguments.[10] In fact, the principle of least suffering, or the principle that traditional ways are the best, are themselves just social practices which we oppose to other social practices. Or perhaps the principle of least suffering is a higher level social practice with which we justify lower level social practices, including the social practice of appealing to tradition. Or is tradition a social practice in virtue of which we justify an appeal to the principle of least suffering? Reasoning at this second level is more complicated than Toulmin has made it out to be.

Peters, however, unwittingly provides Toulmin with at least a partial answer to the above criticism. The appeal to tradition *qua* tradition or to authority *qua* authority is not (as a mere matter of how we use moral language)[11] regarded as a good moral reason to justify a social practice. Peters points out that Edmund Burke, who was perhaps the most subtle of the conservative-traditionalists, based his appeal to tradition on a "sophisticated kind of social utility."[12] Burke points out to radical and eager social and moral reformers that our social practices are the product of a long cultural history and that moral and political conventions represent compromises reached by competing interests. In terms of pure utility, these normative conventions cannot be put aside lightly.[13] But an appeal to authority or tradition *as such* is clearly recognized *not* to be a moral appeal. And to make this last statement is not (as Peter suggests)[14] to make a moral claim, but is to make a logical statement about the use of 'moral appeal'.

There is, however, a further argument that can be made against Toulmin's *second kind* of moral reasoning. If we grant that an appeal to tradition itself, if it is to be a moral appeal, must be based upon a higher order principle, is it clear that, as a mere matter of logic, the legitimacy of an appeal to tradition is always and necessarily based on the principle of utility or the principle of least suffering? That this is so does not seem self-evidently clear. I agree with Paton[15] that Toulmin surely ought to have considered some of the arguments directed against ideal utilitarianism. Certainly, everybody accepts the relevancy of the principle of least suffering. But is it the only principle which can be appealed to in order to justify lower-order moral rules, and is it the final court of appeal? Even a Kantian, like Paton, admits that any "sane morality must accept these utilitarian principles."[16] The intuitionists, in one form or another, have admitted the principle. The point is: is it the *only* principle or the most ultimate principle, or are there competing basic normative principles or more ultimate normative principles? Rawls has put this difficulty very nicely:

Toulmin speaks vaguely of the appeal to consequences, the avoidance of unnecessary suffering, and the like. Now all British moralists with whom I am acquainted admit the principle of utilitarianism in some form, even the intuitionists, e.g., Butler, Price and Ross. The main question is whether it is the *only* principle involved in reasoning about the worth of social practices (waiving for the present the matter of specific actions). Even the utilitarians themselves seem to admit that it is not. Bentham had his Principle about every man to count for one and no more than one, and Sidgwick admitted certain rational intuitions, e.g., that of benevolence. Since Toulmin's view is a kind of utilitarianism, one would expect, even in a small-scale map, some discussion of this crucial question.[17]

Is it so clear, from an appeal to usage, that we must appeal to the principle of least suffering to justify promise-keeping (the moral rule)? Could the rule not just as well be made in accordance with C. I. Lewis's "Law of Justice"? Lewis's principle is: each is to act in his relations with his fellow men so that he will recognize as right, in his human associations, only what he recognizes as similarly sanctioned in their conduct toward himself.[18] This rather Kantian reformulation of the Golden Rule would seem to serve just as well as a principle in accordance with which lower-order rules are justified as does Toulmin's basic principle.

Further, if this possibility is admitted, is the Law of Justice to take precedence or is the principle of least suffering to take precedence? Or are both principles on the same level? Do we just have a plurality of "*a priori* first principles" as the pluralistic deontologists think? Toulmin, as he has worked out his position, must maintain that the principle of least suffering takes precedence; but he nowhere argues for it.[19] It does not seem clear that it does do so.

Now I am not claiming that Toulmin might not solve these puzzles about the principle of least suffering. The frequency with which eudaemonistic theories have arisen in both ancient and modern times, and the seeming commonsensicalness of the utilitarian theory, particularly when a notion of just distribution is built into it, would seem to indicate that utilitarianism (taken broadly) is more than our present dominant criterion. But Toulmin had not *shown* that his criterion is more than the present dominant one; and, *above all,* he had not *shown* that his criterion must *hold* if we are to talk morally at all. He has not even made his criterion clear enough to resolve the classical conflicts between Kantians and utilitarians. (I shall try to show this in IV.) He must clarify his criterion and must show, to make his theory stick, that if we are to talk ethically at all, we must use just his utilitarian standards and *no others* as the final court of appeal. If Toulmin is correct, it would be impossible for a man to dispute about the least suffering principle. But, it is argued, this is precisely what we do, at least in our philosophic moments. Even the classical utilitarians, when they argued for their position, thought they were arguing for it morally.

Toulmin, to avoid the criticism that he has confused a factual issue with a logical one, must show that 'preventable suffering is to be avoided' is not merely *in fact* a universally accepted criterion for judging *prima facie* duties (answering the question why do we have the moral rules we do) but that it is also a logically necessary criterion which follows from the very logic of moral talk so that it would be absurd or senseless (unintelligible) to offer any other criterion (like Lewis's "Law of Justice") as a moral criterion for judging *prima facie* duties.

Here again, Toulmin's theory is not adequate as it stands, and is implicitly prescriptive. Lewis's "Law of Justice" in one sense could well serve as a criterion for judging social practices (*prima facie* duties). This would be merely the step Broad speaks of (though critically) as the step from a pluralistic to a monistic deontology.[20] It is not clear how Toulmin, on logical grounds alone, could reject such an alternative principle.

The following is a simple way in which one might try to amend Toulmin's theory so as to avoid these difficulties. We would have to say that there are three kinds of moral reasoning: first, moral reasoning about specific acts which are clearly subsumable under determinate *prima facie* duties; second, moral reasoning about specific acts and about *prima facie* duties subsumable under general moral principles like Lewis's "Law of Justice"; third, moral reasoning about specific acts, *prima facie* duties, and general moral principles like Lewis's "Law of Justice" testable by utilitarian considerations. General principles like the "Law of Justice," though they yield criteria for judging the moral worth of social practices, must themselves be justified in terms of the principle of least suffering (i.e., utilitarian considerations). Though there is, indeed, this "extra kind" of moral reasoning, the crucial point is that the principle of least suffering is the ultimate criterion for moral rules, whether *prima facie* duties or the more general "Law of Justice."

Yet this amendment of Toulmin's theory is itself hardly adequate; for 'preventable suffering is to be avoided' can, depending on how we understand 'preventable', be regarded quite naturally, as can Bentham's principle of utility, as implicitly containing the "Law of Justice" or as containing a principle of just distribution.[21] This claim is particularly clear when we consider the principle of least suffering in relation to Toulmin's conception of the primary function of morals. What is to count as 'preventable suffering' is determined by which suffering could be dispensed with in the effort to harmonize as many independent desires and needs as possible.[22] Bound up in Toulmin's very principle of least suffering is Lewis's "Law of Justice." The principles, then, do not form a neat hierarchy and are not so distinct as they seemed at first.

IV

In order to unpack the argument I expressed in the immediately preceding paragraph, it will be necessary to make a slight detour. But, once back on the main highway, we will be able to understand more readily how Toulmin's principle is a necessary principle of moral talk as moral talk is presently structured. On the detour, I shall make quite explicit the principle of *universalizability* at work in Toulmin's own criteria. In doing that, I shall *first* make clear what is meant by saying that all moral utterances must be *universalizable* and how Lewis's "Law of Justice" expresses that requirement. *Secondly,* I shall analyze the role of 'preventable' in 'preventable suffering is to be avoided'. I shall show that there are two ways 'preventable' in its above context might be taken. One of these interpretations involves the notion of *universalizability*. I shall argue that the most plausible way to understand 'preventable' as Toulmin uses it is to take it in the sense in which it involves the notion of *universalizability*. If his principle of least suffering is given this interpretation of 'preventable' it implicitly contains, as I shall show, Lewis's "Law of Justice" and similar Kantian principles.

For an act to be moral or for an attitude to be moral, it must be *universalizable*. By this is meant the following. If A is morally right for x, it is similarly morally right for anyone else in like circumstances. For something to be morally right or good, it must be such that its moral rightness or goodness does not depend upon who does the act or who has the experience. The notion of *universalizability* is expressed in the adage: "What's good for the goose is good for the gander." One must, of course, add that there are special circumstances which make a reference to the person involved essential in judgments about the rightness of an act. Thus children (but not adults) have a right to protection by their parents and the mentally ill (but not sane people) have the right to care by the state. But, in turn, to be able to modify our moral appraisals on the basis of these special circumstances, we must be able to apply the *universalizability* principle to the acts or attitudes which would probably issue if we recognized these special circumstances. It is not just patient x or z that has a right to protection in the community, but any mentally ill person in the community. The same *universalizability* principle applies even to moral judgments based on very peculiar and unique circumstances. If we excuse someone from moral blame for a given act because of peculiar circumstances in his life history, we do not excuse him because he is the particular person he is but would excuse anyone else in the same fashion in like circumstances who had similar peculiarities of life history. Any case of moral grading must be capable of passing the *universalizability* test.

Lewis's "Law of Justice" expresses the Kantian notion of *universalizability*. Each is to act in his relations with his fellow men so that he will recognize as right in his human associations only what he recognizes as similarly sanctioned in their conduct toward himself. Lewis is saying that if A in certain circumstances deems it morally permissible to break a promise to B, he must, if he is reasoning morally, realize that in like circumstances, it is morally permissible for B to break a promise to him. If one is reasoning morally one must always be able to ask of any proposed moral action: is it *universalizable?*

Now the interesting question for our purposes is whether or not the principle of *universalizability* is built into the use Toulmin gives to 'preventable'. It is not obvious, by any means, that this is so. Let us first look to the use of 'preventable' in 'preventable suffering is to be avoided'. Here 'preventable', like Mill's use of 'desirable', is subject to at least two quite different interpretations. 'Preventable' can mean (1) that which can in fact be prevented or (2) that which *ought* to be prevented. I shall call them respectively the *first* and *second* senses of 'preventable'.

Now the *first* sense of 'preventable' will not do in certain quite ordinary moral contexts. I shall argue that it is the *second* interpretation that is morally relevant. If we do not read 'preventable suffering is to be avoided' with this second interpretation, it will not do the job Toulmin wants it to do. In trying to establish my point, I shall first examine four moral paradigms; then I shall examine one special kind of paradigm that I think is quite crucial if we are to understand the kind of a job the least suffering principle is intended to do in Toulmin's theory.

Note first two quite ordinary moral paradigms in which suffering that can *in fact* be prevented is not prevented and is regarded, in terms of the morality of the situation, as unpreventable. Many people judge that a soldier is morally obligated to lay down his life, if necessary, for his country. Men, under certain circumstances, are sent into situations in which they will almost certainly be killed or taken prisoner. Now this suffering is in a straightforward empirical sense preventable. It is preventable suffering in the first sense. But, in terms of the moral notions governing the situation, it is unpreventable suffering.

Similarly, the suffering a criminal must undergo in being imprisoned is certainly 'preventable' in the first sense, but nonetheless, *if* it is necessary that he be imprisoned for the common good, it is not preventable suffering in the second sense. *Things being as they in fact are,* this suffering ought not to be prevented. It is again the second sense of 'preventable' that is the ethically relevant sense in this situation as it is in the first situation.

Note now the use of 'preventable' in the following somewhat different moral contexts. Before Queen Victoria's pattern making act, many people in England thought it was morally wrong for mothers to take any anesthetic at childbirth. "Sinful man ought to suffer." Such suffering is obviously preventable in the empirical sense (i.e., it could have in fact been prevented). But in the second sense it is again unpreventable. Note a second example of the same general kind. Recently a priest suffering from cancer refused to take any drugs to relieve his suffering. Rather, he felt he ought to accept his suffering, for it was "God's will." While *morally* we may disagree very much with his moral judgment, there is nothing *linguistically improper* about it such that we could say that it could not count as a moral judgment. Again, we have a clear case of suffering that is preventable in the first sense but not in the second morally relevant sense.

If we take Toulmin to be using 'preventable' in the first sense only, then it hardly can be maintained that his principle of least suffering, functioning as it does for him, is based on purely linguistic considerations about how we use moral language. We have in the above four paradigms of moral reasoning moral appraisals which his principle *cannot* account for.[23] He would merely have to rule them out as moral considerations; but to do this would quite obviously be to engage in moral argument rather than to do the meta-ethicist's task of examining the kinds of argument that can count as moral arguments. If he sticks to his meta-ethicist's job, he cannot rule out the above considerations as not moral. If his theory is to work at all we must understand 'preventable' in the second sense.

There is, however, a further consideration which complicates matters in that it leads us to wonder whether, after all, these four paradigms can serve to bring out and make clear the particular sense of 'preventable' which is relevant to Toulmin's least suffering principle. This can be brought out by the following considerations. *Given the ends* sought in the four examples noted above, it is empirically the case that suffering is a *necessary* means to those ends. In this way, the suffering is unpreventable in the first, empirical, sense of 'preventable', although, if one neglects the *moral goals* sought, the suffering is quite preventable in the same first, empirical, sense of 'preventable'. Thus, taking into consideration means-ends relationships, we must qualify our statement in the preceding paragraphs that the suffering in the four paradigms was preventable suffering in the first sense of 'preventable'. Rather, we must say that it is only preventable if we do *not* accept the limitations set up by the moral goals implicit in our moral paradigms. If we do accept them, then the suffering is unpreventable in the first sense as well as in the second sense. But, it is in terms of the 'moral necessity' inherent in the second sense that the suffering is unpreventable in the first sense. Otherwise, in the first sense, the suffering is quite preventable.

Because of the above feature of the four paradigms, we feel that there is "no real moral choice" about the suffering and that we do not have the moral situation we need in order to bring out the moral force of an utterance like 'preventable suffering is to be avoided'. We might clarify what we mean by this last statement a little more fully. When these paradigms are used to explain the sense of 'preventable' in 'preventable suffering is to be avoided', we feel cheated; for, in those examples, there is never really any "choice" involved at all. Given certain moral ends, the suffering is quite necessary. What we want is a situation in which choices about courses of action involve, or at least seem to involve, choices about whether to seek preventable suffering as an *end*. We want a situation in which "suffering is sought for its own sake." In other words, we want a situation in which the suffering is quite preventable in an empirical sense but where we nonetheless just *choose* to seek suffering for its own sake. Now I do not believe that we can give a pure paradigm for that, for I do not think that we can say meaningfully that suffering can be sought for its own sake. One cannot enjoy, seek, or desire suffering as an end.[24] The very meaning of 'suffering' signifies a state one cannot desire or enjoy. One cannot seek out suffering; rather, one seeks to avoid suffering. Suffering is just the sort of thing that cannot be sought *for its own sake*. This is not an empirical matter, but follows from the very use of 'suffering'.

However, we do have a secondary sense in which we might say, though metaphorically, 'suffering is sought for its own sake'. A paradigm case in which this use is at play will give us the kind of example we need for explicating the second sense of 'preventable' in the way in which I believe it functions in Toulmin's criterion. The paradigm I have in mind is the one in which a man, for no purpose at all other than his own enjoyment, willfully inflicts suffering on others. This, from a moral point of view, is the sort of thing which we are likely to say is "unqualifiedly evil." In the other four paradigms, the suffering was unpreventable in a morally relevant sense. But here we have a situation in which someone inflicts suffering on another person when it is both empirically and morally possible to prevent the suffering. The man, of course, does not seek suffering for its own sake but seeks others' suffering because it gives him pleasure. But, in a metaphorical sense, we can say that he seeks suffering (i.e., the suffering of others) for its own sake. To put it this way brings out an important feature in which this paradigm differs from the other four. Here there is no question of the suffering being sought as a necessary means to a "higher end"; it is sought merely because the sadist likes to see people suffer. He simply chooses to inflict suffering on others. In one quite ordinary empirical sense, the suffering inflicted is preventable (i.e., it can be prevented) and certainly, in another way, it is unpreventable (i.e., it is a necessary means to the sadist's ends) in an equally empirical sense.

But in which sense is 'preventable' relevant to the moralist? In terms of the sadist's ends, the suffering is quite as unpreventable as in the first four paradigm cases in which we agreed that, in a morally relevant sense, the suffering was unpreventable. But, in the last case, we say the satisfaction of the sadist's ends is ruled out by moral considerations.

There is a teasing problem here. It is perfectly true that, *as a matter of fact*, we do say that the sadist's ends are morally irrelevant. But in giving him a bad moral grade are we grading him down on his morals alone or are we also grading him down on his logic? Is the end the sadist seeks an end which we, as moral agents, find morally repugnant still an end which we could understand as being a moral end in someone's morality? It is at this point that the Kant-like concept of *universalizability* becomes crucial. I shall contend that *if* the sadist's ends can be *universalized* then they *could* count as a bit of moral discourse, though I as a moral agent find myself as eager as the next man to reject the sadist's ends.

Some might argue that the sadist's ends are not *universalizable*. They might say that the sadist cannot wish that in like circumstances *suffering* be inflicted on him, although he may wish (assuming he is also a masochist) that *pain* be inflicted on him. This is so because the very meaning of 'suffering' contextually implies that one will avoid suffering unless it is necessary for some higher end. Because here there is no higher end the sadist's end is not *universalizable* and hence not moral.

The above argument, unfortunately, is wrong. The sadist's ends are *universalizable* though it may take some exercise of imagination to see it. Again we have been misled (as so often is the case in philosophy) by forgetting that a metaphor is a metaphor. The sadist doesn't really seek the suffering of others for its own sake but he seeks it as a means of increasing his own pleasure or satisfaction. It may be replied that we cannot correctly say the sadist seeks the suffering of others for the sake of a higher end. This is perfectly true, as we usually use 'higher end' but this *may* not faze the sadist. He may say that the term 'higher end' is a polyguous grading label,[25] that has no set or fixed denotation. "Enlightened humanity," he will urge, "realizes that the only thing really worth seeking as an end in life is the maximum satisfaction for *each individual, no matter how that satisfaction is obtained.*" He—the sadist—is a member of the class of "enlightened humanity." And, as a psychological fact, the only way he (the sadist) can maximize his satisfaction is by inflicting suffering on others.

What can we say of such a bizarre contention? 1) We can convict the sadist of departing from the usual criteria for a 'higher end' and for giving 'higher end' a capricious *persuasive* definition.[26] Yet if he takes his above line of argument, it is clear that he is taking the position of a radical moral reformer who is advocationg *new* standards or criteria for what is to count as a 'higher end'.[27] He is altering the rather vague denotation of 'higher end'. Yet our moral language is sufficiently flexible for his contention to be quite intelligible as a moral utterance. If we criticize his claim here it must be his *morals* not his *logic* that we criticize, though it is worth noting in passing how atypical his contention is. 2) In taking such a stand, our papier mache sadist need not violate the principle of *universalizability,* that is, he need not use a uniquely singular term which is not replaceable by a general term or conjuction of general terms. The sadist could replace his moral claim:

(1) I ought to inflict suffering on others because that and only that maximizes my pleasure.

with a universalized version (2).

(2) Anyone in a relevantly similar[28] position to mine and with a relevantly similar personality ought to inflict suffering on others because that and only that would maximize his pleasure.

If someone directed the ploy at our sadist, "But how would you like it if someone tortured you?" he *might* answer with perfect logical consistency, "Well, I'm not that masochistic! I wouldn't like it and I ought to strive to avoid it. But another sadist has a perfect right to try to inflict suffering on me and he ought to do so. This is one of the irreducible conflicts of the moral life . . . an existential absurdity that we are just saddled with. This is a bit of suffering that Mr. Toulmin would be forced to admit is *not* preventable suffering as long as there are people with personalities like mine." The relevant sense of 'preventable' here is the second, non-empirical sense of 'preventable'. This second sense is governed by the notion of *universalizability*.

Thus the sadist's ends are *universalizable*. And his position could logically count as a 'moral position'. In grading our sadist down, we are grading him down morally; there is nothing wrong with the logic of his moral reasoning. In saying that the sadist's ends are ruled out by moral considerations, we are entering into moral controversy and not just generalizing about moral reasoning. It is important to remember that the sadist does not (and cannot) seek suffering for its own sake; rather, he seeks an end in which each individual seeks to maximize his own satisfaction in whatever way he can, and this end is in perfect accord with the principle of *universalizability*.

Toulmin's principle of least suffering, if it is to count as a principle which sets the limits of moral reasoning, implicitly contains the principle of *universalizability*. The use of 'preventable' in Toulmin's principle is only intelligible if it understood as denoting suffering which cannot be universalized and not just the suffering that can *in fact* be prevented. Interpreted in such a manner, Toulmin's criterion meets the test of ordinary usage, but it also becomes compatible with any and every principle that *could* possibly count as a 'moral principle'. It admits even the sadist's position or a position of an ethical egoism of means. While being compatible with the uses of moral discourse, it is certainly incompatible with our common sense everyday moral principles. This does not, however, convict Toulmin of inconsistency because he wishes to square his contention with ordinary usage and not necessarily with common sense moral principles. The logic of moral discourse has, of course, a wider range of application than even very general actual moral principles. But, since "the least suffering criterion" is so completely "tolerant" of all possible moral principles, it can hardly serve as a guide for deciding which reasons among the various preferred reasons are *good* reasons for deciding between conflicting moral rules or social practices.

The above difficulty can be brought out in another way noting the role the principle of *universalizability* plays in moral assessment. Hare has pointed out that because the notion of *universalizability* is analytically tied with what we mean by a 'moral consideration', *universalizability* is a purely *formal* logical criterion that is compatible with any moral rule.[29] All reasons to count as 'reasons' must be *universalizable* but we cannot by this device alone find out which reasons are *good* or which moral principles are acceptable. If Kant, and more recently Paton, expect the *universalizability* principle to do this job, they have simply misapplied the principle. It will neither tell us specifically what we ought or ought not to do (a point Kant and Paton are quite clear about), nor tell us, in general, what courses of action ought to be sought.[30] Toulmin, himself, puts this point well: "Kant does not pretend to be providing a recipe for the Good Life: rather, he is engaged in a logical or meta-ethical enquiry, setting out to analyze the nature of moral obligation, and to contrast it with prudential and technical advisability."[31] Kant's meta-ethic does not commit one to a "super-ego morality" of sin and renunciation. One can be a "cultural relativist" or "naturalist" and still accept the Kantian contention that moral utterances must be *universalizable*.

In a like manner Toulmin's principle is compatible with any and every normative ethic or substantive ethic.[32] To set the limits of moral reasoning it must be vacuous in this manner, but, in becoming so, it will no longer serve as the criterion for deciding between conflicting moral rules. As it has been interpreted, Toulmin's theory must be inadequate in order to be adequate. And Toulmin is surely anxious to avoid this "philosopher's paradox."

V

We are now ready to take the main road again. Is Toulmin's kind of principle the ultimate criterion we use in justificatory steps in morals? On the detour we found that built into Toulmin's very principle of least suffering is the principle of *universalizability*. We also discovered that *universalizability* is an essential ingredient in moral discourse, but that because of the role *universalizability* plays in Toulmin's principle of least suffering, Toulmin's principle becomes compatible with every and any normative ethic. Finally, from our discussion in IV, it should become obvious why there can be no simple and neat hierarchy of principles, starting with those of a pluralistic deontology, ascending to a Kantian or monistic deontology, and ending finally with the utilitarian principle. The logic of moral discourse is more complex than that. But as long as we are committed to a moral point of view and as long as we are using ethical words as they are usually used it is clear that Toulmin's principle, vacuous as it is, is the ultimate principle of moral assessment.

The above conclusions, nevertheless, ought to make us pause. In a reflective re-appraisal the following objections might naturally occur:[33] What kind of a principle of assessment or appraisal is it when this ultimate principle is compatible with any and every actual morality and every moral rule that could possibly count as a 'moral rule'? This will not enable us to distinguish good reasoning from bad reasoning in ethics. Continuing my reflections, I might conclude that I have put too many "subtle Kantian" qualifications into Toulmin's thesis. I have made 'preventable' and 'unnecessary' bear too big a load. Toulmin's actual criterion is more straightforwardly utilitarian. If the consequences of a moral rule will lead to greater general misery or unhappiness, this is a moral rule that ought to be replaced by one causing less general misery and unhappiness.[34] I have failed, it might be continued, to note that Toulmin's ultimate criterion for moral rules is fixed in terms of the *function* of ethics or morals and this function places the utilitarian criterion in a good light. To decide whether Toulmin's criterion is indeed the ultimate criterion for the second kind of moral reasoning we must consider it in conjunction with Toulmin's conception of the function of morality. As Toulmin remarks, "the scope of ethical reasoning is limited as well as defined by the framework of activities in which it plays its part."[35] It might be said that the characteristic function of ethics is to correlate our feelings and acts in a way which fulfills as many independent desires and wants as possible. Peoples' actions are to be harmonized so that each person can attain the maximum amount of satisfaction that is compatible with the same goal fulfillment by his neighbors.[36] It is Toulmin's contention that once we clearly understand the primary function of ethics, we will also understand why there are natural criteria (good reasons) in morals.

Let us, then, try to follow out Toulmin's suggestion and consider the ultimate criterion of morality vis-à-vis Toulmin's conception of the function of morality.

This effort might be immediately opposed by a denial that morality has a characteristic function. It has been said that since morality is not a kind of instrument, like a hammer or a saw, it—unlike the hammer or saw—does not have a characteristic function. And, unlike science, it is not a definite discipline with discernible functions.[37] Sometimes moral utterances do not function to alter behavior or feelings but function merely to express our own convictions, as when we utter under our breath after reading of some personal or governmental scandal, "He's a bastard." A functional analysis may be appropriate for scientific discourse, but it is not appropriate for moral discourse. Moral discourse is too varied.

To the above, the following reply can be made: It is perfectly true that the uses of moral concepts are protean. Morality, of course, is not like an instrument and it does not have any simple, single function. Toulmin is quite clear and definite about this.[38] Nonetheless, there are some paradigms of moral behavior and moral utterances. The borderline between morality and tabu or self-interest, etc. may not always be clear, but we do have at least some instances of publicly comprehensible utterances or behavior that clearly count as moral utterances or moral behavior. (We must distinguish the ability to pick out these paradigms from the ability to say in general just what makes them paradigms.)[39] Morality, it is reasonable to believe, is at least in part an autonomous activity and a philosopher can discover, by careful attention to the ways in which moral concepts are used, at least some general patterns of this activity. To say that morality is totally patternless or functionless makes inexplicable the fact that there are as a matter of fact paradigm cases of moral utterances or moral behavior. Furthermore, we do not seem to be uttering absurdities when we speak of the purposes or aims of moral discourse. We must only avoid being monolithic about it.

If we grant that morality has some characteristic function or functions, we still must justify Toulmin's conception of the characteristic function of ethics.[40] It is necessary to ask why Toulmin takes the above function of morality to be the central or the most characteristic function. The answer to this can best be seen from the reply to the following question: *"Why is it that we have morals at all?"* There is of course no question that we *have* such an activity. As different as various moral systems are, anthropologists now assure us that morality is a universal category of culture.[41] Assured that morality is pan-human, we can ask *why* do we have morality? Now, because moral utterances are protean in their jobs there is no single, simple answer to this question. To assume the contrary would be again to go after an essentialist will-of-the-wisp. Yet, Hobbes brought out strongly, though in a needlessly polemical manner, one very central part of the answer. Epicurus (among others) had uttered it before, and, most recently, Russell has advocated it in his *Human Society in Ethics and Politics*.[42] Put simply (perhaps too simply), the answer to our question is that we all want to be able to lie down at night in peace and sleep. Man, even if he is not so aggressive as Freud and Niebuhr think he is, needs some social mechanism that will curb his personal desires so they will fit into social and asocial (but not antisocial) patterns. The human animal is a social animal, and in society there will be conflicting desires and goals, not all of which can be realized. Man needs some *impartial mechanism* to adjudicate these desires and strivings so that mankind can live together in reasonable harmony. Individuals, by and large, desire security and they desire a life in which they can maximize their desires and exercise freedom of choice. Morality, which functions (in large part) to harmonize man's desires and goals, is instrumental to the satisfaction of this human need. In view of this function, it is also clear why the principle of *universalizability* (or impartiality, as it is sometimes called) must be built into moral principles. Morality could only successfully harmonize desires and adjudicate wants if it functioned objectively or impartially. A morality without such a rule would be not unlike a car that not only wouldn't but couldn't move.

Difficulties are not at an end. Toulmin's conception of the function of ethics erects barriers to taking it as an adequate instrument for determining what kinds of reasons are good reasons in ethics. The very word 'function' as it is used by Toulmin causes this difficulty. Mackie remarks that when Toulmin speaks of the " 'functions' of science and ethics. . . it is not clear whether a function is what a thing does or what the speaker is telling it to do."[43] We find out the function of something by observation (including observation of linguistic behavior); but, in finding out what the function *is* we somehow also find out that we *ought* to do it. Toulmin seems to be arguing, according to Mackie, that if you don't accept the generally recognized ethical criteria you are simply not arguing ethically. But, this is the "long-discredited" method of saying, "since everyone does so-and-so, therefore you ought to do it."[44] Hare notes the same difficulty: "In order to discover how, by reason, to answer questions of the form 'which of these courses shall I choose?' we first discover what ethics is by seeing how the word is used; to discover what its function is, is at the same time to discover what are good reasons in ethics (note here the passage from a descriptive to an evaluative use of the word function—we find out what the function is by observation, but to discover the function is to discover what are good reasons). . . . "[45]

Now, as I remarked initially, in one perfectly plain sense Toulmin's critics are right. We cannot derive an evaluation from a description. It is one thing to describe and correctly explicate the function of ethics and to describe and explicate what reasons, because of that function, are *taken* to be good reasons in ethics, but we say something of a quite different order when we say that the reasons *taken* to be good reasons *are* good reasons. The first contention is a meta-ethical contention *mentioning* ethical talk; the second contention is a normative ethical or moral claim *using* ethical or moral words.[46] In seeming to muddle this logical distinction, Toulmin's theory is definitely at fault.

Granting all this, there is still an important point to be made on Toulmin's side. Toulmin is not—at that juncture—trying to solve the borderline dispute between self interest and morality. He is not trying to answer the question: "Why be moral?" by saying that it pays in the long run to be moral or that one ought to be moral because one's conscience demands it. Toulmin is not answering *that question* one way or another. He is, however, trying to show that such questions are not *moral* questions, though, as he indicated elsewhere, they are relevant to moral questions.[47] Like Hare, he believes that ultimately the choice between the moral life and the life of amoral self-interest rests on a personal decision.[48] In fact, this element of decision looms so large that it has led another of Toulmin's critics, H. J. Paton, to remark (misleadingly, I believe) that Toulmin contends that ultimately morality is based on personal decision.[49]

Rather than justifying being moral, Toulmin is trying to describe what are 'good reasons in ethics' on the assumptions that 1) people are committed to being ethical, and 2) 'ethics' or 'morality' is being used as it is usually used.

The word 'function' is used descriptively by Toulmin. It is being used as it would be in describing the function of a car or the function of swearing or the function of ritual in the Catholic Church. Toulmin ought to have brought out that we can never *derive* a normative principle, not even the principle of least suffering, from a description of the way ethics functions. He should have added that his arguments about good reasons follow only if we are committed to a moral point of view. Yet if we as moral agents or moralists are reasoning within a moral context, we start on the assumption that we are committed to a moral point of view; or, if we as meta-ethicists are explicating *moral* reasoning, we assume this *moral-ought* context as part of our *explicandum*. Toulmin's view is persuasive only in the sense that it implicitly recommends we reason morally rather than non-morally. It is not prescriptive in the sense that it recommends a limited pattern of ethical reasoning as "ethical reasoning." It does not plump for a morality of conformism (as Mackie suggests)[50] or for a liberal, secularist morality (as Rossi-Landi suggests).[51] And, it takes a good flair for the absurd to believe that it "would serve quite admirably as a support for the perverted racial conception of morality advocated by Hitler," as Dykstra suggests.[52] It would suit one as well as the other, for Toulmin's meta-ethical account of moral reasoning is not that kind of account.

Toulmin's conception of the function of ethics definitely establishes a central place for the utilitarian principle as establishing the literal limits of moral reasoning. The goals men seek often conflict. With acute psychological realism, Hobbes remind us that even "the same man, in divers times, differs from himself; and one time praiseth, that is, calleth good, what another time he dispraiseth, and calleth evil. . . ." The ways of men often are at loggerheads. In a "culture" without a morality, attainment of anyone's goals would be immensely difficult because of the pervasiveness of conflict between men. There is a general tendency among men to want to attain as many of their goals as possible. Morality, in large measures, serves as a social mechanism to make this goal attainment generally possible. Thus it clearly plays a utilitarian role. We appeal to the consequences of acting consistently on those rules. If acting consistently on those rules tends to enable men generally to avoid preventable suffering or avoidable misery, then the rules are good. In morals we cannot go any further. Unhappily, this utilitarian part of Toulmin's theory is not, by itself, enough to do the assessment job Toulmin wishes it to do. The familiar problems of just distribution come trooping in here, too.[53] It is here that Toulmin might have taken a lesson from Sidgwick. It is over these questions of just distribution and equity that our "subtle Kantian" interpretations of Toulmin's analysis become crucial, if we are to make a reasonable case for the adequacy of Toulmin's description of the language of moral conduct. Again we see that while this utilitarian principle ties moral evaluations to human aspriations and goals, it still has built into it, integrally, the completely *formal universalizability* principle. The *universalizability* principle is a logical principle in accordance with which moral principles are made. The statement of the function of ethics is a non-moral, non-evaluative statement which mentions (among other things) the requirement of *universalizability*. *Neither this statement nor the principle of universalizability are moral principles.*

That *universalizability* is built into Toulmin's conception of the function of ethics can readily be seen. Toulmin provisionally defines the function of ethics as that activity which serves "to correlate our feelings and behavior in such a way to make the fulfillment of everyone's aims and desires as far as possible compatible."[54] We might put Toulmin's conception in a more Benthamite way by saying morality generally functions to give as many people as possible as much as possible of whatever it is that they want. But, how do we decide what is to count as 'as far as possible' or 'as possible' in the above formulations? I wish to contend that an empirical statement of what is possible will not do the trick here alone, but, as with 'preventable suffering', *universalizability* must be brought in. With it, however, the same formalistic difficulties will occur that we found occurring in the principle of least suffering. I can best establish this last point by means of the following example. In the example to follow, 'as possible' will be interpreted as what is simply empirically possible rather than as what is taken to be *universalizable.* But, as I shall try to show, such a construing of 'as possible' does not at all square with the ordinary uses of moral discourse.

Let us now turn to the example. Suppose an anthropologist is sent by a large rubber corporation into the Amazon jungle to study the behavior of a given primitive culture. The *raison d'être* for his study is to succeed in understanding the structure of their way of life so well that he can discover what propaganda devices could be used to make the natives work willingly as near-slaves for the large corporation. Suppose further that the anthropologist succeeds in this endeavor and the culture subsequently becomes one in which all the members willingly slave from sun-up to sun-set for bare subsistence wages. Given the aims and desires of the company members, we have, in a sense, made the fulfillment of everyone's aims and desires as far as possible compatible. The natives approve of the state of affairs. So do the executives. And the anthropologist is well paid and happy, basking in the satisfaction of efficient work well done and well rewarded. True, the natives wish they had a little more food now and then, and they universally agree it would be nice to work shorter hours. But such desires are not compatible with the desires of the management to keep up efficient, cheap production. Furthermore, without such a rate of work they could not realize their aim (company-induced it is true) to produce and harvest more rubber more economically than any other tribe in Amazonia. Surely, they chorus, one cannot have everything. But within the limits of existing conditions and given the then *de facto* desires and goals of the people involved, as many desires and aims as are possibly compatible are being fulfilled.

In a plain sense, however, we (or most of us) would say that such a situation is a truly immoral situation. It most probably involves, on the part of the company officals and the anthropologist, not an appeal to morality but to privilege. Assume the company officials are asked: if you were in the natives' place and still knew the situation fully, how would you feel? If they replied that this was not the thing they would wish to have done to them in such a situation we would say they had not *universalized* their principles of action and that they were appealing to privilege not morality. But the sad fact remains that such a situation *could be universalized.* Suppose instead the officials reply: "If we were the natives, exactly the same kind of treatment that we give them ought to be given to us." If we then asked them why this should be so and they offered as a reason the contention that people like these natives were of a lower, "more degenerate" human order, they could be *universalizing* their principle of action. Because the maxims could be *universalized,* we would grudgingly give them a quasi-moral status. 'As possible' in Toulmin's criterion must be interpreted, if it is to fit with the above example, as being controlled not only by straightforward empirical requirements alone but also by the *universalizability* requirement. Toulmin's very conception of the function of ethics has this requirement built into it. If we read Toulmin's criterion in just a straigtforward empirical sense, we cannot correctly explicate the above example.

There is, however, another lesson here that brings out the utilitarian and empirical side of Toulmin's criterion. Note that we did not grant full moral status to the officials' claim even though it was *universalizable.* Instead, we said it had a "quasi-moral status." This was so because being a rational agent is one of the presuppositions of morality and the officials are not making their moral assessments as fully rational agents. Thus their utterances cannot be in the fullest sense moral utterances. They must fully examine the relevant empirical considerations.

The truth of the above contention can be seen from the following considerations. The officials (as most present-day segregationists) are rationalizing and appealing to a "mythical anthropology" in claiming that the natives belong to a lower, more degenerate human order. Contemporary anthropology gives us no scientific warrant for ranking the races as higher or lower. The officials have confused culture with race. Their statement has a factual sound, but in fact it is really a moral recommendation parading as a factual statement used to back up another moral recommendation. It is a bit of ideology, not science.

Why the above kind of manipulation of a primitive culture for the officials' ends is regarded as immoral and why at best we can only give the official's position a "quasi-moral status" can be further explained by the following considerations. The utilitarian material requirement of the maximum possible human happiness or the least possible suffering would also count against the officials' defense. We would insist that Toulmin's reference to 'as possible' be governed not only by the principle of *universalizability* but also by straightforward empirical considerations. And, as a matter of act, more desires could be satisfied under a different (but still *universalizable*) policy. This can be easily seen. Through propaganda, certain secondary needs have been developed in our primitive culture. They conflict with certain other secondary needs and even infringe on certain primary ones. Reflecting on the officials' policy, a disinterested ideal observer might well note that under a different policy more desires (primary and secondary needs) could, as a matter of fact, be satisfied than the participants in the culture thought could be satisfied. This could be achieved by altering certain culturally induced desires (secondary needs). They could achieve good production and still have better living conditions. They would not have quite so high or quite so cheap production; but, on the whole, there would be a greater quantity of satisfaction of primary and secondary needs for all the people involved if another policy were undertaken. The officials' position is not "dictated by the facts." Either they are rationalizing or they are plainly mistaken if they think that under their system the maximum number of compatible desires are being satisfied. Fully moral utterances ought not to be expressions of rationalizations or to involve empirical mistakes that could be reasonably corrected. (The force of the 'ought' here is linguistic and not directly moral; in other words, the preceding sentence is a meta-ethical rather than a moral utterance, though I would not deny that it has indirectly important moral consequences.)

Thus, even if the officials universalize their actions there are good logical reasons for regarding their position as a truly immoral position. We need not directly enter into moral debate with them but we can point out their error on a logical level by indicating (as we have) how they ignore the basic presupposition or contextual implication that 'moral talk' be 'rational talk'. The officials have been irrational in turning from scientific considerations to ideology and rationalization and in refusing to consider objectively what conditions would maximize human happiness and still be *universalizable*. In making their "moral judgments" (policy decisions), they have simply ignored relevant empirical considerations.[55] But I would insist that in saying it is the function of ethics to harmonize as many desires and wants *as possible* Toulmin is also appealing with 'as possible' to these empirical considerations. Both *universalizability* and *utility* are at work here. Both are necessary features.

We can now generalize. To count as 'good reasons' in ethics, reasons must be *universalizable,* although this is not sufficient to determine what is a good reason in ethics. Here, it is tempting to appeal to the other traditional touchstone—human happiness, or (put negatively) to the avoidance of misery. This touchstone indeed is crucial and perfectly natural. Toulmin's statement (in its simplest form) says: if we appeal to human happiness it must be to the greatest happiness for the greatest number. But, the formal requirement of *universalizability* governs in part what is to count as the 'greatest number', and this formal requirement makes the criterion *as a whole* applicable to *any rule.* It will *not* do the job of picking out which reasons are good reasons in ethics. We do know however, that: 1) all reasons, in order to be 'good reasons', must be *universalizable,* and 2) moral judgments based on these reasons should, indirectly or indirectly, guide action so as to generally further human happiness. But we do not know from 1) and 2) which of the reasons that could count as 'good reasons' are good reasons. And we do not know just what makes them *universalizable.*

At this point, the use of imagination and decision by the moral agent and moral critic becomes exceedingly relevant. In such a context, Toulmin's own comment that "in seeking moral justification there comes a point where great generality becomes feckless" is also directly relevant. Toulmin argues, convincingly, I believe, that instead of continually looking for a yet-more-general principle that will cover all principles involved in moral assessment, we must, taking the utilitarian criterion as a sign-post, seek to see in concrete detail how the acceptance or rejection of a given social practice bears upon our lives.[56] Here we must carry out experiments in imagination and, above all, in empathy. The methods of the clinical psychologist or counselor are not at all amiss here, and, in such an experiment in imagination, "the reconstruction of life by a first-class novelist, if vivid and imaginative, provides one with as good a source of vicarious experiences as most."[57] There is no question of demonstration or proof at this point though talk and even argument (rational persuasion) need not be at an end. But above all we must rely on imaginative sympathy here. And, at this point, the Tolstoys and Koestlers of the world are far more valuable than the Kants and Moores.

In bringing in this appeal to imaginative sympathy or empathy, in suggesting that finally we must ask the moral agent to seriously ask himself, "But how would *you feel* if this were done to you," I am not suggesting moral discourse is just "the logic of the emotions." Rather, I am suggesting that such a conception is a third necessary ingredient in moral discourse. In addition, we have also the *universalizability* principle and we have the utilitarian principle as necessary ingredients in all moral assessment at Toulmin's second level of moral reasoning.

Admittedly, the logical relations between the *universalizability* principle and the utility principle have not been worked out, nor has the exact role of sympathy in relation to these principles been mapped. Here we can see some of the classical problems of the history of ethics arising, though, as Bergmann is so fond of putting it, they are now marvelously transformed into a linguistic or conceptual milieu. However, it can also be seen that Toulmin has not succeeded in making these vexing philosophical problems disappear altogether.

What, then, has Toulmin succeeded in doing? First, I think he has succeeded in making it clear that the above elements must be present in moral assessment. If we cut out one of these elements, or overemphasize one, we invariably distort that conceptual area we call morality. Second, Toulmin has dealt a severe blow to the general overall skepticism of the "despairing philosophers," who despair of the rationality of morals. (I shall return to this second point in my concluding paragraph.)

Let me conclude this section by making a few comments on my first point. Though Toulmin has not made clear the logical relationships of the above elements of moral discourse, he has succeeded in making it clear that they are all essential to moral discourse. I have tried in my own way to make it clear why they are essential, but quite apart from the validity or invalidity of my *own argument* it is well to remember that there is a greater *de facto* recognition of the above three ingredients as essential to moral discourse than is commonly realized. Only the polemic and overstatement so frequently associated with philosophy obscures this. We have noted that Bentham, Mill and Sidgwick (as well as Toulmin) built *universalizability* into their theories, and Kant postulated immortality so he could have at least a shot-gun wedding of duty and happiness. This same tendency toward merger is present in one of our most respected contemporary Kantians, H. J. Paton. While still plugging for the Categorical Imperative as the fundamental formal principle of morality, Paton (in a discussion of Toulmin's utilitarian criterion) remarked that any "sane morality must accept these utilitarian principles."[58] To this he has added, in his most recent book, *The Modern Predicament:* "The oldest and best of these material principles (though it has had refinements in recent years) is that a good man is one who aims at the happiness of mankind."[59] The pluralistic deontologists seem most recalcitrant to my above generalization but, as we have seen in II, their own positive claims can be logically accounted for under Toulmin's first level of moral reasoning and their negative criticism of utilitarianism can be met by Toulmin's distinction of two kinds of moral reasoning. The appeal to sympathy or empathy is the hardest to include in my generalization. Anxious to avoid basing morality on emotion, many moralists have played down the importance of imaginative sympathy and empathy. But they have also recognized, though sometimes grudgingly and only half consciously, that moral discourse is a practical kind of discourse with a dynamism and irreducible emotional and attitudinal element. If we could conceive of a man without desires, we could hardly understand how he could comprehend or act on moral advice and exhortation. In fact, such a "man" would be a "robot" and not only poetry but morality would be totally lost on such a being. Russell's talk about the emotions vis-à-vis morals and Santayana's talk of a "pre-rational morality" as the source *and* final base of all morality is terribly important here, extreme and one-sided as their claims are in other respects. It is exactly what is needed after a fascination with Richard Price and the early Moore. To attain a clarity about the uses or functions of moral discourse and reasoning we must keep well in mind all three of these central elements.

## VI

Let me summarize. Basic work needs to be done on the exact role of *universalizability* in moral assessment and analytical work needs to be done on the relation of *universalizability* to *utility;* but, though this work is of crucial importance in an explication of moral discourse and reasoning, Toulmin's analysis (if what has been argued here is at all correct) has at least shaken the "despairing philosopher" from his dogmatic slumbers. It has also put off the mystagogue, though this species never really dies. The routes to skepticism over morality are many and thickly criss-crossed and involuted. Skepticism over many of our work-a-day moral judgments and practices is healthy. Indeed, it is one of the marks of a rational man. Since Toulmin's analysis, however, the *obsessional philosophical* skepticism over the justifiability of *all* of our moral judgments or over the very possibility of reasoned moral judgments has been seriously weakened. There is still room for philosophical skepticism over morality, but in the extremity it will now be forced into, the doubt is rapidly becoming a caricature of a doubt.

NOTES

1. Stephen Toulmin, *An Examination of the Place of Reason in Ethics* (Cambridge: The University Press, 1950), pp. 4, 55, 154, 223-224. Toulmin and Baier, "On Describing," *Mind* 51 (January, 1952): 34.
2. Toulmin, *The Place of Reason in Ethics*, pp. 149-150.
3. Ibid., p. 160.
4. John Rawls, "Discussion-Review of *An Examination of the Place of Reason in Ethics,*" *The Philosophical Review* 60 (October, 1951): 577. See for a fuller development of Rawls's own conceptions that underlie this criticism his "Outline of a Decision Procedure for Ethics," *The Philosophical Review* 60 (April, 1951): 177-197. Since this was first written, Rawls has published an article in which he admits that Toulmin's conception of the

relation of moral judgments to moral rules under which they are subsumed is correct, although—as his last footnote indicates (footnote 27)—he still does not regard moral reasoning as a rigidly rule-governed sort of affair. All in all, his "new position" seems to be like the "middle position" taken by Aiken. The remarks made in my text, however, only take into consideration Rawls's "old position" stated in his critical notice of Toulmin and his earlier article. For Rawls's later position see John Rawls, "Two Concepts of Rules," *The Philosophical Review* 64 (January, 1955): 3–32.

5. Toulmin, *The Place of Reason in Ethics*, p. 150.

6. This in substance is Toulmin's own dialogue. Ibid., p. 146.

7. Rawls, "Discussion-Review of *An Examination of the Place of Reason in Ethics,*" *The Philosophical Review* 60 (October, 1951): 577.

8. Ibid. For further criticism of this first type of moral reasoning see R. Peters, "Nature and Convention in Morality," *Aristotelian Society Proceedings* 51 (1950-51): 229-232. See John Mackie, "Critical Notice of *The Place of Reason in Ethics,*" *The Australasian Journal of Philosophy* 29 (August, 1951): 117–119.

9. Ironically enough, perhaps the clearest statement of this position is made by Rawls himself in his later article where he repudiates his old position stated above. See John Rawls, "Two Concepts of Rules," *The Philosophical Review* 64 (January, 1955): subsection 11 and most particularly pp. 16–18.

10. Peters, op. cit., p. 232.

11. Note Toulmin's remark here. See Toulmin, *The Place of Reason in Ethics*, p. 171.

12. Peters, op. cit., p. 231.

13. Ibid., pp. 231–232.

14. Ibid., p. 232.

15. H. J. Paton, "Review of An Examination of the Place of Reason in Ethics," *Philosophy* 27 (January, 1952): 83.

16. Ibid.

17. Rawls, "Discussion-Review of *An Examination of the Place of Reason in Ethics,*" *The Philosophical Review* 60 (October, 1951): 572–580.

18. C. I. Lewis, "The Meaning of Liberty," *Revue Internationale de Philosophie,* revue trimestrielle (August, 1948): 17.

19. It is no doubt that Broad had this in mind when he remarked that Toulmin, in comparison with Sidgwick, was an unsubtle utilitarian, for Sidgwick has certainly thrashed through these problems.

20. C. D. Broad, *Five Types of Ethical Theory* (London: 1930), pp. 206–207.

21. Note the long quote from Rawls, footnote 17, this paper. I do not necessarily equate Lewis's "Law of Justice" and a principle of just distribution.

22. Note again the appeal to 'as possible'. What considerations control 'as possible'? Are they not considerations of equity?

23. It will not do in any of the above paradigms to say that we were really talking about an act clearly subsumable under a definite *prima facie* obligation, for in the above cases we are either talking about the practice or there are obvious conflicts of *prima facie* rules that will call for the second kind of moral reasoning.

24. We must also separate this question from the question of whether pain can be sought for its own sake. 'Pain' is in a word a definite sensation. But 'suffering' is not equisignificant to 'pain'. We ask where it pains but not where it suffers. Surely, if one is in pain we normally assume that he is suffering; but one may suffer without being

in pain at all, and a masochist may be in pain without suffering. Pain is a sensation; 'suffering' does not denote any kind of sensation at all.

25. Paul Edwards, *The Logic of Moral Discourse*, pp. 74–75.

26. See Stevenson's remarks about Perry and persuasive definitions. Charles Stevenson, *Ethics and Language*, p. 270.

27. See Urmson's remarks about these different roles. J. O. Urmson, "On Grading" in *Logic and Language* (A. G. N. Flew editor) (Second Series), p. 182.

28. 'Relevantly similar' remains undefined above. Nor is it profitably definable though contextually the 'relevantly similar circumstances' could be specified with objectivity.

29. R. M. Hare, "Have I Duty to My Country As Such?" *The Listener* (October 20, 1955): 651–652, and R. M. Hare, "Universalizability," *Aristotelian Society Proceedings* 55 (1954–55): 295, 312.

30. H. J. Paton, *The Modern Predicament*.

31. Toulmin, "Is There a Fundamental Problem in Ethics?" *The Australasian Journal of Philosophy* 23 (May, 1955): 13.

32. For the distinction between meta-ethics or analytic ethics and normative ethics or substantive ethics see Henry Aiken, "Education and Moral Philosophy," *The Harvard Educational Review* 25 (Winter, 1955): 41–44.

33. I am indebted to Roger Buck for the core of the following suggestions.

34. Toulmin, *The Place of Reason in Ethics*, pp. 140–143.

35. Ibid., p. 152. For an exposition, as well as a qualified defense, of Toulmin's conception of the function of ethics or morality see my doctoral dissertation. Kai Nielsen, "Justification and Morals," unpublished doctoral dissertation, Duke University, 1955, chapters 2 and 10.

36. Toulmin, *The Place of Reason in Ethics*, pp. 136, 137, 170, 223. For a further defense and elaboration of this general conception of the functions of ethics, see my article "The Functions of Moral Discourse," *The Philosophical Quarterly* 7 (July, 1957): 236–249 [reprinted as chapter 2 of the present volume].

37. I am indebted to Max Black and Jerome Balmuth for raising this point.

38. Toulmin, *The Place of Reason in Ethics*, p. 185. This same point comes out, in his two later articles "Is there a Fundamental Problem in Ethics," *Australasian Journal of Philosophy* 33, (May, 1955): 1–19 and "Principles of Morality," *Philosophy* 31 (April, 1956): 142–153.

39. See Urmson and Flew on the limits of the paradigm case method in this respect. Urmson, "Some Remarks Concerning Validity," and Flew, "Philosophy and Language," both in *Essays in Conceptual Analysis*, ed. A. G. N. Flew.

40. I would prefer to speak in the plural but Toulmin does not.

41. See Clyde Kluckhohn, "Ethical Relativity : Sic et Non," *The Journal of Philosophy* (November 10, 1955): 663–677 and Ralph Linton, "Universal Ethical Principles: an Anthropological View," in *Moral Principles of Action*, Ruth Anshen ed., pp. 645–660.

42. To be sure Russell has not regarded it as the only function of morality. See Bertrand Russell, *Human Society in Ethics and Politics*, chapters 1, 2, 3.

43. John Mackie, "Critical Notice: *An Examination of the Place of Reason in Ethics,*" *The Australasian Journal of Philosophy* 29 (August, 1951): 115. See Vergil H. Dykstra's related criticism, "The Place of Reason in Ethics," *The Review of Metaphysics* 8 (March, 1955): 465.

44. Mackie, op. cit., p. 116.

45. R. M. Hare, "Review of *The Place of Reason in Ethics,*" *Philosophical Quarterly* 1 (July, 1951): 373.

46. This distinction has been briefly but incisively put by Paul Edwards, *The Logic of Moral Discourse*, pp. 43-45.

47. Toulmin, "Principles of Morality," *Philosophy* 31 (April, 1956): 150.

48. Toulmin, *The Place of Reason in Ethics*, pp. 155-160.

49. H. J. Paton, "Review of *The Place of Reason in Ethics,*" *Philosophy* 27 (January, 1952): 82.

50. John Mackie, op. cit., p. 191.

51. Ferruccio Rossi-Landi, "Review of *The Place of Reason in Ethics,*" *Methodos* III (1952): 127-130.

52. V. H. Dykstra, "The Place of Reason in Ethics," *The Review of Metaphysics* (March, 1955): 464.

53. Paul Ramsey notes this dual source within utilitarian theory. He thinks that such a non-utilitarian element within the principle of utility itself spells the doom of all secular or rationalistic systems of ethics and that ultimately to explain this *universalizability* principle we must turn to an ethic based on a religion. Paul Ramsey, "No Morality without Immortality: Dostoevski and the Meaning of Atheism," *The Journal of Religion* 36 (April, 1956): 90-108. For a more analytical treatment of some of the paradoxes of utilitarianism here see A. I. Melden. "Two Comments on Utilitarianism," *The Philosophical Review* 60 (October, 1951). See also footnote 17.

54. Toulmin, *The Place of Reason in Ethics*, p. 156.

55. Charles Stevenson has pointed out how valuable a scientist with his greater knowledge of human nature and society can be in giving advice as to which moral judgments are the most warranted by the facts of the situation. Moral judgments to be fully rational (and thus fully moral) demand a careful scrutiny of the facts. See C. L. Stevenson, "The Scientist's Role and the Aims of Education," *The Harvard Educational Review* 24 (Fall, 1954): 231-8. See also Abraham Edel, *Ethical Judgement: The Use of Science in Ethics*.

56. Toulmin, "The Principles of Morality," *Philosophy* 31 (April, 1956): 146-150.

57. Ibid., p. 149.

58. Paton, "Review of *The Place of Reason in Ethics,*" *Philosophy* 37 (January, 1952): 83.

59. Paton, *The Modern Predicament*, p. 300.

# 4

# On Moral Truth

When we reflect philosophically about morality we are very typically concerned with determining whether we can have any knowledge of good and evil, whether any moral claims have an objective rationale; that is to say, in thinking about the foundations of moral belief, we want very much to know whether any ethical code or any moral claim at all can be shown to be objectively justified.

In making such an inquiry, we run into trouble right away. What does it mean to say that moral claims can be objectively justified? Presumably it means that some moral claims are objective. But what does *that* mean? Some moral philosophers write as if moral judgments or moral statements would be objective if and *only* if moral values had a real existence apart from any reference to a human mind or to human attitudes. But now we are surely up queer street, for moral values are not objects like a table or even like an electron. To speak of moral values is to speak of what is good or right *to do,* or to *have done,* or what is good to seek, or of what one ought to be or to have been. But then we are surely not talking of what exists but of what is *to be* brought into existence. Sometimes we do indeed make assertions about what is the case when we make moral judgments, e.g., when we assert that someone has an admirable character, but moral utterances usually involve a *telling to,* not a *telling that.* (In talking about the past we are talking about what to have done.) Given this peculiarity of moral discourse, it is absurd to think of moral values as some peculiar sort of "nonnatural object" or of norms as existing in some odd noumenal realm. If we note the actual uses of moral discourse we will immediately recognize that

From *Studies in Moral Philosophy,* in *American Philosophical Quarterly* Monograph Series. Monograph #1 (Oxford: Basil Blackwell, with the cooperation of the University of Pittsburgh, 1968). Reprinted by permission of the publisher.

it is absurd to think of moral values as existing either apart from or as being dependent on human minds. Talk of existence cannot gain a foothold here. Moral values are neither natural nor non-natural objects. To ask whether in that sense they are objective is like asking whether a wife is unmarried. Such a request is self-refuting because it is nonsensical.

Yet, as Westermarck recognized, though he was not entirely free of the above kind of confusions, there are other, quite separable elements in the concept of an objective moral judgment that perhaps can be satisfied. First, if someone is claiming that the statements 'x is good' or 'x is wrong' are objective statements, he is claiming, at the very least, that such statements are not reducible to x is *thought* to be good or x is *thought* to be wrong. If our moral claims are objective, they must be something of which we could correctly say that though people *think* so and so is wrong, they are mistaken, for it is not wrong. There are people who think that the earth is flat but their thinking so does not make the earth flat. Only if we can get beyond "thinking makes it so" can we be justified in claiming that there are objective moral claims.

Westermarck adds another condition that must be satisfied if moral judgments can be correctly said to be objective. This is the condition that some moral judgments can be true and others false. To believe in the objectivity of morals is to believe that some moral statements are true. In short, to correctly claim that a certain "course of conduct is objectively right, it must be thought to be right by all rational beings who judge truly of the matter and cannot, without error, be judged to be wrong." Now we must be careful here to use the word 'rational' in a non-moralistic way, if we are to avoid going in a short and vicious circle.[1] In short, to assert 'x is objectively right' and 'x is objectively speaking the best thing to do' is to give one to understand that statements asserting that x is objectively right or that x is objectively speaking the best thing to do are true and that they are thought to be true by all rational beings who properly consider the matter. But apart from difficulties about 'rational' and 'properly consider the matter', there are notorious difficulties about saying moral statements are true or false. I want here to consider these difficulties.

Most emotivists and other non-descriptivists claim that it is misleading to say that fundamental moral statements are either true or false.[2] They readily admit that it is linguistically quite in order to say of certain very typical moral statements that they are true or false. In that way they differ very markedly from commands or imperatives or mere expressions of emotion. A. J. Ayer puts this general point very well when he remarks:

For, as the English language is currently used—and what else, it may be asked, is here in question—it is by no means improper to refer to ethical utterances as statements; when someone characterizes an action by the use of an ethical predicate, it is quite good usage to say that he is thereby describing it; when someone wishes to assent to an ethical verdict, it is perfectly legitimate for him to say that it is true, or that it is a fact, just as if he wished to dissent from it, it would be perfectly legitimate for him to say that it was false. We should know what he meant and we should not consider that he was using words in an unconventional way.[3]

Ayer stresses all this, but he still argues, as have many others, that it is logically misleading to follow ordinary usage here. These non-descriptivists are recommending a new way of speaking that will be, so they think, logically speaking less misleading than the old way of speech. Ayer argues that when we consider carefully the actual use of moral language—its depth grammar rather than its surface grammar—we will see that moral utterances, even when declarative in form, are not verifiable or even comfirmable. If I say "The dog is in the snow," "The Russians are invading Alaska," or "Frustrated people tend to respond with aggression" you know what factors count in establishing the truth or falsity of my claim. These statements assert certain quite empirically identifiable states of affairs which, if the asserted state of affairs in question actually does exist, will establish the truth of my claim. If it does not exist then my claim can quite correctly be said to be false. My attitudes, my interests, do not at all affect the truth or falsity of what I assert. I may hate to see dogs romping in the snow, I may fear the Russians coming to Alaska, I may deplore the fact that frustrated people keep the whole cycle going by responding aggressively, but all the same the facts are what they are no matter how I or anyone else may feel about them. But how do we verify or confirm, falsify, or disconfirm 'Dogs ought to be allowed to romp in the snow', 'The Russians ought not to invade Alaska', or 'Frustrated people ought not to become aggressive'? We can and do give reasons for these statements, but what would it be like to verify the statements as distinct from verifying whether some of the factual statements given as supporting reasons are true? There seem to be no facts that we can point to that would verify such statements; and if there is no *conceivable* direct verification of them then we cannot sensibly speak of an indirect verification of them either, for where nothing could conceivably count as direct verification the phrase 'indirect verification' could have no meaning. If this is so, we do not know what it would be like for such claims to be true, for we do not know what we would have to apprehend to make them true or, for that matter, false. Because of this, Ayer argues, we had better, for philosophical purposes at least, amend ordinary language and stop speaking of moral statements as true or false.

This, and more complex considerations as well, have counted heavily in favor of the 'no truth' account of moral discourse. But there are difficulties here as well. Even if, as with descriptive statements, there are no facts that moral statements simply describe—even if there is nothing like " 'The cat is on the mat' is true if and only if the cat is on the mat"—it does not follow that it is not proper to say that statements of logically diverse kinds are true. Mathematical and logical statements are true; more generally there are analytic truths even though such a 'correspondence theory' will not begin to work for them. Just as we recognize factual truths and logical truths, why cannot we recognize moral truths as well?

It is here where the good reasons approach and Kurt Baier's analysis in particular can be of considerable help. Baier thinks he has a way around our problem. His first move is indirect. It consists (1) in showing how we determine the truth of claims about what is legal or customary, and (2) in showing how very different moral concepts are from legal concepts or from mere customs. To find out whether it is true that it is illegal for Caucasians and Negroes to marry in Mississippi, we need only to find out what the law is in Mississippi and how this bears on U.S. Federal laws; to find out whether it is customary for white men to flirt with Negro girls in Mississippi, we need only determine what the practice is in Mississippi. Once we discover what the law is or what the custom is, we have unequivocally settled the question of the truth of our legal claim or our claim about what is customary. But this is not so with moral questions. If we make a moral claim, if we assert "It is immoral to prevent Caucasians and Negroes from marrying in Mississippi or anyplace else" or "It is wrong for white men to flirt with Negro girls when they cannot marry them, have no intention of marrying them, and do not even treat them as persons," the truth or falsity of these claims is *not* decided and cannot be decided simply by discovering what are the moral convictions of the group. Morality differs radically from law and custom here. If I know what is demanded or prohibited by the moral code of my society, I do *not* thereby know what is right in my society or elsewhere. Once a person knows what the law or custom of his own or some other culture is, he cannot intelligibly ask whether his convictions about what is legal or customary in *that culture* are true, but this is not so for morality. How then do we determine whether a moral conviction is true?

Baier's answer is very simple: "Our moral convictions are true if they can be seen to be required or acceptable from the moral point of view."[4] When we say that a moral judgment is true we endorse that judgment; we endorse it as a judgment that is rationally warranted; and when the judgment in question is a moral judgment, to say that it is rationally warranted comes to acknowledging it as acceptable from the moral point of view.

But what is it for something to be acceptable from the moral point of view? What is it to take the moral point of view? In chapter 8 of his *The Moral Point of View,* Baier explicates what it is to take "the moral point of view." To take the moral point of view, three conditions must be satisfied.

1. We must adopt rules of conduct not as rules of thumb designed to promote our own individual interests, but as matters of principle. As Baier points out, "this involves conforming to the rules whether or not doing so favors one's own or anyone else's aim."[5]

2. A moral agent must adopt rules to which not only he and his friends conform as a matter of principle, but rules to which everyone can conform as a matter of principle. Moral rules are meant for everybody.[6] There are four subsidiary conditions which need to be noted under this condition.

   *a.* It must be possible to teach a moral rule to everybody.

   *b.* It must be a rule such that its purpose would not be defeated if everyone acted on it.

   *c.* It must be a rule such that it would not be defeated if a person let it be known that he adopted it.

   *d.* It must not be a rule such that it would be literally impossible for everyone to act in accordance with it.

3. Moral rules must be rules which are adopted for the good of everyone alike. The principle of impartiality or justice is involved here, since the interests of all people must be furthered, or at least given equal consideration when some moral rule has to be overridden. Baier gives us a case to make clear exactly what it is that he means. This condition excludes from morality any set of rules "which enrich the ruling class at the expense of the masses."[7] It excludes any rule that is not reversible. This is to say, the behavior in question "must be acceptable to a person whether he is at the 'giving' or 'receiving' end of it."[8]

One further point is important in considering what it is to take the moral point of view. When one takes the moral point of view one must, when one has a specific moral perplexity, review the *facts* in the light of one's moral convictions.[9] The important thing to see here is that if one is reasoning morally, one must attend to the facts relevant to the case.

According to Baier, we can determine true from false moral statements by determining which statements are *acceptable* from the moral point of view. If a statement is acceptable from the moral point of view, it is true; if not, not. Only certain rules of conduct will satisfy these conditions. This means that no moral statement can be true unless it is made in accordance with and acceptable from the point of view of those norms which encapsulate the moral point of view.

This view, if correct, would give us some moral truths, some knowledge of good and evil. But Baier's view and the good reasons approach generally has not escaped thorough criticism. It has been thought by many in some way to enshrine, as *the* logic of moral discourse, the rather limited moral views of some particular men at a particular time and place. Paul Taylor has made this reaction specific and penetrating in his striking article "The Ethnocentric Fallacy."[10] Taylor argues that Baier's effort is reduced in essence to the claim that a moral claim is true only if it is made in accordance with the moral principles of liberal Western society, but these principles in turn are not testable—nothing establishes their truth or falsity. But to argue in this way—to argue as Baier does—is, Taylor argues, to commit the ethnocentric fallacy.

Let me explain exactly what Taylor means when he makes this claim. Baier, Taylor argues, defines 'the moral point of view' in terms of the moral code of liberal Western society.

> As a logical consequence of his definition, all moral convictions which do not accord with those of that particular society are false. But this assumes that one set of moral convictions are true, and does not tell us how we know *this*. In fact, by making moral knowledge relative to or dependent upon these convictions, it places the convictions themselves beyond truth and falsity and hence renders them arbitrary.[11]

This challenge of Taylor's is a powerful one—a challenge that cannot in some form or other but occur to any thoughtful reader of Baier's book. Let us take a close look at Taylor's incisive arguments.

Taylor points out that "if we define the word 'moral' in terms of an impartial set of rules, according to which no act is right unless reversible, then it become *self-contradictory* to talk of the moral code of a society which, for example, places women in a subordinate position to men."[12] But if we adopt this definition, we in effect make the truth of someone's moral convictions "relative to the moral code of what might be dubbed 'liberal Western society'—the society which had adopted a moral code embodying principles of justice, impartiality, and brotherhood extending to all human beings."[13] At this point Taylor drives home his most crucial point. For all his sophistication, Baier has been very culture-bound, very ethnocentric in his characterization of the moral point of view. Taylor remarks that the above liberal code of conduct

> . . . is only one among many. However deeply our own conscience and moral outlook may have been shaped by it, we must recognize that other societies in the history of the world have been able to function on the basis of other codes. There are societies with caste systems, societies which practice slavery, societies in which women are treated as inferior to men and so on. To claim that a person who is a member of one of those societies and who knows its moral code, nevertheless does not have true moral convictions is, it seems to me, fundamentally correct. But such a claim

cannot be justified on the ground of Baier's concept of the moral point of view, for that is to assume that the moral code of liberal Western society is the only genuine morality. This renders it nonsensical to talk about alternative moral codes, unless we place "moral" in brackets or quotation marks . . . to indicate that such codes are somehow alleged to be moral but are not genuinely so.[14]

To proceed in this ethnocentric way, Taylor argues, produces the very reverse effect of what Baier was after. Baier wanted to show how one could correctly assert that the moral convictions of a society, including his own, could be false. But given this ethnocentric definition of 'the moral point of view' and given Baier's definition of 'moral truth', moral truth comes to depend on which codes of which societies are referred to. If a moral claim is acceptable from the point of view of Western liberal morality, it is true; if not, it is false. This is a perfect rationalization for ethnocentrism. Moreover, it will now become senseless to ask whether a person's moral convictions are true if they are acceptable from the point of view of liberal Western morality. But this is itself, Taylor argues, surely nonsense for if this were so (1) 'Act *x* is forbidden by the moral code of society *S,* but is it really wrong?' would become equivalent to (2) 'Act *x* is forbidden by the moral code of society *S,* but is it forbidden by the moral code of liberal Western society?' But the two questions are not equivalent. (2) could be settled in the way we settle questions of what is customary or what is legal, but, as Baier has shown himself, we do not and cannot settle moral questions in this way. Furthermore (1) would make sense when asked of any society, but (2) does not make sense when society *S* is liberal Western society. Thus (1) and (2) are very different questions.

Surely Taylor is right *if* to take the 'moral point of view' is to take a point of view wherein we must, to be even *reasoning morally,* have the ideal of the brotherhood of all men. There have been plenty of societies that have had moral codes that did not even remotely have this ideal. As Westermarck points out,

> Primitive peoples carefully distinguish between an act of homicide committed within their own community and one where the victim is a stranger: while the former is in ordinary circumstances disapproved of, the latter is in most cases allowed and often considered worthy of praise. And the same holds true of theft and lying and the infliction of other injuries. Apart from the privileges granted to guests, which are always of very short duration, a stranger is in early society devoid of all rights.[15]

Westermarck, utilizing a wealth of empirical material, goes on to show how in Greek society, Roman society, among the early Teutonic groups, through the Middle Ages and down into the seventeenth century in Europe, similar moral conceptions were very widespread. Even today, Westermarck points out, such ideas are not entirely dead within Western culture. Modern moral philosophers argue against it, but such tribal moral beliefs—beliefs which come to the fore during wartime and in times of political and economic pressure—are surely not dead among us. As normative ethicists, as moralists, we may surely deplore such "moralities" and seek to argue for a universalistic morality in which the ideal of brotherhood and beneficence is extended to all men, but plainly such alternative moral codes and moral conceptions do exist.

Certainly this is a powerful attack. In a very plain sense of 'adopted for the good of everyone alike' not all rules that as a matter of linguistic propriety can be properly called 'moral rules' or 'moral principles' enshrine such an intent.

Yet this is not the whole tale. What Baier says about the third condition for the moral point of view, perhaps with a little stretching in the direction of Hare, can be *interpreted* in a way that does not fall prey to the ethnocentric fallacy.

A key to what I want to claim here lies in Baier's Kantian claim that moral judgments must be reversible. When we say that a moral claim must be reversible, we are saying that whatever is to count as 'a moral claim' must be acceptable to the agent whether he is on the giving or receiving end of it. Now it has been argued that this reversibility is not analytically linked with what it is for something to count as 'a moral statement'. After all, people have said, "Women should not vote," "Black men should not live in the same apartment blocks as white men," "The ruling classes have a right to enrich themselves at the expense of the masses," "Germans deserve one kind of treatment, Jews another," "People who are shipwrecked may be plundered." But, it has been argued, clearly non-reversible and neanderthal though they be, that these judgments are unequivocally moral judgments. It is, Taylor and others have argued, not a necessary condition for something's being a moral judgment that it be reversible. In thinking that it is, so the argument runs, Baier and Kant reveal an ethnocentric understanding of morality.

I want to argue that these examples not withstanding, reversibility *is* such a necessary condition and this Kantian claim, *properly understood,* does not commit us to an ethnocentric view of morality. There remains a very crucial sense in morals—in which even people who hold such apparently non-reversible views as the anti-Feminist, the racist and the Nazi quoted above, if they are reasoning morally at all, must be applying the criterion of reversibility. Consider this fragment of a dialogue:

A: "Women should not vote. They must always remain in a subordinate place in our society."

B: "If you were a woman you wouldn't say that."

A: "No indeed I wouldn't. I would be quite justified in maintaining that if I were a woman I should have the right to vote, but I still would say that other women ought not to vote."

B: "But then it isn't 'being a woman' that should disqualify one from voting, but 'being a certain kind of a person.' There is something about *you* that entitles you, whether you are or are not a woman, to vote and the women whom you say should not vote lack that quality."

A: "No, I'm not saying anything of the kind. There is—I confess—nothing distinctive about me. I am just saying that women *ought* not to vote. But I am *not* at all willing to say that if I were a woman, in all relevant respects like the women whom I say should not vote, that then *I* should not vote."

When *A* replies in this way he is saying something that is not intelligible as a bit of moral or normative discourse. It is in this sense that reversibility is a necessary requirement of the moral point of view. But such a limitation does not make it self-contradictory, as Taylor thinks, to set forth a moral code that places women in a subordinate position to men. Neanderthals who so argue will come up with some spurious factual claim that women are somehow either naturally or, as a matter of sociological fact, inferior to men and cannot therefore be given the responsibility of voting. But if such a man is reasoning morally, he must—logically must—be prepared to admit that if he were a woman or were inferior in the same specified way, then he too ought not to be allowed to vote. If he is not prepared to so reason, we would not *understand* what he could mean by saying that he was making a *moral* claim. He would not be playing the moral language game. He would not be thinking as a moral agent. The same thing can be said for the other examples I gave. They do not count against the contention that moral judgments must be reversible. This requirement of reversibility is but a facet of universalizability or the generalization principle, a principle that Taylor himself takes to be analytically tied to anything that could count as a normative judgment.[16] It is, Taylor rightly argues, analytic to "say that whatever is right or wrong for one person is right or wrong for every similar person in similar circumstances." In this sense all normative judgments and *a fortiori* all moral judgments must be reversible, and in *that sense,* impartial. As moral agents, we must be committed to such an idea of impartiality.

Yet we must not forget what both Hare and Taylor have stressed, that this requirement *by itself* does not determine the *content* of any moral judgment. It does not, by itself, block a tribal morality. Greeks can (and have) said of Barbarians that they ought not to have the rights of Greeks; Germans can (and have) said of Jews that they do not have the rights of Germans.

But to say this, and make their remarks intelligible as moral remarks, they must contend that there is something about Barbarians or Jews that makes them different from Greeks and Germans.

But, as Westermarck and more recently Hare have recognized, once we dwell on and take to heart this generalizing feature of moral discourse, it becomes very difficult—if we are at all clear-headed—to be a tribalist in ethics, for if Barbarians, Jews, Negroes, women, the proletariat, and the like are not to have the treatment the tribalist claims for himself, there must—logically must—be something about them that justifies that difference in treatment. That is, there must be something that the maker of the moral judgment would acknowledge as justifying a like treatment for him if that characteristic could be correctly attributed to him. It takes a very fanatical and irrational German to be prepared—to really be prepared—to put himself and all his family into the concentration camp if it turns out that they are Jews. We could play the little trick on him Hare proposes. First, by forged documents we get him to believe that he really is what the Nazis would call a Jew and then, if in true fanatical fashion he agrees that he and his family should have a first-class ticket to the gas chambers, we prove to him that the documents are forged and then ask him, what reason he has for claiming in the first place that he and his family should be gassed and why moments later he has changed his mind. What has changed about him and his family that justifies freeing them from this torment? Does he really see or notice anything about his family and children or about his own person in the two different situations that would justify a switch in treatment? He can, of course, continue to say that it is their "Jewishness/non-Jewishness" that justifies the switch in treatment, but then he is really caught up in obscurantism and mystagogy, for our very trick has shown that there is nothing empirically detectable about being a Jew that is relevant to his moral claim. Perhaps Jewishness is a non-natural intuitable, totiresultant quality supervening on all Jews and only on Jews.

In sum, I have tried to argue, as against Taylor, that Baier's characterization of the moral point of view can be interpreted in such a way that it does not commit the ethnocentric fallacy. I have, as Taylor has, concentrated on Baier's third condition, but now I shall show that the first two conditions do not commit Baier to identifying morality with liberal Western morality and that the three conditions, taken in conjunction with Baier's claim that in reasoning morally we must attend to the facts, give us adequate criteria for deciding when a moral judgment is true.

Let us consider Baier's second condition, namely his contention that a rule, to count as a 'moral rule', must be one to which everyone can conform and a rule must be meant for everybody. Our prior discussion should have made it evident that condition two is plausible only under a rather distinctive interpretation. That is, we have to give a distinctive reading of 'rule meant for everybody' or 'rule to which everyone can conform as a matter of principle'. My above remarks about reversibility make it plain how and in what way moral rules are meant for everybody and are rules to which one can conform as a matter of principle. If something is a moral rule it must apply to like people in like circumstances. If it is all right for a starving Brazilian farmer to steal in order to keep alive, if he can't get the means of life in any other way, then it would be all right for anyone like this farmer and in the same kind of situation to steal. In that way, and without ethnocentrism, moral rules are for everyone. But this does not commit us to the absurdity that psychotics and mentally defective people can conform to them, but only to claiming that if, and when, such people can act as moral agents, then they too must, in the relevant circumstances, act in certain prescribed ways.

If a 'rule' to have the logical status of 'a moral rule' must be universalizable in the manner I have described, it clearly must be a rule that can be taught to anyone capable of moral agency to whom the moral rule correctly applies. If a moral rule applies to people of a certain sort, distinctively situated, this commits us to the assertion that when certain conditions obtain they ought to do what the rule enjoins; and this, in turn, implies that they can do it. But surely a necessary condition for their following the rule is that they understand it. Thus the moral rule must be teachable to the people to whom it correctly applies. But in specifying these people we must specify them by pointing to the fact that they have certain determinate characteristics, and *universalizability* commits us to saying that the moral rule in question must apply to anyone who has these characteristics. This would hold for anything recognizable as 'a moral rule'. This is plausible, if somewhat reduced, reading of Baier's claim that a moral rule must be teachable to everybody. I am saying rather that it must be capable of being taught to everyone to whom it can be correctly applied.

Baier's first condition poses more difficulties. Some have thought that there are, or at least can be, 'egoistic moralities', but Baier tells us that to adopt the moral point of view is to conform to rules whether or not conforming to them promotes our self-interest. If something counts as a 'moral rule' or as a 'moral claim' it must (and the force of the 'must' here is logical) override self-interest.

That this is so and why it is so is plain enough when we think of the *raison d'être* or, more modestly and more appropriately, a central *raison d'être,* for having a moral code—*any* moral code at all. Any society needs some device for impartially adjudicating conflicts of interest. Society is necessary for human beings, and when human beings live together, band together in a society with at least the minimal cooperation this implies, they will have conflicts of interest. If, when such conflicts occur, each man were to seek to further his self-interest alone, there would be the kind of conflict and chaos in society that no reasonable man could desire. In fact, if men were to act in this way, it would not even be correct to speak of them as living together in society. Thus to live together, to further one of the main ends of morality, men must adopt rules which override self-interest. To take the moral point of view of necessity involves conforming to such rules. But to conform to such rules is not simply to commit oneself to liberal Western morality. It is rather to adopt a point of view that is and must be implicit in all moral reasoning.

We are not out of the dark woods yet. Granting that moral judgments must be universalizable, granting that in the sense specified they must be for the good of everyone alike, we still do not know and cannot determine *what* is for the good of everyone alike, until we can determine something of the content of 'for the good of everyone alike'. Until we can do this we can hardly be said to have any knowledge of good and evil or any moral truth.

What is it for something to be for the *good* of everyone alike or even for something to be good for me or good period? If we leave the content of 'good' unspecified in stating the moral point of view, then if two moralists both adopt the moral point of view and make logically incompatible moral judgments both of which are—under these circumstances—acceptable from the moral point of view, because they both satisfy Baier's three conditions, then we would have two logically incompatible moral judgments both of which, according to Baier's specifications, would be true. But it is a self-contradiction to assert that two logically incompatible assertions could both be true. Baier would surely add, but, of course, two mutually incompatible statements cannot be true, but the problem remains that if we accept his explication of 'moral truth' there is no possible way of determining which of the two mutually incompatible moral statements is true.

An example may make my claim clearer. Suppose *A* claims that wives ought not to have lunch alone with men who are not their husbands, and *B* claims that this is absurdly medieval, that it is perfectly all right for a woman to have lunch alone with a man who is not her husband. Now these two judgments are both moral judgments, both satisfy Baier's three conditions and they are logically incompatible. We should want to say that they both can't be true, but given Baier's account, as explicated above, we could not possibly say which moral statement was true.

The way out here is to realize that in characterizing the moral point of view, we must *not* speak of 'the good of everyone alike' in such a way that 'good' is used so that it can have *just any* content. But when we claim 'good' must have a certain content, we again run the risk of committing the ethnocentric fallacy. It is tempting to argue that in adopting the moral point of view, we attribute a certain content to 'good' but not everyone would use 'good' in this way; there are, as J. O. Urmson argues, alternative and often conflicting criteria for 'good'. But we must—if we follow Baier—specify moral truth with reference to the moral point of view and here we find that once we consider 'good-making criteria', we get a relativity in the very specification of the moral point of view that defeats Baier's claim that we can develop an objective test for the truth of moral statements.

The question I want to ask here is this: Are the 'good-making criteria' used in such moral appraisals all *that* relative? When we are trying to develop a rational criterion for deciding whether certain actions, rules or practices are good or bad, we are concerned with whether they are, more than any of their alternatives, in the best interests of everyone; and in talking of the best interests of everyone, we are talking about their most extensive welfare and well-being. Now, if you like, you may call 'general welfare' and 'human well-being' grading labels or evaluative terms or prescriptive terms or normative terms or what you will, but they are, all the same, so tied to certain descriptive criteria that actions, rules or practices which did not satisfy these criteria could not be properly said to be in the general welfare or to serve the human well-being.[17] Practices or rules which sanctioned starving everyone to the point where the human animal could just barely keep alive, prohibited all sexual relations, constantly interrupted people's sleep to the point where they were just capable of keeping alive, made both play and work impossible and destroyed all human affection, could not possibly be correctly said to be in the general welfare and serve human well-being. And if they could not serve human well-being or be in the general welfare they could not be in the best interests of everyone and if they could not be in the best interests of everyone they could not be for the good of everyone alike and if they could not be for the good of everyone alike they could not be compatible with the moral point of view.

Such criteria give content to the moral point of view and make it impossible for both the judgments of *A* and *B* to be true. Furthermore, while such an explication of 'for the good of everyone alike' *may* commit what has been called the 'naturalistic fallacy', it does not commit the 'ethnocentric fallacy'. To accept such criteria about human welfare or human well-being does not commit us to liberal Western morality or even to Western morality, it is part of *any* morality.

It could be argued that what I have said above is mistaken; such a conception of 'general welfare' or 'human well-being' is still ethnocentric, for Buddhists striving after nirvana and Plains Indians on the vision quest regard certain forms of behavior as supremely desirable even though they run contrary to what I have said is in the general welfare or for human well-being. After all, we can have an 'ethic of renunciation'. Someone with such an ethic, it is natural to argue, would have a concept of the general welfare very different from the one just put before you. As such ascetics conceive of man's deepest well-being and welfare, we have something that sharply conflicts with what I have said. Such renunciation, they would argue, in reality serves men's deepest well-being and is for the general welfare. 'General welfare' and 'human well-being' are essentially contested concepts.

This objection to my argument will not do. It will not show that my criterion is ethnocentric, for such behavior was never advocated as a basis for social action or as a way of life for *all* Buddhists or *all* Plains Indians to adopt. It was prescribed for the holy man and not for the ordinary Plains Indian or the ordinary Buddhist. Such behavior did not, even for the holy man, serve as criteria for what was for *human* well-being or in the *general* welfare. Here their criteria overlap with the criteria used by what Taylor calls "liberal Western morality"; and the overlap includes the criteria I gave. There is no good reason to think such criteria are ethnocentric.

There is a further consideration that deserves attention here. As we noted before, in adopting the moral point of view, we are committed, when we are able to review the facts carefully, to clarifying these facts for ourselves before making decisions, advocating certain moral rules, or supporting certain moral practices. Now where there *seems* to be some alteration or qualification of the criteria for human well-being that I have offered, it has been in the service of some superstitious, ideological, or wildly metaphysical scheme. That nirvana can be attained, that there is a numinosity answering to the Indian's quest, is either false or without factual significance.[18] Attention to the facts, including the understanding we would achieve if we attained even a minimum of conceptual clarity, would lead us to reject such seeming alterations and qualifications of Baier's characterization of the moral point of view. To carry out moral reasoning fully, we must attend carefully to the non-moral facts and we must seek to be clear-headed. If we are clear-headed and do attend to the facts, we will not go on the vision quest or seek or even expect to attain nirvana.

We must also note that moral judgments are judgments that are ideally made in the light of a full knowledge of the relevant facts and they must, logically must, be made in the light of the facts that it is reasonable to expect the moral agent to have in his possession when he must make his moral decision or render judgment. To take the moral point of view is to reason in this way and it is to use 'good' in the relevant contexts with this factual content. Since this is so, it cannot be the case that two logically incompatible moral judgments, like *A*'s and *B*'s about wives' dining with men who are not their husbands, could both be acceptable from the moral point of view. They have different consequences for human well-being and, everything being equal, if *A*'s judgment is such that it would, if followed, make for greater general welfare than *B*'s, then only *A*'s judgment is acceptable from the moral point of view; and, if there are not other alternatives acceptable from the moral point of view here, then *A*'s judgment is required from the moral point of view and *a fortiori* true.

The concept of good is sufficiently vague and moral reasoning is sufficiently complex to make it the case that for a wide and important range of cases, we cannot determine what we ought to do with any objectivity. But there are also standard cases and contexts in which we can determine moral truth—that is, we can determine how we ought to act from the moral point of view. Moreover, given a sophisticated and a determined application of moral reasoning and an extensive knowledge of man and his world, our knowledge of good and evil can constantly expand. The concept of truth has an application in morals and we have definite ways of determining truth in morality.

## NOTES

1. It is used in a moralistic way in the following examples. "A rational man will never simply use people to further his own interests," "A rational man will not pursue his own lesser good at the expense of the greater good of his society," "A rational man will be fair in his dealings with others."

2. I say *most,* for C. L. Stevenson makes it quite evident that he does not think it is misleading. See C. L. Stevenson, *Facts and Values* (New Haven, 1963), pp. 214-220.

3. A. J. Ayer, "On the Analysis of Moral Judgments" in Milton Munitz (ed.), *A Modern Introduction to Ethics* (New York, 1958), p. 537.

4. Kurt Baier, *The Moral Point of View* (Ithaca, N.Y., 1958), pp. 183-184. In my "History of Ethics," vol. III, *Encyclopedia of Philosophy,* ed. by Paul Edwards (New York, 1967), pp. 109-112, I have given a general characterization of the good reasons approach and tried to place it in contemporary ethical theory.

5. Kurt Baier, op. cit., p. 191.

6. Ibid., p. 195.

7. Ibid., p. 201.

8. Ibid., p. 202.

9. Ibid., p. 185.

10. Paul Taylor, "The Ethnocentric Fallacy," *The Monist* 47 (1963):563-584.

11. Ibid., p. 565.

12. Ibid., pp. 568-569.

13. Ibid., p. 570.

14. Ibid.

15. Edward Westermarck, *Ethical Relativity* (London, 1932), p. 197.

16. Paul Taylor, op. cit., pp. 575-576.

17. In this context see also my "Appraising Doing the Thing Done," *The Journal of Philosophy* 57 (1960); "Progress," *The Lock Haven Review,* no. 7 (1965); "On Looking Back at the Emotive Theory," *Methodos* 14 (1962); and "Problems of Ethics," vol. III, *Encyclopedia of Philosophy,* ed. by Paul Edwards (New York, 1967), pp. 130-132.

18. My remark here may seem brusque and dogmatic, but I could hardly develop my arguments for it here, though I have in some detail in my "On Speaking of God," *Theoria* 28 (1962): Part 2; "Religious Perplexity and Faith," *The Crane Review* 8 (1965); "God-Talk," *Sophia* 3 (1964); "On Fixing the Reference Range of 'God'," *Religious Studies* 2 (1966); and in my book *An Introduction to the Philosophy of Religion,* (London: The Macmillan Press Ltd., 1982).

# 5

# The Good-Reasons Approach Revisited

Philosophy in the twentieth century has taken a Copernican turn. We have developed a keen awareness that philosophical problems are often, if not always, generated by linguistic confusions. We shall be free from philosophical perplexity about certain central concepts such as goodness, probability, God, law and the like when we come to understand how such concepts actually function in ordinary discourse. If we find out how the concept of freedom actually functions and why it functions that way, this will relieve our perplexity as to whether any person is ever free; if we find out how the notion of law is used in living contexts, this will help us, as nothing else will, to relieve perplexities about whether there are "natural laws." In moral philosophy what has been called "the good reasons approach" has utilized this philosophical method in a way that has been of an immense value to our understanding of morality. This method has also been of value in many ways to the legal theorist, the historian, and the social scientist.

I have tried on previous occasions to make a contribution to the forward movement of this approach. Here I would like further to clarify it and advance it by critically examining one of the most searching criticisms of this whole approach. I shall not limit myself simply to a reply to these criticisms but I shall develop the good reasons approach so as to free it from certain obscurities and to advance such an account of morality. The criticism I have in mind is D. H. Monro's "Are Moral Problems Genuine?"[1] I single out Monro's essay because his very central and important criticisms have not been noted and considered as they deserve to be.[2] I have, however, a still more important reason for singling them out: they bring together in an incisive way difficulties with such linguistic approaches to ethics that have also

From *Archiv fuer Rechts und Sozialphilosophie* 40, no 4 (1964): 455–483. Reprinted by permission of the publisher.

been felt by many others. Monro clearly voices what many others have said less clearly. He raises in a powerful form some of the persistent doubts and questions that it is quite natural to have about such an approach. I would exhort readers of this essay to read or re-read Monro's essay, but the scale of my essay is not merely limited to assessing one sharp criticism of the good-reasons approach, but its overarching aim is to re-examine and re-state this whole approach in the light of some basic criticisms of it.

# I

Monro argues that there is a fundamental problem about an "ultimate justification of morals" and that an adequate moral philosophy must solve this problem. It must, in short, provide such an "ultimate justification" for morality. This problem is not, Monro argues, a pseudo-problem engendered by a failure to understand the functions of ordinary moral discourse; it is rather what he labels "a genuine philosophical problem." He holds, as against Toulmin, Hare, Mayo, Baier and Edwards, that there is such a problem and that linguistic analysts are mistaken in regarding such a question as a pseudo-question.[3] The very analyses of these philosophers, he argues, bring this problem poignantly to our attention. The issue Monro raises is a fundamental one and he raises it in an incisive way, but for all of that there are in my opinion some crucial flaws in his argument.

First we need to get a far clearer idea of just what Monro's problem is. Monro seems to be saying that all our practical day to day moral judgments depend for their very soundness on certain ultimate or fundamental moral principles and that it is the crucial problem of moral philosophy to show how we can justify these *ultimate* moral principles upon which all our moral conceptions depend.

This certainly seems like a reasonable claim, but Monro feels fully the difficulties that we encounter when we try to justify these ultimate moral principles. Both Monro and the good-reasons approach philosophers think that the traditional attempts to justify these principles all break down. The good-reasons approach rejects all varieties of intuitionism, nonnaturalism, or transcendentalism. Monro agrees with them here; but they also agree that the point made by non-naturalists about the naturalistic fallacy is well taken and thus Monro finds it impossible to accept ethical naturalism. Subjectivism, though it seems the most palatable position to Monro, "fails to do justice to the way people actually think and behave." And what is most important for our present purposes: none of these traditional positions handle adequately the problem about the justification of fundamental moral principles. Our situation—according to Monro—is just this: Our workaday moral beliefs, rules, and judgments depend for their soundness on certain fundamental principles, but we seem to be completely at a loss to justify these fundamental moral principles. Our crucial philosophical problem about morality consists in examining whether and how (if at all) such fundamental moral principles can be justified. The terrors of Sidgwick remain; this question cannot be dissolved as a pseudo-problem by philosophical analysis. The good-reasons approach has treated it in this way, but this is a mistake. Such a moral problem is genuine.

Yet if we push the matter a bit—if we reflect on the exact nature of this question—we will discover that Monro's question is not as clear as it may seem at first. Monro describes his problem as follows: "What is the ultimate justification of morals? Is morality objective or subjective?" But, as Toulmin and Edwards have pointed out, to ask if morality is subjective or objective can do little more than promote a stutter until we have some clear idea in what way 'objective' or 'subjective' is being used in such a context.

In his examination of Mayo's *The Moral Life and The Ethical Life,* Monro makes reasonably clear what he means by a subjectivist in ethics.[4] A subjectivist is claiming that there is no way of rationally resolving fundamental moral disputes, for fundamental moral judgments or ultimate moral principles cannot correctly be said to be true or false independently of the attitudes of at least some people. The subjectivist is claiming, as Monro puts it, that when we come to "ultimate moral principles we find that we can only accept or reject them, much as our palate accepts or rejects rice pudding."[5]

There is, of course, the difficulty about spelling out exactly what constitutes an 'ultimate moral principle' or 'a fundamental moral judgment'. These concepts have a kind of specious clarity about them. But let us for the sake of the discussion assume we have clarified them.

We, of course, cannot *derive* an ultimate moral principle from another principle, for then trivially our "ultimate principle" could not be ultimate. But this does not entail, or in any way justify, the conclusion that we could not know an ultimate principle to be true and it does not at all distinguish ultimate *moral* principles from other ultimate principles.

The subjectivist, according to Monro, is claiming that there can be no rational resolution to fundamental moral disputes. There is no moral insight or method of validation that will tell us which fundamental moral claims are true or which fundamental moral arguments are sound. If we agree on fundamental principles, then we can rationally resolve our ordinary moral disputes, but if the argument gets really fundamental—if we push our arguments to the limit—we will discover there is no way to objectively validate our fundamental moral claims. Even if as a matter of brute sociological fact we happen to agree on fundamentals, we can recognize, if we are relatively clear-headed, that we could not show that our agreed on fundamental principles were right and that conceivable alternative principles were wrong. Our basic philosophical problem about ethics is to try to determine whether such a subjectivist is right or whether some form of objectivism can be vindicated.


## II

We are still not out of the woods. We have only a specious clarity here, what are we asking for when we ask, as Monro does, for the ultimate justification of *morals?* Even assuming (as we in reality cannot) that we are clear about the sense in which 'ultimate' and 'justification' are being used here, the question still remains ambiguous. It can mean at least the following four things: 1) How can we achieve final agreement about whether or not to try to act morally? 2) How can we attain final agreement about whether or not to try to accept one pattern of moral behavior (one moral code rather than another)? 3) How can we finally justify being moral rather than being amoral or immoral? 4) How can we finally decide which kinds of reasons are good reasons *in* ethics? I shall reject, out of hand, the first two statements of Monro's problem as irrelevant on the grounds that they are not *justificatory* problems at all but are problems of persuasion or goading. Here I am clearly following Hare and Falk in distinguishing between, on the one hand, *telling* and *guiding* and, on the other, between *getting* and *goading*. It is one thing to *get* a group of people to agree to act together toward the achievement of a common goal, and it is a quite different thing to rationally *justify* to them that this is the morally correct thing to do. One might by hypnotism, drugs, threats, propaganda and the like attain agreement about what to do without *justifying* that goal. Moral engineering is one thing; critical assessment of a moral code is another. 1 and 2 are goading problems and 3 and 4 are justificatory problems. If Monro regards his problem as the problems stated in 1 and 2, I shall rest content with the bare challenge that he has not raised a justificatory question at all. If, on the other hand, Monro's basic problem is 3), I shall grant he has raised a justificatory problem but not a problem for *moral* justification. So construed his problem is not a moral problem; it is not a problem about how to justify one moral claim or code rather than another. He is instead asking for a justification for acting morally *at all.* He is asking for a good reason for acting morally rather than for acting on some non-moral basis. 'Moral' here has a descriptive use and it contrasts with 'non-moral'. Monro's question so interpreted is this: to act morally is to act in such and such a manner, but why act in this manner? In asking this question, he is asking for a justification for morality as an activity, as over against a life based on non-moral privilege or some other non-moral policy. It is or should be obvious enough that in such a context we cannot sensibly ask for a good *moral* reason or a *moral* justification for acting morally. As Kant shrewdly recognized, when we ask this sort of question, we are beyond moral reasoning altogether.[6]

The good-reasons approach in ethics shows a clear awareness of the finite scope of moral reasoning. I would argue (and have argued) that 3) is an important problem and an "arguable problem" (a pleonasm), but since Monro and I are in agreement here I shall content myself with insisting that this important problem of human conduct is not a problem that can arise *within* moral reasoning, though surely it is a problem that is *relevant* to morality.

It is 4) that the good-reasons approach has been trying to answer. I shall now try to clarify this question and ask in what senses (if any) it is a *general* philosophical problem requiring a single, overall, monolithic solution. I shall assume, henceforth, that it is 4) that Monro wishes to consider and that it is 4) that Monro regards as inadequately handled by Toulmin, Baier and Hare.


# III

Let us first try to get clearer about just what we are asking for in 4). I shall first re-state Toulmin's statement of this problem and then briefly re-state the kind of answer he takes to be appropriate.

Toulmin, like Hare, points out that whether we like it or not, we cannot avoid taking a stand on moral questions. Moral arguments, in one form or another, are constantly arising in practical life. We are thus faced with a central practical problem: "How are we to distinguish those (moral arguments) to which we should pay attention from those which we should ignore or reject?"[7] Which of the reasons among the many contenders are good reasons and how far can we rely on reason in arriving at moral decisions or moral assessments? In any problematic situation where we must make a moral decision we consider the relevant facts involved and then make our decision. In doing this, we move from factual reasons (R) to a moral decision (E). We want to know if (R) is a good reason for (E). "What is it that makes a particular set of facts, R, a good reason for a particular ethical conclusion E?"[8] More generally, what kinds of reasons are good reasons for certain moral conclusions; and is it necessary to find reasons for these reasons and then reasons for these reasons or does " 'giving reasons' sometimes become supererogatory" in morals?[9] That is to say, what are the limits of moral reasoning and what (if anything) is the ultimate standard or standards of moral appraisal? I take this last question to be the precisification of 4) and I shall assume that both Toulmin and Monro address themselves to this question.

Toulmin is, of course, on the side of virtue. He emphatically asserts that there are good reasons in ethics; and, while he does not think that there is one "fundamental problem of morals," he is willing to assert that the above problem is a problem that is both of central importance to philosophical ethics and is frequently personally bedeviling to the man in moral bewilderment. But Toulmin also emphatically asserts that we cannot give one answer to this question which will cover all situations and all contexts. There are different kinds of reasoning appropriate to different moral contexts. A moral agent in a particular context faced with keeping an appointment where there are no confining *prima facie* obligations applies the moral principle 'Promises must be kept'. Where there are conflicting obligations or where no *prima facie* obligations are relevant, a moral agent seeks to determine which of the proposed actions will cause the least amount of needless suffering for everyone involved. If the moral agent is questioning the moral rule or social practice as such, he will ask whether this social practice or an alternative social practice will be likely to lead to the least amount of needless suffering for everyone involved. If there is an alternative rule or practice to the one he is examining that would involve, were it adopted, less suffering for the people involved, then we would have a good reason for adopting that social practice rather than the one we are examining. The practice, among the alternatives, that is most likely to lead to the least amount of needless suffering for everyone involved, is the practice that ought to be adopted. If the altering of a social practice led to a happier, fuller way of life for the people involved, then that practice ought to be adopted. (Here we have the cash value of social progress.) If alternative social practices have no discernibly different consequences that would establish one as having greater felicific consequences than the other, a choice between them would be a matter of a nonmoral personal decision. If the social practices are so inextricably involved with the very way of life of the community that they cannot be compared without comparing whole ways of life, a decision for or against one would again (according to Toulmin) be a non-rational, non-moral decision.[10] "The only occasions on which one can discuss the question which of two practices is the better are those on which they are genuine alternatives: when it would be practicable to change from one to the other *within one society.*"[11] Thus Toulmin instead of giving us a block answer gives us a contextual answer to questions about how fundamental moral principles are justified.

In different contexts different answers (answers emphasized as *total* answers by the several traditions of philosophic ethics) become relevant. Moral principles are Protean. There is no one single principle that covers all situations. *If* what is to count as an answer to the question 'What is the basic justificatory standard in morals?' must be given in that single-tracked sense then Toulmin must answer in the negative: "Philosophical moral problems are not genuine." But, if a *pluralistic* answer like the one given in the preceding paragraph is allowable then Toulmin must answer in the affirmative: "Moral problems are genuine." There are standards or principles of reasoning in morals; and there are definite limits to moral reasoning. It is at these limits where moral justification comes to a natural end as all justification must. *A* central task, if not *the* central task, of the moral philosopher is to give an accurate paradox-relieving description of these standards and the roles these standards play in everyday moral assessment.

The same point might be put somewhat differently. A crucial task of the philosopher is to define 'morality' in the sense of delimiting its boundaries; that is in "showing how it abuts onto, but is distinct from law, tabu, etiquette, technique, enlightened self-interest, and so on."[12] But there is no single formula which could be an adequate replacement for such a description of moral discourse. We need an actual depiction of the scope of moral reasoning. Single principles can only indicate how some sectors of the boundary run.

After this exposition of how Toulmin would "answer" Monro's question, I think we can see clearly what bothers Monro most. Monro is not exercised by the whole of the problem, but with that part of the problem which deals with the justification of moral principles and with the justification of whole *ways of life*. I think it is also fair to say that it is just this problem which exercises a very great number of the more traditional moral philosophers. It is simply disingenuous of contemporary linguistic philosophers not to recognize this.

Monro rightly enough sees ambiguity and inadequacy in Toulmin's analysis here. Monro points out that Toulmin's conception of the function of morality and his conception of a principle for judging social practices admit of two interpretations. One of these interpretations makes Toulmin's ethics into a universalistic utilitarianism and the other into a form of ethical relativism. Toulmin tends at various points to hold both these positions and it is not at all clear how they could be reconciled. Monro also argues that we cannot solve or dissolve the basic problem of "the ultimate justification" of moral principles by appealing to the function of moral principles or to certain purely *formal* criteria like universalizability.

I agree with Monro that Toulmin's conception of the function of ethics can be interpreted in a manner that will support either a utilitarian criterion or a form of ethical relativism. I also agree with Monro, as against Toulmin and Hare, that moral questions about whole ways of life can arise and to know what would constitute an answer to them is very important. Toulmin seems to have confused a question of immediate social engineering with a question of theoretical moral assessment. To use Baier's way of putting it, Toulmin has confused the practical aim of a moral reformer with the theoretical aim of a moral critic. There is no way of transforming the slave society of Ancient Greece into a non-slave society; reflections on ancient Greek morality are in this way pointless from the point of view of the moral reformer, but there still is a job here for a moral critic. Sometimes it is even perfectly sensible for the moral critic and the moral reformer to make comparisons between whole ways of life. The reformer may not see the immediate steps to be taken in transforming one society into another, but for all that, an administrator of a colonial territory, a contemporary American Indian caught between two ways-of-life, or a Kemal Ataturk can hardly avoid asking: "Which way of life is the better?" That this is not just a theoretical problem is amply demonstrated by Margaret Mead's study of the fantastic transformation of the Manus from a pre-literate society to what we call "civilization" in the space of ten years. Their change brought acute problems for them about which way of life was better. And their choices were not just those concerning the periphery of their culture, for their very central social structures were transformed. Here we have a genuine experiment in living. There are even cases that are closer to home. We may, after our adolescent enthusiasm cools a bit, come to disagree with the more romantic moral assessments of Polynesian sexual morality and family life. We may no longer compare our forms of life so invidiously with the life of the Samoans; but whether we downgrade Tahiti and the Youth Group and upgrade Mother, God and Country or view Polynesia as a superlatively better Sweden, we are still able to make these judgments, because such comparisons and the arguments they give rise to are intelligible to us as bits of moral discourse. (That they are wild impressionistic judgments is here not to the point.) Such comparisons may be highly speculative and the arguments may indeed be very, very loose and very, very anxiety-arousing, but such arguments and such comparisons are still perfectly possible. Monro is right here and a good reasons approach that is wedded to Toulmin's reasoning here has certainly gone astray.

There are, however, crucial points in Monro's analysis that I cannot accept. Monro thinks that even if we take Toulmin's account as a version of universalistic utilitarianism it is still a very tangled and very inadequate account of moral reasoning. I shall try to rebut Monro's argument here. I shall also criticize Monro's claim that in moral discourse there are no formal criteria consistently followed, universally applicable and mutually consistent. I shall argue instead that the formal criterion of universalizability, plus Toulmin's conception of the function of ethics (interpreted so as to be compatible with a non-relativistic utilitarianism) and an appeal to sympathetic imagination, give us the most important sign posts for an adequate map of the moral terrain.[13] If we clearly understand the respective roles and interrelations of these three features of morality, we are well on our way to understanding the logic of moral discourse. But we must never forget that sign posts aren't maps and formulae aren't descriptions.

IV

Monro claims that Toulmin's conception of the function of ethics does not necessarily involve an appeal to the utilitarian conception of the greatest good for the greatest number. Toulmin, it will be recalled, claims that we justify moral rules by asking whether they will harmonize desires. We have a morality—any morality at all—to enable men to live together in society. Society could not survive unless there were some minimal degree of harmony of desires and aims among its members. It will, moreover, very frequently be the case that the members of one community or society will need at some point to co-operate with the members of another community. The communities would then in a certain sense be a part of one "larger community." Again there would have to be a harmonizing of desires and aims to make life together viable. Such a harmonizing of desires, developed along principles of equity, will amount in practice to the classical utilitarian principle of the greatest happiness for everyone concerned.

It is here where Monro balks. We can accept Toulmin's conception of the primary function of morality, he argues, without recognizing its utilitarian offspring.[14] "Two communities C 1 and C 2 might coalesce in such a way that their members become slave and slave-owners respectively." Desires, Monro points out, might even in this case be harmonized to the satisfaction of everyone involved. Masters would have duties to slaves and slaves would have duties to masters. It is even possible that they could all quite genuinely accept the code in question, but the result is that it will not harmonize desires in the sense of putting an equal value on the desires of slaves and slave-owners, though it will harmonize desires so that as many people *as possible* will get whatever it is that they want. It will not accord with what we pre-analytically understand to be the conditions of fairness.

Monro points out that we cannot tell from Toulmin's conception of the function of morality whether we have in such a situation a set of moral principles or whether we simply have non-moral rules of privilege. But whatever Toulmin says, he is in Monro's opinion in trouble. If, on the one hand, he says that the slave society is *not* a moral community, then there can be a community which reasons in accordance with his conception of the function of morality, but is still not a moral community. (Remember that here 'moral' is being used in a descriptive sense where it contrasts with 'non-moral' rather than 'immoral'.) If, on the other hand, Toulmin says it is a genuine moral community "then the criteria to which moral principles must conform are far more varied than he (Toulmin) seems to suppose."[15]

Toulmin in my judgment is not really stuck here. In criticizing Toulmin, Monro has not brought out an essential feature of Toulmin's conception of the primary function of ethics. But this element in Toulmin's account would *not* allow him, as Monro argues, to ignore questions of equity or fairness in dealing with a case like the one of such a slave society.

Let us see how this is so. To do this we must return to Toulmin's conception of the function of ethics. Provisionally defined, the function of ethics is—to quote Toulmin—"to correlate our feelings and behavior in such a way as to make the fulfilment of *everyone's* aims and desires, as far as possible, compatible."[16] Full-fledged moral utterances are, according to Toulmin, categorical imperatives.[17] A moral argument to be a moral argument must be worthy of acceptance whoever is considering it. "If . . . the most general principles to which we can appeal still contain some reference to us, either as individuals or as members of a limited group of people, then our appeal is not to 'morality' but to 'privilege'."[18]

Now consider Monro's case of a slave society. Toulmin's conception of the function of ethics requires that we consider everyone's wishes and interests. In addition he makes it plain that no moral claim can make an irreducible reference to individuals or to members of a class as such, i.e., to slaves and slave-owners. If such an appeal is made, the appeal isn't to morality, but to privilege. Toulmin's very conception of the function of morality necessitates such a conclusion. If we accept it we must accept that conclusion. If Monro's slave society does not consider everyone's interests and if it simply appeals to members of a class (slave-owners and slaves) *qua* members of a class, then, on Toulmin's own showing, such a code of such a society could not count as a morality. Monro is wrong in claiming that Toulmin's conception of the function of morality does not allow us to decide such a case. He is not on Monro's fork. Given the above description of the "slave society," it could not properly be said to have a morality and Toulmin's conception of the function of ethics can show why. But Monro's case is sufficiently indeterminate to allow us to say, again in accordance with Toulmin's conception of the function of ethics, that it is a community with a moral code. In either case the fault is not with Toulmin, but in the indeterminacy of Monro's case.

Let us see how such a community could be consistently taken to have a moral code. Given certain factual beliefs (racist ones for example), one could still in such a society be concerned with everyone's interests—one could still be willing to universalize one's maxims. One need not justify the different treatment of slaves and slave-owners simply by an appeal to their class. One need not abandon morality and make an appeal to privilege here. The slave-owner could appeal to certain features about himself and other slave-owners to establish his natural superiority, and willingly grant that if the slaves had these qualities they too ought to be treated in that way.[19] Furthermore, if the slave-owners were, as a matter of fact, like the slaves, they too ought to be treated as slaves. Meeting the conditions of fairness, no doubt with the help of rationalization, the slave society, even on Toulmin's utilitarian grounds, could correctly be understood to have a moral code, albeit an irrational moral code. (Surely 'an irrational moral code' is not a contradiction in terms.) As a moral agent, I am as concerned as the next man to oppose such a morality, but this does not blind me to the fact that such a code is still a moral code. In short, Monro's case in no way shows the inadequacy of Toulmin's conception of the function of ethics even if it is interpreted as committing one, if one is prepared to reason morally, to an utilitarian criterion for assessing social practices. In deciding whether the slave community was or was not a moral community, we made an appeal to utilitarian considerations, i.e., to whether everyone's interests, desires and wants were being taken into consideration in such a way that everyone, treated initially alike, could as far as possible, as fully as possible, satisfy his interests and desires. Perhaps this requirement is too strong, but it is reasonable to interpret Toulmin's conception of the function of ethics in that way and Monro has not shown, that if such an interpretation is made, we must end up calling something 'morality' that plainly isn't or denying something the title of 'morality' that plainly is morality. Toulmin has neither flaunted common sense nor those pervasive features of ordinary usage that any adequate meta-ethical theory must be responsive to.

But even if we have undercut Monro's criticism about the function of ethics, we still have, apart from difficulties about universalizability to which we shall turn in the next section, difficulties about the utilitarian criterion of happiness or least suffering.

Monro points to the "notorious ambiguities of the term 'happiness' " and to the anthropological fact that whether we are happier in one culture rather than in another "will depend, at least in part, on the community we happen to have grown up in." What will make us happy will depend largely on what secondary needs our culture has instilled in us; and, as Monro (following Malinowski) is concerned to emphasize, once such needs have been created they will be just as important, just as strong motives for action as motives rooted in primary needs. They may, in fact, even become stronger motives.[20]

I think it should be admitted straight off that what *causes* happiness is no doubt quite varied and is in part at least culturally relative. It is also plain enough that 'happiness' is a polyguous term; that is to say, 'happiness' like 'probable' and 'good', refers to a variety of different things. What we are referring to when we use the term 'happiness' or the term 'suffering' will, in part at least, vary from context to context. That is why general definitions of 'happiness' are so unhelpful. But it is also true that 'happiness' normally has a commendatory force; 'suffering' has just the opposite force. While *just what* will count as happiness may indeed vary from tribe to tribe and even from person to person, a consideration of the felicific consequences of social practices is always used as one very fundamental consideration in judging social practices. It was one of Bentham's great insights to see that those moralities which claimed to be opposed to the greatest happiness principle actually employed it in practice. The criteria of application for the word 'happiness' vary, but the force of the word remains the same. Whatever it is that well informed people in a rational frame of mind take as genuinely furthering their happiness is something they ought *prima facie* to seek. They should only *not* seek it when their happiness—that is the happiness of some individual—conflicts with the common good, e.g. with the maximum distribution of happiness for everyone involved or with the good of many others. (Not just with the good of others, for, as W. D. Falk has nicely shown, there is a limit to how much one should sacrifice for others.[21] Sometimes one has the right to put one's own good above the good of others. There is a large area of indeterminacy here that no formula or generalization will adequately cover, but we do have some guide lines. If widespread misery will follow from attaining what one wants, one clearly ought not to seek it.)

To reply to Monro in this way, it might be objected, is really to in effect bring about the strength of his point. If the criteria of 'happiness' are actually so variable, so culturally and even personally relative and if we only have the "hurrah force" of the word in common, we have no common standard at all. To say that 'happiness' has a laudatory force but that there is nothing which 'happiness' in all its uses refers to or signifies is merely a fancy way of saying that of happiness and misery there is no comon measure. If 'happiness' has no common criteria there can be no states of affairs, no experiences, no actions, no attitudes that will constitute or even partially constitute happiness for all rational human beings.

Even if all this were completely true, it would still be important to realize that we do use this word in such a way in appraising our practices. Yet surely this is not to say nearly enough, for it would only disguise the fact that we have no common ground for appraising our practices. But while 'happiness' is polyguous is it so polyguous that it has no common criteria? I don't think this is the case. Certainly there is a close connection between happiness and pleasure or what will give one satisfaction in living. And it is just not so that what is one man's pleasure is another man's pain. It is true enough that one man may gain pleasure from driving through the country or fishing while another finds such activities a great bore; or one man may love bullfighting or gambling while another abhors them or finds them uninteresting. But such differences do not show that there is no agreement about what is pleasurable and what is painful. There are plenty of quite mundane sources of pleasure and satisfaction that are quite pan-human. We like—in normal circumstances—to eat, make love, talk with our friends, listen to music, hear stories, etc., etc. That these are stable sources of pleasure is plain enough. And what will cause pain and suffering is still more obvious. There are also less tangible things that are sources of happiness and pleasure. We (or at least most of us) need to love and be loved; we need some work which will be both meaningful to us and remunerative; we need a life in which we have both privacy and companionship; we need both to keep our self-esteem and involve ourselves with others. Without these things we will be frustrated and miserable; a life that has a preponderance of things of this sort will be a life that is in the main a happy life. Monro rightly points to the ambiguities of 'happiness', but it is certainly a mistake to argue that "of happiness and of despair we have no measure."

V

Monro also criticizes Hare's and Toulmin's position about formal criteria in moral discourse. His criticism is directed in large measure against the appeal to *universalizability* that plays such a crucial role in our above remarks about the primary function of ethics. Monro discerns three related formal criteria. Moral utterances must 1) conform to a maxim or principle, 2) they must be generally applicable in similar circumstances and 3) they must be applicable to others as well as to ourselves.

The only sense that Monro can make out of 1) is the truism that all our acts have motives. But, he adds, if we examine our actual behavior our actions do not always conform to 2) and 3). People are not as consistent as 2) implies and what "really raises" Monro's doubts is the assertion made in 3) that we always act from principle in the sense that we apply to others the same principles we apply to ourselves.

The basic consideration underlying 3) is Toulmin's contention that if "the most general principles to which we can appeal still contain some reference to us, either as individuals or as members of a limited group of people, then our appeal is not to morality but to privilege."[22] We cannot defend this, Monro argues, by contending that since principles, to be principles, must be teach-able, we "cannot teach others to abide by one set of principles while following quite a different set ourselves."[23] We, after all, can and do teach rules of privilege as well as moral rules. Furthermore, it is a mistake to believe that viewed from within moral codes our ways of life are internally consistent or coherent, though he admits that the anthropological evidence suggests "that there is in human societies a drive towards something that can be called an integration of attitudes." But this is compatible with a great deal of actual inconsistency that is masked by cultural myths.

Surely anyone who has ever lived, ever felt the pangs of his own mortality, must grant Monro the above point. Yet Monro's contention does not even begin to touch the problem linguistic analysts are trying to handle when they seek formal criteria in moral discourse. Monro gets a little closer to the mark when he remarks that perhaps "they appeal rather to the way men feel they ought to behave."[24] But even here, Monro argues, the principles we feel we ought to obey are frequently mutually inconsistent; furthermore, there are people who would dissent from or deliberately reject any appeal to a "rational ethic of mutually consistent principles." Instead, after the fashion of D. H. Lawrence, they would argue for a "life of impulse."[25] It is indeed true that a non-evasive glimpse at our world will make it abundantly apparent that "there are certainly people who would defend rules of privilege."[26] Monro sums up his argument in the following remark: "My point so far is that the concept of a way of life consisting of actions regulated by principles which are universally applicable, not rules of privilege, mutually consistent, and consistently followed is an artificial one: it is not derived either from an analysis of the actual behavior of human beings or from their account of how they think they ought to behave. That is why modern moral philosophers have felt that it does stand in need of some justification."[27]

There certainly is truth in what Monro says, but he has again missed his target. First, a rather minor point. Monro has not produced any evidence that people when they believe they are reasoning morally are willing to consciously accept inconsistency in their basic principles. Surely "the Spirit of Middletown" is rife with contradictions. A whole generation of American novelists ambivalently broke with Middletown because they could not accept these internal inconsistencies. But does this establish that the Pillars of Society in Middletown consciously recognize these inconsistencies? Ibsen keenly penetrates more deeply still when he fashions his defenders of the *status quo* so that they only recognize the inconsistencies in their moral code when they are literally forced on them. Until the last—until extreme conditions force this awareness on them—they persist in believing the emperor has fine new raiment. Only then do they have their brief, dearly bought, "moment of truth." Monro's own remarks in another article about rationalization and myth-making in morality would seem to bear out and partially explain the facts about human behavior that Ibsen has placed before us.[28] Myth-making and rationalization are, Monro points out, really expressions of a drive toward rationality and consistency. It is an attempt, by means of myth or ideology, to reconcile what appear at least to be conflicting principles.[29] In our cultural life we have at our disposal here a whole battery of factual *sounding* expressions that actually function as disguised moral recommendations. When these expressions are functioning in this way, they may quite properly be called ideological statements.[30] By means of such statements we manage to believe sincerely that there is consistency where there is actually conflict of principles. The evidence seems to be that human beings seek consistency and will go to great lengths to whitewash any real inconsistency of moral principles. The history of southern thought about segregation is a good case in point. There seems to be no basis for claiming that people do not *feel* they ought to be consistent in their moral assessments. Indeed there are those who will say, rightly enough, that "*foolish* consistency is the hobgoblin of little minds"; and there are those who will claim that we ought to always go around figuring everything out at great length but we ought to give way to our deep heart-felt convictions. But even here it is *"foolish* consistency" that is to be avoided and it is 'we' that ought to do it; and we should also note that a universaliz-able principle of behavior with a definite rationale is being proclaimed in making such a claim. That is to say, there remain with the most impulsive "existentialist type" moralist conceptions of fairness and equity. Both "Kan-tian superego morality" and a "looser Millian morality" accept the principle of universalizability. They have built into their systems just this principle that Toulmin and Hare argue is part of the very meaning of morality.

Monro also claims that people sometimes defend what I would call mor-ally inadmissible rules of privilege. This is perfectly true, but then they have gone beyond strictly moral considerations altogether. An unabashed appeal to privilege where it conflicts with morality is perfectly possible. But here we do not have two rival "moral geometries" but essentially appeals from two quite different vantage points—vantage points Aiken has aptly called "the ethical" and "the post-ethical."[31] Similarly a life of impulse may be more de-sirable—in some non-moral sense of 'desirable'—than a moral life, but if we are careful about how we use language we will not say such a life, where it conflicts with morality, is *morally* desirable. Men may find things person-ally good or desirable that have nothing to do with morality or that even in extreme cases conflict with it. Toulmin emphasizes that strictly moral con-siderations have a limited application and there is a point where we pass beyond the scope of morality to questions of each man's pursuit of the Good. Here for Toulmin, as for Ayer, personal attitudes and choices are paramount.[32] It is quite possible that someone might wish to challenge the desirability of the moral life itself. There is nothing in Toulmin's writings to rule out this move. Rather he is, like Kant, making the analytical claim that such rea-soning is, by implicit definition, not moral reasoning.[33] Thus the fact that there is behavior inconsistent with the formal criteria Hare and Toulmin ap-peal to does not at all upset their claim that these are genuine formal motifs in moral discourse.

## VI

The above two points are minor compared with a general point about for-mal criteria in morals I wish now to make in defense of the good reasons approach. Toulmin, Hare and like-minded philosophers are trying to give accurate descriptions of the *actual uses* of terms like 'good', 'moral', 'mor-ally relevant reason', etc. They are not carrying out a psychological or so-ciological examination of the behavior of people, they are not trying to dis-cover the *causes* of moral behavior and they are not trying to find out how many people generally behave morally as opposed to how many are immoral and the like. They are not even trying to give a description of *feelings* of guilt, remorse, obligation, righteousness, etc.; they are not even concerned in a *sociological way* with moral language: that is to say, they are not out to discover how many (if any) people now substitute 'cooperative' and 'uncooperative' for 'good' and 'bad' behavior. Such discoveries may sometimes be pertinent to their task but their job is to describe accurately the uses of moral language in order to relieve conceptual perplexity over morals. In seeking out formal criteria they are trying to find out what (if any) other words are linked with moral words in such a manner that one could not understand the use of the moral word in question without reference to the other word or words. We could not understand what it means to say a man ought to do something unless we understood what it would mean to say that he could have done otherwise. Similarly in coming to understand that I have an obligation to do something, I of necessity come to understand that anyone like me in such a circumstance should do as well. Hare puts this in a formal way by saying that the link between universalizability and morality is an analytic one. I see nothing in Monro's analysis which would undermine Hare's claim.

If something is *universalizable* it must be applicable in all the same type or relevantly similar type of contexts. The kind of people involved and the circumstances of these people are taken as part of the context. Hare applies *universalizability* to morality in the following way: "If I maintain that it is my duty to do a certain act, but say of another person, placed in exactly similar circumstances, that it is not his duty to do a similar act, I say something which is logically odd, and gives rise to the presumption that I do not fully understand the meaning of the word 'duty'."[34] Moral principles, to count as moral principles, must be impartial. Though we make exceptions in morality, these exceptions are in turn universalizable or impartially statable; that is to say, we have definite principles of priority and differentiation. Thus we say, 'Jones has no obligation to give blood for he has hepatitis' or we issue the moral imperative 'Women and children first' or the prohibition 'Only adults can see this picture', but the one principle of differentiation we cannot appeal to in morals is that of pure self-interest. We cannot make the move 'I do not have to do this but you ought to do it because *I am I and you are you*'. The 'I am I' can serve as *a principle of differentiation* only when it is a short-hand locution to point out that I am a special case because I have certain special characteristics or I am in a special kind of situation. We do this when we make a claim for special treatment as in 'Because I am a Statesman and my value to my country, now that it is at war, puts me in a special position' or 'I am the Mother of four small children but you have none'. But we can never use, as a morally relevant principle of differentiation, the flat appeal to personal interest. Nietzsche, you will recall, never regarded first names as morally relevant; and it was not even simply the class *qua* class that gave *Übermensch* superiority over the herd; rather, it was the characteristics of power, autonomy, and self-discipline that differentiated them.

Let me put my point more generally. In giving reasons why someone or some group ought to have different treatment there cannot—logically cannot—occur in the statement of these a singular term which is not replaceable by a conjunction of general terms; or, in the language of modern logic, for a statement to be universalizable it must be capable of being formulated in a symbolism which employs only predicates, individual variables, operators, and logical connectives.

It is important to note (as Kant did not) that the principle of universalizability is a truth of language and not the supreme principle of morality. As *modus ponens* limits the form syllogistic arguments can take, so universalizability is a principle that limits the form that moral appraisals can take. The principle of universalizability is a second-order principle and first-order non-formal principles (Kant's material maxims) containing material predicates are made in *accordance* with it. These *first-order* principles are not, however, deducible from the universalizability principle anymore than 'If Todas are pacifists then some peoples are pacifists; but Todas are pacifists; therefore some peoples are pacifists' can be *derived* from *modus ponens*, though it is made in accordance with *modus ponens.* Furthermore, to claim that from a logical principle a moral principle can be derived is to commit the *naturalistic fallacy* in the form of trying to derive an ought from an is-statement about language.

I have, in my above remarks, made some grand assertions, but how do I prove that the link between morality and *universalizability* is an analytic one? This claim has been challenged by philosophers of competence. As is so often the case in philosophy, I do not see that there can be a formal proof here one way or another. The best one can do is to give a description of the standard uses of moral utterances and note whether or not to understand them involves understanding that they are *universalizable.* If there are some that are not *universalizable* then the claim that all moral utterances are *universalizable* is not an analytic truth. It seems to me that there is such an analytic link with universalizability; and it seems to me that the most convincing way to show this is to exhibit, by example, how a specimen argument becomes *unintelligible as a moral argument* at the point where this requirement is dropped.

I will proceed by first giving you representative specimens of our common moral language and then by talking about them show their distinctive function. The latter activity amounts to an attempt to describe their use where such a description is directed to relieving certain philosophically paradoxical features of these specimens or paradigms. Hare also does just this with two different examples.[35] His point is to show that, given our conventions of moral discourse, a rejection of universalizability is unintelligible. I shall use a fresh example that will return to Monro's questions about slave morality. S, an advocate of a "slave morality" talks with R, an unrepentant egalitarian.

1. S: "I have a right to have slaves. In fact it is something I ought to do."

2. R: "So you think *people* ought to have slaves."

3. S: "No, I think *I* ought to have slaves. I ought to have as many as I can use."

4. R: "So there is something special about you. Your circumstances put you in a privileged position."

5. S: "No, I ought to have them simply because I am I. I don't say *you* or anyone else ought to have slaves. I simply say that I ought to have slaves because I am like I am and I like having slaves."

6. R: "You really set that forth as a moral judgment."

7. S: "You bet I do."

8. R: "And you are using 'moral' as it is usually used?"

9. S: "Of course."

10. R: "In that event I fail to understand what you *mean*. Your use of 'ought' and 'moral' is unintelligible."

My point is that S's allegedly "moral pronouncements" are simply unintelligible as bits of moral discourse. Anyone familiar with the conventions of our language will have to agree with R's conclusions in (10). S's reply in (3) to R's initial question in (2) begins to puzzle us. With (5) we are completely puzzled. When we learn (8) we come to conclude, as R does in (10), that S simply does not understand the uses of 'ought', 'moral', and the like. As moral utterances, they are unintelligible. This is almost as evident as it is evident that A in the dialogue below does not understand the use of 'birthday'.

A: "I had two birthdays last week."

B: "You mean you celebrated your birthday twice?"

A: "No. I had my 20th birthday last Monday and my 21st the following Thursday."

B: "You are using 'year' and 'birthday' in their usual ways? You're not just joking?"

A: "I'm quite serious and I am using the words you mention in their usual ways."

B: "Then I find your statement utterly unintelligible."

When a child makes A's mistake we simply correct him and say this is not the way 'birthday' is used. One cannot, *not* as a matter of fact but as a *matter of logic,* have two birthdays in one year. A similar point is to be made for the "moral dialogues."

There is, however, a difficulty here. In the two dialogues above (Hare's dialogues have the same effect) the reader is in effect asked to carry out a kind of experiment in imagination about his own linguistic behavior. My comments on the dialogues only prod the reader's own reflections. He must finally simply "see" that what I claim is so as he must "see" that if my pencil is green it must be colored or that my toothpaste cannot be said to be talkative.

Some might not like this appeal to "linguistic intuition." Suppose someone carried out "the experiment in imagination" and said he found nothing unintelligible about S's remarks or A's, then it would simply be his word against mine. I would have no grounds for saying that he was wrong.

It is perfectly true that *if* we had such a clash of "intuitions," I would have to shift to other grounds to make out my case. It is also perfectly true that it is *logically possible* that someone might so react about S's or A's remarks. But if they did "inquiry would not be blocked," for we could still use Naess's techniques of empirical semantics or Ziff's contrastive method to get at what in such contexts it would make sense to say. I do not, of course, rule out the use of such methods *when we really need them.* I only submit that we do *not need them here* for no one really thinks S's remarks or A's remarks make sense. I suspect that *if* anyone felt compelled to say that, appearances to the contrary, they must make sense, he must be under the spell of some metaphysical theory about what it makes sense to say. If anyone will actually and honestly attend to S's remarks and A's remarks, he will surely immediately realize that what they say does not make sense.

## VII

There are other difficulties with the good reasons approach. More specifically there are quite different difficulties with its appeal to *universalizability.* Granted that moral statements must be *universalizable,* is such a formal criterion of any value in judging which reasons or which types of reasons are good reasons in ethics? The principle of *universalizability* will countenance both the maneuvers of the casuist who overloads Kantian maxims and the ideological irrationalist who uses *je ne sais quoi* concepts. Thus even nihilistic or irrationalistic "moral positions" are perfectly *universalizable*.[36] As a logical principle in moral reasoning *universalizability* can not *by itself* outlaw any moral principle, though all moral principles must be made in accordance with it.

It is indeed true that taken by itself the principle of *universalizability* cannot rule out any moral principle. But here Hare's remarks about the value of this principle need careful examination. Hare maintains that the principle of *universalizability* though analytic has "great importance for questions of international morality." Once we accept the notion of *universalizability* as essential for morality, "we have set our feet upon a road from which there is, in the end, no turning back—the road which leads from tribalism to morality."[37] The principle of *universalizability* has, *as a matter of fact,* led men to assent to another principle: this time a moral principle. This moral principle is a basic principle in any truly egalitarian, humanistic morality. It prescribes the following architectonic moral principle: No mere differences as to tribe or race are to count as morally admissible excuses for differentiation or priority: rather from the point of view of morality, men are simply to be considered as men. As members of the human species, they have a *prima facie* right to equal treatment. *Homo sum, nihil humani a alienum puto.* ("I am a man, and I do not regard as morally relevant mere tribal differences between myself and other men.")

It is, however, essential to remember that this basic moral principle cannot be derived or deduced from the principle of *universalizability* alone; nor can it be deduced from any set of premises that do not involve at least one moral premise. Furthermore, it is not the only moral principle which can be made in accordance with the *universalizability* principle. The logical principle *suggests* the moral principle and for someone like Kant they seem to be inextricably linked. It is natural to link these logical and moral principles, but we must never forget that in fact the link is not one of logical derivation.

We can, however, say to the man who advocates a "slave morality": "Be honest about this! Would you really advocate that if you *were* a slave? Think now, think very specifically and take the matter to heart, just how it would be for you and yours." By this persuasive (but not irrational) device we get or provoke him into exercising his imagination. We evoke feelings of sympathy he may have. Yet, he might, with impeccable logic, reply that if he were a slave with a "slavish mentality," he wouldn't object. But since this is extraordinarily unlikely such a worry has the air of the philosopher's closet. Human beings, being what they are, having the desires and needs they have, simply do not react in this way. We all have feelings of sympathy and mateship.

So what? We have here only discovered another *cause* of our acting in some of the ways we do act. But what *reason* do these discoveries give us for claiming that egalitarianism is right and tribalism is wrong? It might seem that we are at an impasse here. There seem to be no further principles of a still greater generality that we can appeal to. The quest for moral certainty, even the quest for moral objectivity, seems to be bogged down here. What indeed can be said here?

I think in all candor we must say this. Over questions of morality and questions of values, we finally reach a point where we can not establish our position from unassailable premises; we must—if we are going to reason morally—finally simply subscribe to some principles of action. The claims of Hare and Nowell-Smith here seem to me to be essentially correct. It is just here where so-called "subjectivism" in the history of moral philosophy has shown strength.

As usual, there is another side to this as well. There is a place for "objectivism" as well as "subjectivism" in any display of the logical geography of our common moral notions. I have tried to prominently locate their respective places on the moral map, seeing them as not mutually exclusive answers to the same problem but as complimentary components of the moral map.

I do not believe that the above concession to "subjectivism" indicates that moral assessments are all subjective in any plausible sense of that word. This can best be seen if we try to ignore the principle of *universalizability* for a moment and consider again our conclusion about the primary functions of morality. If my contentions are correct and morality, as a limited mode of discourse, functions primarily to harmonize desires so that as many people as possible can attain the goals that they as free reflective agents desire, it is easy to see why, in the interests of *this kind* of social harmony, we must develop a sympathetic imagination for the other fellow. Only where people cooperate with each other in attaining their mutual ends can morality successfully function. And if we do not understand what the other fellow wants—what goals he sets for himself—it will be very difficult, if not impossible, for human beings to effectively cooperate. If a person does not use his imagination to consider what others (often very different from himself) would want or what he would want if he were differently placed, he is not reasoning in the way a moral agent should reason. To assert this is not to make a moral judgment about how moral agents should reason; it is rather to make a methodological remark about what counts as effective moral reasoning. An adult to be fair must consider what a child would want in a given situation. A fairminded Catholic must regard what a Jew or a Buddhist would want in order to attain the conditions of life he desires. This takes both an open-mindedness and a lively play of the imagination, but this is required in the moral life if justice is to prevail. (And within moral discourse we cannot sensibly ask: 'Should justice prevail.') A man without feelings or an appreciation of the feelings of others is unable to play the moral language-game (*Sprachspiel*). To play the game to the fullest, we must be able to understand what our fellow creatures aim at and desire, we must understand ourselves and be clear about our own desires, and we must will that what the other fellow wants on reflection should be realized where it does not conflict with a fair distribution of human wants and needs.

It is true, we finally have to *resolve* to play the moral game, but once we have resolved to play it, there are certain requirements, both material and *formal*, that are inevitable—in a perfectly natural sense of 'inevitable'.


## VIII


To sum up, I have maintained, as against Monro, that there is at least one formal criterion, namely *universalizability* that governs the uses of moral talk. Any way of life or pattern of behavior that is to count as 'moral behavior' or as an 'ethos' (e.g., 'a morality') must be *universalizable*. I have *not* disputed Monro's factual claim that there are other patterns of behavior; but I have maintained that these patterns of behavior cannot count as 'moral behavior'. I have not at at all denied that it impossible to question the very autonomy of morals, as moralists do, by asking why be moral. A frank thoroughly amoral egoism is certainly a possibility. I only deny that it is a *moral* possibility. I have also tried to defend and further explicate a Toulmin-like conception of the primary function of morals. I admit that there is the ambiguity which Monro mentions, but I have tried to sketch a consistent utilitarian conception of the primary function of ethics that would adequately account for the pattern that our very varied moral reasoning actually takes. I have further maintained that if we are committed to reasoning from the moral point of view such a conception of the function of morality will give us a basis for saying which kinds of reasons are good reasons in ethics. Such a general consideration will not, of course, always give us a unique answer to problems of human conduct, but it will enable us to establish important guidelines. These two arguments constitute, I believe, a vindication of the kind of linguistic analyses practiced by the good reasons approach; it will serve as an adequate answer to Monroe's charge and more generally to the wider and wilder charges made by others that linguistic analysis in morals is a systematization of the prejudices of an educated contemporary Anglo-Saxon. I have been describing what it is to reason morally: not just what it is for a liberal educated Westerner to reason morally.

Lastly, I would not wish (and I certainly do not think Messrs. Hare, Toulmin, and Nowell-Smith would wish) to deny that moral problems are genuine. Anyone who has rubbed elbows with his fellows knows very well that moral decisions are surely a part of our very human condition. As Toulmin well puts it, "ethics is everybody's concern" and even if we conclude with Freud that the whole idea of value is a chimera we still need to know what to do and how to live.[38] One need not be a Kierkegaard to recognize the truth of this.

But I am being ingenuous. Monro is not denying this commonplace. His title does not mean quite what it says. Rather, it really means "Are Philosophical Problems of Ethics Genuine?" Because of the ambiguity of this question a straightforward answer to it is impossible. The very writing of this essay indicates that, in a sense, I do think they are genuine. Furthermore, I am fully convinced that certain recent philosophical analyses, as well as some parts of some classical analyses, have helped us immensely in getting clearer about the nature of moral assessment. I would even be willing to concede that *perhaps* a sense may be attached to Monro's question: "What is the ultimate justification of morals?" though, as I have suggested, his question could mean several things. But I am also firmly convinced that the good-reasons approach, on the very points that Monro complains about, has given us a reasonably accurate map of the moral copse. Such analyses are not intended to solve particular moral problems; they try rather to make clear to us the logic of our moral reasoning. Such an understanding of the nature of moral reasoning may, in turn, be used to clear away the philosophical underbrush so that moral problems may be seen in a clearer, philosophically unencumbered light. And this in turn may relieve certain kinds of nonphilosophical moral perplexity.

In another way there are philosophical perplexities about morals that do express purely conceptual muddles, and thus in one plain sense they are not genuine problems, however harassing they may be for the man who does not understand their nature. There are indeed general questions about the nature and limits of moral reasoning that are certainly philosophical and certainly genuine. But after determining what moral reasoning is and why we have it and the nature and limits of moral justification, to go on to ask for a deeper moral philosophical justification of morals seems to be but another confused expression of that "Protean metaphysical urge to transcend language." There is and can be no such problem and as philosophers our task here is to show why this is so.[39]

NOTES

1. D. H. Monro, "Are Moral Problems Genuine?" *Mind* 55 (April, 1956): 166–183.

2. Toulmin once remarked to me that he thought them very important.

3. His criticisms of Baier, Mayo and Edwards occur in his searching critical notices of their books. Reference to them will be made in assessing Monro's position in this essay. See D. H. Monro, "Critical Notice of Paul Edwards' *The Logic of Moral Discourse*," *Australasian Journal of Philosophy* 34 (May, 1956): 52–59; "Critical Notice of Kurt Baier's *The Moral Point of View*," *Australasian Journal of Philosophy* 37, no. 1 (May, 1959); "Review Bernard Mayo, *Ethics and the Moral Life*," *Australasian Journal of Philosophy*

37, no. 2 (August, 1959): 176–180. His discussions of the ethical theories of Raphael, Hourani, Ewing and Hartland-Swann are also worth considering in making a thorough appraisal of his claims. See respectively *Australasian Journal of Philosophy* 34, no. 2 (August 1956); 134–140, vol. 35, (August, 1957); 137–146, vol. 38 (December, 1960); 260–274.

4. D. H. Monro, "Critical Notice of Bernard Mayo's *The Moral Life and the Ethical Life*," *Australasian Journal of Philosophy* 37, no. 2 (August, 1959): 177.

5. Ibid.

6. I have tried to show that this is so in my "Is 'Why Should I Be Moral?' an Absurdity?" *Australasian Journal of Philosophy* 36, no. 1 (1958): 25–32 and "On Being Moral," *Philosophical Studies* 16, no. 1–2, (January-February, 1965): 1–4, and I have tried to give a detailed answer to this question in chapter 8 of this volume.

7. Stephen Toulmin, *An Examination of the Place of Reason in Ethics* (Cambridge: 1950), p. 2.

8. Ibid., p. 4.

9. Ibid., p. 3.

10. Ibid., p. 153.

11. Ibid.

12. Stephen Toulmin, "Principles of Morality," *Philosophy* 31 (April, 1956): 150.

13. It should be apparent that Kant, the classical utilitarians and Hume all have their places here, but they are different non-competing places. For a development of this claim see chapter 3. While I do not think that Hare will quite go all the way with me here, there certainly is an affinity between what I am saying here and some of the central claims of his *Freedom and Reason* (Oxford: 1963). Something of the sort is also suggested by Toulmin in his "Is There a Fundamental Problem of Ethics," *Australasian Journal of Philosophy* 33 (May, 1955): 1–19.

14. Monro, "Are Moral Problems Genuine," *Mind* 55 (April, 1956): 176.

15. Ibid.

16. Toulmin, *An Examination of the Place of Reason in Ethics*, p. 137 italics mine. See also pp. 136, 145, 170, 233.

17. Stephen Toulmin, "Discussion of R. M. Hare's, *The Language of Morals*," *Philosophy* 29 (January, 1954): 168.

18. Ibid.

19. Aristotle reasoned in much this way.

20. D. H. Monro, "Anthropology and Ethics," *Australasian Journal of Philosophy* 33 (December, 1955): 174.

21. W. D. Falk, "Morality, Self and Others," in *Morality and the Language of Conduct*, Hector-Neri Castaneda and George Nakhnikian (editors) (Detroit: 1963), pp. 25–69.

22. D. H. Monro, "Are Moral Problems Genuine?" *Mind* 55 (April, 1956): 122. Monro's reference to Toulmin is to p. 168 of his *An Examination of the Place of Reason in Ethics*.

23. D. H. Monro, "Are Moral Problems Genuine?" *Mind* 55 (April, 1956): 173.

24. Ibid.

25. Ibid.

26. Ibid.

27. Ibid., pp. 173–174.

28. D. H. Monro, "Anthropology and Ethics," *Australasian Journal of Philosophy* 33 (December, 1955): 160–176.

29. D. H. Monro, "The Concept of Myth," *The Sociological Review* 42 (1950): 115–132.

30. See my account of ideological statements in my "On Speaking of God," *Theoria* 28, no. 2 (1962): 118–125.

31. H. D. Aiken, *Reason and Conduct* (New York: 1962), pp. 65–87.

32. Toulmin, *An Examination of the Place of Reason in Ethics,* pp. 158–160.

33. Ibid., p. 158.

34. R. M. Hare, "Have I A Duty to My Country As Such," *The Listener* (October 20, 1955): 651.

35. Ibid., pp. 651–652 and R. M. Hare, "Universalizability," *Aristotelian Society Proceedings* 55 (1954–55): 305.

36. Ibid., Ernest Gellner, "Morality and *Je Ne Sais Quoi* Concepts," *Analysis* 16 (April, 1956): 97–103 and R. M. Hare, *Freedom and Reason* (Oxford: 1963).

37. R. M. Hare, "Have I A Duty To My Country As Such," *Listener* (October 20, 1955): 651.

38. Toulmin, *An Examination of The Place of Reason in Ethics,* p. 112.

39. I have tried to show some further ways in which this metaphysical lament may be met in "The 'Good Reasons Approach' and 'Ontological Justifications' of Morality," *Philosophical Quarterly* 9, no. 35 (April, 1959): 1–16; "Appealing to Reason," *Inquiry* 5 (1962): 65–84 and "Wanton Reason," *Philosophical Studies* 12 (Maynooth, Ireland), (1963): 66–91.

# 6

# Class Conflict, Marxism, and the Good-Reasons Approach

I want to commence with an autobiographical remark. I first heard a version of Michael Lerner's "Marxism and Ethical Reasoning" read at the Radical Philosopher's Caucus at the American Philosophical Association. I was struck by its power and importance and was, as I heard it being read, initially strongly inclined to believe that what I had said about good reasons in ethics was simply badly off the mark and that Lerner had smoked out what on my part was in effect a completely unintended apology for the bourgeois order. This, of course, distressed me, for it is the last thing I would want to do, but I was also impressed, and still am impressed, by the way Lerner spotted certain ideological functions of moral discourse and by his recognition of the importance of moral conceptions in attaining and sustaining a socialist order.[1] On reflection, and after a careful study of his essay, I still remain convinced of its importance and power, though I do not now think that the good-reasons appoach generally and my version of it in particular has the baleful ideological implications that Lerner attributes to it. I am also suspicious, as I was when I first heard him read his essay, of his intuitionism.

In this essay I shall endeavor to show (a) (in Section I) that the good-reasons approach does not have the implications Lerner claims it has; (b) (in Section II) that his intuitionist foundations for a Marxist ethic are in shambles and in conflict with the Marxist tradition and (c) (in Section III) that certain further considerations need to be raised concerning a Marxist ethics. I shall in that concluding section indicate—in part using certain fundamental claims of the good-reasons theorists—something of what is needed

---

From *Social Praxis* 2, nos. 1–2 (1975): 89–112. Reprinted by permission of the publisher.

for the resolution of some of the problems emerging from an examination of these considerations.


# I

I have argued that even in class-divided societies dominated by the capitalist ruling class our conception of what it is to take the moral point of view has so developed that it is now correct to say, at least in terms of our conscious attitudes and what even this ruling class feels it must pay lip service to, that for large numbers of people it has become the case that in morality we are concerned with the reasoned pursuit of what is in *everyone's*—that is each and every individual's—best interest.[2] From the moral point of view, we are concerned with the most extensive welfare or well-being of all concerned. (Even the apologists for capitalism pay lip service to such an ideal, though what actually goes on *vis-à-vis* the quality of our lives under capitalism is quite different.) The most central and underlying function of morality—the justificatory rationale for there being such a form of life—is to adjudicate and harmonize conflicts of interest in order to attain a situation in which the most extensive and most fairly distributed satisfaction of interests is obtained for all human beings. That is to say, as I put it in my *Reason and Practice,* ". . . to a very considerable degree the very *raison d'être* of morality is to adjudicate between the frequently conflicting and divergent desires and interests of people in order to give everyone as much as possible of whatever it is that each one will want when he is being rational, when he would still want what he wants were he to reflect carefully and when his own wants are constrained by a willingness to treat the rational wants of other human beings in the same way." (I quote at length my own previous statement because it is one that Michael Lerner fastens on to criticize in a way which I think is importantly mistaken.)

Stated baldly in this way there are many problems with such an account, not the least of which is its mingling of talk of wants and interests as if talk of wants and interests comes to the same thing. They, of course, do not, but I do not think that my skipping over that distinction in my above remarks makes any important difference to the claim I made there. What, however, I do need to confront is the perceptive critique of such an account made by Michael Lerner. Lerner, writing from a radical perspective which I share, argues that my analysis in fact has an unintended conservative ideological function which distorts, as does Toulmin's account and presumably Baier's as well, the social reality that such accounts of morality would comprehend and in some way build their theorizing on. I shall attempt to show that in very important respects Lerner's argument fails, but I shall also try to indicate how Lerner brings to the fore some very fundamental considerations about morality which are crucial to take note of—considerations which I utterly neglected and which Toulmin, Baier and Rawls also neglect. Basically what is missing in our accounts is a sufficiently realistic picture of social reality and a concern with the social and political conditions of rationality.[3]

Lerner argues that only if we accept a certain description of the social world will it be plausible to accept my account (and Toulmin's as well) of the underlying and central function (rationale) of morality. The description of the social world necessary—Lerner claims—to make our accounts plausible is this: We are human beings who, when we are in our adulthood, are of roughly equal strength, intelligence and vulnerability, and we all live in a world in which our historically conditioned positions of power, prestige and advantage are precarious. Given this position, even a thoroughly self-interested person, if he is rational, will see the advantage of human cooperation and an attempt to attain a harmonization of interests and desires to avoid a kind of Hobbesian war of all against all. Lerner, quite simply and correctly, I believe, responds that we do not live in such a world, for "it is certainly not the case today that we are all equally vulnerable to attack . . . equally able to develop and hence to use in any important sense our strength and intelligence, and we are all not in positions equally precarious with regard to the coercive political power we may exercise." This is so because we live in a class-stratified society in which there is a small but at present incredibly powerful capitalist ruling class which owns and controls the means of production, which from its position of strength and coercive power exploits in varying degrees and in various ways that complex and internally stratified group of people—the working class—who work for a salary and do not own the means of production. The ruling class of capitalists, possessing *de facto* control of industry, government, education, the mass media and the economy, has a disproportionate and entrenched political power and has "every reason to believe that their position is not subject to the same fluctuations in vulnerability that most everyone else faces." While just to survive in the system it is in the short-run interests of the working class to harmonize their interests with the ruling class, it is not in the short-run interests of the ruling class to harmonize their interests with the working class in such a way as to adjudicate conflicts of interest in an equitable fashion, though it is in the interests of the ruling class to keep the working class passive. Between the capitalist class and the working class we have a conflict of interests which is not in principle harmonizable in any equitable manner because it is in the interest of the ruling class to remain in a dominant position of economic and political power while the interest of the working class is to eliminate inequalities in wealth and power. Between such forces there is a clash of interests which cannot be equitably harmonized, while such class divisions remain.

These remarks seem to me correct and indeed important remarks, particularly given their extensive neglect by bourgeois moral philosophers. I would only deny that they are in conflict with the account of morality that I and the other good-reasons theorists have developed, though they do make a crucial stress which we utterly neglected. Lerner, by contrast, would have us believe that what is very centrally wrong with the good-reasons approach is that in picturing the underlying function—the point or purpose—of morality as that of seeking a harmonization of conflicting sets of interests the good-reasons approach groundlessly rules out as a conceptual impossibility a moral posture which holds that an interest in the exploitation of the weak is morally illegitimate and indeed not tolerable in a decent society.

As I just indicated, I thoroughly agree with Lerner that we do live in a class-divided society and I also agree that no equitable harmonizing of conflicts of interests is possible while there are such class divisions. Only in a classless society can such a harmonization of desires and interests take place in any thorough fashion. In a society well on its way to classlessness such a harmonization can be approximated, but in our society with its vast differences in wealth and power no such a harmonization is possible. I also, of course, agree with Lerner's moral judgment that the failure to treat the interests of the ruling class in exploitation as morally illegitimate is itself morally unacceptable (to put it conservatively). Yet, as I remarked, I do not believe that my account at all commits me to either of these mistaken beliefs. But, if it does, then my account is mistaken in a very crucial way. I shall show (try to show), after I have remarked some more on Lerner's account, how I do not make the presuppositions Lerner attributes to me. More generally, whatever may be the actual ideological commitments of the moral philosophers defending the good-reasons account of the nature of morality, there is nothing in such an account itself which would commit one to such a conservative posture.

Lerner also tries to show that the good-reasons approach has a definite conservative ideological effect. It is itself, he argues, a reasonably valuable weapon of the ruling class in its campaign to suppress, control and halt the ascendancy of the working class. One ideological ploy the ruling class will try to utilize is to convince most "people that, all things considered, the present order is the best possible world they can achieve, and that any alternative course would be at least as bad, or would be so costly in terms of the personal risk necessary to achieve it and so uncertain as to what would be achieved that it is more rational to accommodate oneself to the established order." Ideologically speaking, the actual, though unacknowledged, function of morality in society—that is the actual morality of society—is to "help to reconcile the majority of people to the rule of a given class over the entire society." The good-reasons approach is itself, though no doubt unwittingly, a weapon in such ideological thrusts, for it, Lerner claims, provides an abstract and philosophically elaborate rationale or model for such a reconciliation. People are in effect told to accept such a reconciliation for it is grounded in a recognition of what it is to take the moral point of view, of what it is to reason morally. In what is in effect a linguistic sleight of hand, it is made to appear that the very use of moral language is such that it makes no sense to say that social harmony should not be promoted if that harmony requires or even involves human exploitation. But such a remark is perfectly intelligible. Whether or not one is justified in believing one ought to fight for certain moral ideals even though they do involve social disequilibrium and the suppression of the interests of exploiters, is a substantive issue in ethics which cannot be established one way or another by an appeal to linguistic usage. It is not a deviant utterance or an incoherent remark to say that "the true ethical order can be established only when the present exploiters are overthrown."

I indeed stress the desirability of giving people what they rationally and reflectively want, when satisfying one's wants is constrained by a willingness to treat the rational wants of other human beings in the same way, but with respect to this Lerner points out that we should not fail to note that the established order helps form people's wants, e.g., desires for snowmobiles, color TV sets, yellow fingernail polish and clothes with a new cut. *What* we want and even *that* we will have certain wants is subject to manipulation and indeed is manipulated by the ruling class. And to adjust the wants of the working class (the masses) to the wants of the ruling class makes them still more dependent on the ruling class and passive in the face of the ruling-class control. Yet this is something that is quite flagrantly done by the ruling class.

What I wholeheartedly agree with in Lerner's account and what I confess I did not but should have had before my mind in giving my account of morality is a description of social reality such as Lerner's. (Lerner details this account and justifies his bald sociological claims in his *The New Socialist Revolution*.) It is surely not the case that, as a matter of fact, all adult human beings are roughly in positions of equality and equal vulnerability and that there is (considering the short term) nothing very precarious about the advantages the ruling class does possess. There is gross exploitation, and, with such an imbalance of power and wealth, we are not in a position—working with some consensus model—to work out, as rough equals, some balance or harmonization of interests that will be equitable and in the bests interests of everyone. What is in the best interests of the working class (the vast mass of the people) is to end capitalist domination by bringing about the demise of capitalism. I wrote—and Toulmin and Baier do as well—as if we were living in a social world in which such conditions of rough equality prevailed, such that even mutually self-interested and rational people could get together and work out with a mutual give and take an equitable resolution of interests; but this would only be possible if the capitalists generally— and not just in isolated instances—would in the interests of fairness and humaneness de-class themselves voluntarily. But it is an idle dream to expect this to happen. They will hold on or try to hold on to their positions of power and privilege. And in our present historical circumstances it is surely not in their self-interest to do otherwise. In such a social situation the conditions which make it possible for morality to function, as I described it as functioning, do not obtain. All the good-reasons theorists (myself included) write as if it did obtain, but it plainly doesn't, and we should be grateful to Michael Lerner for driving this important point home.

However, the soundness of Lerner's above point notwithstanding, the good-reasons theorists should be understood as being engaged in a quite different and non-conflicting task. They should be taken as philosophers setting out the underlying structure of moral reasoning and the rationale of morality and not as social theorists attempting to delineate social reality. I do not mean to give it to understand that those tasks can be adequately carried out independently of each other, but I am claiming they are distinct tasks. The characterization of man in society by the good-reasons theorists can and should be viewed as very like the articulation of ideal types to make more perspicuous the underlying rationale of morality. We want to know what we could reasonably, even in a communist society, have morality for, where it was not simply—in a pejorative sense of 'ideology'—functioning ideologically. I make it plain in my account of morality that I am speaking not of the harmonization of desires of men culturally drugged as they are in our bourgeois culture but of the harmonization of desires and interests of men in a certain condition.[4] The condition that Lerner utterly neglects—and the neglect of which undermines his most central critique of the good-reasons approach—is that on such an account the harmonization of interests and desires must be of a distinctive kind. A condition for the morally acceptable harmonization of desires is that it will "give everyone as much as possible of whatever it is that each one will want when he is being rational. . . ." But surely, if working-class people are typically bamboozled through a manipulation of their wants into wanting the continuation of the capitalist order with its system of exploitation, then it is not the case that these are the things that working-class people would want when they are being rational. The very wanting of such things is a sign that there has been some diminution of their rational understanding of their situation. They have been kept by the conditions of their lives from gaining a sufficiently rational understanding of social reality so that they could have an undistorted conception of their condition. Thus a key condition for the ethically justified harmonization of interests has not and cannot be met in capitalist society and from this it follows that my account of the underlying rationale (purpose) of morality cannot be in effect an apology for the capitalist order, for on my account it is impossible under capitalism to harmonize desires and interests in a morally acceptable way.

It could only have force to respond that I am characterizing the function of morality in such a way as to make morality a hopelessly utopian enterprise, on the assumption that a classless society is a pointlessly utopian conception utterly unrealizable by human beings in any achievable historic situation. Rawls, as Macpherson[5] has perceptively pointed out, does make it his assumption, but it is a rationally challengeable assumption which a thoroughgoing socialist would not make. I did not and would not make it; unless it can be shown that to make my account of the nature of moral reasoning sound I should make it, my account is not flawed with a pointless utopianism.

In addition, Lerner neglects the fact that I stress that a morally acceptable harmonization of desires operates under the limitation that each individual's maximization of the satisfaction of desire is to be constrained by a willingness to treat the rational desires of other human beings in the same way. But with the exploitative system of human relations which is unavoidable under capitalism, the capitalist ruling class could not accept the constraint that they are to seek to achieve an organization of society in which the satisfaction of the rational wants of the working class are to be maximized. In spite of what Lerner says about rationality, the rational wants of the working class or any class would be (though this is not all they would be) the wants they would continue to have if they understood their condition, the alternatives open to them and the like. This would mean they would understand the way they were being exploited, the way their wants were being manipulated and that they would also understand about socialist alternatives to capitalism. With such knowledge they could not rationally want their own continued exploitation or the continuation of capitalism. Thus the capitalist ruling class could not, while remaining such a ruling class, want the working class to achieve a maximization of the satisfaction of their *rational* desires. This would be tantamount to capitalists desiring their own demise. Moreover, for just these reasons, there is, Lerner's remarks to the contrary notwithstanding, no room in my account for treating as legitimate the rational wants and needs of exploiters to stay in their exploitative positions, for these very wants and needs, while indeed being something it is rational for these people to have, are on my criterion *morally* unacceptable, for they are not governed by the constraint that they must be compatible with the maximum equitable satisfaction of the rational wants and needs of all human beings.

What I have been concerned to show in this first section of my essay is that Lerner has not shown that the good-reasons account of morality is a mistaken one rooted in a mistaken bourgeois conception of man and society. It is indeed important to make the stress he makes about the class-ridden nature of social reality in societies we have known and to indicate, as he has done, its importance to morality and its relevance to an understanding of some of the ideological functions of moral discourse, but an unblinkered acceptance of this is perfectly compatible with the good-reasons theorists' conception of the underlying rationale of morality.

## II

Lerner also attempts to articulate a Marxist conception of ethics. I want now to show that this positive account of his has serious defects which should make us very wary of accepting it as articulating the rational foundations for a socialist morality or a Marxist account of morality.

There are, I should say initially, many good things in Lerner's discussion of a Marxist foundation for morality. It is, moreover, a strikingly different account from what we have come to expect of thinkers of a Marxist persuasion. To get anything comparable, we have to go back to Karl Vorländer's attempt in the first part of our century to effect a wedding of Kant and Marx. Lerner's account is also one—given its intuitionist meta-ethic—which will surely be opposed by many Marxists. There are, however, many perceptive and important things in his account which are not dependent on his intuitionism. There are insightful remarks about alienation, freedom, rationality, self-realization and progress; there is also a good account of the problem of relativism as it arises in the work of Marx and Engels, together with a sensible statement of an important way in which their account of norms aims at being an objectivist one while still accounting for pervasive relativistic and contextualistic features in morality. There is also a set of well-taken deflationary remarks about violence, together with a persuasive criticism of some of Popper's crucial arguments against Marx and Engels. Finally, and perhaps most centrally, there is an excellent account of the central moral commitment embedded in Marxism and a perspicuous arrangement of the underlying moral assumptions in Marx and Engels.

All of this is to be welcomed, for there is a good bit of confusion about Marxism and ethics. Vorländer recounts that it was said of Marx that he would burst into laughter when anyone spoke to him of morality. But be that as it may, Lerner perceptively points to certain moral assumptions which are embedded—though hardly explicitly—in the work of Marx and the acceptance of which is crucial to his critique of capitalism, defense of a socialist order and his account of the human condition. Lerner claims that Marx's most central normative assumption is that "human beings ought to be respected and their human capacities for freedom, love, rationality, solidarity and creativity ought to be given opportunity for development." If such a conviction, Lerner argues, were not at least reasonably believed to be true— and indeed objectively true (to utter a pleonasm)—the basis for Marx's critique of capitalism and defense of socialism would be undermined.

The obvious question which arises is that though this is indeed a very fundamental moral conviction which many of us—perhaps almost all of us in our cultural milieux, socialist and non-socialist alike—share there is still the question about how, and indeed even whether, we know that such a principle is true.

Lerner answers this in a very surprising way for a Marxist. He remarks that it is a "basic ethical intuition" which "is the foundation of all ethical knowledge" and "which is known directly and non-inferentially." It is here where we should, I believe, balk, for there are here crucial critical questions of at least two distinct orders. There is in the first place the recognition that the appeal to intuitionism goes flatly against the materialism and ethical naturalism of Marx himself and of such important Marxist thinkers as Lukàcs (1968), Goldmann[6] and Ollman,[7] all of whom resolutely reject the is/ought dichotomy and thereby (or so it would seem) commit themselves to the meta-ethic of ethical naturalism. Secondly, and more fundamentally, there is the question of the adequacy of an intuitionist account of ethics. (It is not the acceptability of the moral ideal that is so much in question but the account of its nature, its logical status and the way—if at all—we can speak of its truth.)

I shall deal with the first consideration first. Marx in his youth, before he studied Hegel, held to the rather commonly accepted belief that there is no deriving an ought from an is and that moral discourse and factual discourse are of two distinct logical orders. But, after his study of Hegel—that is, throughout his mature intellectual life—he rejected such autonomist ethical theories and held (rightly or wrongly), like Hegel, that such traditional dichotomies were quite untenable. And while there have been some socialist thinkers who thought of themselves as somehow in the Marxist tradition who have resisted Marx here, the central philosophical figures in the Marxist tradition have stood with Marx on this issue. Lukàcs and Goldmann, for example, are two Marxists of stature who are the most explicit and the clearest about a Marxist position here. (Though even here the level of clarity over this argument leaves much to be desired.) Lukàcs stressed that human agents, as historical agents, act not as isolated individuals but as members of a group who both constitute history by their collective actions and understand what they are doing. This entails, Lukàcs and Goldmann claim, that our knowledge of man in society will not in its most important aspects be an objective non-normative knowledge. Any separation of judgments of value and fact and any separation of theory and practice is impossible for a correct account of the human estate. As Goldmann[8] put it (paraphrasing Lukàcs), the knowledge we have of history and society is not the knowledge of a "contemplative science; historical action is neither social technique (Machiavelli) nor ethical action (Kant); the two constitute an indivisible whole which is a progressive awareness of the march of humanity towards freedom." In fine this emancipatory knowledge is a knowledge where fact and value are inextricably intertwined; and indeed any consciousness of society, which was not a grossly false consciousness, would be of that general nature. Where the matter is at all complex there is no understanding society in a 'purely factual', normatively neutral way. In understanding society, proper dialectical thought must understand social reality in a totalistic way which admits of no sharp separation of facts and values, means and ends. Judgments and conceptions of value and fact are indissolubly linked; in viewing significant human action, there is no separating out one from the other. Only by snatching propositions out of context is there even the impression that there are these distinct pure statements of value and pure statements of fact standing there independent of any viewpoint. Understanding, explanation and evaluation are strictly inseparable and the whole analysis is set in a materialist epistemological and ontological framework which would hardly admit of any direct non-empirical, scientifically uncheckable, knowledge of right and wrong, good and bad.[9]

Even if Lerner were convinced by the above arguments that his account was in fundamental conflict with the methodological, epistemological and (if one chooses to use that idiom) ontological commitments of traditional Marxism, it is still far from evident that he would abandon it just on that account. He could and would argue, I believe, that his account is essential for the kind of grounding of democracy that Marx gives and that acceptance of Marx's historical materialism, his critique of capitalism and justification of socialism, are not touched by an abandonment of naturalistic assumptions for intuitionist ones. Indeed it is such an intuitionist account of ethics, Lerner claims, which gives us "the best grounding for a justification of democracy" and that, even if it is not compatible with certain assumptions of Marxists and indeed Marx himself, it is "consistent with Marx's approach to ethics" and it "would be wise to adopt an ethical intuitionist position to justify his [Marx's] approach to the world even if Marx did not do so." Lerner could argue that the methodological, epistemological and ontological conceptions in Marx and the Marxist tradition are not really central to Marxism. What is essential is his critique of capitalism and his justification of democracy and socialism. I doubt whether these elements can be so pulled apart without serious damage both to Marxist conceptions and to our understanding of social reality. However, I shall not argue that here. Rather for the remainder of my discussion of Lerner's statement of a Marxist ethic I shall assume, what I do not in fact believe, namely, that Lerner is home and free on the issues discussed above, and I shall turn to my second major point.

What I want now to query is whether it would be wise for a Marxist or indeed for anyone else to adopt such an intuitionist position. I shall argue that there are difficulties of a very considerable magnitude which need to be overcome before it would be wise to make such a claim or to opt for intuitionism, and I shall suggest that it is unlikely that these difficulties can be overcome.

Lerner tells us that "an intuitionist account is the most plausible account of ethics" and that we have a fundamental ethical principle—a postulate (to use Lerner's way of putting it)—which provides us with the ethical foundation for a Marxist theory of society and for a Marxist social critique. This principle which is "known directly and non-inferentially," is said to be "the foundation of all ethical knowledge." The principle, recall, is that all human beings ought to be respected and their capacities for freedom, love, rationality, creativity and solidarity ought to be given maximum opportunity for development.

However, there are the standard difficulties with intuitionism which Lerner, distressingly enough, does nothing at all to meet. It is *perhaps* clear enough what it means to say that I know directly and non-inferentially that there is a yellow pencil lying on the desk in front of me, and it is perhaps even justifiable to say I know whether or not I have a headache directly and non-inferentially. I simply observe the former to be the case, and I simply have the latter. In both cases the sensory mechanisms are well understood, and there are in the former case non-question-begging observational checks on the truth of my claim, and in the latter case a parallel statement, e.g., Nielsen has a headache, can be known to be true by observing my behavior. But in the moral case we need the appeal to intuition because we have no such an observational basis for ascertaining the truth or falsity of Lerner's basic principle. (Indeed, trivially, if we had it, we would not need to speak of intuition.) Lerner's principle is not simply a psychological claim, and yet there is no question of just looking to see if it is true (or false). But then it is quite unclear what it *means* to say it is known to be true directly and non-inferentially. Indeed it is not clear what it means to say it is 'known to be true' at all.

Lerner would presumably respond that it is not a matter of empirical knowledge based on observation, but it is known non-sensuously. That is to say, it is only where observation, direct or indirect, is at least possible that verification is in order. Where non-sensuous apprehension is involved there is no possibility of verification and indeed talk of verification there is senseless. But then there emerge in full force the standard puzzles about this mysterious non-sensuous moral faculty. What kind of evidence do we have for its existence? And what is it to 'non-sensuously apprehend something' and how do we check for mistaken or *ersatz* intuitions? What if someone has or claims to have Nietzschean intuitions rather than Lerner's kind? How do we show that Lerner's are correct and the Nietzschean's are mistaken? People having such at least putative intuitions both claim to have direct non-inferential knowledge of the truth of their conflicting principles. Do we simply count noses at this point to find out who is right? If we do that—particularly given what Marx teaches about ideology—how do we know or do we know that what most people claim they intuit to be true is true and that the people in the minority are mistaken? Do we need another intuition for that? How in fine do we tell a genuine intuition from a mistaken one?

If there is some non-intuitive way of doing that, then an appeal to intuition is superfluous, for then we can know independently of the intuitions which basic moral claims are true. If we say instead that we just have a plurality of conflicting intuitions without any way of ascertaining which, if any, of the often conflicting intuitions give us genuine moral knowledge, then we may call our moral claims objective-knowledge claims if we like, but we actually have, as Bertrand Russell has observed, a form of subjectivism which by a perfectly understandable ideological conjuring trick is labeled as, and indeed regarded as, a form of objectivism.

To say, given the actual existence of conflicting ostensible intuitions firmly held by different agents, that one's intuitions are self-evidently true or synthetic *a priori* truths raises problems which are again standard, important and not easily, if at all, resolvable in a way that would give comfort to intuitionists. Again, given several conflicting claims to possess self-evident truths, how do we decide which truths are really self-evident? Are we to say in good Thomistic fashion that some are *self-evident in themselves* but not self-evident to us? Such claimed self-evidence is at best of little help to human beings and is itself of doubtful intelligibility. But if we cannot ascertain which of several ostensible self-evident truths are really self-evident, we do not have a workable distinction between what is really self-evident and what is only apparently so. There is also the quite distinct problem whether the very notion of a synthetic *a priori* truth is a coherent one. We cannot now so confidently answer that in the negative as we could ten years ago, but it still remains an extraordinarily problematic notion which we can hardly accept just like that (to put it minimally).

It is of no avail to appeal, as earlier intuitionists such as Clarke and Reid did, to a conception of moral blindness in order to pick out inauthentic, mistaken intuitions from authentic, genuine ones. The analogy between color-blindness and moral-blindness is not a good one. With color-blindness we have independent tests of a non-question-begging sort to ascertain when someone is or is not color-blind, such that people, including the color-blind people themselves, will come to agree who is and who is not color-blind. We have, as well, physiological tests for color-blindness. Nothing like this obtains for moral-blindness. We have no physical tests for when it occurs or even a hint of what physical mechanisms (if any) are involved. And morally-blind people will not, unlike color-blind people, agree that they are morally-blind. The case of Hitler, though extreme, is instructive. He was a moral monster—a paradigmatically, monstrously evil man—yet he was thoroughly convinced of the rightness and justice of his cause, and there was a wide following of educated people who agreed with him. He would not, for a moment, nor would they, have agreed that he was morally blind. It was the others—the communists and the bourgeoisie—who were morally blind. And to say that Hitler was simply mad and so can be discounted as a candidate for a paradigmatically evil but still responsible moral agent is to make a mistake. The last few months of his life apart, when he was under considerable pressure (pressure sufficient to crack many a human being), he was not, if we use non-moral criteria, mad, unless we want to use criteria for madness which are so strong that all fanatics are said to be mad. He was evil, reasonably intelligent, determined and unfortunately possessed of an extraordinary amount of charisma which he utilized for vile and destructive ends. He, indeed, had some crazy beliefs, but if we use the having of crazy beliefs as a criterion for or decisive test of madness, then we should indeed judge many, many more people to be mad than we in fact are prepared to do. Many people who function well in responsible positions and relate reasonably within their families and at their workplace are so afflicted. There is no morally neutral way of sifting out morally blind from non-morally-blind people. The very conception is a mistaken one of no use in shoring up intuitionism.

In sum, the intuitionist foundations on which Lerner tries to build are in shambles, and he does nothing at all to repair such foundations. Marxists should remain suspicious of such accounts as they were in the past suspicious of attempts to weld Marxism to a neo-Kantianism. In Lerner's account, more straightforwardly than in a Kantian account, we have unabashed yet undefended appeal to intuitionism. But intuitionism appears at least to be broken-backed when it is construed as Lerner and intuitionists have traditionally construed it. (A kind of Rawlsian 'intuitionism' is not so evidently vulnerable.) There is nothing here on which to found a Marxist or socialist account of morality or a Marxist critique of society. To the extent that there is a problem about progress, development and objective evaluations for Marxists, the problem is not solved by such an intuitionist account.

## III

Where are we then in trying to untangle questions about Marxism and morality? It is beyond my present capacity to say, though I would like in this final section to make some suggestions concerning matters which we need to research and carefully think through.

People solidly in the Marxist tradition have rejected any is/ought dichotomy. Here there are striking resemblances between Marxist thought and that of that much underrated and neglected American philosopher John Dewey. Yet suggestive as the discussion of these topics by such distinguished Marxists as Lukàcs and Goldmann have been, they have not been nearly rigorous enough to dismantle Hume's guillotine. However, there have in recent years been arguments by philosophers from what might in very broad terms be called 'the analytical camp' which have rigorously attacked the is/ought dichotomy. I refer to the work of MacIntyre, Taylor, Searle, Foot, Melden and Norman.[10] But their work in turn has been powerfully criticized by philosophers who defend such an autonomist conception of ethics.[11] We need, if we can, to see if in a thoroughly rigorous fashion we can get to the bottom of this issue. The philosopher in us will, of course, understandably enough be skeptical about whether we can ever get to "the bottom" of such an issue. But be that as it may, we should do the following. (1) We need to become as clear as possible concerning Marx's position about the is/ought and about Lukàcs's and Goldmann's as well; (2) we need to see how Marxist thought joins with contemporary analytical discussions of the issue; and finally, (3), with (1) and (2) reasonably in hand, we need to probe the issue ourselves so that we can come to resolve, if possible, questions about the viability of Hume's (Poincaré's) law. Can we derive a fundamental moral ought from an is? Is there an intelligible and reasonably clear-cut division between moral discourse and factual discourse such that a derivation is impossible or is it the case that there is no such intelligible division yielding such results? (I do not mean to give to understand that these questions suggest all the possible alternatives.) We on the Left need to gain greater clarity about this general issue and we need to think through the implications—including the ideological implications—of whatever position we come to have.

We also need to think through the issue raised by the fact that, on the one hand, Marx and Engels thought of law and morality as mystifying ideological intuitions which, along with religion, have a reactionary pacifying effect on people and indeed distort their understanding of social reality and, on the other hand, produced a critique of capitalism and capitalist society in terms which are plainly and irreducibly moral. (Capitalist systems of production, as Marx put it in *Capital* [Vol. 1, p. 645], "mutilate the laborer into a fragment of a man, degrade him to the level of an appendage to a machine. . . .") Morality is part of the superstructure and yet Marx, as Lerner sees, needs objective moral categories and an objective moral point of view to make his critique of capitalism and capitalist society. Lerner shows well enough how a positivist solution will not work here. But his own intuitionist "new foundations" are, as we have seen, utterly useless.

Tony Skillen in his significant "Marxism and Morality"[12] wrestles with this issue without succeeding in resolving it. He readily sees that none of the following, frequently made moves will do: (1) "Morality is indeed at the root of Marxism but Marx's own bewitchment by a positivistic ideology of science led him to conceal it from himself," (2) "a Marxist science makes no moral assumptions but functions practically to advance the objective interests of the working class" and (3) "Marxism is value-free but Marxist *praxis* presupposes an extra-empirical commitment to socialist ideals."[13] All of these claims fit badly with Marx's text, and they all have obvious difficulties of their own. How do we, or can we, make a coherent account of a view that contains the following two claims: (a) Capitalism is a vicious social order which is to be and will be replaced by a better order with the achievement and consolidation of socialism and (b) morality (the moral point of view) is to be rejected as a mystifying social device which is itself one of the evils of class society? But surely, if we reject morality or moral categories, we cannot coherently speak of the evils of capitalism or of capitalism being a vicious social order or of socialism being a better social order. Such talk, unless it is itself just an ideological smoke screen, presupposes a coherent and objectively justified conception of a moral point of view. Skillen, for all his perceptiveness about the ideological functions of morality, fudges this point; it is to Lerner's credit that he feels its force and squarely faces it.

What we need to do is to assimilate the profound and humanly useful insights that Skillen marshals to show why Marx could and did speak of the evils of morality with an understanding of the rationale behind Marx's moral critique of capitalism. Intelligently borrowing from Marx, Stirner, Nietzsche, Freud, Reich and Anderson, Skillen, even more forcefully than Lerner, drives home how it is the case that in our societies and indeed in most societies morality often functions "to batter people into acquiescing in their own oppression and impoverishment" and how "it domesticates people into a subjected kind of 'sociability'."[14] He shows how Marx attacks moralism and why; indeed Skillen reinforces and further justifies that attack. What he does not show is how Marx or Marxists or anyone else have established that the moral point of view is to be identified with this moralism. *Some* moral points of view are indeed to be so identified and are to be unmasked and rejected. But that is not to identify the taking of a moral point of view with this moralism. Indeed only if the taking of a moral point of view were not identified with this moralism would Skillen's and Marx's critique of moralism make sense, for they do not simply show that this moralism is irrational, they also show that it is inhumane and evil. But this claim only makes sense if there is an objectively justified moral point of view or at least if there are some objectively justified moral norms.

Skillen fleetingly sees this when he remarks, toward the end of his essay,[15] that we "may . . . need a radical-materialist 'conception of morality'." But he makes nothing of this and does not see the problems it raises—most crucially the question Lerner tries but fails to answer concerning the justification of an objective moral point of view which in turn would square with Marx's critique of capitalism and advocacy of socialism. Skillen argues[16] that such a conception, if it were to be justified, would not be justified in terms of any higher power (God or reason) "controlling our inclinations etc." but would find its rationale in the "necessity for human cooperation in conditions of at least relative scarcity." The resulting conception of morality is seen by Skillen as a device for attaining cooperation in terms of conceptions of good and bad such that with all the different and conflicting interests involved the good is maximized and the bad is minimized.[17] In so reasoning Skillen comes very close to taking a position identical with that of the good-reasons theorists.

It is in terms of such a conception of cooperation that the good-reasons approach understands the underlying function of morality. (It is, of course, stated more self-consciously and thus more precisely in the accounts given by the good-reasons theorists.) If such an account succeeds or even partially succeeds in articulating correctly the underlying rationale of what it is to take a rational moral point of view, a Marxist morality will have found rational underpinnings without falling into what Skillen shows are the real evils of moralism. This is one alternative that needs to be carefully investigated and reasoned through.

However, the approach is thought by many to be in one way or another inadequate. (I shall not here, as I have elsewhere,[18] try to assess the justifiability of these criticisms but simply, as a sociological comment, note that they are widespread.) Others have tried to show how other conceptions of morality are at the basis of Marxism. Richard Norman[19] has argued, as have others, that a self-realizationist account is at its base and has stated a self-realizationist account in such a way as to free it from the incoherencies that plague many self-realizationist accounts, though there still remains the problem of whether such an account could be a complete account of the foundations of morality.[20] (We should also worry about whether we have any tolerable understanding of what it would be like to have a complete account here. Maybe we are looking for the color of heat.)

Derek Allen,[21] by contrast with Norman, and running against the stream, has argued that Marx's account is best understood as a utilitarian one and that the self-realizationist motifs can be subsumed under a general utilitarian account. But even if this claim is correct, we are faced with the powerful critique of utilitarian accounts of morality given by John Rawls.[22] If Marx's ethics is a utilitarian one, then it is far from clear whether it provides us with a justification of our socialist moral commitments.

The general problem is an old one in moral philosophy. Marx's account is clearly not normatively neutral and seems at least to commit one to a certain moral point of view and a certain moral assessment of life. But it is not clear that there is any theoretical conception of morality or indeed any intellectual construction at all that can show that this point of view is rationally justified and indeed is the point of view that we should take.

There is, however, a challengeable assumption embedded in my above remarks—an assumption Lerner and Allen also make—namely, the assumption that unless there is some sort of general philosophical ethical theory justifying the taking of a moral point of view or at least justifying the holding of fundamental evaluations such as those that Marx makes, that we are not justified in believing that this moral point of view or these evaluations are objectively justified. But this assumption—particularly since the work of Wittgenstein—ought to be challenged. It is not evident that rational morality requires such *philosophical foundations*.

Allan Wood[23] has argued something very like that. Marx, he agrees, did condemn capitalism in moral terms. But it is a mistake, Wood tells us, to see Marx's critique of capitalism as rooted in any moral theory or particular moral or social ideal. He should not be understood as being fundamentally some kind of utilitarian or as some kind of Kantian or self-realizationist. Rather, Wood argues, Marx appeals to quite unproblematic moral conceptions, "accepted by the 'common man,' with whose moral view nearly every moral philosopher claims to be in agreement."[24] They are such conceptions as the claim that disguised exploitation, unnecessary servitude, economic instability and declining productivity are ills (and indeed the first two are evils as well) to be ended as soon as possible. But there is no serious challenge to this on the part of bourgeois thinkers be they conservatives or liberals. If (in fact) capitalism has, quite unavoidably, these features and another social system could avoid them without bringing on still graver ills, then we have good moral grounds for condemning capitalism. Moreover, there is no doubt that these are ills or evils to be avoided if it is possible to do so without creating still graver ills. Apologists for capitalism only have challenged whether they can in fact be avoided without these results. These moral beliefs are in sum quite unproblematic, and we can have greater confidence of their truth than we can have of any moral theory or meta-moral theory. Marx does not need any challengeable philosophical moral theory to underpin his critique of capitalism.

Such talk about 'morality without foundations' and without skepticism will cause many moral philosophers to balk. They wish to have something systematic such as we have in Kant, Mill, Sidgwick or Rawls. And it is understandable enough that moral philosophers would have such a wish. However, there is a kind of realism in Wood's remarks which should appeal to Marxists. Is it not the case that we can be more confident that these things are genuine ills and evils, than we could be of the truth of any moral theory or philosophical account of morality? After all philosophical accounts of any interest are complex and the grounds for their assessment seem at least to be essentially contested. At the very least there are deep and persistent disputes about them with no clear methodological guides for their resolution. But moral beliefs like those of Marx mentioned above are beliefs all of us would hold in a reflective equilibrium when we were reasonably informed. Moreover, they are the sort of beliefs we would have to appeal to in testing the adequacy of any philosophical statement of a normative ethic. Marx need not have worked out a moral theory to be in a position to defend the objectivity of his moral condemnation of capitalism or to reject charges of relativism or arbitrariness.

Remembering what Gramsci said about common sense being the ideology of the ruling class, if we claim that such common valuations are ideologically skewed, we must keep in mind that this will, if true, affect moral theories resting in part on such common valuations and not just those very fundamental valuations themselves. And if we try to cut free our normative ethical theories altogether from such appeal to common and deeply entrenched valuations, it is difficult to see how these theories are to be assessed.

I, as much as any other moral philosopher, am interested in trying to discover and set out the underlying structure of morality—if such there be— so as to gain a clear understanding of its rationale (if any). I also agree that such an account, if we had it, would be of value in arguments about the viability of different forms of life and different ideological postures, but I think it is entirely unrealistic and unjustified to think that we must resolve such foundational questions before we can make rational moral assessments of the evils of capitalism and the desirability of socialism.

One final point. I agree with Lerner, and thus disagree with Skillen and Wood, that we on the Left need to make such assessments of capitalism and socialism. However, I believe that Wood is quite right in stressing that Marx believed that a "historically potent demand, a genuine and effective *need* for emancipation arises in an oppressed class only under certain conditions."[25] This emancipatory interest arises only where there is a disharmony between the productive forces within a given social system and its existing relations of production. Wood is also justified in claiming that this emancipatory interest (need) "does not appear *merely* as a social ideal, but always as an actual movement within the existing production relations toward concrete historical possibilities transcending them."[26] But to say that this need does not appear *merely* as a social ideal is not to deny that it does appear as an ideal; my claim and Lerner's is only that there is embedded in Marx's critique of capitalism such an ideal and that if that ideal is not justified his critique of capitalism is undermined. This is not at all to deny the claim of Marx and Engels[27] that "communism is . . . not a *state of affairs* to be brought about, an *ideal* to which reality must somehow adjust itself. We call communism the actual movement which is transcending (*aufhebt*) the present state of affairs. The conditions of this movement result from presuppositions already existing." That is to say, to argue as I have and as Lerner has is not to claim foolishly that if philosophers and a few enlightened people, or indeed even many enlightened people, attain a proper moral understanding, we will then be able to adjust social reality to the ideals embedded in this understanding. It is rather most fundamentally the dominant mode of the forces of production which determines the general nature of social reality. There cannot be an end to the evils—the servitude and domination and the alienated labor—of class-divided societies until productive forces exist which could make possible a classless egalitarian society of sisterhood and brotherhood and of human solidarity. Servitude is an essential ingredient of the capitalist system and was essential for the development of capitalism to the stage where socialism becomes a real possibility. This needs to be recognized, but the recognition of this is compatible with a recognition that there is a state of affairs to be achieved, where the productive conditions are right, which has the earmarks of a truly human society—a society far better than the inhuman ones which we have known under the yoke of capitalism.

NOTES

1. In an important article with a much more directly morally educative intent, [K. T.] Fann ("The Ethics of Liberation: The Example of China," *Monthly Review* [April, 1974]: 39) has stressed the importance for socialism of a moral understanding, while remaining sensitive to the ideological distortions to which moral discourse is frequently subject. (Nixon's resignation speech is an obvious and particularly disgusting example of such a perversion of moral discourse.) Fann appropriately remarks: "Liberation from this oppressive system (the class rule of capitalism) requires, first of all, the reintroduction of ethics as a motivating force of the revolution. Commitment to a new ethical order is the first prerequisite of a revolutionary." As different as their political strategies were, such a common conception underlies the thought of both Carlos Marighela (*For the Liberation of Brazil* [Middlesex, Eng.: Harmondsworth, 1971]) and Salvador Allende (*Chile's Road to Socialism* [Middlesex, Eng.: Harmondsowrth, 1973]).

2. Kai Nielsen, *Reason and Practice* (New York: Harper and Row, 1971), chap. 26; Kai Nielsen, *Ethics Without God* (Buffalo: Prometheus Books, 1973), chap. 3.

3. C. B. Macpherson, *Democratic Theory* (Oxford: Clarendon Press, 1973), chap. 4; Macpherson, "Rawls' Models of Man and Society," *Philosophy of the Social Sciences* 3 (4) (December, 1973): 341-347.

4. Nielsen, op. cit.; "A Defense of Radicalism," *Question* 7 (January, 1974): 53-66.

5. Macpherson, op. cit.

6. Lucien Goldmann, "Is There a Marxist Sociology?" *Radical Philosophy* 1 (January, 1972); *Introduction à la Philosophie de Kant* (Paris: Presses Universitaires, 1952); *Sciences Humaines et Philosophie* (Paris: Gallimard, 1962).

7. Bertell Ollman, *Alienation: Marx's Conception of Man in Capitalist Society* (Cambridge, England: University Press, 1971).

8. Goldmann, op. cit., p. 20.

9. Ibid., pp. 14, 20-21.

10. Some of the core writings about this have been collected together by W. D. Hudson (ed., *The Is/Ought Question* [London: Macmillan, 1969]). The essays which argue that an ought can be derived from an is which are particularly worthy of note are the essays of MacIntyre, Black, Searle, Anscombe and Foot. In addition to the essays in this volume, note for further non-autonomist arguments George Mavrodes ("On Deriving the Normative from the Non-Normative," *Papers of the Michigan Academy of Science, Arts and Letters* 53 [1968]: 353-365), A. I. Melden ("Reasons for Action and Matters of Fact," *Proceedings and Addresses of the American Philosophical Association [1961-62])*, Charles Taylor ("*Neutrality in Political Science*," in *Philosophy, Politics and Society*, ed. Peter Laslett and W. G. Runciman, 3d series [Oxford: Blackwells, 1967]), and Richard Norman ("On Seeing Things Differently," *Radical Philosophy* 1 [January, 1972]). The last two essays mentioned should be of particular interest to people on the Left.

11. In the Hudson (1969) collection, the following essays are of particular importance for a defense of an autonomist position: Flew, Phillips, Hare and James and Judith Thomson.

In addition, the following are crucial: Alison Jaggar ("It Does Not Matter Whether We Can Derive 'Ought' From 'Is,' " *Canadian Journal of Philosophy* 3, no. 3 [March, 1974], R. M. Martin ("What Follows From 'I Promise,' " *Canadian Journal of Philosophy* 3, no. 3 [March, 1974]) and A. E. Wengraf (" 'Is' and 'Ought' in Moral Reasoning: Can Hume's Cuillotine Be Dismantled?" *Methods* 16, no. 62 [1964]: 109–126.). Chapters 5 and 6 of Hudson (W. D., ed., *Modern Moral Philosophy* [London: Macmillan, 1970]) provide a useful summary discussion of the arguments pro and con here.

12. Tony Skillen, "Marxism and Morality," *Radical Philosophy* 8 (Summer, 1974): 11-15.

13. Ibid., p. 11.

14. Ibid., p. 14.

15. Ibid., p. 15.

16. Ibid.

17. Ibid., pp. 14-15.

18. Kai Nielsen, "On Moral Truth," in Nicholas Rescher (ed.), *Studies in Moral Philosophy* (Oxford: Blackwells, 1968); "Justification and Moral Reasoning," *Methodos* 9 (1957).

19. Richard Norman, unpublished work titled "Self-realization."

20. This essay is in part a response to Nielsen ("Alienation and Self-Realization," *Philosophy* 48 [January, 1973]. I there try to show how the classical treatments of self-realization, as suggestive as they sometimes are, have not received a coherent statement. While acknowledging the force of much of my case, it does seem to me that Norman has given a coherent and suggestive account of self-realization.

21. Derek Allen, "The Utilitarianism of Marx and Engels," *American Philosophical Quarterly* 10 (3) (July, 1973): 189-199.

22. John Rawls, *A Theory of Justice* (Cambridge, Mass.: Harvard University Press, 1971).

23. Allan Wood, "The Marxian Critique of Justice," *Philosophy and Public Affairs* 1 (3) (Spring, 1972): 244-282.

24. Ibid., p. 281.

25. Ibid., p. 279.

26. Ibid. (italics mine).

27. Karl Marx, *Writings of the Young Marx on Philosophy and Society*, ed. Lloyd Easton and Kurt Guddat. (Garden City, N.Y.: Doubleday, 1967).

# 7

# The Voices of Egoism

Many people think that egoism is simply enlightened common sense. If we are clear-headed and tough-minded we shall come to see that all voluntary actions are and should be thoroughly egoistic. What finally justifies an agent acting in one way rather than another is that it is in the agent's own interest to so act. Our fundamental moral principle should be: 'Everyone should look after his own interests regardless of the interests of others'. That is to say, everyone should seek to achieve that which is in his or her own rational self-interest no matter what its effect may be on the interests of others. Enlightened self-interest is the sole rational standard of conduct or at least it is the finally decisive rational standard of conduct.

This view, or at least something like it, is an ancient and recurring one in the history of ethical thinking.[1] It is a belief that many people who reflect about ethics naturally come to have. This is particularly true of people living in cultures such as our own. However, the vast majority of moral philosophers in the past three hundred years have rejected it as thoroughly confused. I think that in this instance the vast majority of moral philosophers are right. I shall try here to show why, notwithstanding its continued general popularity, these philosophers have been justified in their rejection of egoism.

It is first necessary to give a clear statement of what the egoist is claiming. Some people who like to think of themselves as egoists are simply accepting the common sense observation that people often 'look out for number one' and ride roughshod over the interests of others. But this is a truism that every realistic person must surely accept. In capitalist and capitalist-like societies at least, a not inconsiderable number of people are, for the most part, rather self-centered and often self-serving. They only deceive themselves and people who do not know them well: they appear to care for others,

From *Philosophical Studies* (1984): 83–107. Reprinted by permission of Kluwer Academic Publishers.

to put the interests of others on a moral par with their own, but they actually do not. Bulstrode in George Eliot's *Middlemarch* is a good example. As a pillar of his Church, he conceals from himself as well as from others, the selfishness of his acts. His charity is charity to ease a guilty conscience, i.e., good works to blot out the memory of past transgressions. But when he has a chance to really do something that would right the wrong he has done—though doing it would conflict with his self-interest—he again, though with heaviness of heart and much ambivalence, does something which from a non-egoistic point of view is thoroughly unprincipled. But Bulstrode, defenders of egoism will maintain, is but a microcosm of the macrocosm that is humanity. We all, when the chips are down, act in terms of what we take to be those policies which will further our own interests. And where our interests conflict, or are thought to conflict with the interests of others, we act in accordance with what we take to be our own interests.

It is fairly elementary street wisdom to realize that people, often with rationalization, seek to further their own interests and neglect the interests of others. This is a deep-going human trait, particularly in possessive individualistic societies such as our own, that our official tribal mythology obscures. This much we should indeed recognize. But it is still a long way to the philosophical doctrine of egoism. Of course, if you mean in calling yourself an 'egoist' that you simply believe that most people tend rather frequently to put their interests first and rationalize in their own favor, then obviously you can, *in that sense,* quite consistently be an egoist; but this is not the position espoused by philosophical egoists and it is not a position which requires one to claim that the only thing one *can* have regard for or the only thing one *does* or *ought* to have regard for or the only thing one can *reasonably* have regard for is one's own self-interest.

## II

What then are philosophical egoists espousing? At this point we should make a very important distinction between *psychological egoism* and *ethical egoism.* Some loose philosophical discussions are utterly obscured by a failure to note how very different these positions are.

*Psychological egoism* is a theory of human motivation. It is not an ethical claim, though surely it is relevant to ethics. *Psychological egoism* is the view that *for every individual all of his voluntary acts are acts which are done to further or protect what he believes to be in his own interest or will promote or protect what he judges to be his own greatest good.* He is concerned to help others when and only when helping them or being concerned about them will, in his judgment, further his own interests. The thing that is always decisive in moving anyone to action is the belief that what he is about to do will promote his own good. It is the ultimate motivating force or onsetting factor for all voluntary actions.

Psychological egoists can quite consistently assert that sometimes a man will voluntarily act in a way that promotes the interests of others and involves *some* frustration of his own interests. But when he so acts, he will do this only because he thinks that by so furthering someone else's interests he will, at least in the long run and all things considered, further his own interests. What the psychological egoist is committed to denying is that people ever voluntarily act to promote the interests of others as an *end* in itself or that one ever acts disinterestedly, i.e. acts in such a way that he has the same regard for himself as he has for others. This comes, where there is no relevant difference between the parties involved, to treating them all alike in the sense that all their interests count equally. But the psychological egoist must deny that people ever act that way. They always look out for themselves and put what they at least take to be in their own interests, first.

*Ethical egoism,* by contrast, is not a psychological doctrine at all. It is rather a *normative* principle—allegedly an ethical doctrine—that tells us, or purports to tell us, how we should live. Psychological egoism is concerned with what human beings actually do. Ethical egoism is concerned with what they *ought* to do. *It is the normative doctrine and at least allegedly the ethical doctrine that what each person ought to do is always to seek his own greatest good (his own rational self-interest) regardless of its consequences to others.* The only things *worth* having for their own sakes are those things that promote one's own self-interest. A rational person will only consider the interests of others when considering the interests of others will, in his (her) best judgment, promote his (her) own self-interest.

It is true enough that there is a little of Bulstrode in us all. We are often hypocritical. We often, either consciously or unconsciously, seek our own advantage, seek to push our own interests at the expense of others. This is hardly news. What the psychological egoist must show is that in *all* our voluntary actions, great and small, we act in such a manner; and the ethical egoist must show that this is the only *rational* or *reasonable* thing to do. Cast in this light, it should be evident that neither psychological egoism nor ethical egoism are plainly true—mere bits of tough-minded street wisdom. Rather, they are positions which very much need to be established, if indeed they can be. Are there good arguments which would establish either or both of them?

III

In going in search of such arguments, I believe that one of the first things we need to see is that psychological egoism and ethical egoism are, or at least very definitely appear to be, logically independent. That is to say, one might be a psychological egoist and not be an ethical egoist and one might espouse ethical egoism while not espousing psychological egoism. *After all, a psychological egoist simply makes a claim about the ultimate motivating factors in human nature.* He tells us how he thinks people in fact act. He is not saying anything directly about how they *should* act or about what is *rational* to do or about what is *good* or *bad.* An ethical egoist, on the other hand, need not be claiming that men always or even typically seek their own good or what they take to be in their own self-interest. Rather, he is concerned to claim that this is what they *ought* to do. It is the only rational thing to do. To do anything else is to be foolish and duped.

It is, however, fair to say that the reason that most people give for adopting what philosophers call 'ethical egoism' is psychological egoism. That is to say, they claim that since human beings in fact do seek only their own good, this is what they should do. It is at least reasonable to counter that this does not follow, for we cannot derive a moral statement from a factual statement. We cannot *deduce* an *ought* from an *is.* But even if that is so (and it is at least reasonable to believe that it is) the matter is still not settled, for someone who wished to base his ethical egoism on psychological egoism might still argue that the *best evidence* we can have that someone *ought* to desire something is that human beings pervasively and reflectively *do desire* it or seek it. The *best evidence* we can possibly have for the desirability of something is the fact that it is something that the vast majority of human beings do desire and will continue to desire on reflection, when they are fully aware both of the causes of their desires and of what it would be like to have the relevant desires satisfied. Such a position can and indeed should be carefully weighed, for it is—to put it minimally—not obviously fallacious and it may well be a sound position to take.[2] It is, at the very least, not unreasonable. If an ethical egoist were to accept it and if he believed psychological egoism were true, then he would be grounding his ethical egoism on psychological egoism.

It should be noted, in passing, that if psychological egoism is stated in a much stronger way, it is not only incompatible with ethical egoism, it is incompatible with *any* ethical position or with any normative doctrine, i.e., with any view that tells us how we should act and how we should live our lives. Let me show how this is so. If we beef up our definition of 'psychological egoism' and state it in such a way that the only thing that *can* move anyone to action is the belief that what he is about to do will promote his own good, then, since in some sense ought implies can, it makes no sense at all to tell anyone that he ought to do *anything* at all. If the only thing he *can* possibly do is seek his own self-interest, it makes no sense to tell him that he *ought* to do so, or that it is a good thing for him to do.

I did not, however, state psychological egoism in this strong way. I stated it as the doctrine that the only thing that people *do* do is to act in accordance with what, in their judgment, best serves their self-interest. This is perfectly compatible with saying that man is something to be surpassed. It is quite compatible with claiming that we *should* develop in individuals the capacity for self-sacrifice and for genuinely altruistic or disinterested action. Thus, even if it is the case that we cannot derive (deduce) ethical egoism from psychological egoism, the truth of ethical egoism is not incompatible with psychological egoism and psychological egoism may be used to support ethical egoism.

## IV

Given what we have argued above, the first order of business is to find out whether psychological egoism is true.

At first glance it seems obviously false. People plainly do often act egoistically, but this is not enough to establish psychological egoism. We must establish that they *always* act egoistically. But there are, in fact, plenty of cases where they act non-egoistically. Since this is so, psychological egoism must be false.

Let us consider some plain cases. I have heard of a German farmer and his family in the Black Forest that hid a Jewish family—a mother and two children—throughout the war years. This farmer did this at great personal risk to himself and his family. Detection would mean that he too, and perhaps his family, would go off to a concentration camp where torture and/ or death might very well be their lot. But he acted in the way he did and there were other people who did act in the same way. People acting in this way are certainly not egoists. Their actions are not self-serving acts.

Similarly, many of the actions of men such as Hammarskjöld, Schweitzer, Martin Luther King, or Malcolm X cannot properly be said to be egoistic. We have conspicuous examples of human beings who could not correctly be said to be egoists and we have plenty of cases of actions, such as my case of the German farmer, Japanese Kamikaze pilots, Buddhist monks or nuns frying themselves in acts of desperate social protest, mothers sacrificing themselves for their children, and the like, which are not self-serving, egoistic acts. These cases are obvious enough, not to mention a plenitude of mundane ones, such as giving someone a ride, giving directions, offering a pen to someone whose pen gives out during an examination and the like. And it is in large measure because they are so obvious and so unproblematic that it is quite evident that psychological egoism has been disconfirmed.

Yet there is something fishy here. Cases of this sort are surely obvious enough. Egoists know about them. Yet they never really seem to take them to heart and they do not lead them to question their egoism. In fact they pounce on the more dramatic cases with gusto. Such cases are simply more fuel for their egoistic fire. Egoists, for example, will point out that so-called self-sacrificing mothers are often thoroughly frustrated, neurotic and embittered women who live only through their children. Their own lives are dull and warped. They are sick unto death of their husbands and they try to live their children's lives with a grasping vicariousness. Furthermore, they bind their children to them by acts of sacrifice and they find the little gratification they can find in life in seeing themselves as good, self-sacrificing mothers giving their all to their family. A psychological egoist might say about the German farmer, that he did risk his own life and the lives of his family, but he could not have lived with himself if he hadn't. The Nazi holocaust was too bestial for him to simply stand back and watch. His pride as a German, his sense of human dignity, self-respect and sanity would not allow him to simply ignore such things. Most others did ignore it, and many actively engaged in it, but this man had a keener conscience than the ordinary man and was not so good at rationalizing. But he still wasn't unselfish. He acted as he did because the rub of his conscience was too great for him not to so act. It is true that he saved the lives of three hunted people, but his motives were still ultimately selfish, for he could not stand the sting of guilt, the whip of bad conscience that he would feel if he did not so act. The egoist would tell a similar tale for those Buddhist monks and nuns going in for human barbecues. Surely they gave their lives in a way almost too horrible to consider. But, it is also true that by such desperate acts they put for a moment their little and obscure lives onto the great stage of the world and for a moment became somebody; more importantly still, they carried out something they believed would be commended by their religion, something that will, so they thought, bring them the bliss of nirvana. Their acts, an egoist would maintain, are as calculatingly selfish as those of a Jimmy Hoffa, a Nixon, a Lance or a Bulstrode.

Egoists make basically the same rejoinder about the other cases—both mundane and dramatic. In short, the psychological egoist argues that we must come to recognize, if we wish to be realistic, that everyone is selfish. We must come to see that all people all of the time always act to further what they take to be their own good no matter what the consequences to others. Each person looks out for number one and only number one. It is indeed true that different people get their kicks from different things and have different interests. But deep down we are all selfish. The *content* of what is in a person's self-interest, or at least what he takes to be in his self-interest, varies not inconsiderably with the person, his class and the sort of society he lives in; but when there is a clash between what he takes to be in his own self-interest and what he takes to be in the interests of others, he gives pride of place to his own interests or what he at least takes to be his own interests. That he may suffer from 'false consciousness' does not make him any the less egoistic.

Joseph Butler and Bertrand Russell are indeed correct in claiming that where people have an *enlightened* self-interest, there will be fewer clashes than we ordinarily would assume, but still there are such clashes and when there are, the psychological egoist claims, people always act in accordance with what they take to be in their own self-interest. Not all concern for one's own self-interest need be narrowly or plainly selfish, for one could be concerned for oneself and others as well, but in fact all such self-interested behavior is still in a deeper way selfish, for it is always the case, where the action is voluntary, that, where there is a clash or even where it is believed that there is a clash between one's own interests and the interests of others, an agent will act in accordance with what he takes at least to be his own interests.

Let us take, in trying to probe whether this is so, a mundane case—a case where the images of excellence we create for ourselves are less likely to be hounding us. Suppose some little children, dressed in masks, come knocking at my door. I suddenly remember that it is Halloween and the children are "trick or treating." I hunt around and discover that I do not have any candies or cookies to give to them. I feel mildly bad about this—a little, but only a little, sorry for the kids. I wish I had remembered about Halloween, but I don't feel guilty or ashamed for forgetting or even foolish. Why on earth should I have remembered a thing like that? I just wish I had remembered and purchased some candy to give them. Surely this is a normal and perfectly standard altruistic wish. It wasn't that I wanted to make myself feel better, for I didn't feel bad. I just wanted to give them some candy.

However, the egoist will reply: "Well, you *wanted* to, didn't you? If you had done it, you would have done it because you *wanted* to do it, because it would give you *satisfaction*. So then, after all, you wouldn't really have done it for them, you would have done it for yourself. You would have done it because of your own selfish motives. So there too, you would have acted selfishly as we all do in all the things we deliberately do. You think your wish was altruistic but in reality it wasn't."

There occurs here an unacknowledged and no doubt unwitting shift away from arguing for psychological egoism in a quite straightforward and proper empirical manner: that is by amassing evidence that ostensibly altruistic acts are really egoistic. The straightforward empirical task is to establish that they are not altruistic or even non-egoistic but that they are egoistic in a covert way by amassing empirical evidence for this claim. But in discussions of psychological egoism a slide occurs from making this empirical claim to making an illegitimate *a priori* or conceptual claim that makes it true by *definition* that any voluntary action *must* be egoistic. But these are two quite different sorts of claim. The empirical one is just false for it does not plausibly account on egoistic grounds for many cases of actions that seem at least quite straightforwardly to be altruistic or at least disinterested acts and not at all egoistic ones. By contrast the *a priori* claim—the claim most psychological egoists ultimately rely on—rests on conceptual confusions.

That there is such conceptual confusion on the egoist's part can be shown by the following argument. If the psychological egoist could prove to me that my *only* reason for wishing I had purchased some candy for the children was that by doling it out to the children, I could enhance my stature in the eyes of my wife or in my own eyes, I would indeed have been shown to have, after all, been acting egoistically or selfishly. If instead, he only shows that I did it because I *wanted* to, then we should reply that to show that only shows that it was a *voluntary* act, *not* that it was selfish or even self-interested. If we claim that any act that anyone does because he *wants* to do it is *thus ipso facto* a *selfish* act, we are confusing things that ought not to be confused. (1) below may well be true. It may even be analytically true, i.e. by definition.

(1)  We only voluntarily do what under the circumstances we want most to do or dislike least.

But that (1) is either empirically true or (as I believe it is) analytically true does not entail or justify psychological egoism or any kind of egoism. It only would, if (1) were equivalent to (2) or (3) below. The psychological egoist mistakenly takes them to be equivalent.

(2)  We only voluntarily do that which we think will satisfy our own interests.

(3)  We only do that which we believe will promote our own good.

How can I be so confident that (1), (2) and (3) are not equivalent? Well, first it is evident enough that they are not equivalent in the sense they have the *same meaning*. An examination of our usage makes that plain. Suppose Jones asserts (1) in John's presence and John replies, "Yes, and what I want to do most of all is to always act fairly, to consider the interests of others as well as my own." His remark here is perfectly intelligible—egoist and non-egoist alike understand it—but if (1) is true then John's reply might also be true, and indeed would be true, if he is not lying or self-deceived, but if (2) is true then John's reply *must* be false. But if (1) and (2) actually have the same meaning or are in any other way equivalent what would make one true would make the other true and what would make one false would make the other false. But the very intelligibility of John's utterance shows that they do not have the same truth-conditions, for in understanding John's utterances and in understanding (1) and (2), we see that John's reply is compatible with the truth of (1) but not with the truth of (2).

It might be responded that all we know from the above is that (1) and (2) are not equivalent in meaning, we do not know they are not extensionally equivalent. That is to say, we do not know that in fact they do not have the same truth conditions so that when in fact one is true the other is true and that when the other is true the first claim is true as well. We clearly can *conceive* what it would be like for (1) to be true when (2) was not true; but it might turn out, as a matter of fact, to be true that whenever (1) is true (2) is true and whenever (2) is true (1) is true. But since we can clearly conceive of situations of a quite ordinary sort in which we would assert (1) and deny (2), the burden is clearly on the egoist to show that (1) and (2) are extensionally equivalent by showing that in these cases doing what we want most to do or dislike least is really also either in our own interest or in what we take to be in our own interests. This surely does not appear to be the case, but if the egoist can unearth good empirical evidence in these cases we would have, given some reasonable, though hardly conclusive, evidence to believe that (1) and (2) are extensionally equivalent. But nothing like this has been even attemped let alone achieved. That it could be done seems, at least, to be utterly implausible.

Moreover, we have no reason to believe that whenever (1) is true, (2) will in fact be true. We would only be justified in believing that if we were justified in believing the truth of the claim that we only want that which we think will protect or further our own interests. But that seems at least not only to be groundless but a plainly false claim as well, for there are many cases where people prefer to do things which they know are not in their own interests, as when someone in Canada gives money to a black South African liberation group or (in most circumstances) when a person donates a kidney.

Similar things can be shown about (1) and (3). Suppose Jones asserts (1) in Janet's presence and Janet replies: "Yes, and what I want most of all to do is to be a person of principle and not to be a person who only promotes her own good." But if (1) is true, Janet's assertion can be true; but (3) cannot be true, if Janet's assertion is true, as it very well could be. Then (1) and (3) are not equivalent. And there would be similar problems to those discussed above for (1) and (2), about (1) and (3) being extensionally equivalent.

What the above argument establishes is this: the establishing of the truth of (1) is not sufficient for establishing the truth of (2) or (3). Psychological egoists have perhaps given us a good argument for accepting (1), but this is of no avail for it does not take them to what are straightforward (evident) statements of psychological egoism, namely (2) and (3). They mistakenly think that (1), (2) and (3) are all equivalent and thus having established (1) they believe that they have also automatically established (2) and (3). And to the extent that (1) seems undeniably true, psychological egoism is also going to seem undeniably true too as long as it assumed that (1), (2) and (3) are equivalent.

When we see they are not equivalent in meaning and that no good grounds have been given for claiming they are extensionally equivalent (they are both always true under the same conditions), then we should come to see that even if (1) is in some sense self-evidently true, we have not come within even a country-mile of establishing psychological egoism simply because of it.

There are indeed certain circumstances in which in doing what I want to do I am acting selfishly. Suppose I like the cinema and my wife likes the opera and further, suppose that I always deliberately fail to get tickets for the opera and take her to the cinema instead. Here my act squares with (2) and (3). I am plainly acting selfishly, i.e. egoistically. I am looking out for my interests and neglecting hers. If by doing what "I want most to do" I *mean* only voluntarily doing what, others' wishes apart, satisfies me the most, I am acting in accordance with (1). But that is not the only way we can and do take "I want most to do. . . ." Indeed it is *not* the most natural and straightforward way of construing it. In many contexts, including the one that follows, we would *not,* and could not, reasonably construe it in that egoistic way. Suppose instead of always going to the cinema I act on the policy, "Half the time to the Met, the other half to the cinema." Now if I do that simply because it is fair and because I *want* to do what is fair, my act squares with (1) but is a counter-instance to (2) and (3). Surely I *wanted* to do it, I *chose* to do it, but this only shows that it was a voluntary action. It does not show that it was a *selfish* action—an instance of (2) or (3) or even something I enjoyed doing. The *object* of my choice or preference was not my *personal* advantage but to act fairly—to give an equal distribution of satisfactions. This is an example of an unselfish, though surely not an altruistic, act. It certainly need not be an instance of someone acting to promote his own good, though, as Butler has shown, some actions of this sort can both be in one's rational self-interest and unselfish. But, since it need not be for our own good, it does not square with (3) either. In short we can point to cases which would disconfirm (2) and (3) but would clearly square with (1). This definitely establishes that (1) is not equivalent in meaning to (2) or (3) and sets the burden of proof on the egoist to show that appearances to the contrary they really are extensionally equivalent. That is, egoists must show that in fact it is always the case that when (1) is true in fact, (2) and (3) are true and that when both (2) and (3) are true, (1) as a matter of fact also always turns out to be true.

In this connection we should keep in mind a point first stressed by Butler, namely that it is the *object* of a want that determines whether or not something is selfish. The mere fact that I do something I want to do does not make my action selfish. Whether it is selfish or not depends on *what* I want. If I want only my own good and do not care a fig for others, I am selfish; but if I want the well-being and happiness of others and if I actually act on that desire, I am being unselfish.

Finally, it is not just that we have good reasons for believing that it is false that all people are all of the time motivated by selfish desires, but we also do not have anything like adequate grounds for believing that all human beings are basically selfish in their life-orientation, that, while occasionally they may act unselfishly, their *dominant psychological set* is to preserve what they take to be their own interests even at the expense of the interests of others. Butler was right in rejecting the claim that self-love or a desire for one's own happiness is the basic drive in human nature. We have no good grounds for believing that all people in all social settings are so constituted that they *only* care about what they take to be their own interests and do not care about others except insofar as they believe those others might be useful to them. Besides self-love we are sometimes moved to action by such independent motives as benevolent affections, considerations of conscience and direct passions like hunger, thirst, lust, resentment, curiosity, ambition, pride and the like, where, on certain occasions, the having of these passions and the acting on them are not in the person's self-interest. We, as a matter of fact, have many springs of action other than self-love (cool or otherwise) and no reason has been given for thinking that with all or even most persons that self-love is the dominant or ultimate spring (motivating force) of action.

It is not very clear what psychological egoists assert when they claim all human beings are basically selfish, but, if it means anything tolerably clear at all, it means that they all massively put their own interests before the interests of anyone else, that this is the overall orientation of all human beings. But there seem at least to be all sorts of expectations to this and, once we expose the linguistic legerdemain that would lead us to reinterpret such exceptions into the egoistic straight-jacket, we have no grounds for believing that, in spite of appearances, all people are exclusively, or even typically, dominantly motivated by the desire to maximize whatever it is that they believe is in their own interests even when this is at the expense of others.

V

Psychological egoism is thought to be an empirical claim, i.e. the claim that human beings always seek what they believe to be in their own personal interest. Psychological egoists presumably take this simply to be a pervasive *fact,* a factual statement about how human beings behave. Now a characteristic feature of straightforward factual statements is that we can say what at least in principle would disconfirm them. They may, like 'Human beings have livers', be universally true. But we still know what it would be like for a human being *not* to have a liver. Taken as a straightforward empirical statement about human behavior there are all sorts of counter-cases—apparently disconfirming instances—of psychological egoism. But the psychological egoist waits for these cases with glee. All cases of apparently altruistic or at least non-egoistic behavior are said by him to be at least *covertly* egoistic. It is interesting to note that he does not really investigate with any serious intent the actual cases. He has no need for the psychologist's or artist's probing to find out if there are hidden motives of a conscious or unconscious kind that show the apparently non-egoistic act to be really egoistic. Sometimes, as we have learned from life and literature, if not from psychology, they really are covertly egoistic. But the psychological egoist is not interested in the careful consideration of individual instances or of human psychology. He treats what, on the surface at least, appear to be empirical claims, as if they were *a priori* truth. He is certain they are true and doesn't concern himself with evidence for his claims. He doesn't really have to examine a person's motives, for, after all, whatever he does, if his act is *voluntary,* he does it because everything considered this is what he prefers in that situation to do. As it makes no sense to say x is sleepy but he is not tired, so it makes no sense to say x is a voluntary act but not something one chooses to do. And if one chooses to do it, it must be the act, under the circumstances, one *wanted* to do or at least disliked doing least. This means that it is *logically* impossible to find a *voluntary* act which is not an act that the agent did not want to do more than any of the alternatives available to him in the circumstances in question. But then psychological egoism is no longer a factual claim about human behavior but a tautology. Nothing could conceivably disconfirm it. We have in psychological egoism a tautology masquerading as a law of psychology. Where it has its characteristic *a priori* certainty, it has it only because it has become perfectly vacuous.

Assuming now that the foregoing has established that we can find no adequate support for ethical egoism in psychological egoism and indeed have no good reason to believe that psychological egoism is true and considerable grounds for thinking it is false, we now need to consider whether there are independent grounds for accepting ethical egoism.

A related matter needs consideration first. Philosophers who actually defend egoism usually do not distinguish, as we have, between ethical egoism and psychological egoism. This might be attributed merely to sloppiness on their part, but it could be attributed to something less disreputable. An egoist could claim that the only *rational* thing for an agent to do is to always act in such a way as to protect or further what he *reasonably* believes to be in his own interest. Human beings, he could agree against the psychological egoist, do not always act in accordance with what they believe to be in their own self-interest, but they are fools not to. A rational person will always act in accordance with that which he has good reason to believe is at least in his own long-term self-interest. Enlightened self-interest is the ultimate guide for a reasonable tough-minded human being.

This contention falls between the claims of the ethical egoist and the psychological egoist. It is like ethical egoism and unlike psychological egoism in that it is a claim about how human beings are to act and not a putative description about how they do act. The terms 'rational', 'reasonable', 'fools', and 'tough-minded' have a normative, directive force. It is evident enough from the usage and the context that it is a good thing to be reasonable and rational and that being a fool is plainly a bad thing and that being tough-minded is a good character trait. There is here in effect an appraisal of how a human being should act or at least how it would be wise to act, and not just a description of how he does act. However, the claim is distinct from the claim of the ethical egoist in that there is no avowal here that acting in one's own self-interest is what *morally speaking* one ought to do. What might well be involved is Machiavellian and/or simply prudential advice about how to get on in the world and not at all a claim about what should constitute an ultimate criterion of morality. Such a defender of *rational egoism*—to give it a label—might well believe (though he need not be of that opinion) that one is duped if one commits oneself to acting in accordance with a moral point of view (i.e., a moral vantage point) where it is not in one's self-interest to do so. So he clearly need not be an ethical egoist. He is telling people how to act, though not necessarily how *morally* speaking they should act. A person (*assuming* that we can make sense of ethical egoism) might be both an ethical egoist and what I have called a rational egoist, but a human being—a certain kind of Machiavellian, for example—could be a rational egoist without being an ethical egoist.

Perhaps the first thing that should be noted about 'rational egoism' is that it is not clear just how to take the claim that to be rational one must always act (where such considerations are relevant) so as to protect, enhance or achieve what is in your own self-interest or at least what you believe to be in your own interest. Is this being made true by definition? If this is so, and if it is also taken as a *stipulative definition,* then it is just the egoist's stipulation on how to use 'rational' in this way. There is no reason why we should adopt his stipulation. If, more plausibly, it is claimed that this is a genuine implication built into our very use of 'rational', then this claim needs to be proven or established. It is surely far from obvious that such a claim is true.

By constrast, rational egoism may be something which it is claimed we observe to be true, as it is alleged by psychological egoists that we observe it to be true that all men always seek what they believe at least to be in their own self-interest or, as some claim, that frustrated people tend to respond with aggression. But there is an important difference between rational egoism and the other two cases. We know what counts against the truth of psychological egoism and what counts for its truth. If we observe that many people who profess misguided ideals are in reality fakes out to serve their own interests and are really indifferent to the fate of others, we have some evidence for the truth of psychological egoism. On the other hand, we have some evidence against psychological egoism if we find people acting interestedly and showing concern for others, even when there is no good reason to believe they stand, directly or indirectly, to gain from it. If we tease people or deprive them of things they might legitimately expect and they start striking back, we have some confirmation of the hypothesis that frustrated people tend to respond with aggression. But if often they do not, then we have some disconfirming evidence of the hypothesis. But how, in a similar way, could we simply look and see that people are rational agents, only if they always put (where such considerations are relevant) their own interests first? The point is that this is not something we can simply observe to be true if indeed we can observe it to be true at all.

We are left with the realization that no ground has been given for accepting rational egoism, for we have been given no good reason for believing that the *only* reasonable thing to do, when one's interests are at stake, is to act in accordance with self-interested motives, for it has not been shown to be true by definition and we do not know what would or could empirically establish it or even disestablish it. Futhermore, it has not been established that when one's interest clash with the interests of others, even many others, that one must, to be rational, put one's own interests first. Some rational people will; others won't. We have no good grounds for claiming that those who will must be the more rational.

It is a truism to say that if something is genuinely in one's self-interest then one, *everything else being equal,* ought to do it. It is indeed rational and reasonable to look out for one's own self-interest, others are not likely to. But from this it does not at all follow that the *only* rational thing to do is to look out for your own interest and that the reasonable thing to do is to *always* give considerations of self-interest pride of place when they conflict with the interests of others, no matter how many people's interests are involved. This is what the rational egoist must be claiming, but he cannot get this from the truism that people, if they are reasonable, should attend to their own interests. The rational egoist's claim has not been made out that the reasonable thing *to do* is to *always* give one's own interests pride of place when there is a conflict of interests. That appears to be an utterly arbitrary claim.

If neither rational egoism not psychological egoism have been established, the prospects for ethical egoism seem pretty slim. Let us see whether there are any sound independent arguments for ethical egoism.

VI

Ethical egoism, like Campbell's soup, comes in several varieties, though, as I shall try to show, there is only one basic variety that is even initially plausible as an *ethical* theory. To avoid confusions it is well to get the varieties in front of us. Keep in mind, while considering them, that in order to be normative ethical theories they must contain, as essential features, action-guides which purport to be universal; that is action-guides which tell people how they should act and live their lives and relate to each other in certain reasonably determinate circumstances. They do not simply tell Tom, Dick and Mary how to act and relate, but tell people generally how they are to act and relate.

Keeping this in mind attend to the following varieties:

(1) *Universal Ethical Egoism* (Impersonal Egoism):
Every person should do what will most effectively further and protect his own self-interest and disregard and, where necessary, override the interests of others, except insofar as having a regard for the interests of others will further his own self-interest or will at least in no way harm it.

(2) *Individual Ethical Egoism:*
Every person ought to do what will further *my* self-interest [that is the interest of the individual making the claim] and disregard and, where necessary, over-ride all other interests except where a regard for the interests of others will further, or at least in no way harm, my self-interest.

(3) *Personal Ethical Egoism*:
I [the person making the utterance] ought to do what will most further my self-interest and I should have a regard for the interests of others only when and to the extent that it will be in my self-interest, or at least in no way harm it, to do so.

(2) *Individual Ethical Egoism* can be readily dispatched. It is plainly utterly arbitrary, for no reason at all is given why everyone should do, and only do, where there is any conflict, what is in the personal interest of the person making this 'individual ethical egoist claim'. If the person making the utterance is some extraordinary person, a Shakespeare, Jesus, Goethe, Keynes or Lenin, there may be good grounds for giving him special treatment, but then it has to do with how he (or she) affects others and the world about him. But for such a person, it isn't his interests *per se* which are of overarching importance. The reason they are treated as they are is that by giving his interests special consideration others are affected in a generally beneficial way. The situation in broad scale is comparable to a situation where people

in desperate straits in a lifeboat give special consideration to the interests of the one person in the lifeboat who knows how to navigate. If individual ethical egoism is to be established, we must, *for any person you like,* including a person without any special qualifications, seek to further his interests even if it is at the expense of everyone else. But there is no reason at all why everyone should act to further his interests, simply because he claims it or even if he doesn't, especially when his claims conflict with the claims of others. Why should you—to translate it into the concrete—seek to further the interests of Kai Nielsen or anyone else simply because this person is Kai Nielsen, Rod Smiles, Will Bennett, or Nancy Millhaven?

(3) *Personal Ethical Egoism* is a horse of a different color. When we reflect for a moment, we can see that it is not, and could not be, a moral guide at all for it does not make a moral claim but is just a bit of hard-headed practical advice concerning how some particular individual ought to live. An action-guide, as we have seen, in order to be *moral* must purport at least to be universal in the sense that it tells people—that is everyone—how they should act. It must be a guide for people generally or else it does not even count as a *moral* action-guide. But personal ethical egoism does not even *purport* to tell people how they should act. It only announces a policy of action for the utterer; it does not say that others, even in similar circumstances, should do likewise. It could not function as a rule to guide human conduct and thus it could not be an ethical claim. In short, it is not a key principle of a public code or even a part of a public code which could serve as an action-guide for how people are to live. It only announces how a given individual is to live his life. Others can and surely will ask, "Why should people look out for *a given agent's* interest when it will involve harming their own interests and the interests of others?" They will ask: "Why should I look after *him* regardless of others?" These are perfectly reasonable questions and it is not at all evident how, particularly in 'the spirit of egoism', the personal egoist could answer such questions. The personal egoist may very well respond that that is not really to the point, for all he is claiming is that he, the agent in question, should always give his interests pride of place. But he also shows, as clear as can be, by that very response that he is not giving us a moral action-guide.

Personal egoists may regard people as fools for not, in this exclusive way, looking after their own particular interests, yet a personal egoist would be somewhat of a fool himself if he were to think that it is in his own personal interest that they do not remain so duped. Moreover, persuasion to the effect that one should ignore the claims of morality because morality doesn't pay is not moral persuasion. 'Personal ethical egoism' isn't a malign, satanic or cynical morality because it isn't a morality at all. We might say of some, from our point-of-view, 'far out' moral code—say the Aztec's or the Keroki's moral code—that it was a perverse or even an immoral moral code. By contrast, personal egoism is a mere contempt for, or at least an indifference to, moral considerations altogether and this is not a moral code at all. It is not even something that could be intelligibly or coherently proclaimed as a morality.

Let us now turn to what is a tougher horse to domesticate, namely (1) *universal ethical egoism:* the doctrine that everyone should protect and where possible further his own interests regardless of the interests of others, the doctrine that everyone should pursue his self-interest above all else. I would first like to explicate and examine an attempt by Brian Medlin to show that it is a self-inconsistent doctrine where it is taken as an ethical doctrine which states categorically the ultimate rationale for moral action.[3] Medlin contends that when we say that everyone would act to protect or further his own interests (look out for himself) regardless of the interests of others, we are saying something incoherent. This becomes evident, Medlin claims, when we exhibit the attitudes expressed in such a claim:

| | |
|---|---|
| I want myself to come out on top | I don't care about Tom, Dick, Harry . . . |
| and | and |
| I want Tom to come out on top | I don't care about myself, Dick, Harry . . . |
| and | and |
| I want Dick to come out on top | I don't care about myself, Tom, Harry . . . |
| and | and |
| I want Harry to come out on top | I don't care about myself, Dick, Tom . . . |
| etc. | etc. |

Such a display of what is involved in stating such a principle shows that the principle expressing such an attitude is inconsistent. It in effect tells us that I want my interests furthered above all else and I am indifferent as to whether they are furthered. I want Tom's interests furthered above all else and I don't care about Tom's interests.

Suppose alternatively, Medlin continues, the ethical egoist drops the claim that everyone is to seek his own well-being or self-interest but merely states his position in the following way: Let each man do what he wants regardless of what anyone else wants. Then such an ethical egoist has dropped any positive claim about what is good beyond perhaps giving us to understand that whatever a human being happens to want is good. Moreover, as we have seen in examining psychological egoism, his wants may not be selfish: they may not be directed to furthering his own self-interest. 'He wants only what is in his own self-interest' is not analytic or some other sort of necessary truth. And indeed no good evidence has been given for thinking it true at all.

Furthermore, even if this move on Medlin's part is legitimate, such an 'ethical egoism' still is vulnerable, thought I see no good reason for saying that such a statement of it is inconsistent. Compare:

(a) It is clearly good for X to do because it is in X's self-interest and it doesn't harm anyone else.

(b) It is clearly good for X to do because it is everything considered in X's well-being and it doesn't harm anyone else.

(c) It is clearly good for X to do because X wants to do it and it doesn't harm anyone else.

Suppose one argues for (c) above by claiming that an individual is a better judge than others of what he wants and that the best possible social arrangement—the one making for the most happiness all around—would be one in which as many people as possible are allowed to do whatever they want to do, since each person is the best judge of what it is that he wants. It is indeed true that this may not even invariably be so. But whether or not it is invariably so, it certainly isn't invariably so when we shift from *wants* to *interests* as in (a) and (b). It is not *always* the case that each person is the best judge of what is in his self-interest, though no doubt it usually is the case that this in itself is an important practical moral consideration. Still this is not the crucial issue, for the ethical egoist in so arguing in defense of (a), (b) or (c) has generalized a concern for the individual well-being and thus has *unwittingly* abandoned ethical egoism and has moved somewhere in the direction of utilitarianism, namely the belief that we should do that which makes for the most happiness or satisfaction of interest all around.

Suppose, alternatively, the universal ethical egoist makes a determined attempt to state his position in a genuinely egoistic and consistent manner. Each person is to look out for his own well-being and to consider the well-being of others only when it will further his own well-being. In taking well-being as a good it is plain that he prizes happiness. But this means that in advocating universal ethical egoism, he is giving us to understand that he wants to be happy and he wants Tom, Dick and Mary to be happy, but that he does not care about Tom, Dick and Mary when caring about them adversely affects his own happiness or his own interests., Then he in no unqualified way wants Tom, Dick and Mary to be happy or wants their well-being, but this does not square with his claim, also implicit, that he wants everyone to be happy.

Suppose again the universal ethical egoist restated his position as:

(3) Let each man do what he wants and let each man disregard what others want when their desires clash with his own.

But (3), Medlin claims, commits him to (4):

> (4) I want everyone to be happy and I want everyone to disregard the happiness of others when their happiness clashes with his own.

It is not so evident that accepting (3) does not commit him to (4) as well; but even if it did difficulties remain for the egoist, for, if the egoist got what he wants here, i.e., (4), he would assuredly make himself miserable. But one of the things that he is committed to—even as a universal ethical *egoist*— is to the attainment of *his own* happiness, to the satisfaction of his own self-interest. *One thing he most assuredly will do, if he is any kind of egoist at all, is to seek to avoid making himself miserable and to seek to avoid damaging his own interests.* In saying he wants everyone to be happy he is also giving to understand that he want to be happy. But he also and unavoidably, in proclaiming *universal ethical egoism,* in effect is offering a directive that would make him miserable, for it tells people to disregard the happiness of others, including his very own happiness, when it clashes with their own individual happiness. He is in effect saying "*Always* try to attain p but disregard p under c" but this is an incoherent directive.

Medlin's general point is that no matter how you twist universal ethical egoism you either get a self-inconsistent doctrine or a doctrine which really isn't egoistic, because it presupposes at a more basic level utilitarianism or some other non-egoistic normative ethical theory.

Universal ethical egoism dies hard and to show that an account of such dimensions lacks self-consistency is by no means an easy thing to do. A particular formulation might be so convicted but it might also be possible to reformulate the account so as to escape those difficulties. Indeed it is not unreasonable to expect that this will always be the case. Moreover, the alteration need not be an *ad hoc* adjustment but might be one that continues to capture what initially gave the theory an intuitive plausibility.

John Hospers, for example, has tried in just this way to work around Medlin's argument that ethical egoism is incoherent.[4] He argues that the egoist need not be caught in a web of inconsistency in which he is saying that he hopes Dick will successfully protect his own interests even when they conflict with Tom's and that Tom will successfully protect his own interests even when they conflict with Dick's.[5] What the egoist should say to preserve consistency is this: "Everyone should *try* to protect his own interests and *try* to come out on top when interests conflict." His attitude is like an impartial spectator's at a game.

> Perhaps the egoist likes to live life in a dangerous cut-throat manner, unwilling to help others in need but not desiring others to help him either. He wants life to be spicy and dangerous; to him the whole world is one vast egoistic game, and living life accordingly is the way to make it interesting and exciting.[6]

If he proceeds in this way he is not, Hospers claims, caught in an inconsistency.

Hospers's argument seems to me to be defective and not to meet Medlin's point. Hospers' egoist is in reality no egoist at all. *Any egoist wants to try to protect and enhance his own interests.* That is his over-riding concern. This is as true of the universal egoist or impersonal egoist as it is of the personal egoist. The universal egoist differs from the personal egoist in that he in some sense wants all people to do or at least try to do likewise or at least he believes they, if they are rational, all should do that. But he cannot consistently want others, where there is a reasonable chance they might succeed, to even try to win out against him, for he must want, *as an egoist, to protect his interests* above all else. He believes that, if they are thoroughly rational, they will also put their interests first, and he believes he has no generally good grounds for telling them not to do so. Yet he also says he wants others to try to protect and even further their own interests, giving them the same weight as he gives to his own interests. But in situations where he is or may be vulnerable to them and they might succeed, he is unsaying what he is saying. He is saying p and not-p. Hospers has not given us a consistent version of ethical egoism.

There is a further and independent error in Hospers's account which vitiates his criticism of Medlin. In fact Hospers has done just what Medlin has shown that many do in trying to refute his core argument. In reformulating universal egoism to show that it will not have the disastrous implications of Medlin's formulations, Hospers has unwittingly altered the account from a universal egoism to a non-egoistic account. It is not a utilitarian account, but it is not an egoistic account either. What Hospers calls "one vast egoistic game" is in reality an account which treats living a life that is exciting and dangerous as the ultimate value and not, as a genuine egoist would, the maximizing of self-interest as the ultimate value or rationale of action. We want or should want, on Hospers's view, a dangerous and spicy life, a life in which there is struggle and keen competition and winners and losers. The thing is to have a life which is thrilling; whether it maximizes what is in our self-interest is a secondary consideration. And whether such a life is in our self-interest is surely not evident. Cicero and Epicurus surely would not have thought so. Whether it actually is or whether such an issue is even resolvable depends on *what* our genuine human interests are and whether that concept is sufficiently unproblematic and non-contested to afford the possibility of an objective account of human interests.

However, it is clear enough that Hospers's account is not an egoistic one. Even if it were self-consistent, it still is not advocating or in any way setting out as our ultimate action-guide the maximizing of self-interest. The thing to do, on Hospers's account, is to live a spicy, interesting, keenly competitive life whether or not it is a life which maximizes the interests of everyone or even anyone. Whatever the merits of such a claim, it plainly is not a form of egoism.

I am not saying that others cannot succeed where Hospers has failed. Perhaps, as some critics believe, Medlin has not established conclusively that there is not some form of universal ethical egoism which is not caught in a web of inconsistency.[7] At the very least Medlin has shown how difficult it is to state a consistent or coherent form of universal ethical egoism and how behind its surface coherency there lie myriads of difficulties.

## VII

We can perhaps cut behind these controversies and make a strong but still concise argument for the incoherence of ethical egoism along the following lines. Suppose we take as the core claim of an ethical egoist the proposition that, if x is an agent and if x is acting both ethically and rationally, x will always act (where x's interests are involved) to protect his or her interests, or at least what they take those interests to be, and to put them before the interests of anyone else. But if in this spirit egoism is formulated as for all (x) and for all (y), (x ought to do y if and only if y is in x's overall self-interest), this means that any individual you like, let us call him Smith, should act to satisfy and protect his own interests and any other individual, let us call him Jones, should do likewise. That also means that Smith agrees that Jones should seek to satisfy his own interests even if it hurts Smith's interests. But then Smith is in effect saying, if it is in Jones's interest, he should seek to harm Smith; but since Smith, as an egoist, is also categorically committed to putting his interests first, he can never rationally or justifiably allow it to be the case, where he can prevent it. Thus universal ethical egoism allows two incompatible directives or injunctions, for a world with Smith in it, namely that Smith is to act so that his interests are to be satisfied or protected before all else and, if and when Smith's interests are incompatible with Jones's interests, Jones is not to act so that Smith's interests are to be satisfied and protected before all else. But that surely looks like the self-contradictory position that Smith is to act to protect his own interests and Jones is not to act to protect his self-interest. And an incoherence of this type obtains not only for a world with Smith in it but for any world in which there are individuals with interests of their own which sometimes conflict.

I shall turn to another consideration, turning on what it is to have a morality at all which, I believe, shows that the notion of a universal ethical egoism is an incoherent one. Ask yourselves why it is that we have a morality—any morality—at all. It seems to me evident that the most central reason—or at least *a* central reason—is that we need some way of fairly and equitably adjudicating conflicts of interest. Even in the most humane and progressive of societies some conflicts of interests do occur. And it is evident enough that we human beings need some device for adjudicating them as reasonably and fairly as possible. This then is a very central but not the sole function of, or rationale for, morality.

We should now apply this consideration back to the problem of egoism. If, where interests conflict, we are simply told that each person is always to act to satisfy his own interests, we have no way rationally to adjudicate conflicts of interest. We in effect tell the people who are in conflict to go on conflicting. If we add "And let the stronger win out," or something of that order, we have departed from egoism and offered, as an ultimate action-guide, the claim or principle that the strongest or fittest in a competitive struggle should survive. We are to fight things out and the ideal that should prevail is the ideal that the strongest should survive. If we do not add something like that—as we cannot if we are to remain consistent universal ethical egoists—we must simply say that when interests conflict we can, within the bounds of universal ethical egoism (or for that matter any egoism), offer no rationale for adjudicating such conflicts. Then it is plain that we have no ethical theory at all, for so-called ethical egoism fails to do what most centrally an ethical system exists to do, namely to adjudicate in a fair and reasonable manner conflicts of interest.

## VIII

Many feel dissatisfied with such a demolition of the varieties of egoism. They feel that such arguments do not really get to the heart of the matter. If you do feel this way you are really asking a quite different question—a question that arises naturally out of a consideration of ethical egoism—but is still a distinct question from that which an ethical egoist (*qua* moralist) can ask. It is the question "Why be moral?" It is important to see that that question is *not* and cannot be a moral question. That is to say, it is not a question that can arise *within* morality any more than the question, "Why be scientific?" can arise within science. Ethical egoism tried to give us a more rational foundation for morality than we have in the common sense, received moralities. If my arguments have been correct, or even close to being correct, it has failed in this endeavor. To go on to ask, "But why should an agent commit himself to moral institutions or to what Butler called 'the moral institution of life' and to be bound by the dictates of morality when it is not in his interest?" is to ask an *entirely different* question, which puts us in a very different context. I think this question is often behind defenses of egoism. What is crucial to see is that this question is not itself a moral question, though it does force the individual to consider why it is that he should do what he acknowledges to be the right thing to do. But it does not tell him—as ethical egoism purports to do—what *morally speaking* is the right thing to do.

Ask yourself: "Why be moral? Why not kick the habit, if I can?" But ask, as well, what you are really asking in that question. If you are at all clear-headed in asking "Why be moral?" you are putting the following considerations to yourself: granted that if I am to be a person of principle—to be, that is, a decent human being—I must be fair; and to be fair I must be prepared to put the interests of others on a par with my own interests. Moreover, let us also grant that Thrasymachus is mistaken and morality is not just what is in the interests of the stronger. But, even after we have granted all these things, might we still not individually ask the question: why *do* what I recognize (acknowledge) to be right and indeed through and through morally mandatory, when it is not in my self-interest to do so? This is a question—or so it appears—a non-evasive person will put to himself. And while this is not a moral question, it certainly appears at least to be a perfectly intelligible question about human conduct.

Plato, Hobbes and Butler all try to show that it is always in a human being's rational self-interest to be moral. But it is highly questionable that this is *always* so. For some people some of the time—indeed perhaps for most people most of the time—it is true enough that they would not be happy if in certain determinate situations they did what they recognize to be wrong. But it is also true that some men might (to take an example) embezzle money, believe it to be wrong to do so and indeed specifically wrong in this instance to so act, and still be considerably happier for doing it. Plainly this is something that from their moral point of view they should not do; but what non-question-begging reason can be given to show them that they should *always* act in accordance with what they take to be the dictates of morality? (Remember all 'shoulds' are not 'moral shoulds'. Example: "You should put the glue on here.") Egoism, if my arguments have been near to being correct, is not the rational basis for conventional morality or any other morality, but it still *may* be true that the only *justification,* if such justification can be given at all, for taking the moral point of view, as distinct from some other point of view, is that it is in one's enlightened self-interest to do so. We—as Epicurus and Cicero long ago reminded us—all desire our own happiness. This is something that we seek or at least hope or wish for. Now consider this: what *reason* can be given to us to put the interests of others on a par with our own interests? To be fair, to be moral, is to do so; but why be moral or fair? Bentham and Mill, for example, thought we ought to desire the happiness and well-being of all sentient creatures. But even if we limit our interests here to humankind, what reason can be given for desiring the happiness of all humankind? In morality we have the maxim, 'Each to count for one and none to count for more than one'. But what reason do we have for following that maxim? From the fact that I desire my own happiness and see happiness to be intrinsically good, how do I get to the position that I ought to desire the happiness of others? Indeed if I am going to be fair

I must or at least I must acknowledge that another person's happiness is of equal moral importance to my own. But why be fair? This is but another way of asking "Why be moral?" The ancient doctrine of egoism leads to the question: "Why be moral?" Psychological egoism is false, rational egoism is an arbitrary claim, and ethical egoism rests on a mistake, but we have yet to be given an adequate answer to a crucial question behind these muddled doctrines: *"Why be moral?"*

Before trying to answer that question, or trying to dissolve it as a conceptual confusion, we need first a tolerably clear understanding of what it is to be moral and what justification can be given for accepting one moral standard rather than another. It is of the utmost importance that we do not confuse these questions with the question of "Why be moral?" It is one thing to ask for a *justification in ethics,* a justification *within* the moral mode of reasoning itself, and it is another thing to ask for a justification for taking any moral point of view at all. It is one thing to ask which of the various competing moral claims is justified or even justifiable. It is another to ask: why pay any attention to any moral claims or considerations at all? This last question is the real question behind egoistic doctrines and remains even after the refutation of ethical egoism. It is this, if you will, 'ultimate question' that fuels, though typically in confused ways, a continued preoccupation with egoism.[8]

## NOTES

1. I think the qualification "or at least something like it" is in order, for a strong case could be made for egoism, as I have formulated it above, being pretty much a modern creation, manufactured, if you will, by Sidgwick and Moore. The "great classical egoists," such as Epicurus, Cicero and Hobbes, it is reasonable to claim, were not proclaiming exactly that.

2. Everett W. Hall, *Categorical Analysis* (Chapel Hill, N.C.: The University of North Carolina Press, 1964), pp. 93-132 and Kai Nielsen, "Mill's Proof of Utility" in Henry Garven (ed.), *New Dimensions in Humanities and Social Sciences.*

3. Brian Medlin, "Ultimate Principles and Ethical Egoism" in Paul W. Taylor (ed.), *Problems of Moral Philosophy,* second edition (Encino, Calif.: Dickenson Publishing Company, 1972), p. 122.

4. John Hospers, "Baier and Medlin on Ethical Egoism" in William K. Frankena and John T. Granrose (eds.) *Introductory Readings in Ethics* (Englewood Cliffs, N.J.: Prentice-Hall, 1974), pp. 61-67.

5. Ibid., p. 67.

6. Ibid.

7. Jesse Kalin, "In Defense of Egoism" in David Gauthier (ed.), *Morality and Rational Self-Interest* (Englewood Cliffs, N.J.: Prentice-Hall, 1970), pp. 64-87.

8. See chapters 8 and 14 of this volume.

# 8

# Why Should I Be Moral?

## I

Subjectivism as an ethical theory is dead. As a meta-ethical analysis of what is meant when a moral judgment is made, it claims that all moral judgments are in reality only about the attitudes of the person who makes the judgment. According to this theory, if $A$ says 'The execution of Nagy was vile', he simply means 'I disapprove of the execution of Nagy'. But the truth-values of these sentences are obviously not the same. $A$ might disapprove of the execution of Nagy but he still could reasonably ask if this execution was vile. Autobiographical reports are not in themselves taken as decisive evidence for the truth of moral claims. But in finding out what $A$'s attitudes really are, we discover whether or not $A$ disapproves of the execution of Nagy. Objections of this type have been correctly regarded as decisive objections to such a subjective meta-ethic.

Yet for newcomers (students, interested onlookers, and the like) and for some professionals, too, there is something too easy about this refutation of subjectivism. Variations of subjectivism have been recurrent in the history of philosophy from Gorgias to Bertrand Russell. Some of them have been foolish, some simply confused, but to suggest that these theories have been *simply* foolish and without point seems to me *prima facie* implausible. In this essay I shall attempt to show why this is so; I shall attempt to indicate a plausible line of reasoning, a common sense core, in these subjective ethical theories. (Here again the task will be to elicit a really crucial use of 'subjectivism' in reflections about human conduct. The view often called "naive subjectivism" is for the most part a strawman of certain philosophical analysts). Once I have made explicit what the common sense core of this subjectivism

Originally published in *Methodos* 15, nos. 59–60 (1963): 275–306.

is, I shall examine what considerations can be reasonably brought against it. In order to get more directly to the core of my argument I shall assume here the correctness of two major contentions.

First, I shall assume the general correctness of the claim developed at length in Hare's *The Language of Morals* and Nowell-Smith's *Ethics,* that moral and evaluational utterances are parts of practical discourse and that a complete justification of any practical claim involves reference to the attitudes of the parties involved or to the decisions they would make. I am aware that this is a controversial claim and that unless carefully stated, it is likely to be misleading and unless carefully qualified it is wrong. Nevertheless, I believe there are careful formulations of it that are correct, though I shall not argue for its correctness here.

Secondly, I shall assume what I have argued for elsewhere,[1] namely, that it makes sense to ask 'Why should people be moral?' and 'Why should I be moral?' as long as we do not construe the 'should' in the above two questions as a moral 'should'. Only if the 'should' is construed morally, are the questions above like 'Why are all round things circular?'

Without entering into a defense of this second point, let me leave the reminder that there are a multitude of uses of 'should' and 'ought' which are not moral uses, i.e., 'I should fill my fountain pen for it's writing poorly', 'People ought to mix their TV viewing with a little theater-going', 'The beam should be placed here', 'The level ought to be longer', etc. The second-mentioned sentence is clearly not a technical injunction but gives advice as to how to act in the sphere of human conduct. Yet it is not distinctively moral, for we would not ordinarily say that it is evil to refuse to obey it, though a person who would seriously assert it would say that peoples' lives would be enhanced if they did follow it. There are clearly standard uses of 'ought' that are not moral uses though they are a part of the practical language of human conduct.

'Why should people be moral?' and 'Why should I be moral?' are indeed unusual questions, but the 'should' in them does not function in an unusual way any more than it does in 'Why should people never wear sports jackets to cocktail parties?' A recognition of the intelligibility of the odd question 'Why be Moral?' naturally arises in relation to the old saw, "Egoism and Ethics."

The frequently obscured common sense core of subjectivism can be seen most readily from a natural reaction to a refutation of ethical egoism. It is necessary to recall that ethical egoism is not a psychological doctrine of human motivation, so it is not necessary for the so-called ethical egoist to hold that all men always seek their own good even when it conflicts with the good of others. Rather, the so-called ethical egoist claims each person *ought* to seek his own good as the sole end worth seeking for its own sake.[2] It is important to note the qualifiers 'always' and 'worth seeking for its own sake'.

Many non-egoistic views would claim that we frequently ought to seek our own good or even that we have a *prima facie* right to seek our own good except in those situations where it conflicts with the common good. The ethical egoist is distinctive in claiming we always ought to seek our own good and that we always ought to regard this as the sole aim worthy of pursuit for its own sake; that is to say, the position I am concerned with here is that of an ethical egoism of ends or what Brian Medlin has called a "categorical egoism."[3] But it not only must be a categorical egoism, it must also be a universal egoism if it is to make a claim to be a normative ethic or even a way-of-life. Note I said, "Each person ought always to seek his own good," that is, "everyone ought always to seek his own good as the sole end worth seeking for its own sake." This is very different from an individual egoism which claims that the person making the claim should seek his own good as his only rational end.

Universal categorical ethical egoism will not do as a meta-ethical theory purporting to analyze what is meant when people say something is morally good or obligatory; and if it is offered as a radical normative ethic it likewise gets into intolerable paradoxes. In order to remain intelligible, egoism must be put forth as an individual and not as a universal egoism. But, as such, it also fails to meet the minimum conditions necessary for something to count as a 'morality', as that word is ordinarily and intelligibly used. However, it is just this individual egoism that is at the heart of the matter for the subjectivist. He wants to know why *he* shouldn't be an individual egoist. (Remember the 'shouldn't' here does not have a moral force, though it does have a normative force.)

The dogmatic-sounding contentions of the above paragraph need to be established. I do not want to write another essay on the refutation of egoism.[4] But the following remarks should make the essential points and prepare the way for what is to follow.

To count as an ethical doctrine, an ethical egoism of ends must be understood as claiming that each person ought to seek his own good as an end and consider the good of others only when this would in his judgment further his own good. What purports to be our standard of moral appraisal is personal; that is to say, each of us should always ask ourselves when deliberating on how we ought to act: 'Is this rule or this action or this attitude in my rational self-interest?' If it is in one's rational interest then it ought always to be done, if not, not. But, as Baier has ably argued, such a standard could not be a moral standard for we have moral standards to impartially adjudicate the conflicting interests of individuals and groups; but if each individual's own rational self-interest is taken as the standard, in reality we have no standard by which to adjudicate these conflicting interests. The very *raison d'être* of morality has been frustrated. Thus self-interest, no matter how enlightened, cannot be our standard of *moral* appraisal. "Ethical ego-ism" cannot possibly be an ethical or moral doctrine.

More could be said about this—there are moves and countermoves that could still be made—but I have given what I take to be the most funda-mental reason why egoism is not a possible moral stance.[5] So-called ethi-cal egoism is not a radically different "moral geometry," "a perverse mor-ality" or even an iconoclastic morality. It isn't a morality or even a possible morality at all. If we are to be consistent egoists we must be individual ego-ists, and this is to simply reject the claims of anything that could conceivably count as a morality. As Medlin puts it, such "indifference to morals may be wicked, but it is not a perverse morality."[6]

If individual egoism is not dressed up as a kind of morality—something it can't possibly be—it can be put in a logically impeccable way. It can be a *personal,* rationally thought-out plan or policy of action.

But for a man like Thrasymachus who is willing to question the claims of the whole moral enterprise, why isn't individual egoism a viable alterna-tive? He could admit that Butler is perfectly right—people don't always act egoistically—but he could go on to claim that only a benighted fool insists on trying to be a morally good man. A wise man will not be duped by all the humbug about morality learned at Nannie's knee.

Surely one crucial question that any reflective individual in any age must face is the question, 'What kind of life would be a happy life? What sort of people should we strive to become so that we as individuals can be happy?' The individual egoist, as well as the moral agent, is (or at least can be) vi-tally concerned with this question. Such an egoist, if he is wise, has consid-ered the claims of morality and has decided that he will not attain genuine and lasting happiness by striving to be a morally good man, though it may be good tactics usually to be a man of good morals. It is his belief that the way of morality is not usually the way of happiness. And if and when it is, it ought to be pursued only because it will bring the pursuer happiness. To be sure, an intelligent individual egoist will not go around proclaiming that everyone should only look after himself. He may, if he is so *inclined,* pass on his insight to his family and some close friends, but he will not try to become an ethical egoist or try to base conventional morality on ego-ism. This would be the very epitome of foolishness. In certain contexts, he may even find it expedient to mouth "the high-minded pomposities of this morning's editorial." Such behavior, so to say, gives him a good press. But he has decided to act on the personal principle: Always look after yourself and no one else, unless looking after someone else will benefit you.

True, there cannot be an egoistic way of life or *Weltanschauung philos-ophie* but there could be a deliberate, rationally thought out and consistently adhered to personal policy of individual egoism. Brunton correctly notes, "There can be intelligent, self-controlled people, with a plan of life, who care only for themselves."[7] Egoism cannot be an ethical doctrine but the man committed to individual egoism still has a use for 'I *ought* to consider only my own good' as distinguished from 'I only care about myself.' The first normative (though not moral) sentence indicates a settled policy of action. The latter, by contrast, indicates what may be only a momentary or very impermanent reaction. The token 'ought' when used in such a context has more than just the common mark or noise in common with the token 'ought' used in a moral context. In both instances they are only properly used if in some way they indicate a settled policy as distinct from a momentary whim, emotion, or impulse.

Thus, I do not see anything logically inconsistent about individual egoism so long as we don't try to extend it into a new rival morality or into an iconoclastic world view. A view that exhibits a contempt for all moral considerations whatsoever, could not possibly be a moral view, not even a perverse moral view. But a consistent individual egoism, intelligently pursued, is not a doctrine; it is not something that would be articulated by an intelligent egoist. Yet privately a person might adopt it as his policy of life.

Why shouldn't he? (Recall the 'shouldn't' here is not a moral 'shouldn't'.) Why is he (or is he?) irrational or mistaken if he follows this egoistic policy? Surely it is not in our *interest* for him to act immorally, but why shouldn't he or I or even you? Why should the "existing individual" who is trying to decide how to live happily, or significantly, opt for the point of view of morality rather than an intelligent and carefully controlled individual egoism?

Imagine yourself studying all the meta-ethical treatises, the systems of normative ethics, the sage advice of the wise men, in short, all the claims of morality. Then imagine yourself in the quiet of your own study weighing up—not for others but for yourself alone—these considerations against the considerations in favor of individual egoism. Why should *you* choose to act morally rather than non-morally?

This question, which is at least as old as Plato, has been traditionally imbedded in the thick muck of metaphysics.[8] Often it has been confused with a lot of other questions and recently it has been too lightly dismissed as nonsensical or absurd. The *feeling* emerges that finally there is no real argument here, one way or another; one must just opt for one policy rather than another. Here Sartrean or Kierkegaardian talk about decisions and anxiety *seems* correct. Subjectivism again raises its ugly head. We are tempted to say that here decision or commitment is king. Emotional energy may go into our commitment to morality but in a "cool hour" we cannot discover decisive reasons for acting in either way. There seem to be no decisive reason for our choice here; nor can we conceive of a non-question-begging general procedure that would enable us to decide between these conflicting policies.[9]

Reflective people, uncorrupted by philosophical theories, can be brought by ordinary reflection over morality to recognize the point I have just made.

The non-philosophical idioms 'It's a value judgment' or 'It's finally a matter of what sort of a person you want to be', reflect just this point. The
very anxiety that any slight reference to subjectivism arouses in some people's breasts counts (I believe) for rather than against my claim. We do not
come to a conclusion of this sort unambivalently. In reflecting about morality and human conduct, we are tempted finally to say that you must just
decide what sort of person you want to be. No intellectual considerations
will settle the matter for you here.

It is just this belief that seems to me to be the commonsense core of
subjectivism. But is it a belief that we can and should accept as clear-minded,
rational human beings? Can we rationally defend taking a moral point of
view? Are there decisive reasons for accepting the claims of morality such
that any rational "un-moved spectator of the actual" would have to assent
to them? In the next section I shall turn to this question.


## II

Why then be moral? We need initially to note that this question actually
ought to be broken down into two questions, namely, (1) 'Why should people
be moral?' or 'Why should there be a morality at all?' and (2) 'Why should
I be moral?' As will become evident, these questions ought not in the name
of clarity, to be confused. But they have been run together; in asking for
a justification for the institution of morality both questions are relevant and
easily confused. 'Why be moral?' nicely straddles these questions. In this section I shall first examine some traditional, and I believe unhelpful, answers
to the above general questions. There the general question is not broken down
as it should be and in examining these views I shall not break it down either.
After noting the difficulties connected with these approaches, I shall state
what I believe to be a satisfactory answer to the question, 'Why should there
be a morality at all?' and indicate why it leaves untouched the harder question, 'Why should I be moral?'

There is a prior consideration that we must first dispose of. In considering both of these questions we must be careful to distinguish the *causes*
of a man's being moral from the *reasons* he gives for being moral. If one
is a little careful about the implications of the word 'likes', Bradley seems
perfectly right in saying: "A man is moral because he likes being moral; and
he likes it, partly because he has been brought up to the habit of liking it,
and partly because he finds it gives him what he wants, while its opposite
does not do so."[10] In other words people are moral primarily because they
have been conditioned to be moral. The human animal is a social animal
and (as Butler and Hume observed) people normally tend to consider the
welfare of others as well as their own welfare. People indeed act selfishly

but they also take out life insurance, feel anxiety over the troubles of others, and even have moments of mild discomfort at the thought that life on this planet may some day be impossible. People react in this way because they have been taught or conditioned to so react. But, the 'because' here is explanatory and *not* justificatory. It explains in a very general way what *makes* or *causes* people to be moral. But the question I am concerned with here is a quite different one. In asking 'Why should people be moral?' I am asking the question, 'What good reasons do people have for being moral?' In asking about the justification for acting morally, I am only incidentally concerned with an explanation of the causes of moral behavior.

What good reasons are there for being moral? And if there are good reasons for being moral are they sufficient or decisive reasons?

There is a short, snappy answer to my question. The plain man might well say: "People ought to be moral because it is wicked, evil, morally reprehensible not to be moral. We have the very best reasons for being moral, namely that it is immoral not to be moral." The plain man (or at the very least the plain Western Man and not *just* the ordinary Oxford Don) would surely agree with Bradley "that consciousness, when unwarped by selfishness and not blinded by sophistry is convinced that to ask for the Why? is simple immorality. . . ."[11] The correct answer to the question 'Why be moral?' is simply that this is what we ought to do.

This short answer will not do, for the plain man has failed to understand the question. A clear-headed individual could not be asking for *moral* justification for being moral. This would be absurd. Rather he is asking the practical question: why should people be bound by the conventions of morality at all? He would not dispute Baier's contention that "it is generally believed that when reasons of self-interest conflict with moral reasons, then moral reasons override those of self-interest."[12] It is perfectly true that the plain man regards moral reasons as superior to all others and it is, of course, in accordance with reason to follow superior or overriding reasons, but if a clear-headed man asks "Why should we be moral?" he is challenging the very grading criteria those ordinary convictions rest on. He would acknowledge that it is indeed morally reprehensible or wicked not to act morally. But he would ask: "So what?" And he might even go on to query: "What is the good of all this morality anyway? Are not those Marxists and Freudians right who claim that the whole enterprise of morality is nothing but an ideological device to hoodwink people into *not* seeking what they really want? Why should people continue to fall for this conjuring trick? To call someone 'wicked' or 'evil' is to severely grade them down, but why should people accept any *moral* grading criteria at all?"

There are several traditional replies to this. But all of them are unsatisfactory.

One traditional approach advocated by Plato and Bishop Butler, among others, claims that people should be moral because they will not be happy otherwise. Being moral is at least a necessary condition for being happy.

For Butler the argument takes the following form. Human beings are so constituted that they will, generally speaking, act morally. When they don't act morally they will clearly recognize they were mistaken in not doing so. The human animal has a conscience and this conscience not only causes people to act in a certain way, but is in fact a *norm* of action. Conscience guides as well as goads; the deliverances of conscience are both action-evoking and a source of moral knowledge. Conscience tells the moral agent what to do even in specific situations. It clearly and unequivocally tells him to always act morally and he is so constituted that if he ignores the dictates of his conscience he will not be happy. In other words, Butler agrees with Plato in claiming that Thrasymachus and other amoralists are fundamentally mistaken about the true interests of a human being.

That it is in the human animal's best interest to live virtuously is no more established by Butler than it is by Plato.[13] Plato is reduced to analogy, myth and mystagogy and, as Duncan-Jones points out, Butler is finally pushed to concede that "full acceptance of the conclusion that human nature is satisfiable and only satisfiable by virtue depends on revelation."[14] In the face of what clearly seem to be genuine exceptions to the claim that it is in the individual's self-interest always to act morally, Butler is driven to remark: "All shall be set right at the final distribution of things."[15]

Some intuitionist may argue that while this Butlerian move won't do, it still remains the case that Butler could rightly have said that we just directly (in some sense) perceive or see the fittingness or suitability of always acting morally. To meet this point we would have to argue against the whole logical or epistemological machinery of intuitionism. We would need to question (as Toulmin has) such a use of 'intuition', to point out that neither 'see' nor 'apprehend' is at home here, and challenge the notion that ethical words simply refer to qualities or relations. But in view of the incisive literature criticizing this overall intuitionist claim, I believe it is quite unnecessary to refute this intuitionist claim once more. At any rate, I have no new arguments to deploy beyond those offered by Toulmin, MacDonald, Strawson, Robinson, Nowell-Smith and Edwards.

There is a more defensible answer to the question: 'Why should people be moral?' It was first urged (in the Western world, at least) by Epicurus; later it was developed and given its classical forceful statement by Hobbes. Bertrand Russell elaborates it in his own way in his *Human Society in Ethics and Politics* (1955) and Kurt Baier has clearly elucidated and defended Hobbes's argument in his *The Moral Point of View* (1958). This Hobbesian argument, which within its proper scope seems to me conclusive, can readily be used to meet the objections of those "tough-minded" Marxists and Freudians who do not want the usual fare of "sweetness and light."

Hobbes points out that as a matter of fact the restless, malcontent, foraging human animal wants "the commodious life"; that is, he wants above all peace, security, freedom from fear. He wants to satisfy his desires to the maximum extent, but one of the very strongest and most persistent of these desires is the desire to be free from the "tooth and claw" of a life in which each man exclusively seeks his own interest and totally neglects to consider the interests of others. In such a situation life would indeed be "nasty, brutish and short." We could not sleep at night without fear of violent death; we could not leave what we possessed without well-warranted anxiety over its being stolen or destroyed. Impulses and inclinations would be held in check only when they would lead to behavior detrimental to the individual's own interest. Where peoples' interests conflict, each man would (without the institution of morality) resort to subterfuge or violence to gain his own ends. A pervasive Dobuan-like suspicion would be normal and natural . . . even rational in such a situation. Every individual would be struggling for the good things of life and no rule except that of his own self-interest would govern the struggle. The universal reign of the rule of exclusive self-interest would lead to the harsh world that Hobbes called "the state of nature." And, as Baier puts it, "At the same time, it will be clear to everyone that universal obedience to certain rules overriding self-interest would produce a state of affairs which serves everyone's interest much better than his unaided pursuit of it in a state where everyone does the same."[16] Baier goes on to point out that "the very *raison d'être* of a morality is to yield reasons which override the reasons of self-interest in those cases when everyone's following self-interest would be harmful to everyone."[17]

When people ask: why should we have a morality—any morality, even a completely conventional morality—we answer that if everyone acts morally, or generally acts morally, people will be able to attain more of what they want. It is obvious that in a moral community more good will be realized than in a non-moral collection of people. Yet in the interest of realizing a commodious life for all, voluntary self-sacrifice is sometimes necessary; but the best possible life for everyone is attainable only if people act morally; the greatest possible good is realizable only when everyone puts aside his own self-interest when it conflicts with the common good.

If people ask: 'Why should one choose that course of action which will probably promote the greatest possible good?' we are quite correct in answering as Baylis does: There is probably nothing better one could possibly do instead.[18] I would only add that Baylis's caution here is rhetorical for there is no place at all for the qualifying word 'probably'.

## III

Yet an answer to the question 'Why should people be moral?' does not meet one basic question that the thorough-going skeptic may feel about the claims of morality. The "existing individual" may want to know why *he,* as an individual, ought to accept the standards of morality when it is not in *his* personal interest to do so. He may have no doubt at all about the general utility of the moral enterprise. But *his* not recognizing the claims of morality will not greatly diminish the total good. Reflecting on this, he asks himself: "Why should *I* be moral when I will not be caught or punished for not acting morally?"

Recall how Glaucon and Adeimantus readily agree that Socrates has established that morality is an indispensable social practice. But their perplexity over morals is not at an end. They want Socrates to go on and prove that the individual ought to be moral even when he is perfectly safe in not acting morally. Someone might readily agree that the Hobbesian arguments presented in II establish that the greatest total good will be realized if people act morally, but he still wants to now 'Why should I be moral in those cases where acting morally will not be in *my* rational self-interest?' He might say; to himself—though certainly if he were wise he would not proclaim it—"There is no reason why I should act morally."

Such an individual egoist cannot be refuted by indicating that his position cannot be a moral position. He may grant the overall social good of morality and he may be fully aware that 'Why should I do my duty?' cannot be a moral question—there is indeed no room at all for that question as a moral question, but an individual egoist is not trying to operate within the bounds of morality. He is trying to decide whether or not he should *become* a moral agent or he may—in a more theoretical frame of mind— wonder if any *reason* can be given for his remaining a moral agent. Prichard is quite right in arguing that the *moral* agent has no choice here. To assert 'I'll only be moral when being moral is in my rational interest' is to rule out, in a quite *a priori* fashion, the very possibility of one's being moral as long as one has such an intention. To be a moral agent entails that one gives up seriously entertaining whether one should deliberately adopt a policy of individual egoism. 'X is moral' entails 'X will try to do his duty even when so acting is not in his personal interest'. Thus we must be very *careful* how we take the individual egoist's question: his question is, 'Should I become moral and give up my individual egoism or shall I remain such an egoist?' If he decides to remain an individual egoist he will have made the decision that *he* ought to behave like a man of good morals when and only when such behavior is in his own personal interest. Now what grounds (if any) have we for saying that a man who makes such a decision is mistaken or irrational? What (if any) intellectual mistake has he made? Remember, he doesn't challenge Prichard's remarks about the logical relations of duty to interest or the Hobbesian argument that morality is an essential social device if we are to have a commodious life. But he still wants to know why *he* should be moral rather than non-moral.

The individual egoist may well believe that those who insist on being moral even when it is not in their self-interest are really benighted fools duped by the claims of society. A "really clever man" will take as his own personal norm of action the furtherance of his own good. Everything else must give pride of place to this. He will only endeavor to make it seem perfectly obvious that he is a staunch pillar of the community so as to avoid reprisals from his society.

Can such an individual egoist be shown to be wrong or to be asking a senseless question? What arguments can be given for an affirmative answer to the question: 'Should I be moral?'

Kant recognized as clearly as did Prichard that there is no room for this question within morality, but he felt, in a way Prichard apparently did not, that nonetheless such a question needs answering and that this was one of the main reasons we need God and the graces of religion. Thus, Kant found it necessary to posit God and immortality as postulates of the practical reason so that there would be a heaven in which the morally good man would be rewarded for doing his duty because it is his duty. But these principles of practical reason are, for Kant, finally based on the demands of the moral will. The universe just couldn't be so bad as to allow evil to go permanently unrequited and the man of good will unrewarded. Sidgwick too (strangely enough) created a theological postulate to provide for a harmony between universal and individual happiness. We assume that God so rewards and punishes that it is always in everyone's interest to seek to further the greatest good for the greatest number.

But it is increasingly difficult for an educated modern even to believe in God, to say nothing of making Him such a *deus ex machina*. As J. J. C. Smart rightly remarks: "More and more it seems that man is just part of nature. In the light of modern science he appears to be a very complicated physico-chemical mechanism, who arose by natural selection from simpler mechanisms, and there may well be millions of planets in the universe with similar, or higher, forms of life on them."[19] Yet for the sake of the argument let us assume (what indeed ought not to be assumed) that we have an appropriate use of 'God' and let us also assume that we have some evidence that there is an X such that X is God. Even making these assumptions, it does take the utmost vanity and the epitome of self-delusion to believe that such a Being could be so concerned with our weal and woe. And to postulate God *because* of His practical necessity or to postulate immortality to try to insure a justification of morality is just too convenient. It is deserving of the scorn Bradley heaped upon it.

Medlin does not engage in such rationalization but without further ado plays Dr. Johnson. He comments: "If the good fellow wants to know how he should justify conventional morality to the individual egoist, the answer is that he *shouldn't* and *can't*. Buy your car elsewhere, blackguard him whenever you meet, and let it go at that."[20] A philosopher, Medlin goes on to comment, is "not a rat-catcher" and it is not his "job to dig vermin out of such burrows as individual egoism."[21] Inasmuch as Medlin is pointing out that the individual egoist's position isn't and can't be a moral alternative to conventional morality, he is perfectly right in his strictures; but as an answer to the question as I have posed it, Medlin's reply is simply irrelevant.

Must we say at this juncture that practical reasoning has come to an end and that we must simply *decide* for ourselves how to act? Is it just that, depending on what attitudes I actually happen to have, I strive to be one sort of a person rather than another without any sufficient rational guides to tell me what I am to do? Does it come to just that—finally? Subjectivists say (at such a juncture) that there are no such guides. And this time there seems to be a strong strand of common sense or hardheaded street wisdom to back up the subjectivists' position.

I do not believe that we are that badly off. There are weighty considerations of a mundane sort in favor of the individual's taking the moral point of view. But I think the subjectivists are right in claiming that it is a mistake to argue that a man is simply irrational if he does not at all times act morally. It is indeed true that if a man deliberately refuses to do what he acknowledges as morally required of him, we do say he is irrational or better unreasonable. But here 'irrational' and 'unreasonable' have a distinctively *moral* use. There are other quite standard employments of the word in which we would not say that such a man is irrational.[22] In all contexts the word 'irrational' has the evaluative force of strongly condemning something or other. In different contexts the criteria for what is to be called 'irrational' differ. In Toulmin's terms the criteria are field-dependent and the force of the word is field-independent. In saying a man acts irrationally in not assenting to any moral considerations whatsoever we need not be claiming that he makes any mistakes in observation or deduction. Rather we are condemning him for not accepting the moral point of view. But he is asking why he, as an individual in an ongoing community, should always act as a moral agent. He is not asking for *motivation* but for a *reason* for being a morally good man. He wants to know what intellectual mistake the man who acts non-morally must make. To be told such a man is immoral and in *that sense* is unreasonable or irrational is not to the point.

The subjectivist I am interested in contends that in the nature of the case there can be no reasons here for being moral rather than non-moral. One must just *decide* to act one way or another without reasons. There is much to be said for the subjectivist's claim here but even here I think there are rational considerations in favor of an individual's opting for morality.

## IV

Before I state and examine those considerations I would like to show how two recent tantalizingly straightforward answers will not do. Baier has offered one and Hospers the other.

Baier says that when we ask 'Why should I be moral?' we are asking 'Which is the course of action supported by the best reasons?' Since we can show along Hobbesian lines that men generally have better reasons for being moral than for being non-moral the individual has "been given a reason for being moral, for following moral reasons rather than any other. . . ." The reason is simply that "they are better reasons than any other." *But in the above type situation,* when I am asking, 'Why should I be moral?' I am not concerned with which course of action is supported by the best reasons *sans phrase* or with what is the best thing to do for all concerned. I am only concerned with what is a good reason *for me.* I want to know what is the best thing *for me* to do; that is, I want to know what will make for *my* greatest good.

Baier might point out that an individual has the best reasons for acting morally because by each man's acting morally the greatest possible good will be realized. Yet, if the reference is to men severally and not to them as a group, it might well be the case that an individual's acting immorally might in effect further the total good, for his bad example might spur others on to greater acts of moral virtue. But be that as it may, the individual egoist could still legitimately reply to Baier: "All of what you say is irrelevant unless realization of the greatest total good serves *my* best interests. When and only when the reasons for all involved are also the best reasons for me am I personally justified in adopting the moral point of view."

We can, of course, criticize a so-called ethical egoist for translating the question 'What is the best thing to do?' into the question 'What is the best thing *for me* to do?' In morality we are concerned with what is right, what is good and what is supported by the best reasons, *period;* but recall that the *individual* egoist is challenging the sufficiency of moral reasons which we, as social beings, normally grant to the moral enterprise. (We need to reflect on the sense of 'sufficiency' here. The egoist is not challenging the point of having moral codes. He is challenging the sufficiency of the moral life as a device to enhance *his* happiness. But is this "a goal of morality"? It is not.) He is asking for reasons for *his* acting morally and unfortunately Baier's short answer does not meet the question Baier sets out to answer, though as I have already indicated it does answer the question, 'Why should people be moral?'

Hospers has a different argument which, while wrong, carries a crucial insight that takes us to the very heart of our argument. Like Baier, Hospers does not keep apart the question 'Why should I be moral?' from 'Why should people be moral?' After giving a psychological explanation of what motivates people to be moral, Hospers considers what *reasons* there are for being moral.

Virtue is its own reward and if an act is indeed right this is a sufficient reason for performing the act. We have been operating on the wrong assumption—an assumption that we inherited from Plato—namely, that if it isn't in our interest to behave morally we have no reason to do it. But it does not follow that if a right action is not in our interest we have no reason for doing it. If we ask 'Why should we do this act rather than other acts we might have done instead' the answer 'Because it is the right act' is, says Hospers, "the best answer and ultimately the only answer."[23]

It is indeed true that *if we are reasoning from the moral point of view* and if an act is genuinely the right act to do in a given situation, then it is the act we should do. Once a moral agent knows that such and such an action is the right *one to do in* these circumstances he has *eo ipso* been supplied with the reason for doing it. But in asking 'Why should I be moral?' an individual is asking why *he* should (non-moral sense of 'should') reason as a moral agent. He is asking, and *not* as a moral agent, what reason there is for his doing what is right.

It is at this point that Hospers's reply—and his implicit defense of his simple answer—exhibits insight. It will, Hospers points out, be natural for an individual to ask this question only when "the performance of the act is *not* to his own interest."[24] It is also true that *any* reason we give other than a reason which will show that what is right is in his rational self-interest will be rejected by him. Hospers remarks "What he wants, and he will accept no other answer, is a self-interested reason" for acting as a moral agent.[25] But this is like asking for the taste of pink, for "the situation is *ex hypothesi* one in which the act required of him is contrary to his interest. Of course it is impossible to give him a reason *in accordance with his interest for acting contrary* to his interest."[26] 'I have a reason for acting in accordance with my interest which is contrary to my interests' is a contradiction. The man who requests an answer to 'Why should I do what is right when it is not in my interest?' is making a "self-contradictory request." We come back once more to Prichard and Bradley and see that after all our "question" is a logically absurd one—no real question at all. The person asking "the question" cannot "without self-contradiction, accept a reason of self-interest for doing what is contrary to his interest and yet he will accept no reason except one of self-interest."[27]

His "question" is no real question at all but at best a non-rational expression of a personal predicament. Our problem has been dissolved—the "common sense core of subjectivism" has turned out to be the core of the onion.

But has it really? Is any further question here but a confused request for *motivation* to do what we know we have the best reasons for doing? Let us take stock. Hospers has in effect shown us: 1) That x's being right entails *both* x should be done (where 'should' has a moral use) and there is (from the moral point of view) a *sufficient reason* for doing x ('I ought to do what is right' is a tautology where 'ought' is used morally); 2) That from the point of view of self-interest the only reasons that can be sufficient reasons for acting are self-interested reasons. This again is an obvious tautology. The man asking 'Why should I do what is right when it is not in my self-interest?' has made a self-contradictory request *when he is asking this question as a self-interested question.*

These two points must be accepted, but what if an individual says: As I see it, there are two alternatives: either I act from the moral point of view, where logically speaking I must try to do what is right, or I act from the point of view of rational self-interest, where I must seek to act according to my rational self-interest. But is there any *reason* for me always to act from one point of view rather than another when I am a member in good standing in a moral community? True enough, Hospers has shown me that *from the moral point of view* I have no alternative but to try to do what is right and from a *self-interested point of view* I have no rational alternative but to act according to what I judge to be in my rational self-interest. But what I want to know is what I am to do: Why adopt one point of view rather than another? Is there a good reason *for me,* placed as I am, to adopt the moral point of view or do I just arbitrarily choose, as the subjectivist would argue?

I do not see that Hospers's maneuver has shown this question to be senseless or an expression of a self-contradictory request. Rather his answer in effect brings the question strikingly to the fore by showing how from the moral point of view 'Because it's right' must be a sufficient answer, and how it cannot possibly be a sufficient answer from the point of view of self-interest or from the point of view of an individual challenging the sufficiency of the whole moral point of view, as a personal guide for his actions. It seems that we have two strands of discourse here with distinct criteria and distinct canons of justification. We just have to make up our minds which point of view we wish to take. The actual effect of Hospers's argument is to display in fine rational order the common sense core of subjectivism: *at this point* we just choose and there can be no reasons for our choice.

It will not do for Hospers to argue that an individual could not rationally choose a non-moral way of life or ethos, for in choosing to act from a self-interested vantage point an individual is not choosing a way of life; he is, instead, adopting a personal policy of action in a very limited area for himself alone. Such an individual might well agree with Hospers that a rational way of life is one, the choice of which, is (1) free, (2) enlightened, and (3) impartial.[28] This remark, he could contend, is definitive of what we *mean* by 'a rational way of life.' An intelligent egoist would even urge that such a way of life be adopted but he could still ask himself (it wouldn't be prudent to ask others) what *reason* there would be for *him* or any single individual, living in a community committed to such a way of life to act in accordance with it. (This need not be a question which logically speaking requires a self-interested answer. An existing individual is trying to make up his mind what he is to do).

To reply, 'If it's rational then it should be done', is to neglect the context-dependent criteria of both 'rational' and 'should'. There are both moral and non-moral uses of 'should' and 'rational'. In the above example Hospers is using 'rational' in a moralistic sense; as Hospers puts it, "Let me first define 'rationality' with regard to a way of life" and while a way of life is not exhausted by moral considerations it essentially includes them.[29] Only if 'rational' and 'should' belong to the same strand of discourse is 'If it is rational then it should be done' analytic. Something could be rational from the moral point of view (morally reasonable) and yet imprudent (irrational from the point of view of self-interest). If we were asking what we should do in terms of self-interest, it would not follow in this case that we should do what is rational in the sense of 'morally reasonable'. Conversely, where 'What is rational' means 'What is prudent' it would not follow that what is rational is what, morally speaking, we ought to do.[30]

Thus, it seems to me that neither Baier's nor Hospers's answers will do. We are left with our original question, now made somewhat more precise, 'Is there a good reason for me as an individual in a moral community to always act morally no matter how I am placed?' There is no room *in morality* for this question but this question can arise when we think about how to act and when, as individuals, we reflect on what ends of action to adopt. But as a result of Hospers's analysis, must we now say that here we must 1) simply make a choice concerning how to act or 2) where there is no live question concerning how to act it is still the case that there can be no non-question begging justification for an individual, were he faced with such a choice, to act one way rather than another? (Of course there is the very best *moral* justification for his acting as a moral agent. But that is not our concern here, for here we are asking: why reason morally?)

Here the pull of subjectivism is strong—and at this point it has an enlightened common sense on its side. But I think there is something more to be said that will take the bite out of such subjectivism. In trying to bring this out, I am in *one sense* going back to Plato. It is, of course, true that we can't ask for a self-interested reason for doing what is right where *ex hypothesi* the action is not in our self-interest. But in actual moral situations it is not so clear what is in our self-interest and what is not, and often what is *apparently* in our self-interest is really not. Part of my counter to the subjectivist, and *here* I am with Plato, is that if a man decides *repeatedly* to act non-morally where he thinks he can get away with it, he will not, as a very general rule, be happy.

This isn't the whole of my case by any means, but I shall start with this consideration.

V

Suppose that I, in a fully rational frame of mind, am trying to decide whether or not to adopt individual egoism as my personal policy of action. I ask myself: "Should I pursue a selfish policy or should I consider others as well even when in my best judgment it doesn't profit me?" In my deliberation I might well ask myself: "Will I really be happy if I act without regard for others?" And here it is natural to consider the answer of the ancients. Plato and Aristotle believe that only the man who performs just actions has a well-ordered soul. And only the man with a well-ordered soul will be "truly happy." If I am thrown off course by impulse and blind action I will not have a well-ordered soul; I will not be genuinely happy. But the alternative I am considering is not between impulsive blind action and rational, controlled action, but between two forms of deliberate, rationally controlled activity. Why is my soul any less well-ordered or why do I realize myself (to shift to Bradley's idiom) any the less if I act selfishly than if I act morally? If it is replied, "You will 'realize yourself more' because most people have found that they are happiest when they are moral," I can again ask: "But what has that to do with me? Though I am one man among men, I may not in this respect be like other men. Most people have neurotic compulsions about duties and are prey to customary taboos and tribal loyalties. If I can free myself from such compulsions and superstitions will I be any the less happy if I am selfish? I should think that I would be happier by being intelligently selfish. I can forget about others and single mindedly go after what I want."

To this last statement Plato and Aristotle would reply that by always acting selfishly a man will not fully realize his distinctively human *areté*. By so acting, he simply will not be responding in a fully human way. We say of a man that he is a 'good man, a truly happy man' when he performs his function well, just as we say a tranquilizer is a 'good tranquilizer' when it performs its function well; that is to say, when the tranquilizer relaxes the tense, harassed individual. But can we properly talk about human beings this way? We do speak of a surgeon as 'a good surgeon' when he cures people by deftly performing operations when and only when people need operations. Similarly, a teacher is 'a good teacher' if he stimulates his students to thought and to assimilate eagerly "the best that has been thought and said in the world." We can indeed speak of the *areté* or "virtue" of the teacher, fireman, preacher, thief or even (as MacIver reminds us) of the wife or unmarried girl.[31] People have certain social roles and they can perform them ill or well. In this sense we can speak of 'a good husband', 'a good father', 'a good Chancellor of the Exchequer. . .', but—MacIver rightly concludes—hardly of "a good man."[32] People, *qua* human beings, do not seem to have a function, purpose, or role. A child can sensibly ask: "What are hammers for?" "What are aspirins for?" "What are dentists for?" but if a child asks "What are people for?" we must point out to him that this question is not really like the others. 'Daddy, what are people for?' is foolish or *at the very least*—even for the Theist—an extremely amorphous question. At best we must quickly strike some religious attitude and some disputed cosmology must be quickly brought in, but no such exigency arises for the cosmologically neutral question, 'Daddy, what are napkins for?' or 'Daddy, what are policemen for?' After all, what is the function of man *as such?* In spite of all his hullabaloo about it, is not Sartre correct in claiming that man has no "essence"—no *a priori* nature—but that human beings are what human beings make of themselves? If a human being acts in an eccentric or non-moral way are we really entitled to say he is any less of a human being?

If we counter that we are indeed entitled to say this, and we then go on to say, "By not acknowledging that we are so entitled, we are in effect overriding or ignoring man's 'distinctively human qualities' " are we not now using 'distinctively human qualities' primarily as a grading label? In such contexts, isn't its actual linguistic function primarily moral? We are disapproving of a way of acting and attempting to guide people away from patterns of behavior that are like this. If we say the consistently selfish man is less human than the moral man, are we not here using 'less human' as a moral grading label and not just as a phrase to describe men? 'More human', on such a use, would not be used to signify those qualities (if there are any) which are common to and distinctive of the human animal; but would be used as an honorific moral label. And *if* it is used *only* to describe how people have behaved then it is perfectly possible for me to ask, "Why should I be more human rather than less?"

Most moderns would not try to meet the question 'Why should I be moral?' in this Greek way, though they still would be concerned with that ancient problem, 'How should I live in order to be truly happy?' A rational man might make this elementary prudential reflection: "If I am thoroughly and consistently selfish and get caught people will treat me badly. I will be an outcast, I will be unloved, all hands will be on guard against me. I may even be retaliated against or punished as an 'irredeemable moral beast.' All of this will obviously make me suffer. Thus, I better not take up such a selfish policy or I will surely be unhappy."

At this point it is natural to take a step which, if pushed too far, cannot but lead to a "desert-island example." It is natural to reply: "Clearly it would be irrational to *appear* selfish. But I don't at all propose to do that. I only propose to look out for 'number one' and only 'number one.' I will do a good turn for others when it is likely, directly or indirectly, to profit me. I will strive to appear to be a man of good morals and I will do a good deed when and only when it is reasonable to believe there will be some personal profit in it. Such a policy of unabashed, outright selfishness would be disastrous to me. Obviously, this is something I will strive to avoid. But I shall keep as the maxim of *my* actions: Always consider yourself first. Only do things for others, when by so acting, it wil profit you, and do not be frankly selfish or openly aggressive except in those situations where no harm is likely to befall you for so acting. Take great pains to see that your selfishness is undetected by those who might harm you."

But, at this point our hypothetical rational egoist would need to consider the reply: "You will regret acting this way. The pangs of conscience will be severe, your superego will punish you. Like Plato's tyrant you will be a miserable, disordered man. Your very mental health will be endangered."

Imperceptibly drawing nearer to a desert-island example, the egoist might reply, "But the phrase 'mental health' is used to describe those well adjusted people who keep straight on the tracks no matter what. I don't intend to be 'healthy' *in that sense*. And, I do not recognize the *authority* of conscience. My conscience is just the internalized demands of Father and Tribe. But why should I assent to those demands, when it doesn't serve my interests? They are irrational, compulsive moralistic demands, and I shall strive to free myself from them."

To this it might be countered, "Granted that conscience has no moral or even rational authority over *you,* you unfortunate man, but practically speaking, you cannot break these bonds so easily. Consciously you may recognize their lack of authority but unconsciously they have and always will continue to have—in spite of all your ratiocination—a dominating grip on you. If you flaunt them, go against them, ignore them, it will cost you your peace of mind, you will pay in psychic suffering, happiness will be denied you. But as a rational egoist happiness is supposedly your goal. And it is wishful thinking to think some psychiatrist will or can take you around this corner. Neither psychoanalysis nor any other kind of therapy can obliterate the 'voice of the superego.' It can at best diminish its demands when they are *excessive*. Your conditioning was too early and too pervasive to turn your back on it now. If you are rational you will not struggle in such a wholesale fashion against these ancient, internalized demands. Thus, you should not act without regard to the dictates of morality if you really want to be happy."

It is at this stage that the rational egoist is likely to use his visa to Desert Island. He might say: "But if I had the power of Gyges and that power included the power to still the nagging voice of my superego, would it not then be reasonable for me to always act in my own self-interest no matter what the effect on others? If there were some non-harmful pill—some moral tranquilizer—that I could take that would 'kill' my conscience but allow me to retain my prudence and intelligence why then, under those circumstances, should I act morally rather than selfishly? What good reason is there for me in that situation to act morally if I don't *want* to?"

It is not sufficient to be told that if most people had Gyges ring (or its modern, more streamlined, equivalent) they would go on acting as they do now. The question is not 'What would most people do if they had Gyges ring?' or even 'What would I do if I had Gyges ring?' The question is rather, 'What should I do?' At this point can *reasons* be found which would convince an intelligent person that even in this kind of situation, he ought to act morally? That is, would it serve his "true interests" (as Plato believes) for him to be moral, even in the event these conditions obtained?

It is just here, I believe, that subjectivism quite legitimately raises its ugly head. If the above desert-island situation did in fact obtain, I think we would have to say that whether it would or would not be in your "true interests" to be moral or non-moral would depend on the sort of person you are. With the possible exception of a few St. Anthony's, we are, as a matter *of fact,* partly egoistic and partly other-regarding in our behavior. There can be no completed non-personal, objective justification for acting morally other than non-morally. In certain circumstances a person of one temperament would find it in his interests to act one way and a person of another temperament to act in another. We have two policies of action to choose from, with distinct criteria of appropriateness and which policy or action will make us happy will depend on the sort of person we *happen* to be.

It is here that many of us feel the "existential bite" of our question. Students, who are reasonably bright and not a little versed in the ways of the world, are often (and rightly) troubled by the successive destruction of first psychological egoism and then ethical egoism. They come to see that individual egoism can't be a moral view, but they feel somehow cheated; somehow, in some way, they sense that something has been put over on them. And I think there is a point to this rather common and persistent feeling and I have tried, in effect, to show what this is. I would *not,* of course, claim that it is always the "Why-should-I-be-moral?" question that troubles a reflective student at this juncture but frequently, like Glaucon and Adeimantus, the student wants to know why, as a solitary, flesh and blood individual, he should be moral. He *feels* that he should be moral, but is he somehow being duped? He wants a *reason* that will be a good and sufficient reason for his being moral, quite apart from *his* feelings or attitudes about the matter. He does not want to be in the position of finally having to decide, albeit after reflection, what sort of person to strive to be. It seems to me that the subjectivists are right in suggesting that this is just what he finally can't avoid doing, that he doesn't have and can't have *the kind* of objectivity he demands here. We need not have existentialist dramatics here, but we do need to recognize the logical and practical force of this point. Most rationalistic and theological ethical theories seem to be mythmaking devices to disguise this *prima facie* uncomfortable fact.


# VI


But need we despair of the rationality of the moral life once we have dug out and correctly placed this irreducible element of choice in reasoning about human conduct? Perhaps some will despair but since it is not the job of a philosopher to be a kind of universal Nannie I don't think he need concern himself to relieve this despair. But, I think, if he will remind people of the exact point on the logical map where this subjectivism correctly enters and make them once more aware of the map as a whole they will—now able to see the forest as well as the trees—be less inclined to despair about the rationality of their acting morally. If one is willing to reason morally, nothing we have said here need upset the objectivity and rationality of moral grading criteria. More importantly here, to admit subjectivism at this point does not at all throw into doubt the Hobbesian defense of the value of morality as a social practice. It only indicates that *in the situation* in which an *individual* is 1) very unlikely to be caught, 2) so rationally in control that he will be very unlikely to develop habits which would lead to his punishment, and 3) is free from the power of his conscience, it might, just might, (if he were a certain kind of person) make him happier to be non-moral than moral. But this is not the usual bad fellow we meet on the streets and the situation is anything but typical.

A recognition of the irrelevance of desert-island examples will provide further relief from moral anxiety, over such subjectivism. Critics of utilitarianism invent situations in which a social practice is, as we use moral language, regarded as obligatory, even though there is no advantage in acting in accordance with it in this particular kind of circumstance. They construct desert-island examples and then crucify the utilitarian with them. They point out, for example, that promises made on desert-islands to a dying man to dispose of his effects in a certain way are considered obligatory even if it is clear that 1) some other disposal of his effects would be more beneficial and 2) that there is no reasonable chance that the breach in trust would be detected. The usual utilitarian answer is that disregarding promises of this sort would weaken our moral character; and, in addition, we cannot be quite sure that such a breach in trust would not be detected or that it would really do more good than harm. Further, to ignore a promise of this sort is bad, for it would tend to weaken the utility of the social *practice* of promise-keeping.

Nowell-Smith, however, is quite correct in saying: "The relentless desert-islander can always break such utilitarian moves by adding stipulations to the terms of the original problem."[33] That is, he will say to the utilitarian, "But what would you say *if* breaking a trust in situations of this type would not weaken the utility of the practice of promise-keeping? Surely it is *intelligible* to suppose that such acts would not weaken people's moral fiber, would not be detected, and would not do more total good than harm." To this the utilitarian can only say that this statement of the desert-islander is a very "iffy proposition," indeed. Nowell-Smith rightly remarks: "The force of these desert-island arguments . . . depend expressly on the improbability of the case supposed."[34] "It is difficult to assess their force precisely because the case *is* improbable and therefore not catered for in our ordinary language."[35] The language of human conduct has the structure it has because the world is as it is and not otherwise. If people and things were very different, the structure of moral codes and the uses of evaluative language presumably would be different. The very form of our talk about human conduct "reflects empirical truths that are so general and obvious that we can afford to ignore exceptions."[36] If through desert-island examples we withdraw that pervasive contextual background it is diffcult to know what is the logically proper thing to say. The logic of the language of human conduct did not develop with such wildly improbable situations in view. It, after all, has a wide range of distinct, practical uses, and it only has application in a certain type of setting. If one of these desert-island situations were to obtain, we would have a good reason, as Wittgenstein clearly saw, to make a linguistic stipulation, that is, we would have to decide what is to be *said* here and our linguistic decision would indeed be an intervention in the world; it would indeed have normative import. But it is neither possible nor necessary that we make all such stipulations in advance and we can hardly reasonably accuse the language of conduct of inadequacy because it does not cater to desert-island cases. It would be like saying that "the language of voting" is inadequate because it does not tell us what to do in a situation in which a senior class, consisting of a thousand, tries to elect a president from four candidates and each time a vote is taken each candidate gets exactly 250 votes. This indeed is a logical possibility, but that *this* logical possibility is not considered in setting out the procedures for voting does not at all indicate an inadequacy in our voting procedures.

Our "Gyges-ring situations" are just such desert-island cases. In fact, Nowell-Smith is quite correct in remarking that the Gyges-ring example in the *Republic* is a paradigm of all such desert-island arguments.

"Would I be happier if I were intelligently selfish in a situation in which I could free myself from guilt feelings, avoid punishment, loss of love, contempt of family and friends, social ostracism, etc.?" To ask this is to ask a desert-island question. Surely we can and do get away with occasional selfish acts—though again note the usual burden of guilt—but given the world as it is, a deliberate, persistent though cunning policy of selfishness is very likely to bring on guilt feelings, punishment, estrangement, contempt, ostracism and the like. A clever man might avoid one or another of these consequences but it would be very unlikely that he could avoid them all or even most of them. And it is truistic to remark that we all want companionship, love, approval, comfort, security and recognition. It is very unlikely that the consistently selfish man can get those things he wants. At this point, it may be objected: "But suppose someone doesn't want those things, then what are we to say?" But this is only to burgeon forth with another desert-island example. The proper thing to reply is that people almost universally are not that way and that in reasoning about whether I should or should not be selfish, I quite naturally appeal to certain very pervasive facts (including facts about attitudes) and do not, and need not, normally, try to find an answer that would apply to all conceivable worlds and all *possible* human natures. To think that one must do so is but to exhibit another facet of the genuinely irrational core of rationalism.

## VII

It seems to me that the above considerations count heavily against adopting a thoroughly consistent policy of individual egoism. But do such considerations at all touch the individual who simply, on occasion, when his need is great, acts in a way that is inconsistent with the dictates of morality? Will such a person always be happier—in the long run—if he acts conscientiously or is this a myth foisted on us, perhaps for good social reasons, by our religions and moralities? Are all the situations desert-island situations in which we can reasonably claim that there could be rational men who would be happier if they acted non-morally rather than morally or in which we would have to say that any decision to act one way rather than another is a matter of arbitrary choice? Are there paradigm cases which establish the subjectivist's case—establish that it is altogether likely that some clear-headed people will be happier if, in some non-desert-island circumstances, they deliberately do what they acknowledge to be wrong and/or in some non-desert-island circumstances some people must just decide in such circumstances what they are to do?

Let us examine three *prima facie* cases.

Suppose a man, believing it to be wrong, decides to be unfaithful to his wife when it is convenient, non-explosive and unlikely to be discovered. Usually it is not, on the part of the knight-errant husband, a deliberate and systematic policy but it might be and sometimes is. Bored husbands sometimes day-dream that this is a return to paradise; that is to say, it might earn, at least in anticipation, a good score in a felicific calculus. In order to make the example sufficiently relevant to the argument, we must exclude those cases in which the husband believes there is nothing wrong in this behavior and/or gives reasons or rationalizations to excuse his behavior. I must also exclude the guilty weak-willed man with the Pauline syndrome. The case demands a man who deliberately—though with sufficiently prudent moderation—commits adultery. It is important for our case that he believes adultery to be immoral. Nonetheless, while believing people ought not to be adulterers, he asks himself, 'Should I continue to live this way anyway? Will I really be happier if I go the way of St. Paul?' He does not try to universalize his decision. He believes that to choose to remain an adulterer is immoral, but the immoral choice remains for him a live option. Though people may not put all this to themselves so explicitly, such a case is not an impossibility. People may indeed behave in this way. My example is not a desert-island one. I admit there is something odd about my adulterer that might make him seem like a philosophical *papier maché* figure. There is also something conceptually odd about saying that a man believes x to be wrong and yet, without guilt or ambivalence and without excusing conditions, rationally decides to do x. With good reason we say, "If he knows it to be wrong or really believes it to be wrong, he will (everything else being equal) try to avoid it." Still there is a sense in which he could say he believes x to be wrong even though he seeks x. The sense is this: he would not wish that people generally choose or seek x. When this is the case he says 'x is wrong' even though he makes a frank exception of himself without attempting to morally justify this exception. It is important to note that this is a *special* though perfectly intelligible use on my part of 'He believes it to be wrong'. While it withdraws one essential feature, namely that non-universalizable exceptions are inadmissible, it retains something of the general sense of what we mean by calling something morally wrong.

Yet for the sake of the argument at least, let us assume that we do not have a desert-island case. Assuming then that there are such men, is their doing what is wrong here also for *them* the personally disadvantageous thing? Can any individual who acts in such a way ever be reasonably sure he won't be caught—that one of the girls won't turn up and make trouble, that he won't run into an acquaintance at the wrong time? Even if these seem to be remote possibilities, can he ever be free enough from them in his dream life? And if his dreams are bothersome, if he develops a rather pervasive sense of uneasiness, is it really worth it? He must again consider the power of his conscience (superego) even though he rationally decided to reject its authority. Will it give him peace? Will the fun be worth the nagging of his conscience? It is difficult to *generalize* here. Knowledge of oneself, of people, of human psychology and of imaginative literature is all extremely relevant here. I think the individual egoist can correctly argue that it is not *always* clear that he would be unhappier in such a situation if he did what was wrong. A great deal depends on the individual and the exact particular circumstance but the moralist who says it is never, or hardly ever, the case that a person will be happier by pursuing a selfish policy certainly overstates his case.

Let me now take a different paradigm for which much the same thing must be said. It is important to consider this new case because most people would label this man a "veritable moral beast" yet he stands to gain very much from acting immorally. The case I have in mind is that of a very intelligent, criminally experienced, well-equipped, non-masochistic but ruthless kidnapper. He is a familiar type in the movies and thrillers. Now, Hollywood to the contrary, why should it not sometimes be the case that such a kidnapper will be happier if he is successful? Indeed, he may have a murder on his hands but the stakes are very high and when he is successful he can live in luxury for the rest of his life. With good reason our *folklore* teaches that he would not be happier. It is of the utmost value to society that such behavior be strenuously disapproved. And given the long years of conditioning we are all subject to, it remains the case that most people (placed in the position of the kidnapper) would not be happier with the successful completion of such a kidnapping if it involved murdering the kidnapped child. But then most people are not kidnappers. They have very different personalities. Such brutalities together with fear of detection would haunt them and it is probably the case that they also haunt many kidnappers. But if the kidnapper were utterly non-moral, very, very clever, etc., why wouldn't *he* really be happier? He could live in comfort; he could marry, have children and attain companionship, love, approval, etc. "Well," we would say, "his conscience would always bother him." But, particularly with modern medical help, which he could now well afford, would it bother him enough? "Well, there would always be the awful possibility of detection and the punishment that might follow." But, if the stakes were high enough and if he were clever enough might it not be better than a life of dull routine, poverty or near poverty? And think of the "kicks" he would get in outwitting the police? We all have a little adventure in our souls. "But"—the dialogue might go on—"if he were intelligent enough to pull off this job successfully, he would certainly be intelligent enough to avoid poverty; and to avoid making his living in a routine, boring way." The dialogue could go on interminably but I think it is clear enough again that even here there is no one decisive, clear-cut answer to be given. The case for morality here is stronger than in the previous paradigm, but it is still not decisive. Yet there are paradigms in which doing what is clearly wrong (and understood by the individual in question to be wrong) is in the rational self-interest of some individuals. Our first more typical paradigm is not completely clear, but the following third and less typical paradigm given by Hospers is a clear example of a case in which it is in a man's self-interest not to do what is right.

There is a young bank clerk who decides, quite correctly, that he can embezzle $50,000 without his identity ever being known. He fears that he will be underpaid all his life if he doesn't embezzle, that life is slipping by without his ever enjoying the good things of this world; his fiancee will not marry him unless he can support her in the style to which she is accustomed; he wants to settle down with her in a suburban house, surround himself with books, stereo hi-fi set, and various *objets d'art,* and spend a pleasant life, combining culture with sociability; he never wants to commit a similar act again. He does just what he wanted to do: he buys a house, invests the remainder of the money wisely so as to enjoy a continued income from it, marries the girl and lives happily ever after; he doesn't worry about detection because he has arranged things so that no blame could fall on him; anyway he doesn't have a worrisome disposition and is not one to dwell on past misdeeds; he is blessed with a happy temperament, once his daily comforts are taken care of. The degree of happiness he now possesses would not have been possible had he not committed the immoral act.[37]

Clearly it was in his rational self-interest to do what is wrong.

Someone might claim that it is too much to expect that he could arrange things so that no blame would fall on him. This could happen only in desert-island type situations. But unless we began to have the doubts characteristic of traditional epistemologists about 'the blame could not fall on him', there are plenty of cases in which crimes of this general sort are carried out with success. There is no good reason to think such an individual in such circumstances would not be happier.

But it is also crucial to recall that our cases here only involve certain specific acts that do go against the requirements of morality. The cultured despiser of morals we described in the last section is a man who rejects the authority of *all* moral considerations and systematically pursues a selfish policy in all things. Thus, we would need to project risks similar to those of the wayward husband and the kidnapper through his entire life. But are there really any realistic paradigms for such generalized egoistic behavior that would hold any attraction at all for a rational man? I doubt very much that there are. Yet, our three paradigms indicate that for *limited patterns of behavior,* no decisively good reasons can be given to some individuals that would justify their doing the moral thing in such a context. (It would be another thing again if they repeatedly acted in that way. Here the case for morality would be much stronger.)

In pointing this out, the subjectivist is on solid ground. But it is also true that even here it is not just a matter of "paying your money and taking your choice," for what it would be rational for you to do depends, in large measure, on what sort of person you are and on the particular circumstances into which you are cast.

There is a further more general and more important consideration. Even if large groups of people read and accepted my argument as correct, even if it got favorable billing by Luce publications, it still remains very unlikely that kidnapping and crime would increase one iota. For the most part, people get their standards not from ethical treatises or even scriptural texts or homely sayings but by idealizing and following the example of some living person or persons. Morality or immorality does not typically (or perhaps even ever) arise from precept or argument but from early living examples. The foundations of one's character are developed through unconscious imitation way before perplexity over morality can possibly arise. Unless a man is already ready to run amok, he will not be morally derailed by the recognition that in deliberating about how to act one finally must simply decide what sort of a person one wishes to be. Since most people are not ready to go amok, the truth of my argument will not cause a housing shortage in hell.

There are further considerations that will ameliorate this subjectivism. It seems reasonable to say that in different societies the degree of subjectivism will vary. All societies are interested in preserving morality; they have a quite natural and rationally justifiable vested interest in their moral codes. Now, as societies gain a greater know-how, and particularly as they come to understand man and the structure of society better, it seems reasonable to assume they can more effectively protect their vested interests. In other words, I believe, it is reasonable to assume that it will become increasingly difficult to be successfully non-moral as a society gains more knowledge about itself and the world.

This also poses a puzzle for the intelligent individual egoist. In such advancing culture-studying cultures, it will become increasingly more difficult for *him* to be non-moral. But it is in his rational interest for *others* to be moral so he should not oppose this more efficient enforcement of morality. And if he does choose to oppose it, it is very probable that he will suffer a fate not unlike Camus's stranger.

More generally, it will not be in the interest of the individual egoist to oppose morality and even if he, and others like him, do find that it pays to act non-morally their failure to act morally will of necessity be so moderate that the set of social practices that help make up morality will not be disturbed in any extensive way. (This puts the point very modestly.) And, if too many go the way of the rational individual egoist, then it will no longer pay to be non-moral so that large numbers of individual egoists, if they are rational, will become men of good morals.

Though the plain man committed to the moral point of view will probably not jump with joy over this state of affairs, I think the considerations in the last three paragraphs give him genuine grounds for being sanguine. The subjectivism I have pin-pointed need not create a generation of "despairing philosophers" even if my argument is accepted as completely sound.

NOTES

1. Kai Nielsen, "Is 'Why Should I be Moral?' an Absurdity?" *Australasian Journal of Philosophy* 36, no. 1 (1958): 25–32.

2. Charles Baylis, for example, defines 'ethical egoism' in this way in his *Ethics: The Principles of Wise Choice* (New York, 1958), p. 169.

3. Brian Medlin, "Ultimate Principles and Ethical Egoism," *The Australasian Journal of Philosophy* 35 (1957): 111–118.

4. See my "Egoism in Ethics," *Philosophy and Phenomenological Research* 19 (June, 1959).

5. Some of these are made by John Hospers in his "Baier and Medlin on Ethical Egoism," *Philosophical Studies* 12 (January–February, 1961).

6. Medlin, op. cit., p. 113.

7. J. A. Brunton, "Egoism and Morality," *Philosophical Quarterly* 6 (1956): 298–299.

8. It received a new coat with Donald Walhout's essay "Why Should I Be Moral? A Reconsideration," *The Review of Metaphysics* 12, no. 4 (June, 1959): 570–588. Consider only ". . . the final theoretical answer" to our question is that ". . . one should be moral because this fits into a pattern of universal harmony of all things. . ." and the "universal harmony of all things can be regarded as the ultimate culmination of all existence, not indeed as a description at any particular moment of time, but as an all-pervasive ideal." But such an ideal is not left to the whims of mortal will for we are told "it may be regarded as rooted in the ultimate power of being that produces what is." Apparently it is too much to expect that the days are over when this kind of philosophy could be written. Walhout sees there is a problem about justifying the moral point of view that was not adequately met by Bradley and Prichard but in answering what he calls "the ultimate question" he gives us this nonsense.

9. See W. H. Walsh, "Skepticism About Morals and Skepticism About Knowledge," *Philosophy* 35 (July, 1960): 218–234.

10. F. H. Bradley, *Ethical Studies* (New York: The Liberal Arts Press, 1951), p. 7.

11. Bradley, op. cit., p. 6.

12. Kurt Baier, *The Moral Point of View: A Rational Basis of Ethics* (Ithaca: Cornell University Press, 1958), p. 308.

13. John Hospers effectively marshalls the points that need to be made against Plato here. See John Hospers, *Human Conduct: An Introduction to the Problems of Ethics* (New York: 1961), pp. 176–183.

14. Austin Duncan-Jones, *Butler's Moral Philosophy* (Pelican Philosophy Series, 1952), p. 181.

15. Quoted by Duncan-Jones, op. cit., p. 182.

16. Baier, op. cit., p. 309.

17. Ibid.

18. Charles Baylis, op. cit., pp. 172–173.

19. J. J. C. Smart, "Philosophy and Religion," *The Australasian Journal of Philosophy* 36, no. 1 (1958): 57.

20. Medlin, op. cit., p. 113 (italics mine).

21. Ibid., p. 114.

22. I have discussed this issue in my "Appealing to Reason," *Inquiry* 5 (Spring, 1962): 65–84.

23. John Hospers, *Human Conduct,* op. cit., p. 194.

24. Ibid., p. 194.

25. Ibid.

26. Ibid.

27. Ibid., p. 195.

28. Ibid., p. 585.

29. Ibid.

30. See here William Dennes, "An Appeal to Reason," in *Reason, University of California Publications in Philosophy* 27 (Berkeley, Calif., 1939), p. 3–42 and *Some Dilemmas of Naturalism* (New York, 1960), chapter 5.

31. A. M. MacIver, "Good and Evil and Mr. Geach," *Analysis* 18, no. 1 (October, 1957): 7–13.

32. Ibid., p. 8.

33. P. H. Nowell-Smith, *Ethics,* p. 240.

34. Ibid.

35. Ibid.

36. Ibid., p. 132.

37. John Hospers, *Human Conduct,* op. cit., pp. 180–181.

# 9

# Morality and Commitment

## I

Philosophers out of the idealist tradition—Kant, preeminently F. H. Bradley and H. J. Paton among our near contemporaries—have tried to set out a kind of objectivist grounding for moral principles which, I shall argue, moral principles do not and indeed could not possess. There have been many sadly defective rhetorical arguments against both absolutism and subjectivism in ethics; and rhetoric, in a quite different and indeed legitimate sense, has been employed to show that many anti-absolutist and pro-subjectivist arguments rest on conceptual confusion and rhetorical exaggeration. Close attention to the logic of our language—it has been claimed—would lead us to see that all grand talk of either objectivism or subjectivism is just so much rhetoric— switching once more to the pejorative sense of 'rhetoric'.[1] Still, more recently, some philosophers have tried to specify a sense of 'subjectivism' which is coherent and which does pose a rational challenge to the claims of those idealist philosophers and to the claims of others as well that there are objectively true or objectively justified categorical moral claims or whole moral accounts of how we ought to live.[2]

I shall argue, building on my arguments concerning 'Why be moral?' that there is: a) a reasonable sense to the contention that moral claims are 'subjective', b) that it is the case that in an important but frequently unrecognized way moral claims are subjective, and c) that the truth of such a subjectivist account does not at all warrant the alarms sounded by such idealist philosophers as Bradley and Paton; that is to say, (referring now to c), even if such a form of subjectivism is a correct account of how things are in morality, it remains the case that such considerations alone do not afford sufficiently good

From *Idealistic Studies* 8, no. 1 (January, 1977): 94–107.

reasons for believing that our moral universe is shaken and nihilism is upon us.

## II

I have argued that while so-called subjectivist ethical theories have been undermined by contemporary philosophical analysts, the feeling is likely to persist with many reflective people that somehow there still is a point to these subjective theories. I believe that this feeling is justified and I sought in my "Why Should I Be Moral?" to bring out what was behind it that justified it.[3] To do this most effectively, I had to move rather indirectly. I first argued that so-called ethical egoism could not possibly count as a morality or a moral point of view. But I also argued that while categorical universal egoism (an ethical egoism of ends) is incoherent, individual egoism is not, though it could not possibly be a moral point of view (not even an iconoclastic moral point of view). It could, however, be a nonmoral *personal* policy without it at all necessarily being irrational. I then argued that 'Why be moral?' is a perfectly sensible question. It is, however, not a question that can be asked within morality, and someone committed to a moral point of view cannot seriously entertain it and remain so committed. (This is intended as a conceptual or grammatical remark.) But in challenging the good or the value of the whole moral enterprise, this question is perfectly at home. Yet when we intelligibly ask "Why be moral?" we can be asking at least two questions: 1) "Why should people be moral?" and 2) "Why should I be moral?" I argued (as have others) that Hobbes gives a generally satisfactory answer to the question "Why should people be moral?" or "Why ought there be such a social practice anyway?" The answer (to put it very baldly) is: we should be moral because morality is an essential device for group life without which our individual lives would be miserable. But I also argued that the answer to 2) must finally be of a more personal and less definitive sort. It is at this point that subjectivism becomes a genuine issue.

In many cases it is perfectly clear that I should be moral, for in one way or another I will be made unhappy if I am not. But in a situation in which my acting immorally will not be detected, must I always be moral? Here I warned against the use of desert island examples but I also indicated that there are some rather limited circumstances in which it *might* be true that *an* individual would be happier in being immoral. Whether he would in fact be happier would in part depend upon the sort of person he was. But I also argued that the world being as it is and people being as they are, a rational individual egoist is very much like a unicorn: his existence is indeed possible but we do not expect to find him in our zoo; and such behavior is not the way to human happiness for flesh and blood individuals.

But this remark is in no way a necessary proposition and it remains at least logically possible that some people might find not only a summer, but a life of happiness in this way. It is just this point that many traditional moral philosophers have worked hard to deny and that subjectivists—often in a highly misleading form—have asserted. However, it seems to me that here— as I argued in detail in "Why Should I Be Moral?"—the subjectivists have a sound point. I went on, however, to try to show that there still are ameliorating conditions which make it clear that generally speaking an individual would be happier in taking a moral point of view. Given the world and the people we find in it, the systematic rational egoist is a purely philosophical artifact. In practical deliberation we can rightly afford to ignore such artificial possibilities; the language of human conduct—our instrument of practical deliberation—was not developed to handle such cases nor need it be. The subjective elements in reasoning over how to act, which I have brought to the fore, do not really give us any cause for Joadian or Patonian worries over the rationality of morals.

I am reasonably confident, however, that those jealous defenders of absolutism in morals will say that *if* what I have claimed here and in "Why Should I Be Moral?" is correct, then the rationality and intelligibility of the whole moral institution of life has been destroyed. F. H. Bradley in a rather Edwardian and chauvinistic manner warns us that morality is "an end to be desired for her own sake, and not as a means to something beyond. Degrade her, and she disappears; and to keep her, we must love and not merely use her."[4] There is a universal, categorical quality to moral principles. To ask seriously if morality pays is not at all to act as a moral agent. It is, in effect, to place oneself outside the moral community; to make it quite clear that one is a blackguard. Basic moral principles such as 'Unnecessary suffering is evil' or 'Obligations are to be kept' or 'Good is to be sought and evil avoided' are not *at all* conditional or hypothetical. They are unconditional, universal in scope, and rationally unquestionable. As central moral concepts they are certain. H. J. Paton is expressing this point of view when he remarks, at the end of a penetrating criticism of the emotive theory, "Whatever be the theory of it, I am as certain that cruelty is wrong as I am that grass is green or that two and two are four. If this certainty is merely contingent, then my whole universe is shaken."[5]

## III

At least two things need to be said here. First, the self-evident, necessary character of certain moral utterances derives from their tautological or quasi-tautological nature. To say, 'Murder is wrong', like saying, 'A father is a parent', is to utter a tautology.[6] Any act to which the word 'murder' correctly applies is also *eo ipso* called 'wrong'. We cannot understand the meaning of the word "murder" without realizing that this must be so. Those acts of killing that are labeled 'unjustified killing' or 'murder' are also called wrong acts; that is to say, the class of acts called murders is included by definition in the class of wrong acts. Similarly to say, 'Good is to be sought and evil avoided' is to utter a tautology. If something is called 'good', it is something that is (everything being equal) to be sought. The reverse is true for being evil. This first, necessary, self-evident principle of the natural moral law is a plain tautology. The necessity we discover in examples of this sort is in language and not in some 'super-sensible' or 'noumenal' or 'ontic' 'realm of values', whatever it is that these odd phrases may mean.

The second problem is more taxing. In arguing as I have, I have assumed with such writers as Toulmin, Hare, Nowell-Smith, and Paul Edwards that moral discourse and the language of human conduct generally is a form of practical discourse addressed to answering questions like "What shall I do?" "What should I have done?" or "What attitude and indeed, where relevant, what policies of action should I take toward what has been done, is being done, or probably will be done?" I have assumed what they have explicitly argued for, viz., that a complete justification of any practical claim necessarily involves making a choice or a decision. But this assumption, as the work of Foot has made evident, cannot simply be accepted without any questions asked. What I will try to do here, without challenging anything Foot claims, is to show how this assumption, in a important way, is justified, though the relation between "goodness and choice" is not to be understood in exactly the way Hare and Nowell-Smith take it.

Something of what is involved in this second problem can be best brought out if I expand my above remarks a bit. When we say '$x$ is good', or '$x$ ought to be done', we are referring directly or indirectly to certain natural features of $x$ in virtue of which we call $x$ good. Grading labels not only typically express attitudes, decisions or wishes, but also have distinctive empirical criteria of application. If someone says '$x$ is good', or '$x$ ought to be done', it is always possible and legitimate to ask why it is good or why it ought to be done. When in reply he gives his reasons for saying '$x$ is good or obligatory', his reasons will either be factual statements or further moral statements. If his warrant for his original moral claim is itself a moral principle, then that principle will frequently have for its backing or support statements of a factual kind. But if it is the case that we cannot have a categorical normative conclusion unless we have at least one (implicit or explicit) categorical normative premise or rule of inference, must it not be the case that in arguing such a normative question (in arguing over what finally we must do) there must be at least one warrant which is itself a categorical normative principal? For there to be any sound reasoning over what to do, must we not assume, without justification, at least one such normative warrant? (Note that here there is no denial that one can derive an 'ought from an is', but there is a denial that one can get a categorical ought from an is.)

Still, how does choice or decision come in here? The following considerations should answer this question. They attempt to show a crucially different way in which non-normative and normative arguments are resolved. Justification only ends for categorical normative judgments when people choose or would strive to choose the *justificandum* if they could.

While it is trivially true that in any form of life we cannot prove (i.e., demonstrate) ultimate principles (or else they would not be ultimate), it does not follow that we cannot choose such principles wisely or foolishly. If a principle is ultimate it cannot possibly rest on another principle, but, as Aristotle well argued, what is reasonably believed is not necessarily believed for a reason. While we must finally choose what ultimate principles we are going to act in accordance with, there is indeed a proper way of choosing such principles, though it still may be the case that even with this proper procedure, we will not know what principles to subscribe to. In reasoning over what is the case, we frequently have some statements of antecedent conditions ($c$) and some general empirical laws or warrants ($l$). And sometimes ($c$) and ($l$) conjointly entail some description ($e$). Pressed for our support or backing for our warrant or law ($l$), we may cite another law or warrant ($l'$) and in turn that may be supported by a further law or warrant ($l''$). But alternatively we sometimes support or back our warrant or law by certain observations, since it is presumably an empirical generalization of universal scope. And pressed for the justification of such an empirical law, we would *finally* give a description which was not itself a law or law-like statement. And asked for the justification for the description, we would finally be reduced to saying: "It just happens to be that way. Look for yourself!" But if we press in a like manner for justification of moral warrants, we do not finally end with descriptions and logical rules. If someone will not accept the moral warrants governing human conduct, then it is not necessarily the case that the man has made some faulty observations or some faulty inferences from his observation statements or empirical generalizations. It may instead be that he is a kind of Meursault with attitudes radically different from those of most people who assent to such moral warrants. He may simply feel differently from the solid pillars of his community about the matter at hand, and a point may finally be reached in which there is nothing more to be said. This is why people such as Edwards and Nowell-Smith say that in ascertaining which reasons are relevant and justifying reasons for categorical normative judgments, we must *finally* appeal to the attitudes of the people involved. If I say, "The Chilean Junta is an evil regime because it condones distortion of fact for political purposes, ruins the Chilean universities, murders workers, and tortures political prisoners," my reasons will only be accepted as good reasons if I, and the people to whom I address my remarks, have an unfavorable attitude towards those features of the Junta's behavior. Within a given community or culture (at least), there are certain quite stable criteria of moral goodness. Yet, it is argued, that since 'good' and 'ought' are expressive and directive as well as descriptive, there is in moral contexts no analytic connection between 'good' and any set of criteria. It is always possible to reject the more typical criteria for moral goodness while still using 'good' with its usual commendatory force.

Justification of moral and categorical normative questions must involve a reference not only to facts but to attitudes as well; and if, as I have urged, it makes sense to ask 'Why should I be moral?' then this question too cannot finally be answered without reference to attitudes. We can and must offer good reasons for normative judgments, for after all they are appraisals; but a disagreement about a normative issue will be rationally resolved (and not just terminated) only if the disputants agree in attitude. That is a necessary though not a sufficient condition for such a resolution. A moral principle is not establishable as an acceptable moral principle unless people are willing to assent to it. And, while I might act in accordance with a command out of fear, prudence, or habit, a putative moral principle becomes an effective moral principle for me only when I assent to it. To assent to it means that I subscribe to it, universalize it, and try to act in accordance with it; and acting in accordance with it entails that I do not act simply because of what I may get out of so acting.

## IV

As it is presupposed that $x$ believes that $y$ is colored when he honestly asserts '$y$ is red' so it is presupposed that $x$ has a pro-attitude toward $y$ when he asserts '$y$ ought to be done' as a moral principle he actually subscribes to.

If the rationalist in morals pushes us with "Why approve this rather than that?" or "Why make this decision rather than that?" we can go on to point to certain natural features of the object of our approval in virtue of which we approve what we approve. If he continues to push us, we may finally give him a very extensive specification of a way of life—indeed as nearly complete as we can reasonably make it. If someone, for example, challenges us to give reasons for not being Fascists or male chauvinists, we could in principle at least be pressed into specifying for him our whole way of life. But the determined rationalist could still reply: But finally you choose this way of life rather than some other way of life (if such a choice is at all possible) because you prefer to want or (more adequately) you have a pro-attitude toward this way of life. Your reasons are good reasons only if you approve them. But such reasons are not good enough reasons for me—the rationalist continues—for they make morality finally rest on what we *just happen to want.*

Hare (in effect) responds to this point when he remarks:

> If the inquirer still goes on asking "But why should I live like that?" then there is no further answer to give him, because we have already, *ex hypothesi,* said everything that could be included in this further answer. We can only ask him to make up his own mind which way he ought to live; for in the end everything rests upon such a decision of principle. He has to decide whether to accept that way of life or not; if he accepts it, then we can proceed to justify the decisions that are based upon it; if he does not accept it, then let him accept some other, and try to live by it. The sting is in the last clause. To describe such ultimate decisions as arbitrary, because, *ex hypothesi,* everything which could be used to justify them has already been included in the decision, would be like saying that a complete description of a universe was utterly unfounded, because no further fact could be called upon in corroboration of it. This is not how we use the words "arbitrary" and "unfounded." Far from being arbitrary, such a decision would be the most well-founded of decisions, because it would be based upon a consideration of everything upon which it could possibly be founded.[7]

Now Hare, as well as Edwards who makes a similar argument, do not seem to differ on any substantive issue from the subjectivist who says that finally the choices we make are based on our tastes—on the pro-attitudes we happen to have. They disagree only on how best to describe the situation. The subjectivist says that finally ultimate decisions are arbitrary and Hare and Edwards deny this.[8]

There is indeed a difficulty about the use of 'arbitrary' here. Hare argues that it is a linguistic outrage to suggest that a decision or choice which was made after a full consideration of all the facts is an arbitrary choice. In everyday contexts we do not correctly use the words 'arbitrary choice' for such choices. But Vincent Tomas has indicated (*pace* Hare) that there is a perfectly ordinary and respectable sense for 'arbitrary choice' here.[9] He points out that Hare's analogy between a complete description of the universe and a complete specification of a way of life is not a good one. Two complete descriptions of the universe would entail that predictions made with one would be identical with the predictions made by the use of the other. Since they have the same predictive value, a choice between them would be a matter of indifference or at best a matter of convenience. But rival ways of life, even when they are completely specified, would still entail different answers to the question 'What shall I do?' So, as Tomas goes on to say, "the decision that the answer entailed by one, and not that entailed by the other, is the 'correct' answer, is, after all, arbitrary in the usual sense of that word."[10] Unlike the case about alternative complete descriptions, complete specifications of alternative ways of life would involve some different decisions. But, *ex hypothesi*, there would be no possible grounds for choosing one rather than the other in this context. We would just have to decide here which way of life to adopt, and it is quite in accordance with ordinary usage to say that such a decision is both important (not a mere matter of convenience) and arbitrary. Indeed, this is not only plain man's talk; it is the case—if the situation is as Hare hypothesizes—that any choice between the different ways of life is an arbitrary one.

In a similar way, a decision between a personal policy of individual egoism and a moral policy is an arbitrary one. In the last analysis we must just decide what sort of people we want to be.

I do not think that it can reasonably be denied that a recognition of this—at first at least—causes in many people a certain amount of anguish. The existentialists, I suspect, are frequently pointing, though often in an exaggeratedly romantic fashion, to just this human problem. It is, however, of considerable importance to examine this situation with a cold and steady eye and to approach some writings on this subject in a deflationary mood. When Sartre contends that because of this we have in making moral decisions no known guides to turn to but must in anguish and forlornness make some goal—some project—our 'authentic good' without any knowledge of better or worse, and when a rationalist such as Paton suggests that if we lack certainty in moral matters his "whole universe is shaken," they are both being romantic and unrealistic. We are not without guides in moral reflection, and no rational man, including the rational individual egoist, denies the value of morality as a social activity.[11] And we all (as Russell reminds us) "desire and need food and shelter and clothing; security from injury, happiness, joy of living, freedom." If we did not share these very general pro-attitudes, there would be no basis for agreements over the problems of human conduct. They are some of the very crucial phenomena in the contextual background of both moral agreement and disagreement. Phenomena such as these make morality as we understand it possible.

*If* a man did not care about his life, liberty or happiness, *if* he had no desire for security or companionship, then there might very well be no basis on which we could agree with him on a correct plan of human action. If the individual egoist does not want to achieve security and happiness, he may choose a very different course of action than ours and there is finally no proving him wrong, though, it is fair to say, this would be a strange egoist indeed, so strange that we now find it difficult to understand the meaning of 'egoist' here. For the unmoved spectator of the actual, as Hägerström and Russell have remarked, there can be no good or evil; what we take to be good or bad is *finally* determined by our attitudes and what attitudes we have is a factual matter. If someone has a completely different set of attitudes from ours about what is to be done, there is finally no proving him wrong. If we disagree in attitude and he sees all the factual implications involved in the beliefs linked with his attitudes as clearly as we do and yet continues to disagree in attitude with us, there is no proving one party right and the other wrong.

Russell's and Dewey's comments about the unity of human attitudes only tell us about the way human beings in fact happen to behave. They set no natural limits for natural kinds. Human beings may radically change or they may make heroic efforts to initiate change. They may come to have very different attitudes towards life, and if they nonevasively do so there are no objective grounds for saying they are wrong.

Even here, however, it is crucial to note the radically different senses of 'may'. When we suggest that human beings may so radically change, we may be doing nothing more than indicating how it is not *logically* impossible that men could be different; that is to say, it is not self-contradictory to assume that people do not want security, happiness, freedom from pain, and the like. But there are, as well, many rather more ordinary employments of 'may'—as in 'There may be a frost tonight'—which make no such stringent requirements and are not concerned with mere logical possibilities. However, philosophers tend to ignore these plain man's uses and, as Toulmin has shown in *The Uses of Argument,* all manner of philosophical and conceptual ills follow from ignoring them and from insisting on the logico-mathematical criteria for modal qualifiers. And *vis-à-vis* our present question there is something painfully unrealistic in thinking that such future contingencies could topple "the moral universe." Some philosophers induce a kind of self-hypnosis that generates philosophical fantasies by constantly reminding themselves that since the contradictory of any existential statement is not self-contradictory, it may then be true and the existential statement may be false. I suspect that moral philosophy needs its Don Quixotes, but after a session or so with the windmills, we need the clear realistic vision of a Sancho Panza.


V


It is frequently said, often by people who should know better, that the kinds of arguments that I have espoused are too Edwardian. I will content myself here with the counterassertion that if to argue as I have here, or as Toulmin, Nowell-Smith, or Baier have, is to be Edwardian, then to be Edwardian is to attempt to be clearheaded and realistic. Such approaches do not deny that there are moral perplexities. That this is so should be evident enough to anyone with mortal coils. There is, rather, an effort made to help us regain our philosophical sanity by recognizing that rationalist and existentialist speculative worries are like much metaphysical speculation, a strange amalgam of conceptual confusion and unrealistic fantasy that need have nothing at all to do with the realistically troubled engine of our moral life. Concerning good and evil choice, subscription and decision are unavoidable, but this truism need no more totter a rational morality than the revelation that the number two is not an object to be gazed at with a microscope or a telescope need totter mathematics.

If people were very, very different, they would in all likelihood make choices very different from those they in fact make. If human nature, like a kind of kaleidoscope, were continuously and rapidly changing, there would probably not be any reliable guides in choosing between good and evil. These are indeed possibilities—*but mere logical possibilities.* To say, as Paton does, that because of this his universe is shaken or to say, with Camus or Sartre, that because of this man's lot in the world is an absurd one, is to be absurd, to be caught, perhaps unwittingly, by what Toulmin calls an impossibly unrealistic "analytic ideal."[12]

Because of *these* future contingencies our universe need not be shaken and only on some bizarre and question-begging use of 'reliable' need we say that we have no reliable guides for wise choice. More fundamentally still, that such wildly improbable, contrary-to-fact conditionals ever would be anything other than contrary-to-fact conditionals is, in a plain sense, an impossibility. 'If men were 700 feet tall our houses would be inadequate' gives us no sound reason for concern over our houses. Doubts about the justifiability of the whole moral enterprise *on the above grounds* are of just this nature. They are pointless laments.

The idealist rationalist or absolutist may persist in saying: "No, we must have a surer, more certain foundation for moral judgments. We must have some foundation that roots out even the small element of subjectivity I have discovered and above all rules out every element of decision in practical reasoning." But this is like asking for the taste of red. Such an absolutist is simply asking for something that he cannot—logically cannot—have. I can point out to him that a reasoned practical decision to count as such must be deliberate, reflective, fact-regarding, and *universalizable;* but if he says: "There must be absolutely no uneliminatable reference to decisions or to preferences, but instead there must be self-evident, universal, completely impersonal principles which would obtain even if there were no sentient beings at all," I can only say that he has made a radical category mistake. He is, in effect, asking that practical reasoning and the problems of morals and human conduct cease to be practical reasoning, etc., and become something else altogether different. Like the philosopher who demands a deductive justification for induction, such an absolutist moral philosopher is demanding a nonpractical justification for a practical problem. No conceivable answer would satsfy him, for in effect he is asking that practical reasoning cease to be practical reasoning and become some other kind of reasoning, just as some people claimed that inductive reasoning was not at all sound because it was not deductive, while by their very arguments making it quite clear—as it should be anyway—that it could not become deductive without ceasing to be inductive.

## NOTES

1. Paul Edwards, *The Logic of Moral Discourse* (Glencoe, Ill.: The Free Press, 1955).

2. See, for example, D.H. Monro, "Relativism in Ethics," *Dictionary of the History of Ideas,* Vol. IV, ed. by Philip P. Wiener (New York: Charles Scribner's Sons, 1973), pp. 70-74, and his *Empiricism and Ethics* (Cambridge, England: Cambridge University Press, 1967), and my "Varieties of Ethical Subjectivism," *Danish Yearbook of Philosophy* 7 (1970): 73-87, and "Does Ethical Subjectivism Have a Coherent Form?" *Philosophy and Phenomenological Research* 35 (1974): 93-99.

3. [See chapter 8 of this volume].

4. F. H. Bradley, *Ethical Studies*, 2nd. ed. (Oxford: Clarendon Press, 1927), p. 3.

5. H. J. Paton, *In Defense of Reason* (London: Hutchinson's University Library, 1951), p. 212.

6. Some would prefer to speak of "being analytic" rather than "being tautological" here, reserving 'tautology' for statements of logical identity such as 'a brother is a brother' and 'a brother is a male sibling'. I use 'tautology' rather than 'analyticity' for stylistic reasons and if anyone wants, rather more strictly, to reserve tautologies for a limited species of analyticities, the appropriate substitutions can be readily made in my above argument. The force of my argument will not be changed one whit.

7. R. M. Hare, *The Language of Morals* (Oxford: Clarendon Press, 1952), p. 69.

8. Leonard G. Miller has well brought this out with respect to Paul Edwards in his review of *The Logic of Moral Discourse, The Philosophical Review* 65 (1956): 560–562.

9. Vincent Tomas, "Review of *The Language of Morals,*" *The Philosophical Review* 64, no. 1 (January, 1955): 132-135.

10. Ibid., p. 135.

11. W. D. Falk, "Moral Perplexity," *Ethics* (1956).

12. Stephen Toulmin, *The Uses of Argument* (Cambridge, England: Cambridge University Press, 1958), pp. 126-127.

# 10

# Rationality and the Moral Sentiments
## Some Animadversions on a Theme
## in *A Theory of Justice*

I

Moral philosophers have repeatedly argued that there is an intimate bond between rationality and morality. It is pervasively believed that a thoroughly reasonable person must be a morally committed human being; amoralism or indifference to morality must involve some failure of rationality: a rational human being must also be a morally committed human being.

John Rawls in his monumental *A Theory of Justice* defends this traditional bit of moral rationalism. I shall display the core of Rawls's argument for the claim that reason determines the ends of life in such a manner that it must be the case that the through and through rational person will also be a person of moral principle. I shall then proceed to argue that Rawls has not shown this to be so and that, Rawls apart, such moral rationalism, though appealing, remains a very problematic matter. In making this assessment of Rawls, I shall first very schematically characterize some of the core features of Rawls's moral theory, including his account of rationality. I shall then turn to those features of his account designed to establish this key thesis of moral rationalism.

As reviewers have repeatedly stressed, *A Theory of Justice* is a powerful, seminal and intricately orchestrated work which will be discussed many years hence. It is a massive, deeply reflective and complex work with a rondo-like and often confusing structure. These features practically ensure that the

From *Philosophica* 22, no. 2 (1978): 167–191. Reprinted by permission of the publisher.

initial appraisals, many of which have been reprinted in Norman Daniels's *Reading Rawls,* will be first approximations in a continuing dialogue.

*A Theory of Justice* is no less than an attempt to articulate and justify a conception of the principles of justice, together with an account of the values of community and an ideal of the human person, which will provide "an Archimedian point for judging the basic structure of society,"[1] Yet, its ambition and scope notwithstanding, the fundamental idea in Rawls's theory is not at all complex: it is the idea that the principles of justice, and indeed the principles of morality generally, are the principles which free and equal rational persons would come to agree on (mutually accept) as the principles which are to regulate their lives together. He takes the central problem of moral and social philosophy to be the problem of "how society should be arranged if it is to conform to principles that rational persons with true general beliefs would acknowledge in the original position," i.e. (roughly) in a position of impartiality (*TJ,* 547).

Rawls assumes that by sustained rational inquiry we can come to specify principles which will render determinate the rationale for and the proper assignment of rights and duties and the distribution of benefits and burdens among people whose conflicting interests require resolution in some morally acceptable manner. The principles of justice which he believes would be the outcome of such a rational inquiry and would be the principles which rational persons would choose were they to choose impartially, and where conditions of life are not too harsh, are the following: (1) "each person is to have an equal right to the most extensive total system of equal basic liberties compatible with a similar liberty for all" and (2) "social and economic inequalities are to be arranged so that they are both (a) to the greatest benefit of the least advantaged, consistent with the just savings principle and (b) attached to offices and positions open to all under conditions of fair equality of opportunity" (*TJ,* 302). In moderately favorable circumstances, these principles, together with true factual knowledge, are taken to give us an Archimedian point to assess the morality of institutions and social designs. In such circumstances they are to be taken strictly in their order of priority, i.e. the second principle is to be satisfied only if the first one has been satisfied. The aim is to arrive at a scheme which benefits all and in which the only morally acceptable inequalities are those which are, everything considered, to the advantage of the worst off strata of the society. Rawls would not accept as just a utilitarian principle maximizing either total or average utility, for this might involve sanctioning as just representative members of the society ending up with lower life chances for the benefit of others. Rational persons judging in ignorance of their particular positions in society and judging impartially would not accept such utilitarian principles. They would instead accept, for moderately favorable circumstances, the two principles of justice stated above and would in less favorable circumstances fall back on what Rawls calls a more general conception of justice, to wit the principle that all "social primary goods—liberty and opportunity, income and wealth, and the bases of self-respect—are to be distributed equally unless an unequal distribution of any or all of these goods is to the advantage of the least favored" (*TJ*, 303).

These, Rawls would have us believe, are principles all rational human beings would choose where they have full general knowledge of society and human life and where they must be impartial. But to assess this claim and to make headway with the central problem of this essay, we need to have some understanding of what Rawls is talking about when he speaks of rationality.

## II

Rawls construes rationality in the self-consciously minimal and antiseptic way in which it is usually understood in bourgeois economic theory. He does not start out by stipulatively defining 'rationality' or by elucidating the concept but proceeds indirectly. We find out whether a person's interests and aims are rational by finding out whether "they are encouraged and provided for by the plan that is rational for him" (*TJ*, 409). We, in turn, find out whether a person's plan of life is rational for him by finding out whether "(1) it is one of the plans that is consistent with the principles of rational choice when these are applied to all the relevant features of his situation, and (2) it is that plan among those meeting this condition which would be chosen by him with full deliberative rationality, that is with full awareness of the relevant facts and after a careful consideration of the consequences" (*TJ*, 408). Thus for Rawls, in determining the rationality of action and of moral conduct and generally the rationality of our aims and interests, it is essential to determine what are the *principles of rational choice* and what it is to choose with full *deliberative rationality*.

Rawls, in keeping with his general philosophical program, does not analyze the concept of rationality any more than he analyzes the concept of justice. He gives the principles of rational choice, as he remarks, "by enumeration so that they replace the concept of rationality" (*TJ*, 411). The cluster of principles, which are the core principles of rational choice and are, as Rawls puts it, the most central "aspects of rationality," are the following: (1) *the principle of effective means,* (2) *the principle of inclusiveness,* and (3) *the principle of the greater likelihood.* They are mutually compatible principles, all of which Rawls takes to be tolerably unproblematic (*TJ*, 411-415). They would be a part of any coherent conception of rationality. Stated cryptically they are the following:

1. Given a determinate objective, it is to be achieved with the least expenditure of means or, given the means, the objective is to be fulfilled to the fullest extent. (*TJ*, 411-412)

2. Of two or more alternative plans, that plan is to be preferred which would most extensively achieve the desired aims of the other plans and in addition its own desired aims. (*TJ*, 412)

3. Where two plans are closely similar, then, *ceteris paribus*, the plan withe the greater likelihood of success is to be favored. (*TJ*, 412-413)

It is important to realize that in using these principles we do not address the rationality of our wants or desires *per se*. The principles are principles of instrumental rationality enabling us to estimate most adequately how we are most likely to be able to maximize the satisfaction of these wants or realize most fully the maximum of our aims. The *principle of inconclusiveness* combines with the *principle of effective means* to "define rationality as preferring, other things equal, the greater means for realizing our aims, and the development of wider and more varied interests assuming that these aspirations can be carried through" (*TJ*, 413). However, Rawls does not limit his principles of rational choice to the above three principles. He also takes as an essential aspect of rationality the following:

4. We are to take that course of action which is most likely to realize our most important aims.

In addition to (4) and the other above 'counting principles', Rawls adds two further at least putatively unproblematic principles of rationality:

5. *Ceteris paribus*, in choosing like plans, an individual is to choose those plans which will best advance his or her interests. (*TJ*, 142)

6. *Ceteris paribus*, people are to try to protect their liberties, widen their interests and enlarge their means of promoting their aims, whatever they are. (*TJ*, 142)

Lastly, as a final principle of rational choice, we should enunciate what might be called the *principle of rational self-development*.

7. Given that, *ceteris paribus*, people tend to prefer activities that depend upon a large and more complex repertoire of realized capacities to activities that depend on a smaller and simpler repertoire, we are to "realize and train mature capacities." (*TJ*, 428)

These are the core principles of *rational choice* enunciated by Rawls. They, as I have remarked, together with *deliberative rationality,* determine membership in the class of rational life plans. And it is only in the light of a life plan, which has been found to be rational, that an individual's aims and desires can correctly be said to be rational. That is to say, to be rational they must be in accordance with such a plan of life. If they do not square with a plan of life which is rational for him, then they will not be rational aims or desires. (We might very well have Parfitian worries about this last cluster of claims.)

However, a rational life plan must not only be in accordance with the principles of rational choice, it must also not contravene *deliberative rationality.* By the latter Rawls means a way of reasoning and acting. A person committed to such a way of reasoning and acting will choose that plan of action, consistent with the principles of rational choice, which he would decide upon "as the outcome of careful reflection in which [he] reviewed, in the light of all the relevant facts, what it would be like to carry out these plans and thereby ascertained the course of action that would best realize his more fundamental desires" (*TJ,* 417).

We have here what is fundamentally a very Humean-Russellian conception of rationality. Of such a conception it could be justly argued that it does not capture all of what it is we are talking about when we speak of rationality. Rawls, however, is well aware of that but he also realizes that many of the *other* aspects of our common conception of rationality are problematic and morally and perhaps even ideologically non-neutral. If we used instead, in a context similar to that in which Rawls employs his conception of rationality, a morally non-neutral and indeed problematic conception of rationality, we would hardly have a widely accepted base from which we could in some sense derive or ground moral principles of an admittedly problematic sort or preserve the possibility of establishing that taking the moral point of view and rejecting amoralism is something that reason requires.

I could, and on another occasion will, criticize Rawls's conception of rationality, but here I shall accept it as it stands and endeavor to show that, given that conception or any related plausible antiseptic account of rationality, Rawls has not established that amoralism must be irrational or that an amoralist need, because of his rejection of morality, show any loss or diminishment of rationality. Rawls's conception of rationality, even on its own terms, could be refined but that refinement will not make an essential difference to the arguments I shall make about morality and amoralism.

Rawls takes it as a crucial task, in thinking about morality, to determine "whether being a good person is a good thing for that person, if not in general . . . at least [in the circumstances] of a society well-ordered or in a state near justice . . ." (*TJ,* 397–398). His claim is the rather bland one, "that being a good person is indeed a good" (*TJ,* 398). I say 'bland,' for (a) it is truistic and (b) it does not even suggest an answer to the related and more perplexing question that has exercised some philosophers, namely, whether a human being in such a society who is a through and through rational and informed person must also be a good person (a humane person of moral integrity and decency). In an ordinary way we can, as Rawls acknowledges, assess the rationality of a person's desires (*TJ*, 407-408). Given this capacity, what we want to know is whether in a well-ordered society an amoralist must be an irrationalist or whether in being an amoralist he must have irrational desires. Is his not desiring to be a just man—a man of moral principle— but rather simply desiring to be a man of good morals an irrational desire?

## III

Let me begin the central task of this chapter by putting the above problem in Rawlsian terms. Is a desire to act justly regulative of anything that would count as a rational life plan (*TJ*, 456)? Is acting justly part of any person's good? In answering these questions, part of the task is to show "how justice as fairness generates its own support." In chapter 8 of his *A Theory of Justice*, Rawls sets himself this task.

If we are to have a well-ordered society with stable institutions, it is crucial, Rawls contends, that there be a shared sense of justice within that society. Recognizing that "a moral view is an extremely complex structure of principles, ideals, and precepts, and involves all the elements of thought, conduct and feeling," Rawls stresses that "many kinds of learning ranging from reinforcement and classical conditioning to highly abstract reasoning and the refined perception of examplars enter into its development" (*TJ*, 461). In showing how justice as fairness generates its own support, we need a reasonably realistic account of how moral development would occur in a well-ordered society in which such principles are instantiated. [We should recall that Rawls characterizes "a well-ordered society as one designed to advance the good of its members and effectively regulated by a public conception of justice" (*TJ*, 453)].

Rawls attempts a sketch of moral development. The first stage of moral development, he refers to as the *morality of authority*. It is in this form that morality first becomes a reality for children, though elements of this form of morality carry over into our adult lives (*TJ*, 462). Children in being introduced to morality are not in any position to assess the validity of the precepts or injunctions addressed to them by those in authority. Children, when they are very young, cannot reasonably doubt the propriety of parental injunctions; without an understanding of the rationale for the injunctions and without the needed background information, they must, to act rationally, simply submit themselves to the *authority* of their parents. Their parents may very well have biased and distorted moral and social views, but the children are in no position to recognize that. Though, we should remember, in a well-ordered society this unfortunate condition of their parents would not (by definition) obtain (*TJ*, 454).

In the context of moral learning, love and trust between parent and child is central and essential, for without it a child is unlikely to accept their moral authority. And without this familial relation, unless he is fortunate enough to have effective and rather constant parent surrogates, he is not likely to gain any effective moral understanding at all. Where there is no such love and trust, he will sense that his parents have a power over him and he will fear them and hence obey them, but he will not accept their authority, where 'authority' has any sense other than their 'power to constrain and instill fear'. He will not, at least *vis-à-vis them*, develop a sense of what it is for there to be a moral or a *de jure* authority. Indeed it is unlikely in such a circumstance that he will develop any such sense in any very effective manner. This is why relations of love between parent and child are so crucial to a well-ordered society. They are, in short, essential empirical conditions for the reciprocity between human beings essential for justice.

So, for moral learning and development to take place, parents must first come to manifest love to the child, meaning very centrally by that that they will "be concerned for his wants and needs" and, most crucially, to affirm his sense of worth as a person (*TJ*, 464). Initially, a child's actions are motivated by "certain instincts and desires" and to the extent that his aims are regulated at all they are motivated by a limited rational self-interest. In a well-ordered society, his parents' relations to him are such that they will do for him as his rational self-love would incline him towards, where this rational self-love is compatible with the principles of justice (*TJ*, 463-464).

Looked at normatively, for the morality of authority to be a genuine part of morality, it must be subordinate to the principles of right and justice. Where this obtains, the parents' authority is, given the child's distinctive circumstances, a legitimate moral authority. The steps whereby we come to introject the moral point of view reproduce the structural scheme of morality. The claim is that children have a 'morality of authority' and that an appeal to authority has a genuine if limited place in the moral firmament (*TJ*, 461).

The second stage of moral development is what Rawls calls "*the morality of association.*" It is, in short, the morality of my station and its duties. The content of this morality is "given by the moral standards appropriate to the individual's role in the various associations to which he belongs" (*TJ*, 467). It, of course, takes many forms, since after all there are many associations and roles into which individuals enter. In a well-ordered society, and that *ex hypothesi* is what we are talking about, the principles of justice will regulate the ideals governing these varied associations (*TJ*, 472). In talking of associations, we are talking about everything from the family, school, neighborhood, professional bodies, sports associations and the like up to the community as a whole (*TJ*, 467-468). But in a well-ordered society everyone will have the role of citizen and there will be a full equality of citizenship; everyone is meant to have political views concerning the common good. Thus there will be in such a society "a morality of association in which the members of society view one another as equals, as friends and associates, joined together in a system of co-operation known to be for the advantage of all and governed by a common conception of justice" (*TJ*, 472).

Starting with the family itself, one finds oneself in various associations, embedded in certain social structures, in which each member has certain rights and duties. Indeed, as Dahrendorf has argued, we wouldn't even have a social structure or a society if this did not obtain.[2] In a well-ordered society, a child, trusting his parents, is simply taught by his parents to do the proper thing in the various associations into which he willy-nilly enters. He is taught *what* it is to be a member in good standing in such associations and he is taught *to be* in such good standing. Children learn what it is to be a good daughter, student, mother's helper, companion, sport, choir-boy, neighbor and the like. And indeed, as Rawls points out, our moral understanding increases as we move in the course of life, through a sequence of stations with their attendant duties. And in doing this we will come to have certain ideals appropriate to those roles.

As our understanding of ourselves and our society increases, we will move beyond a morality of association in the direction of having *a morality of principles* as we work out "a conception of a whole system of co-operation that defines the association and the ends which it serves" (*TJ*, 468). But in doing this, we will of necessity come to understand the roles of others and to see things from their perspective. Without this we can have little in the way of moral understanding. This leads us, in a way a child operating exclusively under a *morality of authority* will not do at all, to take note of the importance in morality of motives and intentions (*TJ*, 469).

What generally must obtain for there to be a functioning cluster of associations in a well-ordered society? One central thing is that there must be relations of friendship and mutual trust, where people can rely on one another to do their part. There must be developing relations of *reciprocity*. The situation of an agent entering into an organization in a well-ordered society is parallel to that of a child in his family in such a society. Finding people well-disposed toward him and willing to "live up to their duties and obligations" in the associations into which he enters, he develops, as a matter of psychological fact, "feelings of trust, and confidence" *vis-à-vis* them.

And he acquires attachments to them and a desire to live up to the ideals of the associations. The system will be stable where participants in a system of social co-operation regularly act with evident intention to preserve its just (or fair) rules and where bonds of friendship and mutual trust develop among them, thereby holding them ever more securely to the system (*TJ*, 472).

The principles of justice will be part of the ideals of many of the more complex associations and since this is so, people in those associations move very easily and naturally to a morality of association of the community as a whole, where everyone is viewed as a member of a society of equals and where, as associates, they are joined together in "a system of co-operation known to be for the advantage of all and governed by a common conception of justice" (*TJ*, 472). Here the key virtues are "justice as fairness, fidelity and trust, integrity and impartiality" (*TJ*, 472). The principal vices are "graspingness and unfairness, dishonesty and deceit, prejudice and bias" (*TJ*, 472). Such moral attitudes, Rawls contends, are bound to exist when people become attached to those, who co-operate with them in a fair scheme (*TJ*, 472).

The third and final stage of moral development is labelled by Rawls as the *morality of principles*. In it he tries to account for "the process whereby a person becomes attached to these highest order principles themselves" (*TJ*, 473). He recognizes, even in the more complex forms of the morality of association, where a concern develops for the equal citizen, that there is an acceptance of the principles of justice. But our complying with them at such a stage of development is not because we, on reflection and with vivid awareness, simply want to act justly and advance just institutions, but the motive for acceptance "springs largely from . . . ties of friendship and fellow feeling for others." Rawls wants to understand how we become attached to the highest order moral principles themselves and come to accept them as intrinsically desirable. This means that our moral attitudes "are no longer connected solely with the well-being and approval of particular individuals and groups, but are shaped by a conception of right chosen irrespective of these contingencies" (*TJ*, 475). The *morality of principles* includes, of course, the virtues of the morality of authority and association. But it is more as well, for it organizes the ideals of these moralities "into a coherent system by suitably general principles" (*TJ*, 478). We at this stage of moral development become fully mature moral agents. As such we not only want to be cooperative and attain approbation from those around us, we wish, as well, to be *just persons* (*TJ*, 473). We come to recognize how social arrangements in accordance with the principles of justice have promoted our own good and the good of those with whom we are associated and this tends to engender in us "a desire to apply and to act upon the principles of justice" (*TJ*, 474). And the having of this desire leads us beyond simply caring about the welfare of those to whom we are bound by particular family-molded, association-molded, ties of fellow feeling. The building up of such sentiments is crucial in morality. Friendship and the ties of association are not enough, for "while every citizen is a friend to some citizens, no citizen is a friend to all"

(*TJ*, 474). Our moral psychologies need to be developed to the point where there is the general "acceptance of public principles of justice," the common allegiance to which "provides a unified perspective" from which we can adjudicate our differences. Our psychological development naturally leads to the having of such a *morality of principles* and the having of such principles by human beings is essential to our individual and collective well-being.[3]

## IV

What seems puzzling is how we come to desire, *for its own sake,* to promote just institutions or to act in accordance with the principles of justice. Would they not always be principles which were desired for some other end? They, of course, could be desired for some other end and for themselves as well. Yet it is the latter which remains puzzling. How is it that we come to "want to do our part in maintaining" just arrangements even when doing so may not be beneficial to people we happen to care about, including ourselves? A man with a sense of justice will have such wants, but how does he come to have them and sustain them? That is to say, *how* does he become and remain a man with *a sense of justice?* It is also the case that a man with a sense of justice is a man who will be willing "to work for (or at least not to oppose) the setting up of just institutions and for the reform of existing ones when justice requires it" (*TJ*, 474). In a well-ordered society, we simply desire to do or have these things. We in short have a pro-attitude toward morality and indeed value it for its own sake (*TJ*, 527).

How is it that we come to have these desires? Rawls seems to rely here principally on associationist psychological principles or a kind of Skinnerian reinforcement.[4] He remarks that once attitudes of love, friendship and mutual trust have been generated, the very recognition that we and those for whom we care are the beneficiaries of established and enduring just institutions tends to produce and continue to reinforce in us the corresponding sense of justice. That is to say, once we have these other dispositions and we live in a society with just institutions, we will come to have *a sense of justice.* We develop a desire to apply and to act upon the principles of justice once we realize how social arrangements answering to them promote our good and that of those with whom we are affiliated. "In due course we come to appreciate the ideal of just human co-operation" (*TJ*, 474). In such circumstances, when we do not live up to these principles, we also feel guilt. (*Pace* Skillen and Collier we need not and indeed should not believe that such feelings of guilt must be irrational.)

It looks at least as if this prizing of morality *for its own sake* is just a brute fact about us and, furthermore, it does not look—someone might argue—as if Rawls has even unearthed an explanatory reason let alone a justificatory reason why this should be so.[5] We (or rather most of us) just want to be moral. I do not wish to make such a strong claim, but I shall argue that Rawls has not shown that there is or can be a reason or set of reasons for prizing morality for its own sake which are sufficient to undermine a consistent amoralist's challenge by showing the irrationality or even the inferior rationality of the consistent amoralist's alternative point of view. This may be one of the points where the giving of reasons comes to an end. This is particularly evident if we stick to Rawls's rather antiseptic conception of rationality.

There is, however, a passage in which Rawls does try to provide us with such a rationale and to show that "the desire to act justly is not a form of blind obedience to arbitrary principles unrelated to rational aims" (*TJ*, 476). Put just like that, with the umbrella phrase 'unrelated to rational aims,' it may be little better than a truism on Rawls's part. But put somewhat more strongly, as I think is his intent, the claim would come to the contention that if a man has rational aims and is in a well-ordered society, then he will just desire—and for its own sake—to act justly: a perfectly just society must be part of an ideal that *any rational* man will have, if he has full knowledge and vivid awareness of what is involved.

But his argument why this must be so does not seem to me very clear or convincing. (Indeed, as we shall see, he even makes remarks of his own which hardly square with that claim.) The principles of justice are prized because rational persons can see that it is in their interests to have them when they need to adjudicate competing claims. But this seems only to show their *instrumental* value. It does not show why a rational individual has a sound reason for prizing them for their own sake. It shows why he will want them to be the principles of adjudication between people, but it does not show why he will always want to use them himself rather then always just appear to use them when it is in his interest to do so. That is to say, a rational individual will never want to be *seen* to be unfair and he will see the overall value of principled behavior in society. That is, he will see why rational individuals will want people to act in accordance with the principles of justice. But it is not so clear that a rational person *must* actually want to be fair, when it is not in his interest to so act, as distinct from wanting simply to seem to be fair. And it is not clear that it is always in a rational individual's interest to be fair. My point is that while it is plausible enough to claim that for rational persons generally it will advance their collective interests if they act in accordance with the principles of justice, it does not follow that it will always be in the rational self-interest of any given individual to be fair or to desire to be fair in every situation in his life where competing claims and questions of justice arise. Rawls typically (but not always) seems to think that being fair will be what reason (rationality) requires of him, but—as far as I can see—he has not given any persuasive grounds for this belief. He has not shown that being fair is something we should do for its own sake, that it is desirable for its own sake or that it is something to be wanted in itself.

Rawls claims—and I agree—that it is a first class blunder to maintain "that the highest moral motive is the desire to do what is right and just simply because it is right and just, no other description being appropriate" (*TJ*, 477). Such a doctrine "of the purely conscientious act," Rawls holds, "is irrational" (*TJ*, 477). It makes the sense (sentiment) of right and the sense (sentiment) of justice into something quite arbitrary, something without rhyme or reason. Rawls, of course, believes that this sentiment of justice is not a different desire from that of acting "on principles that rational individuals would consent to in an initial situation which gives everyone equal representation as a moral person" (*TJ*, 478). And, in a very Kantian fashion, he takes that to be equivalent to "wanting to act in accordance with principles that express men's nature as free and equal rational beings" (*TJ*, 478). We need not à la Ross or Prichard take the sense of right to be a desire for something which is unique and unanalyzable. Alternatively, and by a de-mythologization or at least de-mystification, we can construe it, as Rawls does, in terms of a *desire to be rational:* to "want to live with others on terms that everyone would recognize as fair from a perspective that all would accept as reasonable" (*TJ*, 478).

I shall make two general comments about this claim. First, the acceptance of the above is perfectly compatible with saying as well that being just is something to be wanted for its own sake, desirable in itself, i.e. intrinsically and not just instrumentally desirable. That the desire to do what is right could only be properly characterized in those Rossian terms could be quite mistaken, even incoherent, while it could very well still be true that being just is something which has intrinsic worth—something which a rational person would want for its own sake. This being so my questions developed two paragraphs back are quite intact. Second, it may be—I do not say it actually is—clear enough that Rawls' principles of justice are principles "everyone would recognize as fair from a perspective . . . all would accept as reasonable" and it still could be the case that an individual (any individual at all) could recognize that while that is the *collectively* reasonable thing to do, it still is not necessarily the rational thing, at least in certain circumstances, for him (as an individual) to do and thus he might *not* come to believe or (more likely) to continue to believe that to be a rational person, it must be the case that he desires to be *just,* particularly where that is construed as something to be wanted for its own sake. He might very well believe instead that when he considers things strictly from his own point of view it would depend on the circumstances whether being just is something which is everything considered desirable.

It no doubt is the case that for most of us —though not for the characters in *Last Exit to Brooklyn*—"among our final ends are the attachments we have for persons, the interests we take in the realization of their interests, and the sense of justice" (*TJ,* 494). But the truth of that at least putative sociological fact is perfectly compatible with its not being the case that there must be a failure in *rationality* in an agent, if he did not desire to be—let alone to strive to be—a just person where (to put it crudely) being just did not pay.

Perhaps in going through the stages of moral development Rawls outlines—a psychological development necessary for the proper understanding of morality—we would come in "due course . . . to appreciate that ideal of just human cooperation" (*TJ,* 474). But here we must disambiguate 'appreciate'. Presumably Rawls takes it to mean 'to come to see the importance of and *accept as an ideal to govern your life'*. An amoralist—perhaps someone who had once been a full-fledged moralist—could not, of course, appreciate it *in that way* and be an amoralist, but he could appreciate it in a manipulative way. That is to say, he could see that human cooperation was necessary both to ward off a Hobbesian state of nature and for people to realize their rational life plans. But he can—without any loss of rationality—be a free rider or take a purely class point of view and gain the values of human cooperation, while not himself being committed to any principle of fairness. He appreciates the social value of human cooperation, but he has no appreciation of such an ideal as something to which he must commit himself. And in not so committing himself, it is not clear to me that he denies his nature as a free and rational agent any more (or any less) than if he did so commit himself (*TJ,* 572). Yet Rawls denies this, though he also says things (as we shall see) that would lead one to think that he should accept it. (See his remarks about first-person and free-rider egoism [*TJ,* 486-487].)

What appears at least to be the case is that while sometimes Rawls sees the force of something very much like what I have been arguing, he still characteristically in his arguments fails to acknowledge its force. This is particularly, and crucially so, when he thinks about what a rational person must commit himself to. Rawls, like many a moral philosopher, understandably enough, wants to show that there is a cluster of moral principles which are uniquely rational such that, for certain situations of a determinate kind, any rational agent or at least any fully informed, fully rational agent would have to adopt them as governing his behavior or be diminished in his rationality. If the above argument is correct, it is very doubtful indeed whether Rawls's key claim is so. But Rawls has some further arguments and before we settle with that conviction about convictions we should look at them.

## V

Rawls's second argument for the claim that rational individuals *must* desire to be just, turns on the claim that "the sense of justice is continuous with the love of mankind" (*TJ,* 478). But even if this is so—and that it is so is at least plausible—how do we know that rational individuals *must* love humanity? It is rational in a well-ordered society, under normal circumstances, to love one's parents, friends and the like. And it is not irrational to love mankind as well. But why is it, or is it, that a man is in any way faulted in his *rationality* if he does not love mankind? As far as I can see there are no sound grounds for claiming he has been so faulted if he does not love humanity.

Lastly (in this passage) Rawls argues, following Kant, that in reasoning in accordance with the principles of justice men "express their nature as free and equal rational beings. Since doing this belongs to their good, the sense of justice aims at their well-being even more directly" (*TJ,* 476). But (as I put it in another context) why *must* it be the case—or is it necessarily the case—that an amoralist, a thoroughly unprincipled man, is any the less a free and rational being for not being a morally good man, as distinct from being merely a man of good morals? It would, in anything like normal circumstances, be disastrous for an individual to be *seen* to be through and through unprincipled, but it isn't clear that he must have engaged in any irrationality if he keeps his unprincipled behavior a well-guarded secret.

It may be the case that rational individuals in the initial situation would adopt Rawls's principles of justice. But this does not show that a rational individual in a well-ordered society or even in a not so well-ordered society must, where he is only considering his own rational plan of life (a plan for himself), (1) desire to be just or (2) always find it in his rational self-interest to be just. Has Rawls given us adequate grounds for believing that the "common nature of man" is such that if an individual does not act in accordance with the principles of justice, then he has denied his common human nature or has shown that he is not a free rational agent? (I shall return to this question.)

What Rawls has shown, I believe, is that we, or at least most of us, do, as a matter of fact, have such moral sentiments, including a sense of justice, and that this is to be expected on psychological developmental grounds, given our moral education (indoctrination). And, in addition, he has shown that rational agents in the initial position would recognize that these principles—that is at least *some* distinctively moral principles, not necessarily Rawls's own principles—are the standards it is most reasonable for them to adopt to govern their relations with each other. He may even have given us reason to believe that such a capacity for and propensity towards principled behavior is, as an outcome of natural selection, an adaptation of humans to their place in nature (*TJ,* 503). But all of this does not establish that it is the most rational thing for *an individual* to do or to want to do. What is in everyone's interest, taken collectively, and what is in most people's interests, taken distributively, need not be in an individual's interests taken individually. Rawls stresses this himself, though in another context, when he writes:

> To be sure, from the standpoint of the original position, principles of justice are collectively rational; everyone may expect to improve his situation if all comply with these principles, at least in comparison with what his prospects would be in advance of any agreement. General egoism represents this no-agreement point. *Nevertheless, from the perspective of any one man, both first-person and free-rider egoism would be still better.* Of course, given the conditions of the original positions neither of these options is a serious candidate. Yet in everyday life an individual, if he is so inclined, can sometimes win even greater benefits for himself by taking advantage of the co-operative efforts of others. Sufficiently many persons may be doing their share so that when special circumstances allow him not to contribute (perhaps his omission will not be found out), he gets the best of both worlds: on these occasions anyway things transpire much as if free-rider egoism had been acknowledged. (*TJ,* 496-497 italics mine)

It is evident enough that the first-person and the free-rider egoist is an amoralist or immoralist. He doesn't have an eccentric or self-serving morality, he just doesn't have any morality at all. But what is not crystal clear is why he necessarily must be an irrationalist or indeed why he could not even be a thoroughly rational individual. Rawls recognizes that from the "perspective of any one man" such an egoism "should be still better" than acting from the moral point of view. But, since this is the case, why can't such an egoist be a rational agent? (Remember 'rational' for Rawls is to have no moral force.) Rawls denies that he can be rational. But isn't he just mistaken here? It is irrational in most circumstances to be *seen* to be unfair but need it be irrational *to be* unfair?

Someone might plausibly remark that we should not give a direct—yes or no—answer to this. If Rawls's account of the dynamics of moral learning is even near to the mark, rational agents in a well-ordered society—and even in a society with an endurable moral order—are people who have a sense of justice and this means that they will with some regularity act in accordance with it. We will thus, after all, have good *explanatory* reasons why they are moral. But what about *justificatory* reasons? Can we show the free-rider egoist or the classist amoralist who only considers the interests of his class or those he just happens to like that he must have made some *intellectual* mistake in opting for such a plan of life? Can we know that being fair must be an integral part of any *rational* plan of life?

We could show an individual that it was rational for him to want a well-ordered society and that in a well-ordered society his moral education would be such that he (most likely) will feel guilty if he really does act as such a free-rider egoist or classist amoralist. He will, whether it is rational or not, end up with a sense of justice and this sense of justice will make him miserable for being such a free-rider or classist amoralist.

However, such an egoist or classist could respond that once he has such a clear insight into the situation and, if he is rational through and through, he can discount the early effects of moral indoctrination and come to understand what it would be like to view things and indeed to prudently act from an amoral perspective. He wants to know whether it can be known or justifiably believed that such an amoral perspective must be irrational. He could, even more cautiously, put it counterfactually: if he could discount the effects of early indoctrination in the moral point of view so that he could become more autonomous, would there be anything irrational in taking such an amoralist's perspective?

To this, it might be replied, that there would be such reason, if his very humanity and self-respect are to count for anything, and if they are to be important to him in his image of himself and in the living of his own life. Here we return to some Kantian themes previously mentioned. (In this connection, section 74—particularly pages 486-489—and section 86 are crucial in *A Theory of Justice*.)

Rawls argues powerfully that "the moral feelings are a normal feature of human life. We could not do away with them without at the same time eliminating certain natural attitudes" (*TJ*, 487-488). He goes on to add "among persons who never acted in accordance with their duty of justice, except as reasons of self-interest and expediency dictated, there would be no bonds of friendship and mutual trust. For when these attachments exist, other reasons are acknowledged for acting fairly" (*TJ*, 488). A natural attitude would be the attitude of love and trust. They overlap with moral feelings, for moral feelings, include centrally such things as remorse, indignation, guilt, shame, approval, joy, trust, love and friendship. But these things could not—logically could not—be part of the psychology of a thorough amoralist. Even resentment and indignation are not—though they are natural attitudes—attitudes an amoralist or free-rider egoist could have. If I have as a rational plan that I will only treat people justly where it pays, I cannot, by definition, have friends or love someone. 'Bonds of friendship' does not, semantically speaking, even allow such a relationship. It is a grammatical remark to say "If X is my friend, then I cannot deliberately and regularly treat X unjustly when it simply suits my interests to do so." And it is another grammatical remark to say "I cannot simply regularly ignore the interests of those I love when all that is involved in doing so is that I would gain from it." "He loves her but he doesn't at all care about what happens to her" is an incoherency. Similarly, while the amoralist could feel anger and annoyance, he could not feel resentment and indignation (*TJ*, 488). As moral feelings, resentment and indignation must be elucidated in terms of principles of right and justice. To have them is to accept such principles as regulative for one's behavior. The central thrust of Rawls's argument occurs in the following passage:

> One may say, then, that a person who lacks a sense of justice, and who would never act as justice requires except as self-interest and expedience prompt, not only is without ties of friendship, affection, and mutual trust, but is incapable of experiencing resentment and indignation. He lacks certain natural attitudes and moral feelings of a particularly elementary kind. Put another way, one who lacks a sense of justice lacks certain fundamental attitudes and capacities included under the notion of humanity. Now the moral feelings are admittedly unpleasant, in some extended sense of unpleasant; but there is no way for us to avoid a liability to them without disfiguring ourselves. This liability is the price of love and trust, of friendship and affection, and of a devotion to institutions and traditions from which we have benefitted and which serve the general interests of mankind (*TJ*, 488-489).

This is the Kantian (or for that matter 'natural law') motif that a man's common human nature, his humanity, commits him to taking the moral point of view. The natural attitudes of friendship, love, affection, and mutual trust are things he would have reason to want if he has *reason* to want anything. If anything is a rational desire, wanting these things are rational desires and the having of such attitudes is the having of rational attitudes. *If* to be rational is to act on those desires that one would have when one is fully informed and vividly aware, then these are things it is always rational to desire. But one cannot desire these things without also being committed to the principles of justice: to trying to act in accordance with these principles not just as a man of good morals would, but as a morally good man would. In short, it is never rational to abandon the moral point of view.

Note that while it might be objected that the use of 'humanity' and 'disfiguring' is normative in the above passage and that they might be thought to be contestable notions, Rawls need not argue against that claim to make his core point, for it is just our unavoidable involvement with the natural attitudes cited above that makes it rationally mandatory on us as individuals to adopt the moral point of view.

However, Rawls cannot justifiably make so strong a Kantian claim on the basis of the evidence he has given us. What he has done is to establish that one cannot be a first-person or a free-rider egoist and have such *natural* attitudes. He has not shown that if one prizes friendship, love, trust and the like, one must have a sense of justice and be committed to principles of right and justice, for one might simply take 'a class point of view' or perhaps even 'a familial point of view' limiting one's concern for people quite deliberately to one's own family and relatives or small circle or class and yet experience friendship, love and trust. That is to say, one would have the attitudes appropriate to 'taking familial point of view' or 'a tribal point of view' or 'a class point of view' and still have those natural attitudes. Such a man, committed, say, to 'a familial point of view', rejects principles of justice as firmly as the first-person egoist, but he still has these prized natural attitudes.[6]

There are certain passages in Section 86 of A Theory of Justice that might be construed as an implicit reply to the above argument. Once we have conceded, as I have, that there are principles of morality which are collectively rational and that it is in the interest of each that everyone comply with them, I cannot, without error, maintain the equal rationality of taking something like a purely class point of view. Recognizing that principles of morality are public and setting myself—my relations to my class and circle of friends and close associates aside—"on a systematic course of deception and hypocrisy, professing without belief" the accepted moral views as it suits my purposes and the interests of myself and my friends, I still make, Rawls claims, a mistake, for the psychological costs, given my indoctrination, will be too great to make such deception worth it (TJ, 570). The necessity of taking precautions, maintaining a pose with its consequent loss of spontaneity and naturalness will make the price of acting too high to make it a reasonable option for a rational man in a well-ordered society. (Rawls recognizes that what should be done in exploitative and corrupt societies such as ours is another matter.) (TJ, 570)

What Rawls says may be so; it is surely not unreasonable to believe that it is so. But it is precisely the sort of claim that requires considerable, carefully sifted empirical evidence linked with a rather more sophisticated social theory than we have at present. Here we cannot simply rely, as Rawls does, on what it seems reasonable to believe. We need here actual sociological research. Sticking to our armchairs, we can easily develop different scenarios than Rawls's, including one in which we have Mafia-like people in positions of security in their own clan or class ignoring moral considerations and still attaining the various psychological reinforcements of which Rawls speaks, while avoiding threats to their security and any extensive need to put on a pose or take elaborate precautions. No doubt such an outlook usually involves rationalizations about the worthlessness of 'the others' outside the clan, but it is not clear that it must. They might not, where they are powerful (say a ruling class), extend their caring beyond their own circle. They might have no love for mankind; indeed they might be quite indifferent to the fate of people beyond their circle and not suffer any failure in rationality, security or ease of life. Indeed the latter two might be enhanced. They would want to be fair to friends and give justice to those they happen to care for, but their familial, clan or class points of view would be their reference points and not the principles of justice—principles partially constitutive of the moral point of view. Yet these amoralists could very well have the indispensable natural attitudes of which Rawls speaks (TJ, 580).

Rawls could reply that I am forgetting that he is speaking of a well-ordered society and in such a society these natural attachments, which are so necessary for human flourishing, would be extended rather more widely than I allow. But it still remains the case that even in such a society a rational agent, rather like a free-loader in our societies, could recognize that his conditioning would very likely take such a moralistic form, and still could conclude—given the admitted strains and costs of moral commitment—only to keep such commitments where he would not be hurt by ignoring them or where he would not hurt his friends and the people closely associated with him by ignoring them. It is not my concern to show that people actually so reason and so act—we do not have any well-ordered societies either— but simply to claim that there is no reason to believe that such an amoralist, if indeed he exists, would be less rational than Rawls's man of moral principle.

It is rather unrealistic on Rawls's part to counter that such an agent could not select who would be hurt by his unfairness and thus he might very well inadvertently harm those for whom he cares. A moment's consideration of Rawls's own example of tax-evasion shows that. In a world of non-tax evaders an individual's intelligent and reasonably prudent tax-evasion is going to do precious little general harm but it can be very advantageous to himself and to those close to him. Rawls is being Quixotic when he claims that in all recognizable human contexts there are "strong grounds for preserving one's sense of justice" (*TJ*, 371).

The social nature of human nature and the important role of what Rawls calls the Aristotelian principle in our life is also not sufficient to make amoralism irrational. We indeed need people to bring to fruition our latent powers, the proper functioning of which is essential for our well being, but there is no reason why, at least for some rational agents powerfully placed, a familial or at least a purely class point of view could not so serve as readily as a moral point of view.

Perhaps, borrowing far more heavily from perfectionist moral theory than Rawls is prepared to do and stressing his seventh principle of rational choice, someone wishing to reconstruct slightly his account to meet these objections, could develop and clearly articulate a more satisfactory self-realizationist account of morality in which he would have established that to realize ourselves—to achieve our full human flourishing—we must be just men and not just men of good morals. That is, of course, a humanly attractive doctrine, yet it is fraught with obscurities and has not been worked out by Rawls or, as far as I know, by anyone else.[7]

Rawls is adamant that "in order to realize our nature we have no alternative but to plan to preserve our sense of justice as governing our other aims" (*TJ*, 574). I would no longer make the curt rejection of the coherency of talk about 'realizing our nature' I once did, but it still is a very obscure formula requiring a careful elucidation and defense for it to be something to which we can legitimately appeal.[8] Marx and some Marxists make something of a beginning here; but Rawls does nothing with this and it is at best a first step.[9]

Similar considerations obtain for the attractive but unestablished doctrine that "the desire to express our nature as free and equal rational beings can be fulfilled only by acting on the principles of right and justice as having priority" (*TJ,* 574). Perhaps if we stress 'equal' something can be done towards its rather truistic establishment; but where 'equal' is dropped, or not given prominence, it remains a morally attractive but quite unsupported claim. We have been given no good grounds for believing that if we would be rational we must be committed to it.

Rawls in an ancient and honorable tradition in moral philosophy wants to get out of reason more than reason can establish. This is not to say that reason is wanton but it is to give to understand that it cannot provide the decision procedure in morals that Rawls envisages (*TJ,* 574-575). The sentiment of justice does indeed reveal what a person is and expresses in a very fundamental way a conception of oneself. But this does not mean that the achievement and sustenance of an individual's rationality, even in a well-ordered society, is tied to that sentiment. Thoroughly rational people might be unprincipled bastards.

NOTES

1. John Rawls, *A Theory of Justice* (Cambridge, Mass.: Harvard University Press, 1971), p. 584. All references to Rawls are from *A Theory of Justice* and they are given in the text in parentheses.

2. Ralf Dahrendorf, *Essays in the Theory of Society* (Stanford, Calif.: Stanford University Press, 1968), pp. 151-178.

3. For two striking and indeed important statements of a contrary view see Tony Skillen, "Marxism and Morality," *Radical Philosophy* 8 (Summer, 1974) and Andrew Collier "On The Production of Moral Ideology," *Radical Philosophy* 9 (Winter, 1974) and "Truth and Practice," *Radical Philosophy* 5 (September, 1973). While such a morality of principles with its deontological elements, can and indeed often does have the mystifying and harmful ideological effects which Skillen and Collier characterize, it by no means follows that such a morality must be such an ideology or that to attain this last stage of moral development just is to become firmly captive of such a moral ideology. Moreover, without some sense of justice, it is impossible to attain the solidarity, fraternity and, indeed moral freedom, essential for a fully human society, answering to Marx's conception of such a society. Some of this is brought out in Peter Binn's reply to Skillen and Collier in his "Anti-Moralism," *Radical Philosophy* 10 (September, 1975). See as well Philip Corrigan and Derek Sayer, "Moral Relations, Political Economy and Class Struggle," *Radical Philosophy* 12 (Winter, 1975).

4. Not entirely, however, for see what he says about rationalism on page 495.

5. The need for drawing this distinction and some of the crucial ways we can fall into confusion here has been importantly re-stressed by E. J. Bond, "Reasons, Wants and Values," *Canadian Journal of Philosophy* 3, no. 3 (March, 1974): 333-347.

6. I owe this last point to Professor Grace Dyck. I should also add that there is a curious passage in chapter 9 (page 568) of *A Theory of Justice* where Rawls tries to go around the considerations I have been taxing him with in this essay. He points out there that he is "not trying to show that in a well-ordered society an egoist would act from a sense of justice, nor even that he would act justly because so acting would best advance his ends." He is not even arguing "that an egoist, finding himself in a just society, would be well advised, given his aims, to transform himself into a just man." But then what happens to the tight link between rationality and morality that Rawls is concerned to forge, namely to show that in the world, as we know it, a rational human being *must*—not merely *may*—strive to be a moral human being, e.g. not only do the things a just man would do but do them for the just man's reasons? Rawls in this passage seems to be saying, as I think he should, that there is no such tight link, but then he has lost a grip on what for him is a very fundamental claim, namely that moral principles are the principles that rational human beings would choose to govern their actions. This claim, of course, needs disambiguation but, in one important way—if my central arguments have been correct—it is false and Rawls in this passage in effect agrees that it is false. To counter by remarking that an individual egoist's policies and strategies are not principles, comes down too hard on what may be a correct perception about the ordinary use of 'principles'. However, the essential point is that the individual egoist could have quite teachable strategies that appear at least to be no less rational than moral principles.

7. Richard Norman makes a start in his unpublished work "Self-Realization." His essay is in part a response to my attempt to exhibit the extensive obscurities and incoherencies in a self-realizationist ethics in my "Alienation and Self-Realization," *Philosophy* 48 (January, 1973).

8. For these earlier curt rejections see my "On Taking Human Nature as the Basis of Morality," *Social Research* 29 (Summer, 1962) and "Conventionalism in Morals and the Appeal to Human Nature," *Philosophy and Phenomenological Research* (December, 1962).

9. See here Michael P. Lerner, "Marxism and Moral Reasoning," *Social Praxis* 2, nos. 1-2 (1974): 63-88, and my "Class Conflict, Marxism and the Good-Reasons Approach," see chapter 6 of this volume.

# 11

# Critique of Pure Virtue
## Animadversions on a Virtue-Based Ethic

## I

Goal-based ethical theories, duty-based ethical theories and rights-based ethical theories have all been well represented and well canvassed during the modern era. But it has also become evident, particularly since the extensive examination of Rawls's, Dworkin's and Nozick's views, that none of these accounts are without very fundamental difficulties—difficulties which are not just difficulties in detail but difficulties in the basic structure and the programmatic intent of such theories. Just as with the deadlock in ethical theory of some twenty years ago there were scattered voices telling us to go back to Kant, so in our present circumstances it is understandable that some should try to return to a virtue-based ethics.

Virtue-based ethical theories in a way go back to Aristotle. We have with them a turning away from an ethics of principles, including an attempt to find the supreme principle of morality such as we find in Kantian or utilitarian theories. Kantian and utilitarian theories take the central task of moral theory to be the formulating and justifying of fundamental moral principles or principles of human conduct which would guide both individual and collective choice. A virtue-based ethics, by contrast, seeks to delineate the ends of human life (the good life for man) and to characterize what it is to be a good person. On such an account we find out what it is to be a good person and what are the ends of life by finding out what the distinctive human virtues are. This is the key, we are told, to discovering what human flourishing is.

From *Virtue and Medicine,* edited by E. E. Shelp, (Dordrecht, Netherlands: 1984), pp. 133–149. Copyright © 1984 by D. Reidel. Reprinted by permission of Kluwer Academic Publishers.

It is because of this that such an ethics of ends is called a virtue-based ethics. Where, in a goal-based theory or a duty-based theory, we have an ethics of principle, virtue is an ancillary concept. Virtue, on such an account, is characterized in terms of the disposition to act on principles of right conduct. Virtue-based theorists, following Aristotle, are distrustful of such gestures in the direction of precision. What we need instead is a theory of the virtues explaining the good for man and what it is to be a good person. We, in turn, will, in many circumstances at least, come to understand right action in terms of what a good person would do.

There has of late been a sprinkling of newly minted virtue-based theories: James Wallace's careful and insightful *Virtues and Vices*, Philippa Foot's lead essay in her collection of essays with the same title, and Peter Geach's *The Virtues*. But to my mind, the most significant and the most challenging of them all is Alasdair MacIntyre's *After Virtue*. It is a historicized Aristotelianism jettisoning Aristotle's metaphysical biology and his conception of the function of man. Employing a distinctive moral methodology, it uses, much more than traditional moral philosophy, historical analysis, a narrative method and the human sciences to first critique the dominant goal-based, duty-based and rights-based traditions in ethical theory and then to present his own positive alternative account—his historicized Aristotelianism.

It is with this positive account that I shall be concerned here. Since I am not inclined myself to take a virtue-based turn, though I am not disinclined to use some elements of it, I turn to a critical examination of MacIntyre's account as constituting what I take to be the most significant attempt, with which I am acquainted, to develop such a theory.

## II

Before I turn to critique let me set out the bare bones of his account with the warning that this can hardly begin to convey the nuance and the subtlety of MacIntyre's view.

MacIntyre believes that not only moral philosophy but morality itself in our time is in disarray. Indeed, the disarray of morality and moral philosophy go hand in hand, for MacIntyre would have us believe, we cannot properly understand a moral philosophy without understanding its social embodiment in a culture. Morality, for the Greeks, for the Icelanders represented in the Sagas, and for the Medievals was, MacIntyre believes, whole, but in our culture it is no longer whole and our moral philosophers in their attempts to understand morality are like philosophers trying to understand science after, because of some great catastrophe, a scientific culture has disappeared for several centuries. Such philosophers, living after its disappearance, would be trying to piece some understanding of it together from the fragmentary accounts still available to them of what it was like. Our moral philosophers, MacIntyre believes, are people with analogous disabilities; they have available to them no more than fragments of a conceptual scheme which has lost its context—a context which once made that a conceptual scheme intelligible but which we now have lost.

To try to make it intelligible our philosophers invent moral fictions like natural rights or utility. In such fragmented conceptual schemes, we come, naturally enough, to use moral utterances to express our emotions and the very idea of moral knowledge becomes a Holmesless Watson. MacIntyre claims that with this employment of moral discourse, we show, and indeed further instantiate, how we have lost our grip on the distinction between treating people as ends and manipulating them. And these conceptualizations in turn have their social embodiment in the bureaucratic manager and the therapist, both elitist paternalists, dedicated, though in different ways, to manipulation to achieve certain ends which themselves are never, and never can be, rationality defended.

MacIntyre thinks that there is but a slight chance for us to escape this cultural condition, but to the extent that there is a way, it is, he believes, through recapturing something of the Aristotelian notion of the virtues. We have lost our firm sense, a sense that came naturally to the Greeks and the Medievals, of what the virtues are. MacIntyre develops the notion of a practice—a cooperative activity in pursuit of goods internal to that activity—to explicate the virtues and their role in the moral life. Our various social roles, when they actually are engaged in, are practices such as being a parent, a teacher, a partner or ombudsman.

We not only have practices which, with their internal goods, define virtues, but we need as well some conception of a human life as a whole which like a narrative would have some unity. The making sense of our life as a whole comes to seeing its *telos* as it is revealed when we come to see the narrative unity in our lives. And this means that we need, as well, to recapture an understanding of tradition in which we see that we are what we are in large part because of our history, though this does not mean that we cannot be critical about the traditions which mold us, though we must also recognize that the very direction our criticality can take us is in turn determined by these traditions.

The virtues are necessary in the sustaining of traditions, traditions that in turn make possible a life in which the good for man is realized. But what is this good for man? It is a life with the unity of a narrative quest, a life, which, as MacIntyre puts it himself, is "spent in seeking for the good life for man, and the virtues necessary for the seeking are those which will enable us to understand what more the good life for man is."[1] To make sense of our lives, to make sense of morality, we must, in a way that is almost impossible for people caught in the culture of liberal modernity, see our lives as a unity, see our individual lives as a whole. To do this we need to have a full-fledged narrative understanding of our lives; with such an understanding, it is possible, though for us extremely difficult, to come to an understanding of the good of a human life as a whole viewed as a narrative unity.

## III

In the preceding section I gave you the core of MacIntyre's historicized Aristotelianism. I now want to turn to reflective commentary and critique. I am inclined to believe, where it is really crucial, where MacIntyre really needs to deliver, he doesn't deliver the goods, that his account is as empty or at least nearly as empty as the liberalism he despises. It may be, however, that I am asking too much, expecting something which is too determinate where that expectation is unreasonable.

The above remarks without any elucidation are a cluster of dark sayings. I will try to make them clear as I go along. In querying MacIntyre, as I am about to proceed to do, I want to make one thing perfectly clear at the outset. I think he asks the right questions or, to put it both more guardedly and more adequately, I think he, where for years we have neglected these questions, forces us to ask some very old and some very important questions that contemporary moral philosophy has been the poorer for not asking.

MacIntyre maintains that what we need to articulate and persuasively defend is some reasonable account of an "overriding conception of the *telos* of a whole human life."[2] We need to start with a recognition of how practices define the virtues, but to gain an adequate understanding of morality and the place of the virtues in morality we need to go beyond a careful attention to practices and even to traditions to an understanding of the ends of life. We need, if we can get it, some reasonably determinate conception of the good of a human life conceived as a unity. Without this being the case, MacIntyre contends, both "a certain subversive arbitrariness will invade the moral life" and it will also be the case "that we shall be unable to specify the context of certain virtues adequately."[3] Moreover, he further contends, we shall not have provided any viable alternative to the typically goal-based but sometimes duty-based or rights-based Enlightenment tradition and to liberalism, traditions he has argued are bankrupt.

It may well be, MacIntyre to the contrary notwithstanding, that not everything is lost if we cannot articulate some common conception of the good, for it may be that ethics in the form of a system of coordinative guidelines will still be of a not inconsiderable import in enabling us to forge forms of cooperation that will give some coherence to our lives together even though we do not have much in the way of any common conception of the good.

But still a lot would be lost if we are incapable of specifying, and making a social reality, both a reasonably determinate and a rationally vindictable conception of the good of a human life conceived as a unity. To achieve this, MacIntyre argues, we must understand human action. And to do this—to render human action intelligible—we must provide an alternative, more holistic understanding than the reigning atomistic conception which tries to analyze actions in terms of some conception of 'basic action'. To make actions intelligible we need to see them as a part of an ordered narrative sequence at least in part understood by the agent. In understanding this narrative sequence, it is important (a) to recognize the agents will have some primary intentions and (b) for us, the spectators, to understand what those intentions are. It is principally these primary intentions which give both the narrative and the actions which are part of it a teleological cast. We need, to make sense of our actions and our lives, to see them as having a narrative unity, including some image of the future in terms of which our actions tend to be ordered. It is important for each of us to know the stories of which we find ourselves a part. Our personal identity is a social identity in which we find ourselves in some enacted narrative of which we are a part.

MacIntrye thinks, or at least seems to think, that if we come to accept his view of what intelligible actions are (with its rejection of atomism), come to accept his view of personal identity, his views on how our lives are enacted narratives and his views on the importance and role of tradition in morality and in life more generally, we will come to believe that he has explained to us in what the unity of human life consists and how it is that there is a distinctive human *telos*. I am inclined to accept *something* like his account of the above matters but I do not see how they are sufficient to give us a sense of what the unity of human life consists in or of what our human *telos* consists in, if indeed we even have that sort of thing. What I am suggesting is that we can agree with him about his characterization of human action and personal identity and still be very skeptical about whether that will do much to solve his problem about giving an objective characterization of what the good for man is or even help make plausible that there is such a thing. We might even agree with him about his very general conception of what the unity of a human life consists in and still doubt that he has given us any determinate theory or even a conception of what the good for man consists in or what our human *telos* is.

The unity of a person's life, according to MacIntyre, would consist in "the unity of a narrative embodied in a single life."[4] What is good for that person is how she could best live out that unity and bring it to a completion. To ask, 'What is the good for man?' "is to ask what all answers to the former question must have in common."[5] To see what the human good consists in (what the end of human life is) would come to giving the correct answers to this question. (We must not forget, in examining this question, that there will be a not inconsiderable number of people who will either deny that there is something called 'the human good' or be skeptical about its reality.)

However, even with MacIntyre's appreciation of the import of tradition, even with his holistic understanding of what an intelligible action is and his understanding of personal identity, how are we to specify in any reasonably determinate way what this human good is? How can we, or can we, even specify what the good of a human life is?

Suppose I try for myself. After all, I should know myself better than anyone else. I view my life as a narrative, I ask myself what have I been doing and with what intentions, how have I been relating to others and what is the point of these various activities and the various relations into which I enter, what were my primary underlying intentions in engaging in such activities, what kind of unity do they have? How am I to sum them up and bring them to a completion to give unity and point to my life?

Suppose I do put something like this quite personally and non-evasively to myself as I, or anyone else, would have to to make the question at all real, to make, that is, the question have any real thrust or point. But what am I to say? There are a number of primitive certainties with which I could start. There are a number of people around me who regularly in one way or another enter into relations with me. Do I respond to these people or relate to them in a decent way and with kindness, understanding, and with a genuine caring for them as persons or am I largely indifferent to them or do I manipulate them or treat them with callousness or arrogance? (What I just called "primitive certainties" could just as well have been called à la Rawls, "very deeply embedded considered convictions.") A lot of evaluative terms are coming into play here and *sometimes* their meanings are *somewhat* troublesome and certainly we would have a lot of trouble, in every case, with their definition. But remember that useful definitions are about the last thing we can give after we have fully mastered not only operating *with* the terms expressive of these concepts but after having mastered operating *upon* them as well. It is a Platonic fallacy to think we do not understand a concept until we can define it. So I use in the above remarks terms like 'decency', 'kindness', 'integrity', 'caring', 'indifference', 'manipulation', 'callousness', and 'arrogance'. In some contexts these concepts can be tricky but I think in the context in which I used them I could in most instances in most situations perfectly well know whether I had acted in any of these ways. There is, of course, room for self-deception but that is also corrigible. It is one of the primitive certainties (*our* primitive certainties, if you will) that callousness, arrogance, manipulation, and even indifference should be out and that kindness, decency, caring, and understanding are required of a human being.

If I really do these things, if, that is, I act in the way I described above, I have given a certain unity and purpose to my life. But only a certain unity, for I could do those things and still be a lost human being utterly astray in Eliot's Wasteland. I could be a drunk or even a person thoroughly hating myself and convinced, and perhaps rightly so, that my life was a loss and still so relate. Moreover, it is not true that everyone whose life has had the unity of an enacted narrative, not everyone who has lived such a unity and who has brought to completion with integrity and purpose her life, has lived something that can be correctly called a good life. Some pretty unsavory characters here had such a unity to their lives. Think here of Hitler, Franco, or Stalin. They have lived lives that have had the unity of a narrative quest. They have violated some of these primitive certainties but then, in evaluating these lives, it is these primitive certainties that are carrying the day in our moral evaluation and not the fact one's life has the unity of a narrative quest. One's life could be through and through evil and still have such a unity and it could, in certain respects, be a good life and lack that unity.

It could be countered, the 'in certain respects' gives the game away. Suppose I look at my life again and convince myself that I treat those around me with decency, kindness, and integrity. But I know full well that I could, that notwithstanding, still be 'a lost soul'. My life, for all of that, could still lack anything like the unity of a narrative quest. So I ask myself, as you might ask yourselves, how best am I to live my life to give it such a narrative unity and to bring it to an appropriate completion? But there are so many ways I can go here. I have, in a society like ours, with a history like ours, so many role-models. I have nothing like the certainty of the people portrayed in the Icelandic Sagas or even that of the turn of the century Quebec farmers around Lac St. Jean portrayed in *Marie Chapadaline*. I have been a university professor for the greater part of my adult life and that concrete particularity gives me a few additional primitive certainties. I know I must try to teach my classes with integrity. That is, I know, I must try accurately to understand and comprehensively master the subject matter I am trying to teach and then try to convey it in comprehensible and truthful ways. These virtues are goods internal to the practice of teaching. And I also know I must treat my students fairly and, it should go without saying, that the earlier mentioned primitive certainties about kindness, decency and integrity must obtain in my relations here as well.

Is this enough, if I can really carry it out, to give my life the requisite narrative unity? Some would say so if the other primitive certainties continue to obtain in my family life and the like. Many university professors have so seen themselves, have so picked out such a unity of the narrative quest. Others, and I am one of them, have also seen themselves as intellectuals, as members of the intelligentsia, and have seen this as a central part of their vocation and as determining certain roles—determining certain ways to act and how to relate to others. But not all university professors so view themselves. Some see themselves merely as professionals, members of a certain profession with a certain expertise such as an engineer, an M.D., or a lawyer would view herself.

If the particularity of your life is being a university professor, and, let us say, a philosophy professor at that, how in that area of your life should you view yourself to fill out the narrative of your life? Which way should you fill it out for it to have the narrative unity of a good life? In this domain I have no doubts, subjectively speaking, how I should try to fill it out. But I know that there are others, at least as well educated as I, who see themselves simply as professionals. Which way do we have to go to best live out the unity of a narrative embodied in a single life if we are philosophy professors working in a university in the second half of the twentieth century in North America? I opt for trying to be an intellectual and not merely being a professional with a certain expertise. I think this is essential for an adequate self-definition for a person placed as I am placed, but what reasons could I give for this and how objective would they be?

Let us run with that a bit. I would say I was teaching and trying to understand philosophy and to develop some philosophical notions and I would further contend that the attaining of these things does not merely come to the having of a certain expertise—I am not just around to make distinctions—but very centrally involves the attempt to see steadily and as a whole how things of some human importance and social significance hang together, what sense we could make of our lives together and what it would be like to have more adequate societies and ways of relating to each other such that our lives together would be better lives. Beyond that, I would want to know, if I could, what steps we need to take to achieve such a truly human society. These hedgehoggy questions are not technical questions, though it may be that the answering of some technical questions are not irrelevant to the answering of those questions. These questions go beyond anyone's domain of competence and technical expertise. There is no expert we can turn to to grind out an answer here. It is not at all like asking what conceptions of necessity are essential for understanding modal logic or how material implication is related to our ordinary notions of 'if then' or how entailment is to be understood. These are technical questions and technically trained professionals can come up with the proper answers to them. Yet it is these non-technical questions (the questions about life and society) I raised above that are at the nerve of my own impulse to do philosophy.

Even if, in facing such questions, the last word we could with clarity and honesty give is that such 'questions' do not admit of any kind of genuine answer and that we are only mystifying ourselves and others if we give to understand that, at the end of some long inquiry or some long quest, perhaps carried out over many generations, we would, or at least could, attain answers to them like someday we might find a cure for cancer. But even if we on reflection judge that to be the proper response, we still take it as the response of a certain kind of intellectual and we also recognize, if we know anything, that it is but one of many responses and not, by any means, the only response we could give and that, at any rate, what is the proper response here could not be determined by any profession or even be a matter of some professional expertise.

Since it is intimately a matter of my own self-definition to try to face such perplexities felt as questions, this is an intimate part of my search for a narrative unity in my life. But what if someone says resolutely to me, "Nothing like this is built into the role of being a philosophy professor. Philosophy is not the name of a natural kind. Look about at your colleagues. They have, to put it mildly, not an inconsiderable variety of rather different conceptions of their role. Why should your conception of your way of living out and completing the narrative unity of your life be the right one? To think that it is is both foolishness and *hubris.*"

If I reply, "Because it is my life with my enacted narrative so I should be the one to decide how best I might live out that unity and bring it to completion," I have embraced just that individualism and liberalism MacIntyre so detests and thinks, not without reason, is so intellectually and morally bankrupt.[6] Moreover, it also seems to be a false claim, for it does not seem very probable that we are *always* the best judges here of what would be the best for ourselves. It is not very likely that we always best understand what would be the best life for ourselves. We are not always even the best judges of what is in our own interests even on a particular occasion. No matter how anti-paternalist we are resolved to be we need to recognize that. Why should it be the case, or indeed is it the case, that we are always, or perhaps even usually, the best judges of how best to live out our lives so that we, severally, could give our lives a unity and, like a narrative, bring it best to completion? That is a much more complex question than even the rather complex question of judging what in some determinate but fairly complex situation is in our own interests. That each of us, no matter who we are, and how we are situated, could best judge what would give our lives as a whole unity and integrity is, to put it mildly, highly improbable. (What morally we should do in the light of this is another question.)

If, in turn, it is responded "Oh no, it is not, for there is nothing to be known here or warrantedly believed or reflectively assessed, for such matters are really matters of just *deciding* how we are to live and what sort of persons we are to try to become," we have now fully embraced the non-cognitivism of the tail end of the enlightenment project, a non-cognitivism and decisionalism that MacIntyre was concerned to reject as the confused end product of a fragmented morality.[7] He does not want to say that the unity of my life is whatever I decide to make the unity of my life. He does not want to say that however I forge the unity of my life and bring this unity to completion, then, if that is done with integrity, that is the best life for me. He does not want to have anything to do with such rampant individualism, liberalism, and non-cognitivism.

Still, MacIntyre tells us that "the only criteria for success or failure in a human life as a whole are the criteria of success or failure in a narrated or to-be-narrated quest."[8] But what are the criteria of success here? I am not just a university professor and a philosopher but I am a husband, a father, a Canadian, a socialist, an atheist, an owner of a dog, a writer, and a lot of other things besides. What are the criteria of success of my human life? In answering this I would have to put these various activities into some unity and see them as being woven together in some narrative which would have some appropriate unity and ending. Perhaps I can put this together in a way that I find satisfactory or at least in a way that does not seem to me wildly wrong or alienating. But when I reflect on it in a non-evasive manner I can also see that I could have gone in other directions here, have taken other paths in a yellow wood. I might even have a sense of sorrow that I could not travel them both and be one traveler. But, as I reflect, I would also be aware of a myriad of paths that could be taken, of the many different ways of ordering and completing a narrative. Would I not have further to ask myself "What reason do I think we have for believing that we have anything even close to objective criterion for success or adequacy here?" MacIntyre talks of criteria for success or failure of a narrated or to be narrated quest. But he never gives us any sense of what these criteria are or could be. I have taken just one segment of my life, namely, my being a professor of philosophy, in thinking about how it fits into the narrative quest of my life. But even with this one tolerably determinate sequence there seem at least to be no tolerably objective criteria about how I should fulfill that role. Moreover, surely somewhat earlier in my life there were other things I could have been. Perhaps there are other things that I still could be. Besides being a university professor, I am also a Marxist committed to a socialist transformation of society. I care very much about what I am doing in doing philosophy but I not infrequently wonder if I should have done political economy instead (notwithstanding that it bores me) or whether I should have become an M.D. or an engineer and have gone off to some place like Angola and built bridges or spent my time doctoring in the backcountry. If I had it to do over, I am not so sure that I shouldn't have done these other things rather than what I am doing now. (Again, let me ask, as an aside, is it at all plausible to believe that each person, no matter who that person is, can best answer such a question for himself?)

Even with the particulars of my life reasonably well stamped in, I sometimes wonder whether, in my situation, I should abandon or cut down on doing the academic Marxist work I do and become a more directly political creature spending more time involved in actual concrete political struggles in my immediate environment or whether, when I was younger, I should have chucked up academic life altogether and tried to organize workers or to have become a soldier in some liberation army? Some of these, given who I am and what I can do, may be far-fetched but at least some of these are possible ways of narrating out my life. Which of these various possible activities would narrate out, or would have narrated out, my life best and give it (would have given it) the best unity, integrity, and completion?

It is possible to doubt that there are any objective answers here while very much wanting something with some objectivity, if it is to be had. But what would it be like to obtain anything making even a reasonable approximation to objectivity here? MacIntyre does not give us even a hint as to how such an answer is to be found. Here I have been talking about one person, namely, me. When I reflect on what is as obvious as obvious can be, namely, that my life is but one token of a type of thousands of types of ways a human life could be narrated out and given unity, it is possible to get very nervous indeed about 'true narratives' here or about the 'truth of narratives' or about the having of any even remotely adequate criteria for objectivity here.


IV


MacIntyre is not insensitive to such problems of contextuality (to call them problems of relativity begs some questions and exploits some ambiguities). He writes: "What it is to live the good life concretely varies from circumstance to circumstance even when it is one and the same set of virtues which are being embodied in a human life. What the good life is for a fifth century Athenian general will not be the same as what it was for a medieval nun or a seventeenth century farmer."[9] That is all well and good, but if we are to have some determinate conception of a *final telos* for human beings, something MacIntyre agrees with the medievals in thinking we need, we must also be able to ask and answer such questions as these: will a society and an assemblage of human lives which has the role of fifth century Athenian general, a medieval nun, a seventeenth century English farmer be a better society than one without these roles or with altered roles or quite different roles? Being a nun or a general or a slave or a serf or a proletarian or a lumpenproletarian or a capitalist—having that possible cultural space—goes with a certain kind of society with a certain set of practices and, as MacIntyre stresses himself, carries with it certain internal and external goods and rather different conceptions of the good life for humans. Would a world without nuns and/or without capitalists be, in conditions of productive abundance, a better world than a world with them? I think, and MacIntyre at one time thought, and perhaps still thinks, that, at least in circumstances of productive abundance, a world without them would be a better world. But, if our judgments are to be nonarbitrary here, we need criteria for such judgments (or so, at least, it would seem), but it is just this that MacIntyre does not provide us with or even make a gesture at how we might discover or construct. But surely answers here are necessary if we are to give an answer to what is the good life for man.

Am I quite right in saying he gives us no hints? Let us examine some very key paragraphs on page 204 of *After Virtue*. We have to be able, he remarks there, to in some reasonably determinate way answer the question, "Quest for what?" if we are to make any sense out of the notion of the good life having the unity of a narrative quest. And this means MacIntyre avers that the medieval Aristotelians were right in believing that we must have "some at least partly determinate conception of the final *telos*."[10] MacIntyre believes that this conception of the good for human beings is to be drawn from the questions we ask and what we learn from our "attempt to transcend that limited conception of the virtues which is available in and through practices."[11] When we examine practices, we learn, MacIntyre argues, that they all require trustworthiness, courage, and justice and also, knowing we very much need practices, we rightly conclude that a good life for human beings must contain these characteristics as virtues. It also becomes apparent to us—that is apparent in the history of development of ethics and of moral philosophy—that we are "looking for a conception of *the* good which will enable us to order other goods."[12] But we are also looking for "a conception of *the* good which will enable us to extend our understanding of the purpose and content of the virtues . . . "[13] Thirdly, and lastly, we are looking for "a conception of *the* good which will enable us to understand the place of integrity and constancy in life."[14] Plainly and understandably, as his discussion of Jane Austen makes plain, MacIntyre wants, in addition to trustworthiness, courage and justice, to add integrity and constancy to the list of virtues which must be a fixed part of a good life. Some might say that constancy overstresses the value of a certain unity of the person. Why not give greater weight to the having of intrinsically valuable experiences at a given time and perhaps to the maximizing of such experiences and less to constancy? But even if we do give such weight to constancy and integrity (our considered judgments are likely to pull us along here), it can come to very different things in different contexts. The Inquisition sometimes showed considerable constancy and integrity and so did the Conquistadors even when they brutalized in almost unimaginable ways the Andean and Mexican populations. And similar things have been said about the Black Angel of Auschwitz and a similar case might be attempted for Hitler or Stalin. Even the virtues of trustworthiness, courage, and, by their own lights, justice could be exemplified in the lives of Inquisitors and Conquistadors, even in those Conquistadors who slaughtered Indians all over the place, melted down their silver and gold religious objects, and drowned while crossing a body of water literally under the weight of the plundered silver and gold with which they were laden. They had a conception of the good and they had these central virtues. Admittedly, these are extreme cases and MacIntyre, no doubt, as much as any other morally reflective person living in our time, or perhaps any time, would reject these things as gross immoralities which could not be a part of the good life for human beings. But, putting him on the side of the angels does not gainsay the fact that the various virtues he has been able to show a rationale for are all capable of being exemplified in such behavior. They all can be seen as being a part of such narrative histories and as being a part of such narrative quests. Recall that for him justice is nothing more than the getting of what you deserve. He rejects Nozick's account, Rawls's account, and more radically egalitarian accounts of justice. Justice, as he characterizes it, could come to many different things in many different contexts. It is, on his understanding at least, a very indeterminate essentially contested concept. Moreover, these extreme cases aside, there are, over cultural space and historical time, and even in our own moral cultures, plenty of exemplifications of situations in which we could have these virtues in place and still have radically divergent and often deeply conflicting conceptions of the good for humans. Moreover, we can and do have very different orderings of the various goods and schedulings of the different virtues.

We indeed would reflectively want to be able to extend "our understanding of the purpose and content of the virtues."[15] We would indeed want to do this in order to have a conception of the good life and of what a critical morality could come to. MacIntyre does give us *something* of that here, though it has a certain daunting vagueness about it. But what he does not do is give us a sufficiently clear understanding of the purpose and content of the virtues so as to give us a reasonably determinate conception of the end for man (man's distinctively human good) even when we bring in the concept of a moral tradition.

MacIntyre might respond that his concept of a quest for the good is not something that should be thought to be adequately characterizable all at once. It is something like a *Bildung* which would emerge, as a kind of moral education, that occurs in the course of the quest in the face of all the "particular harms, dangers, temptations, and distractions" that we will encounter along the way. It is a kind of pilgrim's progress or a Wilhelm Meister's apprenticeship. It is in this way that we gain our moral education and through such an apprenticeship, as our self-knowledge grows, the goal of the quest finally is understood.

Should not the response be this: Such moral education has been going on for a long time and, except where we have had very sheltered and homogeneous societies, e.g., in our reconstruction of the Heroic Age and in certain, but no means all, primitive communities, we have not attained a consensus about the good for man, we have not obtained a consensus, let alone anything close to what we could characterize as a rational consensus, about what, if anything, our final *telos* is where that notion is given a reasonably determinate content. And the various *consensi* of limited communities have just been such limited and varied *consensi,* local affairs both temporally and spatially.

The virtues, it is surely at least plausible to maintain, are "those dispositions which will not only sustain practices and enable us to achieve goods internal to practices, but which will also sustain us in the relevant kind of quest for the good, by enabling us to overcome the harms, dangers, and distractions we encounter. . . ."[16] Though this may be how to characterize virtue, still MacIntyre's virtue-based moral theory has not told us what the good is. The increasing self-knowledge we gain from our increasing understanding of the virtues is supposed to give us a better understanding of the good and it indeed does give us an understanding of some elements (the virtues I have been adverting to) of the good, but, as we have also seen, it is still far from taking us to a knowledge of the good that is also a knowledge of our final *telos* or of just our *telos sans phrase.* We still do not know what that is or what it would be like to attain a knowledge of such a *telos.* Indeed we cannot even be confident that such a conception makes sense. So when MacIntyre remarks that we "have arrived at a provisional conclusion about the good life for man: the good life for man is the life spent in seeking the good life for man, and the virtues necessary for the seeking are those which will enable us to understand what more and what else the good life for man is," he has not told us very much.[17] It may even be a mistake to place such a weight on the *seeking* instead of the *having.* A good life for humans might very possibly be one in which there was not much to be done on the questing side for what was taken to be the good life was (sociologically speaking) fairly secure. Given that security, a person could turn her creative powers to other things. But that plainly contentious point aside, without a better idea of what successful seeking would come to here than MacIntyre has been able to give us, we are looking at best for the holy grail and at worst for the color of heat. MacIntyre understandably wants something more determinate by way of the knowledge of the good than what the reigning liberalism and individualism has been able to give us. But here at least he has not been able to deliver on that.


V


In arguing as I have, I have not rejected MacIntyre's insightful understanding of the role of tradition in morality and in our social-political life and his claims about the need to start from the particularities set in part by our varied traditions. (The particularities in question will, to a not inconsiderable extent, vary with what tradition we are in and with where we stand in that tradition and with other contextual features distinctive of our cultural and historical situation.) Nothing I have said in the previous sections commits me to a search for a *purely* universal conception of the good life for human beings that would try massively to set aside distinctive historical identities in determining the good for human beings. But I have maintained that, along with these contextually variable elements, there must, for such an appeal to be viable, be a sufficiently universally determinate conception of the good for humans so as not to so mire us in a historicism such that we are deprived of any critical vantage point in accordance with which we can assess societies or whole moral traditions.[18]

Also, nothing I have said would commit me to siding with J. L. Austin against MacIntyre over the following central consideration:

> It has often been suggested—by J. L. Austin, for example—that *either* we can admit the existence of rival and contingently incompatible goods which make incompatible claims to our practical allegiance *or* we can believe in some determinate conception of *the* good life for man, but that these are mutually exclusive alternatives. No one can consistently hold both these views. What this contention is blind to is that there may be better or worse ways for individuals to live through the tragic confrontation of good with good. And that to know what the good life for man is may require knowing what are the better and what are the worse ways of living in and through such situations. Nothing *a priori* rules out this possibility; and this suggests that within a view such as Austin's there is concealed an unacknowledged empirical premise about the character of tragic situations.[19]

I do think there are tragic confrontations between goods and there are also tragic situations in which our best moral choice is the lesser evil. But, as MacIntyre concedes, there are better and worse ways to respond in such situations. We are not left here with utter incommensurabilities. In saying this I do not mean to disagree with MacIntyre that there are tragic situations where we must just choose between evils. My complaint is that he has not given us a sufficiently determinate conception of the good for humans to give us much of a basis for any beliefs we might come to have about what those better and worse ways are when we have to choose between evils. We do not know, from what he tells us, how they even remotely to be determined here. Sometimes the choice of the lesser evil also involves the choice of what in that situation is the greater good. We indeed should recognize in such situations that "both of the alternative courses of action which confront the individual have to be recognized as leading to some authentic and substantial good," but we do not have a sufficiently determinate conception of a core concept of the good for humans for us to use it to determine in such a circumstance which of several responses that we characteristically make is the more appropriate.

VI

In spite of what I have argued is a central failure of MacIntyre's Aristotelianism, I would not want to maintain that it is as centrally and as irretrievably flawed as is traditional Aristotelianism with its metaphysical biology and its conception of the function of man. Perhaps someone working out of that tradition, demythologized in something like the direction in which MacIntyre has demythologized it, perhaps supplementing it with a theory of needs, could articulate and rationally defend a more determinate conception of the human good that was neither ethnocentric nor as empty as MacIntyre's conception. I do not see any *a priori* objections against it, though it is also reasonable to entertain considerable skepticism about the likelihood that such a research program will pan out. However, I think anyone trying to work it out or anyone setting himself to do moral philosophy period would do well to accept the following core claims of MacIntyre:

> . . . if [as it does for MacIntyre] the conception of a good has to be expounded in terms of such actions as those of a practice, of the narrative unity of a human life and of a moral tradition, then goods, and with them the only grounds for the authority of laws and virtues, can only be discovered by entering into those relationships which constitute communities whose central bond is a shared vision of and an understanding of goods. To cut oneself off from shared activity in which one has initially to learn obediently, as an apprentice learns, to isolate oneself from the communities which find their point and purpose in such activities, will be to debar oneself from finding any good outside of oneself.[20]

I think this is right. Anything else would hardly lead to or leave us with any moral understanding at all. Indeed it would not even allow us to have what MacIntyre calls a powerful Nietzschean moral solipsism. But while what MacIntyre characterized above is essential for moral understanding and moral culture, it will not give us, as I have argued, anything even remotely like an objective conception of the good for man. But, that notwithstanding, it will provide us with a good starting point.

NOTES

1. Alasdair MacIntyre, *After Virtue* (Notre Dame, Ind.: University of Notre Dame Press, 1977), p. 201.
2. Ibid., p. 188.
3. Ibid.
4. Ibid., p. 203.
5. Ibid.
6. Kai Nielsen, "Linguistic Philosophy and 'The Meaning of Life'," in E. D. Klemke, (ed.), *The Meaning of Life* (Oxford: Oxford University Press, 1981), pp. 177-204.

7. Ibid.
8. MacIntyre, op. cit., p. 203.
9. Ibid., p. 204.
10. Ibid.
11. Ibid.
12. Ibid.
13. Ibid.
14. Ibid.
15. Ibid.
16. Ibid.
17. Ibid.
18. Ibid., pp. 205-206.
19. Ibid., p. 208.
20. Ibid., p. 240.

# 12

# Against Ethical Rationalism

I

I

Sometimes, rightly or wrongly, a philosophical account, even a closely reasoned and elaborately constructed philosophical account, will strike us as being so utterly wrongheaded as not to be worth taking the very considerable trouble it would take to sort it out or to refute it. McTaggart's metaphysical theory is one such theory, and, many have felt, Malcolm's account of dreaming is another. It is just dotty, as J. L. Austin was said to have remarked, to think that to dream is to have a propensity to tell a story upon awakening. Modern attempts to refurbish the ontological argument are perhaps the most important examples of what I am speaking of in our contemporary life. Unless we happen to love solving puzzles, we are very likely, if we are interested in the philosophy of religion, to sigh with ennui at the appearance of yet another baroque but carefully crafted argument to prove that a denial of God's existence is self-contradictory. There has to be, we think, something wrong somewhere in such an argument: the problem is, can it readily be located? If the argument is very clever or very complicated, the person who loves solving puzzles may still want to have a go at it, but persons primarily concerned with the great debate between belief and unbelief and knowledgeable about the history of philosophy will, unless perhaps the new defender of the ontological argument has a lot of cultural clout, very likely just want to ignore the whole thing and to turn their attention to more important matters.

I must confess that that is something like the attitude I had toward Professor Alan Gewirth's central thesis about ethics when I first read about it

From *Gewirth's Ethical Rationalism,* edited by E. Regis (Chicago: University of Chicago Press, 1984), pp. 59–83. Copyright © 1984. Reprinted by permission of the publisher.

and first quickly read his initial statements of his core thesis about the foundations of ethics.[1] To believe that there is a substantive supreme principle of morality, the denial of which is self-contradictory, from which all other moral principles can be derived, and which all rational persons must accept, is the equivalent in ethics of accepting the ontological argument in the philosophy of religion. It just has to be wrong, and the task, if one deals with it at all, is to locate the place or places where such an argument went wrong. After studying *Reason and Morality*, I have come to appreciate the skill, the dialectical care, the thoroughness with which Gewirth has constructed his argument and the integrity of his project, but about his central claim I continue to feel the same way.

However, it is not unnatural in turn to respond that that is being a little dogmatic and that, if everyone were to react that way, cultural advance would be impeded. One should, as Malcolm once urged about the ontological argument, actually look and see how the terrain lies and how the arguments to which one so responds go, and not fall back in a mechanical way on a pervasive and unquestioned doctrine that is simply accepted as canonical in our philosophical culture. Such dogmatism, it is not unnatural to remark, is intellectually stultifying. We, given any careful challenge to a canonical doctrine, should rise to the occasion and follow the argument wherever it leads. I do not think that things are quite that simple, but there is enough force in that response to motivate trying here to come to grips with such an ethical rationalism.

It should also be noted that Gewirth is acutely aware that he is running against the stream. He has in his *Reason and Morality* and in several essays and responses to critics stated and elaborated his paradoxical claims with great care. I think it is probably fair to say that there is scarcely an even prima facie plausible criticism of his account that Gewirth has not anticipated and made some effort to respond to. That he has responded to criticisms does not, of course, mean, as Gewirth himself stresses, that his responses are adequate; but it does clearly attest to the care, thoroughness, and philosophical self-consciousness with which Gewirth has argued his case. Yet I still think, after reading through his work and some of the critical response to his work, that Gewirth is engaged in a kind of circle squaring—that such an account just could not be right. It could not provide us with a sound ultimate justification for our or any moral beliefs and it could not provide us with a secure foundation for ethics.

If I am at all to appraise Alan Gewirth's carefully articulated work, I must search out sound arguments for these hunches and test them against the bar of reason as Gewirth has forthrightly sought to test his own work. Though his central thesis can be stated rather succinctly, it is, as I have remarked, elaborately elucidated and defended by him in his extensive statement of it in *Reason and Morality*. Yet there are a number of places in

*Reason and Morality* where critique is in order. In casting about for a possible short cut that will go to the heart of the matter, I came on the following strategy: after placing Gewirth's account on the ethical map—indeed following his own typology—I shall first state his own latest succinct statement of his core argument, and then I shall take the very similar criticisms of Gewirth's core account made by such very different philosophers as Richard Brandt and Alasdair MacIntyre and, after stating them, proceed to see if there are resources in Gewirth's account to adequately meet those very fundamental criticisms.[2] I start from these critiques because they perspicuously make much the same criticism I fumblingly but independently came to on a first reading of Gewirth. These arguments criticize a very fundamental part of Gewirth's theory and do so without making (or so it seems to me) assumptions in philosophical methodology alien to Gewirth's approach which would then have to be argued out before we could come to anything approaching a conclusive case one way or the other. By sticking with these arguments, we give fewer hostages to fortune. If these criticisms cannot be successfully rebutted, Gewirth's account does not fail just in some peripheral part but at its very heart. (*RM,* 355) This being so, it behooves us to sort things out here if we can. I shall now turn to Gewirth's own account.

II

Gewirth wishes "to inquire into the moral power of reason."[3] Rationalist moral philosophers "have engaged both in the meta-ethical task of examining how moral principles and judgments can be justified and in the normative ethical task of actually presenting and developing on a rational basis what they regard as justified moral principles and arguments" (*RM,* 355).

In pursuing this very central question Gewirth quite properly inquires into the meaning of 'rational' in such a context. In claiming that morality is a rational enterprise, rationalist positions come, he claims, in two fundamentally different kinds: *substantive rationalism* and *procedural rationalism.* Substantive rationalists use 'reason' in such a way that they talk in ethics of 'a reason' in the sense of a "ground, including a principle or proposition that is presented to explain or justify actions" (*RM,* 355). Procedural rationalists, by contrast, mean by saying that morality is a rational enterprise that we have reliable "procedures or operations of reasoning or inference" in morality (*RM,* 355). What the *substantive* rationalist appeals to "as a reason or ground in some argument or action may not have been ascertained by reasoning" (*RM,* 355). Thus, a substantive rationalism need not rest on or presuppose a procedural rationalism, and the reverse is true as well.

Gewirth himself defends a form of procedural rationalism. He rejects substantive rationalism of both the traditional intuitionist sort and the good-reasons approach of Stephen Toulmin and Kurt Baier. (This is a position I once argued for myself.) The defects of intuitionism are well known, so Gewirth turns his critical attention to the good-reasons approach. In virtue of what it is for something to be a 'good reason in ethics' certain principles are by definition morally right. Such philosophers believe, Gewirth gives us to understand, that by definition moral reasons must be for the good of everyone alike and the function of morality is to harmonize people's actions in such a way that the good of everyone alike is achieved. But, Gewirth responds, moral issues cannot be settled by such linguistic legislation any more than they can be settled by "dogmatic pronouncements" the nature of which are but slightly disguised by calling them intuitions. The good reasons approach is really not an advance over intuitionism. It "ignores the existence of rival moral principles and 'reasons' and it offers no argument in support of its own principles" (*RM,* 355). Moreover, and perhaps most damagingly, it does not reveal the "moral powers of reason," for it does not show how 'good reasons' in ethics have been ascertained by reason such that any rational agent who understood what was involved in morality would find them supremely authoritative and categorically binding. 'Reason', on such an account, is persuasively defined and, in its morally non-neutral status, it, by what in reality is a conventionalist sulk, opts without justification for a particular moral view—a moral view that in reality is but one contender among several, though it is not recognized as such by the good reasons theorists.

Gewirth, as I have already remarked, defends a form of procedural rationalism, though it is a distinctive form, and he contrasts it with two, in his view, less adequate forms, forms paradigmatically exemplified in the work of Richard Brandt and R. M. Hare respectively. But all forms of procedural rationalism are, he claims, superior to substantive rationalism in that they use 'reason' and 'rational' in a morally neutral manner: they do not incorporate any morally favored principles into the very meaning of a good reason for a moral judgment (*RM,* 19).

There are, as I have remarked, two general forms of procedural rationalism and a subdivision of the second form. One form, the form ascribed to Brandt, is called *probabilistic procedural rationalism*, and the other form is called by Gewirth *apodictic procedural rationalism*. It in turn has two varieties, *full apodictic procedural rationalism* (Gewirth) and *partial apodictic procedural rationalism* (Hare). All forms of procedural rationalism try "to show how morally right principles and judgments can be ascertained or established by reasoning" (*RM,* 19). At the center of such moral philosophy is a direct concern with *moral justificatory argument.* (Its concern is with something which should always be at the heart of moral philosophy.) Probabilistic procedural rationalists stress inductive methods and the linking of moral philosophy closely with the empirical sciences. Finding out what is to be done and indeed even what must be done is very centrally dependent on empirical investigation, while for apodictic procedural rationalists such as Hare and, even more severely, Gewirth, the emphasis is far more deductionist. In certain fundamental ways we can ascertain what must be done by attention to "considerations of consistency or avoidance of contradiction" and by showing in the domain of the moral and vis-à-vis human action, certain revealing "logically necessary connections" (*RM,* 19). The apodictic rationalist, unlike his probabilistic brethren, seeks to establish certain necessary truths as foundational conceptions in ethics (*RM,* 19). *Partial* apodictic procedural rationalism—the position Gewirth sticks on Hare—imposes a logically necessary form on contents which are themselves contingent, while full apodictic procedural rationalism (Gewirth's own position) takes the contents themselves to be logically necessary. Gewirth criticizes both partial apodictic rationalism and probabilistic rationalism. I shall pass over his critique here and turn to his own articulation and defense of a very strong form of ethical rationalism, namely *full apodictic procedural rationalism.*

## III

Gewirth's moral rationalism is very strong indeed, for he seeks to justify a moral system *tout court* and not just for or to some person, perhaps a person with unselfish or caring pro-attitudes (*RM,* 26). He, like Kant, wants to achieve a justification that any rational agent must accept when it is fully and carefully displayed to her. Unlike a probabilistic procedural rationalist, or even a chap like R. M. Hare, Gewirth seeks to establish a morality as a categorically "normatively binding set of requirements" (*RM,* 27). He tries to give us an unassailable grounding, a grounding that does not at all depend on what attitudes or inclinations people have, for categorical and determinate moral obligations (*RM,* 29). This is something that the other positions do not even aspire to. Moreover, it is a grounding which purports to give us a supreme substantive principle of morality that could not be denied without self-contradiction. This is giving very strong moral powers to reason indeed.

Gewirth's theory is fully and carefully adumbrated in *Reason and Morality,* but I want to start with his most recent succinct statement in his article "The Future of Ethics." Gewirth tries there to establish that there are moral principles and judgments which in both their form and their content are logically necessary. "The contents in question consist in the generic features of action"—"features that necessarily pertain to all action" (*RM,* 29). A conceptual analysis of action is said to reveal that there are certain "right-claims" for all agents that are entailed by this conceptual analysis of action. This holds for all agents. "The supreme principle of morality is derived by applying to these right-claims the logical form of consistency. For it follows from this application that every agent, on pain of self-contradiction, must admit that all other agents as well as himself have rights to the generic features of action, namely freedom and well-being" (*RM,* 29). From this we can derive a determinate categorical imperative: an imperative addressed to all agents and categorically binding on all agents, to wit, a principle which directs each and every agent to "act in accord with the generic rights of your recipients as well as of yourself." (This principle Gewirth calls the *Principle of Generic Consistency* [*PGC*]). As I regard it as essential that my own freedom and well-being be protected, so I must, on pain of inconsistency, have a like re- gard for the freedom and well-being of every agent. As conceptual analysis reveals, the generic features of action "necessarily pertain to every agent." They all want and indeed need freedom and well-being. These generic features of action "impose themselves with normative necessity on every agent." There is no possibility of a contradiction-free rejection of "moral requirements set forth in the *PGC*" (*RM,* 29). The moral powers of reason are such that no matter what our desires and inclinations may be there are certain things that are quite categorically morally required of us. Gewirth believes that he has established that certain substantive "deontic judgments are necessarily true, and this can be shown only by establishing that the denials of the judgments are self-contradictory."[4] He believes he has shown, as he summarizes it in *Reason and Morality,* "that determinate criteria of moral rightness are logic- ally derived from the generic features of action" (*RM,* 198). As he goes on to say,

> Every agent, by the fact of engaging in action, is logically committed to the acceptance of certain evaluative and deontic judgments and ultimately of a moral principle which requires that he respect in his recipients the same generic features of action, freedom and well-being, that as rational he necessarily claims as rights for himself. By virtue of this logical necessity, the PGC is rationally justified as a categorically obligatory moral principle. (*RM,* 198)

## IV

Richard Brandt and Alasdair MacIntyre have both made succinct criticisms of Gewirth's full apodictic procedural rationalism. At the end of a discussion of various accounts of rationality (an account that concludes by remarking that it would be "clarifying all around" if we could drop talk of rationality), Brandt remarks correctly that Gewirth (*RM,* 89) utilizes "a very astringent notion of 'rational': as accepting observed facts and the principles of deduc- tive and inductive logic."[4] On this astringent sense of 'rational', as distinct from the more ramified sense utilized by Kurt Baier, it is plain and uncon- troversial that we ought to be rational. However, a very central thing that is controversial on Gewirth's account is his claim about the link between the failure to accept moral principles and being irrational. For him a failure to accept moral principles is a severe failure in rationality. "It would clearly be a tremendous *coup* if Gewirth could show it is irrational in the sense [Gewirth's astringent sense] not to accept important moral principles" (*RM,* 89). Brandt believes, not surprisingly, that Gewirth has not succeeded in carrying out that *coup.* Brandt agrees with Gewirth "that agents want their motivating goals and also want freedom to act and their own purpose-fulfillment generally" (*RM,* 89). All people who understand what they are doing want freedom and well-being as something which is necessary to any goal achievement. And goal achievement is something they all want.

It is not at this early stage but at the next stage of Gewirth's argument that Brandt balks. Gewirth claims that a person who understands the above must also claim a right to freedom and well-being, on the ground these are necessary for all purpose-fulfillment. The right-claim is based on a reason that also applies to others. Moreover, others can make similar demands, and the agent who makes the right-claim, if he is to be consistent and accepts symmetrical reasoning, must accept these demands as being as valid against himself as they are against others. Recognizing they are valid against others (who in the relevant respects are no different from himself), he must, to be consistent, acknowledge that they are valid against him as well. Thus we get, in Gewirth's account, to the general moral principle that all human beings have a right to freedom and well-being; indeed we are not, Gewirth argues, being consistent if we deny that all people have such a right to freedom and well-being. But, Brandt claims, Gewirth's argument is not sound, for he has not shown why the reciprocal prudentially based demands that they have a right to freedom and well-being are "demands which the persons addressed are in any way bound to honor" (*RM,* 89). In particular, Gewirth has not shown how, in accordance with his very astringent, morally neutral sense of 'reason', a person must have acted against reason if he does not honor these demands. How, if he so behaves, has he contradicted himself, what observed facts must he have ignored, what inductions has he failed to make? Gewirth, the argument goes, has not shown that the immoralist must have suffered any of these lapses.

MacIntyre, in the course of trying to undermine what he calls the Kantian project of showing "that any rational agent is logically committed to the rules of morality in virtue of his or her rationality," mounts an argument against Gewirth that is similar to Brandt's, though surely he would maintain as well that Brandt's own positive account also rests on a mistake.[6] He would take it to be the latest in a long line of empiricist and utilitarian accounts which try to carry out what MacIntyre calls 'the enlightenment project': a program in ethics which MacIntyre takes to be fundamentally misconceived. But against Gewirth, MacIntyre and Brandt make common cause. Like Brandt, MacIntyre accepts the claim that (1) every rational person has to acknowledge that a "certain measure of freedom and well-being" are "prerequisites for his exercise of rational agency" and thus (2) a rational agent must will, if he wills at all, that he have "that measure of these goods" (*RM,* 89). But the trouble comes when Gewirth claims that every person has a *right* to these necessary goods. The claim, as Gewirth recognizes himself, "that I have a right to do or have something is a quite different type of claim from the claim that I need or want or will be benefited by something" (*RM,* 89). That I want something or even that I need it does not establish that others ought not to interfere with my attempts to get it, but, where I have a right to something, others ought not, whether I need it or not, interfere with my attempts to get it. Appealing to *universalizability* will not enable us to go from a recognition that such and such are necessary goods to a right-claim to these goods. "It is," MacIntyre claims, "of course true that if I claim a right in virtue of my possession of certain characteristics, then I am logically committed to holding that anyone else with the same characteristics also possesses this right" (*RM,* 65). But, MacIntyre continues "it is just this property of necessary *universalizability* that does not belong to claims about either the possession of or the need or desire for a good, even a universally necessary good" (*RM,* 89). The fact that I find freedom and well-being to be necessary to goods and you do as well does not entail that I acknowledge your right to these goods or even that you acknowledge my own right to these goods. Gewirth has not built such a logical bridge here, and he fares no better than did Kant in showing how, or even that, the immoralist or amoralist must be an irrationalist or even necessarily to have acted contrary to reason.

V

Let us now consider whether there are resources within Gewirth's account adequately to meet this core criticism. Gewirth believes that, since I regard it as essential that my own freedom and well-being be protected, I must, to be consistent, have a like regard for the freedom and well-being of every agent. What he has perhaps shown (at least it is something Brandt and MacIntyre do not dispute) is that agents (that is, each one of us) want and need freedom and well-being and will typically take steps, where necessary, to protect their access to these goods. In that way each individual, or at least each rational individual, regards it as essential that his freedom and well-being be protected. But it doesn't follow that he must believe, if he is rational (Gewirth's sense), that he has a right to his freedom and well-being. He could quite consistently believe that the protection of his own freedom and well-being were for him necessary goods which it was essential for him to protect, if he could, and still, like Bentham, regard talk of rights as nonsense on stilts.

He might be mistaken in that belief, even obviously mistaken, but it is not at all evident that he has contradicted himself, either directly and plainly, or even indirectly and unobviously, so that dialectical reasoning would be necessary to make the contradiction apparent.

Can Gewirth show, appearances to the contrary notwithstanding, that a moral agent really must have contradicted himself if he believes that no such rights have been established on the basis of such needs or on the basis of his true claims that the protection of such needs is essential for him? Indeed, it is one thing for him to believe that it is essential for him that people believe that he has such rights, but it is quite another thing for him to believe that he actually has such rights—to believe that to protect his interests or his agency or to make sense of his life he need invoke such right-claims or even that such rights-talk makes coherent sense. After all, one is not necessarily being inconsistent if one wants other people to have some incoherent beliefs. (That is one rationale for the construction of ideologies.)

Gewirth intends to employ the concept of action and the concept of reason in a morally neutral manner; still, he believes that "deontic judgments on the part of agents are logically implicit in all action" (*RM*, 25-26). The nature of action, he tells us, enters into the very content of morality such that agents must have these rights. (Keep in mind that Gewirth's ethical rationalism is very strong. For him to obtain an objective standpoint in justifying the supreme principle of morality we must have a "whole structure of argument which consists only in rationally necessary propositions." We also must apply what he calls "the dialectically necessary method.") Using this method, the necessary propositions that can justifiably be used in such an argument are those "that follow from the concept of action." So we need to show, if Gewirth's argument is to succeed, that if a rational agent gets thoroughly clear about what is entailed by the concept of action, he will come to see that he has such rights. Indeed, he will be led beyond that to Gewirth's supreme principle of morality.

Action, let us grant, has some normative structure (*RM*, 48). But how can we derive from that the particular normative structure that agents have rights to freedom and well-being or even that they must believe that they have such rights—rights they must claim as "a prospective agent who has purposes he wants to fulfill?" (*RM*, 48). What Gewirth must do is show how he can establish the hardness of the logical 'must' in his central claim that "since the agent regards as necessary goods the freedom and well-being that constitute the generic features of his successful action, he logically must also hold that he has rights to these generic features and he implicitly makes a corresponding right-claim" (*RM*, 63). He must show that there is this tight conceptual connection "between rights and necessary goods" (*RM*, 64). Still, how does he show (or does he show at all) that 'My freedom and well-being are necessary goods' entails 'I have rights to freedom and well-being' (*RM*,

64)? The claim is that if I recognize my freedom and well-being are necessary goods, then I must also recognize, if I am being thoroughly rational, that I am entitled to them or ought to have them as my due. Rational beings, that is, will recognize the analyticity of 'If my freedom and well-being are necessary goods, then I am entitled to them' (*RM,* 66). But that proposition doesn't appear to be analytic. It certainly looks as if we could deny it without contradicting ourselves.

It is not—or so, at least, it appears—self-contradictory for someone, say a gangster, to say that he regards his freedom and well-being as necessary goods and that he will struggle to protect his secure possession of them and will demand that others not interfere with him, hoping that such demands will have the requisite effective force, without asserting, or at least without believing, that he has a right to this protection or even that it is something he ought to have or that reason requires.[7]

Gewirth responds that when we take ought-talk and right-talk, as we should in such a context, to be properly prudential, as "made from within the agent's own standpoint in purposive action," then we must recognize that when the agent makes a judgment based on his "necessary prudential needs of agency" it would be self-contradictory to say that, though these are his needs, he ought not to have them and has no right to them (*RM,* 71-71). Or, at the very least, it would be self-contradictory for him to say that. But, *au contraire,* why does the gangster or amoralist contradict himself if he says, "I don't know about these rights. I don't claim anything about my rights or what I ought to have—such talk may be, for all I know, subjective or ideological twaddle— but what I am saying, in making my demands, is, 'Leave off me or else I'll make you wish you had' "? Perhaps such a flat amoralism is not the most effective way to argue—indeed, it may in most contexts even be very counter-productive—but that is not to the point. What is to the point is that Gewirth has not shown how such a gangster must be saying contradictory things if he so holds forth. Yet the burden of proof is surely on Gewirth, given the appearances, to show that the gangster actually is contradicting himself.

Prudential justification, which is what is most at issue here, would come to showing that such claims to the right to freedom and well-being would securely back up the agent's interests. But the gangster need not deny that empirical claim (putative empirical truth) to avoid self-contradiction. And it is not that the gangster need deny that the strongest ground a person could have for claiming rights, relevant to his actions, is that "their objects are necessary for engaging in any purposive actions at all or for his succeeding in any such actions" (*RM,* 72). But what he could without inconsistency deny is that he need claim any rights at all to obtain the same objects (the necessary goods of freedom and well-being) that the rights-claimant is trying to secure.

Both the amoralist (the gangster generalized) and Gewirth's prudential rights-claimant can demand, and recognize that it is in their interest to have, "certain general goods that every other prospective agent can likewise recognize as necessary for his respective agency" (*RM,* 72). But the amoralist, except perhaps as a bit of mythmaking or as an ideological mystification to serve his interests, does not claim anything is his due or right. And he need not acknowledge any obligations to others or acknowledge that he is bound to acknowledge any right-claims. (What manipulative mystification he might enter into for ideological purposes or purposes of advantage is another matter altogether.) He doesn't, except perhaps in the service of ideological mystification or personal advantage, play the language game of entitlement-talk, and even then he employs that talk for purposes alien to morality. What Gewirth must show is why such a bad fellow must be inconsistent if he doesn't talk about, appeal to, or at least acknowledge to himself what is his prudential due (*RM,* 72-73). Even when he uses such talk manipulatively, in a way parallel to how an ideologist would use it, he need not believe that anything actually is his due even where that notion (assuming this is possible) is construed in a purely prudential sense. Gewirth has not shown that "generic rights are constitutive of the whole context of agency" (*RM,* 73). It is not a logical truth or an analytic truth, if indeed it is true at all, that "every agent must hold, from within his own prudential standpoint in purposive action, that he is entitled at least to noninterference with his freedom and well-being" (*RM,* 73). He might be a Social Darwinian or an error theorist, as far as deontic concepts go, who views life as a struggle for existence and who rejects the very category of entitlements or things being his due.[8] He recognizes that there are certain necessary human goods and he will make certain demands for them and he will hope these demands will do their work and he will seek to see that they are causally effective, but he does not regard talk of rights or entitlements as legitimate. (That does not mean that he need regard them as illegitimate. He might not regard things in this normative way at all. But he has his needs and wants and he seeks to satisfy them.) He does not accept that such deontic norms, or anything else, have any moral or normative authority over him. He does not view the world in these terms. The whole notion of legitimacy/ illegitimacy in such spheres seems to him a Holmesless Watson. At most he will use these moral concepts, when they are useful to secure his ends, in an ideological or manipulative manner. He can deny, at least to himself, that in providing agent-based prudential justifying reasons he need make any appeal to entitlements or rights. The ball is squarely in Gewirth's court to show, against appearances, that the amoralist in reality must have contradicted himself.

## VI

Let us come at this general matter from a different direction. Gewirth remarks that the final ground for maintaining that the agent must hold that he has rights to the generic goods of freedom and well-being is that, unlike the particular goods or purposes for which he may act, the generic goods are the necessary conditions not merely of one particular action as against another but of all successful action in general. Right-claims are thus essentially linked to action because, just as actions themselves are conative and evaluative, so right-claims are demands on the part of agents that the essential prerequisites of their actions at least not be interfered with. It was very likely for this reason that Jefferson included life, liberty, and the pursuit of happiness among the inalienable rights of man. If 'happiness' is understood as well-being, these rights are inalienable because, being necessary to all action, no agent could waive them or be deprived of them and still remain an agent. (*RM*, 77)

Again, even if the generic goods are the necessary conditions of all success-ful action, it does not follow that rational agents must claim, to avoid being inconsistent, that they, or anyone else, have (has) a right or an entitlement to these necessary goods. Moreover, while all right-claims may be demands, not all demands are right-claims. Rational agents, where this is necessary, will make demands that the essential prerequisites of their action not be interfered with, but they need not make these demands by way of a right-claim either moral or prudential. They need not believe or even claim that anything is inalienably theirs or that anything is due them or that people are bound to respond to them in particular ways, though they will, if they are rational, under most circumstances try to secure their life, liberty, and happiness. But Gewirth's ethical rationalism tries to establish something much more stringent than that. He has not shown that agency or rational agency logically requires the making of right-claims.

It is essential for Gewirth's movement from necessary goods to rights that he be able to show that it is necessarily true that "other persons ought at least to refrain from interfering with the agent's freedom and well-being" (*RM*, 63, 78). It is certainly tempting to respond that this is contingently false so it can hardly be necessarily true. Certainly we cannot assert anything so unqualified as 'Other persons ought to refrain from interfering with a per-son's freedom and well-being'. We at least need a *ceteris paribus*, for we need to know *what* other persons and *what* circumstances are being referred to. There are plainly at least imaginable circumstances in which such a claim would not be true. Suppose the agent in question were Hitler. But assume a qualified circumstance in which the proposition would be asserted and a reasonable reading of it given and then consider whether in that circumstance it is correct to construe it as necessary truth. Isn't it, to pursue this, a necessary truth that all other persons ought at least to refrain from interfering with the conditions necessary for a person's agency? This is to give to understand that there ought to be no interference with an agent's freedom and well-being. But unless a *ceteris paribus* is added it is more likely that this also is a con-tingent falsehood rather than a necessary truth. Paternalism may be mistaken but it is not incoherent. And even a very destructive and neurotic agent, as some of Eugene O'Neill's characters illustrate, might (ambivalently) want such interference. That we can intelligibly consider such a matter shows that Gewirth's putative necessary proposition isn't one.

Gewirth, however, thinks that he has shown that, since agents hold that their freedom and well-being are necessary goods for all their actions, they then must also hold that it is necessary that they not be interfered with in having freedom and well-being. But, to the contrary, what at most he has shown is that generally speaking it is desirable that people not be interfered with in having freedom and well-being. Moreover, an agent, indeed a rational agent, could be "opposed to whatever interferes with his having freedom and well-being" without believing for a moment that he or anyone else is *entitled* to freedom or well-being (*RM,* 79). From discovering his necessary goods and following out what their internal relations are, he cannot discover what, if anything, he is entitled to, including discovering that he is entitled to protection from interference by others (*RM,* 79). Gewirth believes that there are conceptual (logical) connections here, but he has not established that there are such connections. To do this he would at least have to show, against appearances, that anyone who says what I have just said must have contradicted himself. But there is nothing in his analysis which shows anything like that. Unless a careful analysis undermines 'appearances' we are entitled to stick with appearances.

## VII

In chapter 2 of *Reason and Morality,* Gewirth develops a distinct argument which he believes "shows more explicitly that if any agent denies that he has the generic rights, then he is caught in a contradiction" (*RM,* 80). This is, as we have seen, a crucial point for Gewirth, and he, trying to secure that point, states essentially the same argument in three different ways. We must examine them in turn. He puts his first argument thus:

> Suppose some agent were to deny or refuse to accept the judgment (1) 'I have rights to freedom and well-being'. Because of the equivalence between the generic rights and strict 'oughts,' this denial of (1) would entail the agent's denial of (2) 'All other persons ought at least to refrain from interfering with my freedom and well-being'. By denying (2), the agent would have to accept (3) 'It is not the case that all other persons ought at least to refrain from interfering with my freedom and well-being'. But how can any agent accept (3) and also accept (4) 'My freedom and well-being are necessary goods'? That he must accept (4) we saw above; for by virtue of regarding his purposes as good the agent must also a fortiori value his freedom and well-being as required for achieving any of his purposes. Hence, insofar as he is a purposive agent, that is, an agent who wants to achieve the purposes for which he acts, he

must want his freedom and well-being to be kept inviolate, so that they are not interfered with by other persons. He must want this, moreover, not as a mere favor from other persons but as setting a requirement for their noninterference that they are obligated to obey, such that from his own standpoint as a purposive agent, severe censure and even coercion are warranted if they violate the requirement. Hence, the agent must accept (2). Consequently, since (2) is logically equivalent to (1), the agent contradicts himself if he denies (1). He must therefore accept, on pain of contradiction, that he has the generic rights. (*RM*, 80)

Similar difficulties surface here to the difficulties we have spotted in his previous arguments. Let us accept that as a purposive agent a human being will want "to achieve the purposes for which he acts" and that since he wants to achieve those purposes "he must want his freedom and well-being" not to be "interfered with by other persons" (*RM*, 80). In that sense he must want them to be inviolate though he need give no stronger reading to 'inviolate.' While he need not at all regard this as a favor from others, he also need not think of their noninterference as something they are obligated to or have an obligation to accept. And he may not believe that censure and coercion are *warranted* if they do interfere. He may view the situation simply as a clash of interests and not conceptualize it in normative terms at all. There is nothing in the logic of the situation which logically compels him to conceptualize the situation as one of setting requirements which people may violate and which they are obligated to act in accordance with on pain of doing something which is unwarranted, illegitimate, or morally untoward. He can continue to view the situation in a nonmoralistic way without self-contradiction.

He, of course (or so let us assume), recognizes that he must value his freedom and well-being as conditions necessary for achieving any of his purposes. He will see that it is a very vital interest of his to secure a situation where his freedom and well-being will not be interfered with. He will, if he is rational, take the steps necessary to protect his vital interests, or at least what he takes to be his vital interests, but he is not compelled to think of this in terms of something he is either warranted (justified) or not warranted (justified) in doing. He need not, at least as far as conceptual possibilities are concerned, view the matter in such normative terms. He could see life as a struggle in which he is just trying to secure and enhance what he takes to be in his own interests. It isn't that he is justified, as over against the next guy, in securing his interests; it is just that he does it because he wants to secure them and (perhaps) needs to in order to survive. He can look a gift horse in the mouth and, in a way, accept (3) while perfectly consistently continuing to accept (4). He might—spelling out what I mean by 'in a way'—think that all this talk about both 'ought' and 'ought not' is rhetoric (perhaps ideological rhetoric) without any warrant, so that any presumption for legitimately asserting *or* denying (3) would be rebutted; nevertheless he would continue to assert (4) and believe (4) to be true. He is willing to engage in teleological talk but not deontological talk. The latter he regards as incoherent or at least mystificatory. I neither assert nor deny that this is the most reasonable position or even a plausible position to take here. My point is, at its most minimal, that Gewirth has not shown it to be self-contradictory. And this is all that is at issue *here*.

Gewirth's second argument to show that if any agent denies that he has generic rights he is caught in a self-contradiction is no better than his first. He starts from his claim in the first argument that if an agent accepts his freedom and well-being as necessary goods, he must also believe that they are, as far as that is possible, to be kept inviolate. Then, referring to propositions (1) and (3) of the first argument, Gewirth sets out his second argument in the following terms.

> If he accepts (3), which is entailed by his denial of (1), then he accepts that it is permissible that other persons interfere with or remove his freedom and well-being. He hence shows that he regards his freedom and well-being with indifference or at least as dispensable, so that he accepts (5) 'It is not the case that my freedom and well-being are necessary goods', where 'necessary' has, as before, a prescriptive force and not only a means-end sense. Therefore, if the agent were to deny that he has rights to freedom and well-being, he would again be caught in a contradiction: he would be in the position of both affirming and denying that his freedom and well-being are necessary goods, that is, goods that he values as the necessary conditions of all his actions and that must hence not be interfered with or removed from him by other persons. (*RM*, 80-81)

But in one sense to accept (3), as we have seen in examining Gewirth's first argument, it is not necessary to accept any 'oughts' or 'ought nots' at all or even to think such talk is coherent. One can, in one way of rejecting (3), in effect, be rejecting all the deontic concepts employed in (1), (2), and (3). A denial of (2), which is what (3) is, could be a denial of the coherence or the very suitability of such talk or such a way of conceptualizing things. 'It is not the case' in (3) could be taken to range over that. In so reasoning in accepting (3), an agent need not accept the normative notion that it is *permissible* that other persons interfere with or remove his freedom or well-being. He recognizes that he has no ground for saying they ought not, but this does not imply that they ought or that they can, i.e., that it is permissible for them to do so. He can just refuse to engage in such normative conceptualizings at all, and this is compatible with accepting (3) on at least one reading of what this acceptance could come to. So in not accepting that it is either permissible or impermissible for others to interfere with his freedom and well-being, he is not committed to regarding his freedom and well-being with either indifference or as being dispensable. Indeed, there is no reason to think that is the way he feels about it. Thus, right at the start, Gewirth's second argument collapses.

Gewirth gives a third argument for the same point which I think is no more successful than his first two arguments.

> This contradiction may be brought out still more explicitly by using the practical-prescriptive 'must' to render both 'necessary' and 'ought'. Thus (4) 'My freedom and well-being are necessary goods' may be rendered as $(4_a)$ 'I must have freedom and well-being', for this expresses the agent's resolve to have what he recognizes to be indispensable for his engaging in purposive action. Similarly, (2) 'All other persons ought at least to refrain from interfering with my freedom and well-being' may be rendered as $(2_a)$, 'All other persons must at least refrain from interfering with my freedom and well-being', for this 'must' also expresses the agent's resolve that the necessary conditions of his engaging in purposive action not be obstructed. Now $(4_a)$ entails $(2_a)$. For if the agent must have freedom and well-being, then, from the standpoint of his own purposive action, whatever interferes with his having these must be rejected or removed, including interference by other persons. . . . It would be contradictory for him to accept both that he must have freedom and well-being and that other persons may interfere with his having these, *where the criteria of the 'must' and the 'may' are the same, consisting in the agent's own requirements for agency.* Hence, from the agent's standpoint, the necessity of his having freedom and well-being entails the necessity of other persons' at least refraining from interference with his having them. This latter necessity is equivalent to a strict practical 'ought' that he implicitly addresses to all other persons, and hence is also equivalent to a claim that he has a right to the necessary goods of freedom and well-being (*RM*, 81).

Let us assume, at least for the sake of this argument, that $(4_a)$ entails $(2_a)$. Since the agent "must have freedom and well-being, then, from the standpoint of his own purposive action, whatever interferes with his having these must be rejected or removed, including interference by other persons" (*RM*, 81). The 'must' in both cases here firmly expresses his resolve to have what he recognizes to be indispensable for his engaging in purposive action. Moving from $(4_a)$ to $(2_a)$ shows the consistency and thoroughness of his intent (his resolve). But simply in expressing this resolve he does not yet say what is morally required of him or what he is obligated to do or what he ought to do. Only if 'must' is construed, à la Stuart Hampshire, and as we normally would, in its strong moral sense, do we get that; but then, if that is the way $(4_a)$ is read, $(4_a)$ is not equivalent to (4), and $(4_a)$ is not something that is self-contradictory or otherwise conceptually impossible to deny.[9] The 'must', on Gewirth's reading, simply expresses the agent's firm resolve to protect his interests. It does not yet tell us or him what he ought to do, what he has a right to do or whether he should so morally or normatively conceptualize the world at all. It does not tell him or us what others are obligated to do, have an obligation to do, are prohibited from doing, legitimately can do or what they ought or ought not do. We have, rather, taken them, as Gewirth takes them in $(4_a)$ and $(2_a)$, as expressions of firm resolve. Such expressions of resolve do not, by firm entailments from additional rationally necessary (analytic) premises, take us to any deontic propositions at all. So, even if Gewirth is justified in asserting that it would be contradictory for an agent to accept both that he must have freedom and well-being and that other persons may interfere with his having these, *where the criteria of 'must' and 'may' are the same, consisting in the agent's own requirements for agency*, we still have not shown that he has a *right* to the necessary goods of freedom and well-being. That would only be shown if, in the above sentence from Gewirth, the 'may' in 'may interfere with his having these' is construed as 'can legitimately interfere' or 'can justifiably interfere' or as 'what is permissible for him to do' or something of that order. But Gewirth's own italicized part of his above sentence makes clear that that is not what he is saying. The 'may' must remain parallel with the 'must' of resolve. In denying that others may interfere with him, he is, as Gewirth has set it up, not asserting anything about what is permissible, legitimate, or justifiable but only about what he is firmly resolved to stop if he can. On Gewirth's reading of 'must', it is *not* self-contradictory for an agent to say 'I must have my freedom and well-being but others can legitimately interfere with it' or 'I must have my freedom and well-being but it is permissible for others to interfere with it'. Where 'may' has roughly a like meaning (does similar work in such a linguistic environment to 'permissible'), there is no contradiction in asserting 'I must have my freedom and well-being but others may interfere with it'. It is only when 'may' has the weaker sense of 'let have' that we perhaps get a contradiction.

Consider however, 'I must have my freedom and well-being but I will let others interfere with it'. Here the agent seems at least, at one and the same time and way, to be resolving and not resolving. He seems at least, given that linguistic behavior, not really to mean it when he says he must have his freedom and well-being. But appearances here are deceiving. For the 'may not interfere' to generate 'they are obligated not to interfere', so that he cannot consistently deny that he has generic rights, the 'may not interfere' must be construed *normatively* as 'it is impermissible to interfere' or as 'interfering is illegitimate or unwarranted'. But with these readings, as we have seen, it is not a contradiction to assert at one and the same time both that he must have freedom and well-being and that other persons may interfere with his having them. Moreover, putting it in the first person does not change matters here. So Gewirth's third argument also collapses. He has not shown that the necessity of the agent's freedom and well-being entails that others must (in the requisite sense of 'must') refrain from interference with his having them. He has not established a very central thesis of his, namely "that every agent necessarily claims for himself the rights to freedom and well-being" (*RM,* 88).

An argument he makes later in *Reason and Morality* is also unsuccessful. (I leave aside what seems to me at least an unwitting shifting of his grounds in that later passage away from purely conceptual considerations.) Gewirth remarks there that once a person has purposes as a prospective agent, he necessarily claims to have generic rights, for "otherwise his having purposes would be futile" (*RM*, 126). If he didn't claim these rights, he "would be in the impossible position of both wanting to achieve some goal and being indifferent to the necessary conditions of his achieving the goal" (*RM*, 126). We have already seen (contra Gewirth) why, even if the agent claims no rights, he need not be at all indifferent to having the necessary conditions for achieving his goals. But, even if having purposes would be futile without having the generic rights, it still would, being an empirical matter, not make 'I must have these rights' an analytic truth or in any way support its claimed analyticity. Yet it is its analyticity that Gewirth needs in order to establish his distinctive brand of ethical rationalism.


## VIII

As I remarked in my first section, there is hardly an objection that can plausibly be made to Gewirth's account that he has not given some consideration to (see Appendix I to this chapter). Neither Brandt's and MacIntyre's criticisms are exceptions, nor is the line of criticism I developed in previous sections. Gewirth states the general thrust of these objections in the following passage, which I shall quote *in extenso;* my task in this section will be to try to show that and how his own response to his own stated objection to his own account will not do. But first let us see how Gewirth puts the type of objection in question.

> Let us now consider another kind of objection against my above argument that every agent must accept or hold on pain of self-contradiction that he has the generic rights. This objection is that the agent need make no right-claim or 'ought'-judgment at all, either positive or negative. He need not accept either statement (2) given above or its negation (3), for he might be an amoralist who disavows for himself all uses of moral or deontic concepts. Thus, in refusing to accept such a judgment as (1) 'I have rights to freedom and well-being' and hence also (2) 'All other persons ought at least to refrain from interfering with my freedom and well-being', the amoralist agent would not therefore have to accept (3) 'It is not the case that all other persons ought at least to refrain from interfering with my freedom and well-being'. He would indeed accept (4) 'My freedom and well-being are necessary goods', in that these are required for his pursuit of all his purposes. But on the basis of this evaluative premise he would not make or accept any right-claims or 'ought'-judgments, either positive or negative, so that he would not be in the position even of denying that persons ought to do or refrain from doing certain things, such as interfering with his freedom and well-being. For, as an amoralist, he would deny that concepts like 'ought' and 'right' have any valid application, at least in his own case. Instead, he would commit himself only to such a resolutive statement as (6) 'I'll do what I can to get what I want'. He might, for example, be the kind of person who holds, like Callicles, Thrasymachus, or Nietzsche, that power is the only thing that counts, so

that normative claims about rights and justifications are useless and unnecessary. Such a statement of his as (6) would not involve him in the contradictions elicited above, for these all depended on the agent's having to accept the negative 'ought'-judgment (3). (*RM*, 89)

In responding to this objection, it seems to me that Gewirth unwittingly abandons his strict ethical rationalism. Remember that his dialectically necessary method commits him only to accepting in the structure of his normative ethical argument for a logically necessary supreme principle of morality "those propositions . . . that logically emerge succesively from the conceptual analysis of action and the agent's necessary beliefs" (*RM*, 83; see also 97, 109-112, 124, 171, 176-177, 187). But in beating back what he calls the amoralist objection, he first remarks that (1), (2), and (3) stated in the above passage are prudential rather than moral judgments (*RM*, 89). Never mind that there are problems about that, but consider, to get at my response, his second remark. The amoralist, Gewirth remarks, cannot disavow any of the above deontic yet prudential judgments, for they are judgments that a rational and a "conatively normal person" must make. Even assuming that this is so, the point I want to make here is that in making the assumption that the amoralist is a "conatively normal person"—a person, as Gewirth explains it, who "has the self-interested motivations common to most persons and is willing to expend the effort needed to fulfill them"—Gewirth deploys a proposition about the assumed motivation of the agent that is plainly a contingent one. But this is incompatible with both his avowed aim of sticking to the dialectically necessary method and with his commitment to *full apodictic procedural rationalism*. On the one hand, he cannot excise that assumption about conative normalcy for he needs it to make his argument work. On the other hand, to fulfill his own severely rationalistic requirements for a proof of what he takes to be the supreme principle of morality, he must proceed by a chain of entailments to a necessary proposition from a series of necessary propositions much as a mathematician proves a theorem from axioms using rules of formation and transformation. Or so, at least, is the picture we get and so goes the official program. Remember that Gewirth, like Kant, is trying to get categorically binding moral principles (principles binding on every rational agent)—including categorical right-claims—from the sheer concept of agency. Since trying to get so much out of a bare concept of agency is like trying to squeeze blood out of a turnip, it is hardly surprising that a material condition like conative normalcy will be illicitly inserted somewhere.

We could halt our examination of his response to the 'amoralist's challenge' here. However, let us assume now that there is some way that Gewirth could go around that Great Bog and follow out his subsequent argument.

A rational conatively normal person, whether he thinks of himself as an amoralist or not, must, Gewirth argues, "make or accept for himself at least prudential 'ought'-judgments" (*RM,* 90). If something, Z, threatens such an amoralist's basic goods and hence his basic well-being, "and he believes that the necessary and sufficient condition of his avoiding Z is his doing X," then, if he believes that he can do X, and he does not believe that by doing X he will do something that will harm his well-being even more or as much, then, according to Gewirth, "he must make or accept for himself such a prudential and prescriptive 'ought'-judgment as (7) 'I ought to do X' " (*RM,* 90).

I would counter that he is not logically required to do anything of the sort. He could perfectly well stick with the considered expression of his intentions and assert instead 'I will do X' or 'I certainly will do X' and eschew any 'ought'-judgments, prudential or otherwise. He will instead continue to operate on the maxim 'I will do what I can to get what I want,' while regarding talk of 'ought' as mystificatory.

To say that ought-talk here just comes to expressions of intentions is to commit oneself to a very problematic reductionist meta-ethical thesis indeed. Surely it would be something which is too problematic to support ethical rationalism. We should conclude, I believe, that Gewirth has not shown that "an amoralist . . . so long as he is rational and conatively normal . . . must use the practical concept of 'ought' " (*RM,* 90). (We should not forget the illicit appeal here, given Gewirth's own methodology, to conatively normal people.)

He will, no doubt, believe that there are necessary goods, namely freedom and well-being. He will try to secure those goods for himself. He will, as well, acknowledge that others, if they are rational, will also recognize there are these necessary goods and that they will also try to secure them for themselves. And he will also recognize that he (the amoralist) is in no relevant respects different from them. It will also be the case that the amoralist will acknowledge that in certain circumstances it will be prudent for him to help them to secure these generic goods or it may just so happen that he cares about some others and, because of this caring, wants to help them secure these necessary goods. But there is no necessity here; there is not the categorical prescriptivity that Gewirth seeks. "Rights," as Gewirth puts it, "are goods to which individuals are entitled as their due" (*RM,* 98). But the amoralist, though he recognizes there are necessary goods and is concerned to secure them, at least for himself, either has no concept of entitlement or due, or he does not accept such concepts as ones which will constrain or guide his behavior (the latter is rather more probable). Such an amoralist, for anything Gewirth has shown, can be perfectly consistent and not be ignoring any of the relevant facts or making mistaken inductions from these facts. In fine, he need be neither an irrationalist nor someone flying in the face of reason or acting in any way contrary to reason (*RM,* 10 -103∫ 109-112, 124, 166, 168, 187).[10] It may be that one cannot be an agent without having freedom and well-being. But a recognition of this does not entail that one will claim, if one is rational, the *right* to freedom and well-being. If an agent confines himself to what he is logically justified in claiming from within his own context of purposive action, he will perhaps claim that his very agency requires having freedom and well-being but he need not, to avoid inconsistency, necessarily claim for himself the rights to freedom and well-being (*RM,* 88) (See Appendix II to this chapter).

APPENDIX I

Gewirth in his first response to E. J. Bond's criticisms exhibits a sensitivity to the type issues I have been discussing. He stresses there the value of the dialectically necessary method for escaping these difficulties. "Each agent," he tells us, "thinking or speaking *in propria persona,* and as concerned with his own purposive pursuits as an agent, must hold that he has rights to freedom and well-being because, if he denies this, then he accepts that it is permissible for other persons to remove or interfere with *his* freedom and well-being. But if he accepts this, then he must contradict what it has been previously established that he must accept, namely, that freedom and well-being are necessary goods *for him* so that he must hold that it is impermissible *for him* to be deprived of them."[11] But, as we saw above, an individual (most clearly an amoralist) might reject the whole category of permissible/impermissible as incoherent or mystifactory while (1) still believing that his freedom and well-being are necessary goods for him and (2) being quite categorically resolved to protect them: not to permit, if he can help it, others interfering with him. He might consistently and firmly hold (1) and (2) and still not make any claim about what it is impermissible for others to do even vis-à-vis him. He sees the above situation as an arena for the conflict of interests— a situation where people with at least potentially conflicting interests may be set against each other—and he is resolved to protect his interests come what may, but he need not, even implicitly, conceptualize things in terms of rights or entitlements or in terms of what is permissible and what is not. (If a person refuses to permit something, it does not follow that he thinks it is impermissible, any more than if he desires something he must think it is desirable, at least where both 'impermissible' and 'desirable' are taken in the strong normative sense required.) Moreover, if I deny that I have rights to freedom and well-being (perhaps because I regard rights-talk as incoherent or otherwise unsuitable), it does not follow that I must regard interfering with my freedom and well-being as permissible. I might regard such a concept as itself incoherent or otherwise unsuitable and talk instead of contingent and necessary goods and of what I could do to protect them. I have argued that Gewirth has *not* shown that if we as agents get very clear about what agency is, including what it entails, we will recognize that we have the generic rights to freedom and well-being. In arguing this I neither have to affirm nor deny a claim which Gewirth takes to be very important, to wit, "that there are arguments which are sound only when given from a certain point of view or relative to a given perspective."[12] I need neither affirm nor deny that in arguing from agency to rights one must deploy arguments that are "agent-relative" and which "lose their soundness when taken out of relation to the agent's conative pursuits." What I have argued is that Gewirth is mistaken in holding to a certain belief of his—a belief which is very central to his ethical rationalism—namely that from 'A regards his freedom and well-being as necessary goods', or 'A implicitly says, "My freedom and well-being are necessary goods," ' it follows that 'A rationally holds that he has rights to freedom and well-being', or that 'A rationally says, "I have rights to freedom and well-being" ' (*RM*, 161).[14]


APPENDIX II

In his "Must One Play the Moral Language Game?"[15] Gewirth deploys some arguments to show the necessary irrationality of the amoralist. We should also have a brief look at them. It may be "that even an amoralist, so long as he is rational and normal [sic] . . . must use the concept of 'ought' " in the broad sense that he must realize that he has reasons for doing certain things and not doing others (*RM*, 111). But this does not take him to the claim that he must believe that he has rights to certain things or to the belief that there are others who have an obligation not to interfere with his exercising those rights. He can, as far as the logical possibilities are concerned, recognize there are constraints that he must put on his conduct without acknowledging or believing that he has any entitlements. An agent, as far as logical possibilities go (and that is what is at issue here), can acknowledge "a requirement for or constraint on his conduct, justified by reasons" without even implicitly bringing in rights or obligations (*RM*, 161). An amoralist, who does A when what morality requires of him is not-A, still need not be violating any universalizability requirements. In acknowledging that A is a reason, though not a morally acceptable reason, for his doing Y (something immoral), he need not deny that A would also be a reason for anyone else similarly situated and with similar desires. He need not, indeed he had better not, deny that "it is a logical feature of all reasons that they are implicitly general" (*RM*, 112). He doesn't want others to act on A and will try, in his own self-interest, to persuade others to believe that A is not a good reason for doing Y or that Y isn't worth doing in the first place. But such manipulative activity is one thing; irrationality or self-contradiction is another. Gewirth has not shown that an amoralist recognizing the generality of reasons, and having certain purposes that require certain means for their achievement, could not consistently remain an amoralist. Even if the amoralist must engage in ought-talk, it need not be moral ought-talk. Even if his 'I ought to do Z' entails 'It is right for me to do Z', this does not (given Gewirth's minimum reading of 'right') entail 'I have a right to Z'. That it is right (prudentially right) for me to cheat him does not entail I have a right to cheat him. Moreover, 'It is right that I do Z' may not (again on a minimal reading) entail anything stronger than 'I have good reasons for doing Z'. It has not been shown that, if it is right that I do Z, that I must have any moral rationale for doing Z. (All good reasons for acting are not morally good reasons for acting.) Even if it is the case that 'I ought to do Z because I want to have Y' entails 'All persons who want to have Y ought to do Z', this does not show that, if the particular 'I' in question is an amoralist, he must not interfere with others getting Y or acknowledge that they have a right to Y. The amoralist only needs to acknowledge (at least to himself) that they have as much reason to go after Y and to have Y as he (the amoralist) has, and that, if they are reasonable, they will go after Y. But this does not entail that the amoralist endorse their pursuit of Y or that he be bound not to interfere with that pursuit or that he respect their efforts here (*RM*, 114). Gewirth tries to resist this by claiming, plausibly, that " 'All persons who want to have Y ought to do Z' entails 'All persons who want to have Y ought to be free to do Z'." But again the amoralist is deliberately refusing to take the universalistic stance of the moral point of view. Given the aims of others, aims relevantly similar to his own, they (the others) indeed ought to do Y; and, since 'ought implies can', they ought to be free to do Y. But the amoralist is not logically forced to consider things from the moral point of view or from others' points of view or to give others' points of view the same weight as his own or, indeed, any weight at all (*RM*, 116). So for the amoralist, 'they ought to be free to do Z' does not entail that 'I ought to refrain from interfering with other persons doing Z if they want to have Y' (*RM*, 111). There is no movement by way of entailments from a person's "own self-interested acts and judgments . . . to a system of mutual rights and duties" (*RM*, 116). Gewirth has not shown that the amoralist, if he is through and through rational, must take any moral norm or plurality of moral norms as supremely authoritative and thereby cease to be an amoralist. The amoralist need not contradict himself in sticking with this stance. All bad fellows, it is sad to note, need not be irrational.

NOTES

1. Alan Gewirth, *Reason and Morality* (Chicago: University of Chicago Press, 1978). All references to Gewirth are from *Reason and Morality* unless otherwise noted and they are given in the text in parentheses.

2. R. B. Brandt, "The Future of Ethics," *Nous* 15 (March, 1981): 31-40; and Alasdair

MacIntyre, *After Virtue* (Notre Dame, Ind.: University of Notre Dame Press, 1981), 63-65.

3. Alan Gewirth, "The Future of Ethics: The Moral Powers of Reason," *Nous* 15 (March, 1981): 29.

4. Alan Gewirth, "Comments on Bond's Article," *Metaphilosophy* 11 (January, 1980): 57.

5. Brandt, "The Future of Ethics," p. 39.

6. MacIntyre, *After Virtue,* p. 64.

7. Our gangster-type, if he asserts those right-claims, can be asserting them disingenuously or manipulatively without believing in what he is asserting.

8. The error theory is articulated by Edward Westermarck, but it has perhaps its most forthright statement in J. L. Mackie's various discussions of ethics. See here, for the latest such accounts, the discussion by myself and by Mackie in Timothy Stroup, ed., *Edward Westermarck: Essays on His Life and Work,* vol. 33 (Helsinki: Acta Philosophica Fennica, 1982).

9. Stuart Hampshire, "Morality and Pessimism," in *Public and Private Morality,* ed. Stuart Hampshire (Cambridge: Cambridge University Press, 1978), 1-23.

10. I have tried to show how strong the amoralist can make his case, both in chapter 10 and in my exchange with Bela Szabados, "Symposium: Morality and Class," *Philosophical Studies* (The National University of Ireland) 27 (1980): 67-93.

11. Gewirth, "Comments on Bond's Article," p. 69.

12. Gewirth, "Reason and Morality: Rejoinder to E. J. Bond," *Metaphilosophy* 11 (April, 1980): 142.

13. Ibid.

14. See also here Jan Narveson, "Gewirth's Reason and Morality—A Study in the Hazards of Universalizability in Ethics," *Dialogue* 19 (December, 1980): 652-674.

15. *American Philosophical Quarterly* 7 (April, 1970): 107-118.

# 13

## Must the Immoralist Act
## Contrary to Reason?

### I

Kurt Baier argues that the relation between the moral and the rational is such that it is necessarily contrary to reason to be immoral.[1] I shall argue that while being moral can be *consistent* with reason it is not *required* by it and that in certain circumstances it can be the case that an immoralist need not be irrational or even less rational than even a well-informed person of moral principle.

Baier contends that we can establish a correct moral method: a method that will show that reason requires us to commit ourselves to the principle that, where there is a conflict, moral considerations *always* override nonmoral considerations. We can do this, he believes, "without laying ourselves open to the objection that we are imparting substantive conclusions into our deliberations under the pretense of having found them by a neutral (meta-ethical) inquiry." While Baier concedes that the nature of the moral point of view is indeed currently contested, he denies that it is essentially contested. Rather, the "moral point of view" can be "properly identified in terms of a set of demands on a method for determining what to do." We need not talk tendentiously of the function of morality. Instead, we can show that these demands are demands that this method "must satisfy if the resulting moralities are rightly to be regarded as constituting paramount practical reasons." The correct moral method is the "one that can best satisfy these demands."

The various conceptualizations of a correct moral method can be con-

From *Morality, Reason and Truth,* edited by David Copp and David Zimmerman (Totowa, N.J.: Rowman and Allanheld, 1985), pp. 212–227. Reprinted by permission of the publisher.

strued as rival hypotheses about which method best satisfies the crucial constraint: that the moralities that would result from its correct application are rightly to be regarded "as constituting paramount practical reasons."

Baier articulates five demands that a correct moral method must satisfy. The first demand is what he calls, somewhat misleadingly, the demand for *soundness*.[2] A system of coordinative guidelines is sound, according to Baier, if "everybody has *equally good* reason to regard its precepts as paramount practical reasons." A morality is something that by definition makes a claim to soundness. It makes no sense for me to assert that these are my moral views but I know they are unsound. If I believe at $t_1$ that $p$ is morally required of me and I come to believe at $t_2$ that my believing $p$ is unsound, I must at $t_2$ change my morality—change in that respect at least what I think is morally required of me. Furthermore, for a morality to be sound, Baier argues, it must be established within that conception that it is a good thing if people are moral and a bad thing if they are not. ('Good' and 'bad' here are of course used in a non-moral sense.) The second demand of practical reason captures that. It is the demand that it is a good thing if people have a morality because it is a good thing if people are moral and a bad thing if the are not. Without a morality, Baier argues, they cannot perform the cognitive and executive tasks that are essential if they are to act reasonably. The morality that this demand requires is one in which people act in accord with not only a morality that *purports* to be sound, but one that *actually is sound*.

The third demand of practical reason is "for everyone to be moral and for social pressures to be applied in support of the precepts of morality." The fourth demand, closely related to the third, is that *the precepts of morality are to be taken as overriding* all other guidelines, including the guidelines of self-interest. The demand is that "people treat moral precepts as supreme guidelines." That everyone must always be moral is, on Baier's account, taken to be a demand of practical reason.

Baier's fifth demand of practical reason is that "morality be in accordance with reason and immorality contrary to reason." If it is not, then we need not, Baier would have it, take much notice of the dictates of morality. Moreover, we could not have the fourth demand without also having the fifth. Baier does not say this explicitly, but it is natural to take him to be claiming here that the fourth demand implies the fifth. If the precepts of morality (a genuine sound morality) are overriding, then "these precepts must themselves be treated as *reasons* outranking all other types of reason." Since the moral point of view is the highest point of view of all the guidelines for action, when viewed from what he calls "the point of view of reason," it must also "be the case that being moral *really is* in accordance with reason, being immoral contrary to it."

II

However, we need to ask for the justification for taking these five demands to be the paramount demands of practical reason. How can it be shown— or can it be shown—that these demands "correctly express crucial requirements of practical reason itself"? Why are these demands the crucial requirements of practical reason? Indeed, do they really have such a status? To show that they do, Baier needs to articulate and defend a distinctive conception of practical reason and, as well, to bring into the foreground "two important facts about interaction between people." And this is precisely what he does do in both "The Conceptual Link Between Morality and Rationality" (1982) and in "Rationality, Reason, and the Good."

Baier distinguishes reason from "mere intelligence." He takes reason to be the name "of several interrelated powers." The powers Baier has in mind are (1) the ability to apply suitably "certain general guidelines of a culture to particular problem cases"; (2) the ability to assess the merits "of the currently prevalent guidelines and of improving them in light of the relevant ideal"; (3) the ability (in some approximation) to ascertain theoretical truths (including knowledge of what is the case) for "problems of what to believe"; and (4) the ability to ascertain or appreciate "the good in the case of practical reason for problems of what to do." Rationality "is the possession of the power of reason, the skill of using it, the tendency to use it, and success in its use up to a certain standard of excellence." Guidelines of practical reason in a particular society function "to enable members of a culture, by suitably applying them to particular problem cases," to improve their lives over what their lives would be if they simply followed their own inclinations or without these guidelines tried to solve their own practical problems. They are guidelines that tell us what to do in certain circumstances.

Baier believes that there are facts about the *interaction* of people such that when they are thought through and considered in relation to the above conception of practical reason it will be evident that we should accept these five demands (putative demands) of practical reason and that a sound morality is necessarily in accordance with reason and immorality is necessarily contrary to it. Baier lists two such facts:

1. The best life for human beings is one in which they interact with one another and cooperate in common enterprises and pursuits.

2. In common cooperative enterprises, sometimes a certain outcome pattern results which fits the pattern of the Prisoner's Dilemma. That is to say, if each person in such a situation does what will answer best to his own interests, given what others are or may be doing, then everyone will achieve only their third best results. Alternatively,

if others follow a certain coordinative guideline, everyone will achieve their second best results. Thirdly, if some take the first alternative and some the second, the first group will achieve their best results and the latter their worst.

Baier's claim is that if we take into consideration these facts about inter-action—genuine social facts about our lives together—and if we are clear about what practical rationality is, then we will in such circumstances come to see, if we are rational, that the five demands on moral method do express crucial requirements of practical reason. In reasoning about what to do, a rational and well-informed person will reason in accordance with them.

He claims that this holds even of those people who take rational ego-ism as the supreme general principle of practical rationality for individuals, namely the principle: 'Always do what is in your own best interest'. In situa-tions of human interaction, such egoists will always translate this into the corollary principle: 'Always do what, considering what others are or may be doing, best answers to your interests'. Even such rational egoists will come to see, if they are tolerably intelligent and well informed, that in prisoners'-dilemma situations, situations that are pervasive in our lives, that it is more rational for them to opt for living in a social order that has coordinative guidelines, generally understood and generally accepted, than to opt for a society in which everyone tried to do what best answered to their own inter-ests, given their understanding of what others are or may be doing. A ra-tional agent will recognize that the prospect of stern penalties indeed is great if people one-sidedly follow a policy of trying to further their own intersts in the light of what others predictably will do, hoping thereby to gain greater rewards than they would gain by sticking with the general adherence to coordinative guidelines. Being a free-rider in such a circumstance is very risky indeed. Rational agents will design social policies to detect and discourage such otherwise attractive behavior (attractive at least to rational egoists). In short, such rational egoists are not likely to get away with such directly self-serving behavior, and the penalties for so acting are great. This being so, it is rational for everyone to have a set of coordinative guidelines in place, spelled out, promulgated, and backed up with sanctions sufficient to deter rational egoists who will not act in accordance with the dictates of morality.

To reason in such a way is to support the second and third demands; namely (a) that it is a good thing that people be moral and a bad thing for them to be immoral, and (b) to support the recognition that social pres-sures are to be applied to ensure that everyone act in accordance with the moral point of view. Even when they are inclined to be immoralists (inclined, that is, to take as the supreme principle for their own actions the principle that they always do what would "constitute their best reply to whatever others are or may be doing"), rational and informed people will recognize that immoralism will not pay. Indeed they will see, Baier claims, that it will never pay. They will see, if they carefully reflect, the desirability of making social sanctions supporting morality so effective, so stringent both in terms of severity and certainty, and thus very costly for themselves, that immoralism (or amoralism, if you will) would not pay. If *people* take as their supreme principle of action 'Always do what constitutes your best reply to whatever others are or may be doing' and act on that principle, they would not lead as good a life, *as a group of people,* as they would if they would accept instead as supreme principles of practical reason certain coordinative guidelines, even purely conventional coordinative guidelines, which would be in accordance with the moral point of view. But this shows that such a principle of self-anchored egoism, as Baier calls it, could not be the correct formulation of the supreme principle of practical reason. It would have suboptimal results.

## III

Baier next introduces a very controversial thesis. He argues not only that rational agents would in prisoners'-dilemma situations want a social order utilizing coordinative guidelines, but he also argues for the controversial thesis that a person starting from rational egoism would want, or would come to want if he deliberated carefully, to follow those guidelines himself even in circumstances in which following them did not constitute his best reply to whatever others are or may be doing. Any egoist, if he were rational, would come to regard such nonegoistic principles to be the supreme principles of practical reason. This surprising claim is a crucial point for Baier because only if it is so will it be the case that rational agents will follow—or so he claims—such coordinative guidelines *voluntarily.* They see, for the reasons already given, that general adherence to such guidelines is plainly desirable. But if they, as individuals, stick with rational egoism as their supreme principle of rationality, they will then still not follow these coordinative guidelines voluntarily, but only when the sanctions were so certain and so severe that not following these coordinative guidelines will be counterproductive. This shows, if correct, that Baier's fourth demand—that the precepts of morality are overriding—is also a crucial requirement of practical reason. People will want such a system of coordinative guidelines for *its own sake* and not simply as a means to an end.

## IV

Baier concludes his case by arguing that rational people will want not only some system of coordinative guidelines or other rather than none, but they will want a distinctive set of coordinative guidelines. Baier, unlike David Gauthier, is not settling for a conventional morality.[3] This comes out with particular clarity in "Rationality, Reason, and the Good." Some systems will afford people significantly better chances of leading a worthwhile life than others; for example, a set of coordinative guidelines favoring ruling class interests will not do this as well as a set of guidelines answering to the interests of everyone alike. In finding the crucial requirements of practical reason, we will want not just some set of coordinative guidelines, but *sound* coordinative guidelines. We will want, that is, coordinative guidelines where everyone has equally good reason to regard its precepts as paramount practical reasons. This shows, Baier claims, that rational people will accept the first demand as a crucial requirement of practical reason. A satisfactory system of coordinative guidelines must be such that "everybody subject to these guidelines have adequate reason to regard them as paramount practical reasons." *Everybody* must have as good reason so to regard them as *anybody* can in reason demand to have. This will be so if *everybody* has as good reason as *everybody* can *have* for so regarding a distinctive system of coordinative guidelines. "No one," Baier maintains, "can in reason demand a better reason than that, since from the point of view of reason no one is *ab initio* in a privileged position to ask for a better reason than anyone else."[4]

Baier's talk of soundness is rather peculiar. In showing a system of coordinative guidelines to be sound, he is not claiming that they can be reduced to a set of valid arguments with true premises. Rather, for Baier, when we are trying to articulate a method for determining what to do, a criterion of soundness will tell us how the relevant properties of the various actions open to us are to be evaluated. The requirement of soundness, Baier avers, is very likely the most important demand on a method for determining what to do. It is a demand we make on anything we would accept as a legitimate morality. But in spite of the importance he attaches to it, what he means by "soundness" is not explicated, though, as we have seen, he does tell us that a system of coordinative guidelines is sound if "everybody has equally good reason to regard the precepts as paramount practical reasons." So we, on his conception, have a sound morality where all rational agents have equally good grounds to regard its moral principles as having overriding rational authority in situations where questions of the guidance of conduct arise. A fair number of questions arise about this conception of soundness, but since the critique that follows does not turn on the details of this conception, I shall not pursue them here.

Baier also believes that he has shown that "to be sound, a morality must be such that it is a good thing if all people are moral and a bad thing if they are not," and he also concludes that the five demands have the backing of practical reason and can thus be "used to define or delineate the correct method for arriving at normative moral conclusions." This, in turn, Baier would have it, means that morality is *necessarily* in accordance with reason and immorality *necessarily* contrary to it.


## V


I want now to turn to an assessment of Baier's account, an assessment that will also involve some further explication of his complicated and nuanced view. (I will not, however, try to sort out everything that needs to be sorted out in his account, but only those things that are germane to the points that I wish to criticize.)

Baier maintains that a group of rational people, starting out with a sub-scription to rational egoism, would not just want a sound system of coordi-native guidelines taught as something for others to follow but not for them-selves to follow, except where following such a system would also coincide with the principle of self-anchored egoism—that is, "Always do what consti-tutes your best reply to whatever others are or may be doing"—but they would also want those principles taught in such a way that they themselves would be socialized into reasoning and acting in accordance with them even when so reasoning and acting would not for themselves (as individuals) be justified in terms of the principle of self-anchored egoism. Even as an indi-vidual member of such a group he will, if rational, will to be so socialized. He will see this, Baier maintains, as a requirement for his own rational ac-tion. He would accept, according to Baier, as his supreme principle of practi-cal reason, what he, at least, believes to be a sound system of coordinative guidelines and would thus be led to abandon his rational egoism. He would so act even in individual situations where so acting did not serve his own interests. He would strive to be not just a man of good morals but also to be a morally good man.

Baier is not just saying that rational egoists would want each other so to act, but that each such egoist would will that he would himself be so socialized that he would come to embrace the moral principles of a system of sound coordinative guidelines as ends in themselves. He would want, if he had perfect rationality, to so order his life that he would always act as these coordinative guidelines dictate. He would, like a good Hobbesian, see the danger of not doing so—that is, the destabilizing effects on the social order and thus the disadvantage to himself—but beyond such instrumental considerations, he would also believe that any other way of orienting his life would offend against rationality.

Baier has not shown anything that strong. A rational individual could without error reason as follows: I, for roughly the reasons that Baier gives, want a sound system of coordinative guidelines to be firmly entrenched in my society. This requires a certain socialization of the people in the society and I cannot in reason desire that such socialization be withheld from me, for others are not going to accept such an exemption. And, even if they did, I do not want to see the practice started, for if this became a practice, it would be applicable to others as well and that would hardly be in my interest. But I still rationally can and do wish that such socialization not be successful in my own case. I wish, speaking for myself alone, that socialization to stick only to the extent that I am able successfully to simulate acting on sound coordinative guidelines, to have the ability actually to act on them when it is my interest to do so and clairvoyantly to recognize situations in which this is so and situations in which this is not so. I indeed recognize the value of the existence of social arrangements in which everyone, including myself, is taught to adhere to these coordinative guidelines, but I hope that such teaching will not be successful in my case because what I want to be able to do, in every case where I prudently can, is to give my interests pride of place and do what I have the best reason to believe, everything considered, furthers my own interests. I hope that I will always be able to take the interests of others to be subordinate to what I have the best reasons for believing will, everything considered, best further my own interests. This may not show a lot about what I actually will do, but it does show something important about the order of my commitments.

Such a person is an immoralist, but Baier has not established that such an immoralist in thinking as he does and in hoping that he can act in such an unprincipled way, where it suits his advantage, is being irrational or even less rational than a person of sound moral principle. What Baier has at most shown is that such an immoralist would want a sound system of moral guidelines in place in society and would recognize the value of devices in the society that successfully socialize everyone into that morality. But Baier has not shown that reason requires that such a person desire that such socialization stick in his own case beyond giving him the ability successfully to simulate acting on principle, and to act, if he so chooses, to counteract the effects of such socialization where it plausibly threatens to become catching and thus to make his society unstable. And he has not shown that such a person must be less rational than reasonable persons of sound moral principle. Baier may have established that it is rational to have a sound system of moral practices and irrational not to have one, but he has not shown that a person who acts immorally necessarily acts irrationally or indeed in any way acts with diminished rationality or makes any intellectual mistake at all. He has not shown that immoral behavior must be contrary to reason. We still have the problem of Hume's sensible knave.

## VI

Such a person could not give a public defense of his position, and he would probably be ill-advised even to defend it privately to his friends (if indeed he could have "friends"), but everyone when they hear such a description of a possible scenario for how a person might act can come to recognize that such immoral behavior need not necessarily be either irrational or even contrary to reason where it is tolerably plain that it will not be copied. Thus Baier fails to establish a necessary connection between being immoral and being less than fully rational. He has not shown that the immoralist must suffer from some defect of reason.

It might *in fact* always turn out to be the case that the social sanctions might be sufficiently stringent and efficient such that it would always transpire that it never was in his interests not to act in accordance with them. But that turn of events would not make them his supreme principles of practical reason or make his acting immorally *necessarily* irrational or even contrary to reason.

Baier might try to rebut this, arguing that a rational immoralist would recognize that if this is the way he rationally responds, then this is also the way others would too, and if people generally acted like that, then the commonly recognized public good of achieving conformity to coordinative guidelines would then require a very effective and very certain system of social sanctions. If he were thoroughly rational, he would also have to recognize that the achieving of *such* a system of sanctions would have to require an extensive amount of coercion in society, a coercion sufficient to get chaps like himself to act morally. He would further recognize, if he were through and through rational, that he could not rationally wish for so much coercion in society, including coercion directed against himself, so he must, to be consistently rational, opt for a society in which he would, and others would as well, *voluntarily* accept such guidelines. He would not want a Hobbesian sovereign.

In reply to this attempt at a rebuttal we should recognize what Baier seems at least to miss; namely, that this is just another situation in which our putatively rational immoralist (Hume's sensible knave) accepts these guidelines because he sees it is in his long-range self-interest to do so. If others could be so conditioned to adhere to coordinative guidelines, even when adhering to them is not rooted in the principle of self-anchored egoism, and if our putative immoralist could escape such a conditioning (without others emulating him), then he could still rationally wish that such a state of affairs obtain. He could rationally want it to be the case that he *not* be so successfully socialized that he would become a person of moral principle. He could rationally wish to be a man of good morals without wishing to become a morally good man. What he would not of course want is for this to be publicly noticed.

That this is so unlikely a possibility that it is desert islandish is not here to the point. After all, it is Baier who is maintaining that there is a conceptual (logical) connection between being immoral and having a defect of reason. It should also be noted that it is not so evident that each person's rationale for action is so transparent to others that such situations would not in fact obtain, but even if they did not, this would not establish the necessary connection that Baier seeks. Whether immorality is irrational or contrary to reason would be very much dependent on what in fact people can get away with. The choice for *an individual* may not between accepting coordinative guidelines voluntarily or by coercion, but between accepting them voluntarily as his supreme principles of practical reason and accepting them voluntarily, but still conditionally on their best answering to his own interests.

I agree with Baier that if the *social* choice (a choice that involves considering everyone in the society) is between a system governed by the principle of self-anchored egoism and a *system* governed by coordinative guidelines, the latter *system* is clearly preferable, that is, the better social alternative, the better system to see instantiated in society, for such a social acceptance of the former would have suboptimal results. But this does not establish that an individual's acting immorally in certain determinate situations must be, or even is, contrary to reason.

## VII

I think Baier makes a well-taken and important point when he argues that rational persons, when considering the interests of everyone alike, would opt for the acceptance of what they at least believe to be a sound system of coordinative guidelines and that they would take such a system as overriding systems not so constituted. Moreover, a sound system of coordinative guidelines, and thus a sound moral system, must be such, when viewed from an agent-neutral perspective—that "*everybody* subject to these guidelines have adequate reason to regard them as paramount practical reasons." For this condition to be satisfied it must be the case that "*everybody* has as good reason so to regard them as *anybody* can in reason demand to have." This in turn is satisfied if "everybody has as good reason as *everybody* (not *anybody*) can have for so regarding a system of coordinative guidelines." Baier, again trying to block the immoralist's option, remarks that "no one can in reason demand a better reason that that, since from the point of view of reason no one is *ab initio* in a privileged position to ask for a better reason than anyone else."

The immoralist can respond in at least two ways. First, he can perfectly coherently reject the idea Baier tries to defend in "Rationality, Reason, and the Good" that there is anything properly called 'the point of view of reason'. Instead, we can only properly speak of what it is rational to do from a particular point of view, such as a technical point of view, a prudential point of view, a self-interested point of view, a moral point of view, an aesthetic point of view, and the like. The unity of practical reason that Baier speaks of is a myth. What we have seen is that it is at least conceivable that what it is rational for an individual to do on a given occasion from a self-interested point of view. There is no coherent sense of what it is rational to do *sans phrase* enabling us to show that an individual always acts irrationally or less than perfectly rationally, if he does not in all situations act from the moral point of view. Where he views the matter disinterestedly, treating his own interests as having no privileged place, trivially, the moral point of view wins out over the self-interested point of view.

Where, alternatively, he sees things from the point of view of his own interests, always giving his own interests pride of place, again, trivially, the self-interested point of view wins out. But there is nothing in "pure reason," including "pure practical rationality," driving him to accept one point of view rather than the other. Whether certain sentiments would so drive him is another matter. Learning to be moral may essentially involve learning to come to *care* in a certain distinctive way. Still he can intelligibly ask why he should (nonmoral "should") cultivate such caring. He can perfectly intelligibly ask why he should take the disinterested point of view required by morality. (The kind of caring needed involves being disinterested in a certain way.) In determinate but partially different ways, both points of view, and other points of view as well, say, an aesthetic point of view, can be objective. (However, it is the case that the concept of objectivity is sufficiently ambiguous and many faceted so as to be of little use here.)[5]

Thomas Nagel has given us a useful way of generalizing such a rejection of the claimed unity of practical reason. Nagel believes that there is a "distinction between reasons that are relative to the agent and reasons that are not," and that this distinction is an "extremely important one" (*PA*, 102-103). He calls them (following Derek Parfit) "agent-relative reasons" and "agent-neutral reasons." An agent-neutral reason is a reason that "can be given a general form which does not include an essential reference to the person to whom it applies" (*PA*, 102). Agent-relative reasons, by contrast, "include an essential reference to the person to whom it applies" (*PA*, 102). Nagel's paradigm case of an agent-neutral reason for action is that it would reduce the amount of wretchedness in the world. It is, he maintains, a reason for anyone to do or want something that doing it would reduce the amount of wretchedness in the world. Such a reason, if there are such, is an agent-neutral reason. His paradigm of an agent-relative reason is that it is in his interest: "If it is a reason for anyone to do or want something that it would be in *his* interest, then that is an agent-relative reason" (*PA,* 102). In such a case, if something were in Sven's interest but contrary to Axel's, Sven would have reason to want it to happen and Axel would have the same reason to want it not to happen. Agent-neutral reasons are reasons for doing things or wanting something to happen that anyone would have even if he were "considering the world in detachment from the perspective of any particular person within it" (*PA,* 103).

Agent-relative reasons, by contrast, although they can be just as objective as agent-neutral reasons (anyone can come to appreciate their force), only commit us to believing that someone has reason to act in accordance with those reasons if they are related to a particular agent in the right way. That it would improve his talents is an objective reason, but it is still an agent-relative reason for that person to do it. But, as Nagel puts it, "someone who accepts this judgement is not committed to wanting it *to be the case* that people in general are influenced by such reasons" (*PA,* 103). Her judgment commits her to wanting something only when its implications are drawn for the individual person she happens to be. So far as others are concerned, "the content of the objective judgement concerns only what they should do or want" (*PA,* 104). It says nothing vis-à-vis that particular action or state of affairs, about what they should want to be done or to be the case for that particular person in that particular case. That it would develop her talents, if it is a genuine agent-relative reason, is an objective reason (if that isn't a pleonasm) for her to do it, but not a reason for me to want her to do it.

There is nothing in what I have said that entails or even suggests that there are no genuine agent-neutral reasons or that, where agent-neutral reasons and agent-relative reasons clash, agent-relative reasons always or even ever override agent-neutral reasons or vice versa. What I have argued is that where agent-neutral and agent-relative reasons clash, there is no point of view of reason that shows that agent-neutral reasons must always, for any thoroughly rational agent, override the agent-relative reasons.

I do not deny that both agent-relative reasons and agent-neutral reasons can be objective, "since both can be understood from outside the viewpoint of the individual who has them" (*PA,* 102). What I am claiming is that there just are these different kinds of reason with no further court of reason to appeal to to tell an agent what she is to do when, on a given occasion, they dictate different courses of action. Baier's ethical rationalism commits him to the view that agent-neutral reasons are overriding or superior reasons, but he has given us no adequate grounds for believing that they are. They of course are *if* an agent is considering the world in detachment from the perspective of any particular agent within it. But Baier has not shown why or even that a clear understanding of her world (including her own situation) always requires *an agent* to adopt that perspective. Even a person who has what Baier calls "perfect rationality" need not always, or perhaps even ever, give such pride of place to agent-neutral reasons. When the immoralist deliberately lets certain agent-relative reasons override agent-neutral reasons, she need not in any way be acting contrary to reason.

Indeed, the best agent-neutral reasons that *anyone* could in reason demand are the best possible reasons *everyone* could have. Where we are thinking of agent-neutral reasons and about the role they play in society, it is clear enough, as Baier puts it in "Rationality, Reason, and the Good," "that the best reasons *anyone can in reason demand* are those *that everyone* can have." But that does not obtain for agent-relative reasons, and there is no sound argument in Baier's account to show that agent-neutral reasons are superior reasons to agent-relative ones such that the individual who does not treat them as overriding must somehow be flaunting the "enterprise of Reason."

There is a second way the immoralist can respond to Baier. Even accepting, for the sake of discussion, that there is something legitimately called 'the point of view of reason' and even accepting that from that vantage point no one individual is '*ab initio* in a privileged position to ask for a better reason than anyone else', it still does not follow that the immoralist acts irrationally or with less than perfect rationality in not, on a given occasion, accepting 'the point of view of reason'. This sounds paradoxical, but consider the fact that the immoralist need not in acting immorally be acting against his own interests (even long-term interests); he need make no mistake in deductive or inductive reasoning; he can have a clear picture of what the facts are, including the various outcomes portrayed in prisoners'-dilemma situations; and he can, as well, Plato to the contrary notwithstanding, be quite thoroughly in control of his passions. All these are plain and paradigmatic marks of rationality. In these ways, it need not at all be the case that the immoralist is defective rationally.

Baier, in spelling out the several interrelated powers that he takes to be constitutive of rationality, provides some additional characteristics or features of rationality. But there is nothing here that the immoralist could not consistently possess. He could readily apply 'certain general guidelines of a culture to particular cases', although he would sometimes do it for ends different from those of the person of moral principle, including ends that might be manipulative. He could, without compromising his immoralism, also assess the merits of these guidelines and indeed know how to improve them in the light of moral ideals. One can understand the moral point of view without being moral just as one can drive fat oxen without being fat. No reason has been given for thinking the immoralist's power of reason need be weaker than that of the person of sound moral principle.

Baier might argue that since the immoralist does not use his power of reason to improve coordinative guidelines, he is, to that degree, defective rationally. But it should in turn be replied that the immoralist very well could use his powers of reason to improve the prevalent coordinative guidelines in the light of the very conception of morality Baier defends. He could, just as much as Baier's persons of moral principle, regard morality (even a sound morality) as consisting "in following what one has adequate reason to think is required by guidelines for interaction among members of a moral community" and even strive, quite consistently with his immoralism, to improve the extant morality in the society in which he lives along these very lines, while still, consistently and rationally, as an individual, although not as a moral person, refusing to act on what he acknowledges is *publicly* required. Doing this need not be at all Dostoevskian perversity. The rational immoralist (Hume's sensible knave) just wants to be a prudent free-rider with stable and sound moral institutions in place. Even with the acceptance of that vague rationalist something called the "point of view of reason," we need not believe that the immoralist need be at all irrational or even defective in his rationality. Whether such a person is someone we are likely to meet up with is not to the point, for Baier's claim about the connection between immorality and rationality is a conceptual one. His claim is that immorality is alays *necessarily* contrary to reason.

## VIII

'Morality is necessarily in accordance with reason and immorality necessarily contrary to it' needs disambiguation. There are at least two ways it may be taken. (1) 'It is rational for everybody in a society to have a sound system of moral practices and irrational not to have them', and (2) 'A person who acts morally necessarily acts rationally and the person who acts immorally necessarily acts in a way that is contrary to reason'. Baier may well have established, given his reading of 'rational', the truth of (1), if it indeed needs establishing. I have not disputed that, but I have argued that he has not established the truth of (2), and that there are indeed very good grounds for doubting that (2) is true.

   This is, some might have noticed, in effect a replay with new arguments and in new terminology of an old dispute between Baier and myself.[6] Some decades ago we both argued, running against what was then orthodoxy, that "Why be moral?" need not be a pseudoquestion. But Baier thought that he had given a satisfactory argument establishing both that we (that is, people generally) should be moral and that, when an individual asks on a given occasion "Why should I be moral?" he had shown that we have a sound argument for saying that he should; that is, to correct a possible ambiguity, if he is rational he should, even when viewing things strictly from his own point of view, conclude that he should. I argued in the early exchange that Baier had successfully answered the question "Why should we be moral?" but not the question "Why should I be moral?" In this respect our positions have remained unchanged. Whether this reflects a hardening of the intellectual arteries on the part of one or another or both of us is better left for others to judge.

NOTES

1. I am principally concerned here with Kurt Baier's "The Conceptual Link Between Morality and Rationality," *Nous* 7 (1982) and his "Rationality, Reason, and the Good" in David Copp and David Zimmerman (eds.) *Morality, Reason and Truth* (Totowa, N.J.: Rowman and Allanheld, 1985). The quotations given in the text, unless otherwise specified, are from these two essays.

2. Baier never defines 'demand' or explains what he means by it or indicates that he is using the term in any special way. I would surmise, looking at his employment of the term, that he means by 'a demand' something it sometimes means in ordinary use; namely, something that is strongly required or claimed as being necessary. Baier introduces his talk of demands as follows: "My thesis is that the moral point of view is properly identified in terms of a set of demands on a method for determining what to do, demands which this method must satisfy if the resulting moralities are rightly to be regarded as constituting paramount practical reasons." I take it that Baier means by 'demands' here 'authoritative requirements' for a proper method for determining what to do. These demands (authoritative requirements) are demands that Baier seeks to show are demands that thoroughly rational people would regard as central constitutive elements of the moral point of view.

3. David Gauthier, "Bargaining Our Way into Morality," *Philosophic Exchange* 5 (1978): 15–27. It is instructive to contrast Gauthier's views and Baier's with those of Derek Parfit. See Parfit, "Prudence, Morality, and Its Prisoner's Dilemma," *Proceedings of the British Academy* (1979): 539–564.

4. It is important to keep in mind here what Baier has said about universalizability. See, for example, "Moral Reasons," in Peter French et al. (eds.) *Midwest Studies in Philosophy* (Minneappolis, Minn.: University of Minnesota Press, 1978), pp. 62–74.

5. Thomas Nagel, *The Possibility of Altruism* (Princeton: Princeton University Press, 1979). All references to Nagel are from *The Possibility of Altruism* and they are given in the text in parentheses.

6. The previous stating of these issues occurred in Kurt Baier, *The Moral Point of View* (Ithaca, N.Y.: Cornell University Press, 1958), pp. 257-320, and in chapter 8 of the present volume.

# 14

# Why Should I Be Moral?
# Revisited

I

To ask "Why should I be moral?" is to ask "Why should I do what is right?" But this in turn presupposes that we understand what it means to claim that something is right or wrong and that we can determine, on at least some occasions and to some extent, what is right and wrong. If nihilism is true and talk of right and wrong is illusory or incoherent or if a really thorough-going moral skepticism is justified such that we can in no measure ascertain or determine what is right or wrong or even what is approximately right or wrong, then it is senseless to ask the question "Why be moral?" If the question is a coherent one, it presupposes that at least some of us, at least in some circumstances, can have some tolerably determinate idea of what is right and wrong and it further presupposes that at least some of us some of the time can be moral: can do what is right and avoid what is wrong.

I am of the view that nihilism and ethical skepticism—particularly some versions of ethical skepticism—are less easy to refute than many philosophers believe and most of our ethics textbooks give to understand. There are indeed versions of nihilism and ethical skepticism that are manifestly absurd, but there are versions of it which are more resilient. Be that as it may, I shall assume here that nihilism and ethical skepticism, even in their strongest forms, can be met and undermined by cogent philosophical argument and I shall concern myself with the quite different question—or (so as to not beg any

From *American Philosophical Quarterly* 21, no. 1 (January, 1984): 81–91. Reprinted by permission of the publisher.

relevant issues) putative question—*why should I do what I acknowledge is the right thing to do?*

Suppose an individual—a Dostoevskian undergroundling if you like—is trying to decide in a very fundamental sense how he or she shall live, what sort of person he or she wishes to become or strive to remain. Such a person knows that it is routinely, indeed, culturally speaking, unquestionably, believed that he should always do what everything considered he believes to be the right thing to do, but he wants to know what justification, if any, can be given for that claim. (Or is this one of the places where justification comes to an end?) He wants to know why he should do what he acknowledges is the right thing to do. And he could indeed even be asking this in the spirit of Glaucon and Adeimantus in Plato's *Republic.* That is, he could be firmly determined to do what is right but still want to know if any non-question begging reason could be given why he should do so. It is that question I want to wrestle with.

This is not ethical skepticism, as I have characterized it, but it is a skepticism over morals. It is not ethical skepticism for it presupposes that we acknowledge that certain things are right or wrong (moral or immoral). We acknowledge these things and then ask, all the same, why should we do what is right and avoid what is wrong? A person of principle (a person committed to the moral point of view) is a person who will insist that moral considerations override all other considerations. I am asking, in reflecting on how I shall try to live, why, and even whether, I should be a person of moral principle.

Nothing substantial turns on it, if you insist on claiming that that is what *real* ethical skepticism really is, because, you claim, that challenge most fundamentally challenges the claim to an objective basis for morals. I say "nothing substantial turns on it," for, if you insist on talking this way, "ethical skepticism" for you simply means what I have called "skepticism over morals" and we will still have to distinguish, at least two kinds of "ethical skepticism," the ordinary garden variety which is skeptical over whether we can even know or reliably ascertain what is right and what is wrong and the more radical kind which asks, even if we can know or can reliably ascertain what is right or wrong, why should we do it? It is this question or putative question that I shall consider here.

II

Let us put some more flesh on this. Taking the moral point of view requires a sensitivity to the pain and suffering of human beings. Generally speaking the less pain and suffering there is in the world the better. That surely is obvious enough. Moreover, morality has developed in such a way that reflective moral agents, at least in societies thoroughly touched by modernity, have also come to an acknowledgment (in theory at least) of the necessity of affirming the inherent dignity and the intrinsic worth of all human beings.

The things I have mentioned above are not all that taking the moral point of view comes to and it has not been part of the moral point of view of all societies at all times and places. Some moral points of view have been rather more parochial. But this acceptance, often in lip service only, of what could be called a commitment to *humaneness* (to lessen suffering) and a commitment to *humanity* (treat human beings as having an intrinsic worth) has become with us pervasive and partially definitive of what it is to take the moral point of view. (That this, not infrequently, is lip service only is something else again.)

The skeptical question I am putting to you should be formulated as follows: suppose, in a thoroughly non-evasive way, you put it to yourself, very carefully and very fundamentally, what sort of life do I want to try to live, what sort of person do I want to become? Most of us, I suspect, would, among other things, want to be people of moral principle, be people who have a commitment to humaneness and humanity. But there may be some of us who really do not have such aspirations. I find that distressing to contemplate, but I ask myself or you ask yourselves: why should I, if I don't feel like it, take this moral point of view with its commitment to *humaneness* and to *humanity* or indeed any moral point of view? That is the skeptical question I am asking you.

## III

Some philosophers have resisted the very posing of this question. They have taken it to be a pseudoquestion. I first want to respond to them in a rather brisk manner. That is, I will respond to those who want to reject the question not because it is immoral to ask it but for the reason that it is—or so they believe—senseless to ask it. It makes about as much sense, they claim, as asking "Why are all scarlet things red?" If we reflect carefully on the occurrence of the word "should" in the putative question "Why should I be moral" we will come to see, the claim goes, that we are trying to ask for the logically impossible: we are asking for a moral reason to accept any moral reasons at all.

That objection evaporates as soon as we reflect on the fact that not all intelligble uses of "should" are moral uses of the term. When I ask, "Should I put a bandage on the cut?" I am not normally asking a moral question and the 'should' does not here have a moral use. When I ask, "Why should I be moral?" I am not asking, if I have my wits about me, "What moral reason or reasons have I for being moral?" That indeed is like asking "Why are all scarlet things red?" Rather, I am asking, can I, everything considered, give a reason sufficiently strong—a non-moral reason clearly—for my always giving an overriding weight to moral considerations, when they conflict with other considerations, such that I could be shown to be acting irrationally, or at least less rationally than I otherwise would be acting, if I did not give such pride of place to moral considerations?

Those who want to reject the very question can in turn respond. The very context of the situation, where the question "Why be moral?" could be raised, is a context, as the above in effect shows, in which it is assumed that acting morally is not in the interest of the agent asking that question, but, if that is so, the question is, after all, senseless, because it is asking for a reason which must be a self-interested reason for being moral, while, at the same time, it is assumed that being moral is not in the agent's self-interest. But that comes to asking for a self-interested reason for doing what is not in his self-interest and that plainly is nonsense. In asking the question the questioner is asking something which is incoherent for he is asking for a reason of self-interest for doing what is contrary to his self-interest.

It could be, and indeed it has been, denied that it only makes sense to ask the question "Why should I be moral?" when it is assumed that acting morally is not in the questioner's self-interest. But, that response aside, there are the following difficulties with that attempt to exhibit the meaninglessness of that question. It is not a logical or conceptual truth (if indeed it is true at all) that, everything considered, the most rational thing for an individual, any individual at all, to do is always to do that which will promote his self-interest. It is not true by definition and it also appears not to be a "universal law of rationality" for it apppears to be the case at any rate— to take what would be a disconfirming instance—that there are circumstances in which it would not be in an individual's short term or long term self-interest to donate a kidney, yet it still would not be irrational or contrary to reason for him to do so. If there are cases of this sort (as there most certainly appear at least to be), then it cannot be the case that *the* rational thing for an individual to do is always to do that which is in his self-interest. There are rational individuals, for example some kidney donors, who are neither being irrational nor acting irrationally in donating a kidney. There are things which are not *required* by reason which are still plainly not *contrary* to reason. Kidney donating, even against your self-interest, can sometimes be one of them.

Moreover, in asking "Why should I be moral?" in contexts where it is not in my self-interest to be moral, it is not clear that, if I am not confusedly asking for a moral reason for not doing what, everything considered, I regard as immoral and indeed actually is immoral, I must then be asking for a self-interested reason for not doing it. It might instead be an aesthetic reason, an economic reason, a political reason such as acting out of pure class solidarity, or indeed the questioner may not be quite sure what kind of reason he will take as overriding—that itself is one of the elements in the question. So that road is also blocked in the attempt to show that the question is a pseudoquestion.

Alternatively, it can be argued that the question is a pseudoquestion because, as we have seen, to ask "Why should I be moral?" is to ask "Why should I do what is right?" and that putative question, it is claimed, is a senseless question, because saying that an act is right just means that one should do it. This is, some will say, the final answer to a challenger of the hegemony of morality. And this, it will be claimed, obtains even for an individual agent in an ongoing moral society. For questions concerning what to do, the moral point of view just is the ultimately overriding point of view. The short of the matter is that if one understands what it is for an act to be right or wrong, it is senseless for one to try to turn around and ask why one should do what one acknowledges, and acknowledges correctly, is right and avoid what is wrong. Doing what is right is just what one should do and indeed must do or at least try to do.

This is plainly not "the short of the matter," for indeed to try to settle the matter thus is utterly to fail to appreciate the force and the point of the putative question. Not all 'shoulds', as we have seen, are moral 'shoulds'. In asking why he should take moral reasons as overriding, a person is asking "Why take the moral point of view?" or, at least, "Why always take the moral point of view as always the overriding guide for all his actions where moral considerations are relevant?" The person asking that question can perfectly well understand that, *from the moral point of view,* "I should do what, everything considered, I regard as right" is analytic or at least unchallengeable. But while not for a moment challenging that, he can perfectly relevantly point out that he is concerned with a different matter. He is asking why take the moral point of view at all? Whatever discoveries we might make about what the moral point of view requires will not *ipso facto,* or perhaps not at all, answer that question. Knowing, assuming now that we can know such a thing, that an act is right or is morally required, is, from the point of view of the person contemplating so acting, a sufficient reason for his doing it, only if the person in question is already committed to acting morally. What is a *morally* justifying reason may be neither a *motivating* reason nor a *justifying* reason *sans phrase.* But the question "Why should I be moral?" is to be construed as a request for reasons to justify that commitment to morality. From the moral point of view, moral reasons are taken as the overriding reasons for action, but why should he, as an individual, accept them as such, or, what comes to the same thing, reason in accordance with the moral point of view? That is the question we are trying to ask and it can't be, non-question beggingly answered or dismissed, by simply telling us that morally speaking it is the right thing to do.

Suppose an individual acknowledges that putting limits on the pursuit of rational self-interest just is acting morally. But he can still ask, "Why should I do that rather than pursue my rational self-interest without any limit?" This is one prominent form of the question "Why should I be moral?" and it has not been shown to be a senseless question.

## IV

So let us now proceed on the assumption that the question is not a pseudo-question. Still, "Why be moral?" is indeed a strange question which requires a reasonably determinate reading or set of readings if any headway is to be made with it. We have already done some of that but we still need to refine it a bit.

One, at least seemingly straightforward way of asking it, is to ask: why move beyond self-interest? Why adopt the so-called, or perhaps even the not so so-called, impartial, universal moral point of view? Some will, on various grounds, deny that there is such an impartial, or even partially impartial, moral point of view. But let us grant there, for the sake of the discussion at least, that we have a coherent conception of such an impartial moral point of view and then ask the hard "Why-be-moral?-question": so what, why should I adopt it?

It is plainly and unequivocally in our collective interests that we have a morality and that people generally act in accordance with it. Life in a world without reasonably functioning moral institutions would in Hobbes's famous phrase be nasty, brutish and short. In living we all need moral institutions. Even if the particular morality is only a conventional morality that we as rational egoists bargain ourselves into, it is much better than no morality at all. It is plainly in our interests to have moral institutions and practices in place and functioning. But that shows why *we* should have a morality, why it is in *our* interests to have a functioning morality, it does not answer the question of why *I* should be moral.

That *we* should be moral—that taken collectively we require moral institutions—does not show why an individual in a society with reasonably functioning moral institutions should himself be a person of moral principle. He should simulate such behavior all right, but why should he not be a free-rider and give the appearance of moral commitment while always, or at least typically, feathering his own nest when it is safe to do so? The correct answer to the question "Why should *we* be moral?" is not necessarily the correct answer to "Why should *I* be moral?"

Some will respond that it is. That an answer to the question of why people should be moral is automatically an answer to why an individual should be moral because of the very nature of what a reason is or what reason is. If to preserve my health is a good reason for me to exercise, it is a good reason for any person like me in circumstances like mine to exercise as well, so if $X$ is a good reason for $Y$ to do $Z$ then it is also a good reason for anyone else like $Y$ in $Y$'s circumstances to do $Z$. Moreover, if some things, $A$, $B$, $C$, and $D$, are such that for anyone in any circumstance there is good reason to have them, then there is trivially reason for each of them to have them. Reasons are general; we can't sensibly say of two similarly inclined and generally relevantly similar people in identical circumstances that $X$ is a good reason for $Y$ to $Z$ and not a good reason for $W$ to $Z$. Contrary to what I have said above, if we have a good answer, as we do, to why *we* should be moral, we also have a good answer to why *I* should be moral— why any given individual in an ongoing tolerably moral society should be moral. This response fails, among other things, to keep in mind the distinction between an *agent-neutral viewpoint* and an *agent-relative viewpoint*. Both may be concerned with what happens or what is done or is to be done. But they view these questions from a very different vantage point (perspective). When our aims are held in common, they are agent-neutral. The above critical response to my argument for splitting the "Why should I be moral?" and "Why should we be moral?" question is from a resolutely agent-neutral viewpoint. If $X$ is a reason for $Y$ to do $Z$ it is plainly a reason for anyone else relevantly like $Y$ and similarly inclined and situated to do $Z$. If there is reason for me to protect my interests in a certain circumstance, I cannot consistently deny that it is a reason for you to protect your interests as well, if you are like me and similarly circumstanced. But all the while we are viewing things from an agent-neutral viewpoint. The immoralist free-rider on morality grants that that plainly is what to do from an agent-neutral viewpoint but he is in effect asking "Why should I take an agent-neutral viewpoint rather than an agent-relative viewpoint?" From an agent-neutral viewpoint, there is as much a reason for you to do something as for me to do it. I can't deny that you have a reason to do it if I do, unless I can show some relevant difference between you and me. But when I am viewing things from an agent-relative viewpoint, I can with perfect consistency ignore that and I can relevantly ask why should I abandon that agent-relative viewpoint. And that plainly is the viewpoint the person who is asking why he should be moral is asking that question from, if he at all has his wits about him. No non-question begging reason has been given why he must override that viewpoint or shift to an agent-neutral viewpoint to remain a rational individual rationally acting in the world.

V

Is it not at least logically possible that the immoralist (amoralist if you will) might be satisfied with his life? Can it be shown that, no matter who I am, no matter what preference schedules I happen to have, that my long-term self-interest is more likely to be satisfied if I, in conjunction with everyone else or even with the greater majority of the people, am doing what morally speaking is the right thing to do, than, if everybody else or even (perhaps) most people are so acting, and I, undetected, am not so acting? Must a prudent intelligent immoralist make himself unhappy or harm even his own long-term self-interest by continuing to be such an immoralist?

Such an at least putatively rational immoralist will be an adroit free-rider. He will have an interest in other people being moral, since the other people's immorality, particularly when they are close by, will, or at least very likely may, adversely affect his own life, and the lives of people he just happens to care about. He, no more than the moralist, will want a Hobbesian state of nature. He will also, and for the same reasons, have an interest in the effective enforcement of the principles and precepts of morality. He will, if he is thoroughly rational and reflective, want others to restrict their exclusive pursuit of their self-interest. But what he reflectively wants for himself is another matter.

## VI

Philosophers, as radically different as Hobbes and Kant, have told us that immorality—any kind of immorality—is necessarily against reason. For both Aristotle and Kant the life we ought to lead is the life dominated by reason. They see, or think they see, an intrinsic relation between a life disciplined by reason and the life we ought to live. There is on such an account a demand for a single ultimate end at which all action ought to aim. There is also here a picture of life in which reason rules. Traditional philosophy, including much moral philosophy, views philosophers as presiders over a tribunal of pure reason, able to determine the structure of other disciplines, the rightness of social practices and the moral appropriateness of various courses of action. There is reason to be skeptical, and perhaps even ironical, about this flattering self-image.

Talk of a "life dominated by reason" or of the notion of "reason ruling" is not pellucid talk where it is taken as being something more than a metaphorical way of referring to the tolerably plain requirements of consistency, coherence, control of one's passions and the taking of the most efficient means to achieve one's ends. But in these plain senses, the immoralist, as we have seen, need not be an irrationalist.

Is there something in our reflective interests or in the very emotional foundations of our lives—the sentiments, affections and attitudes toward the world that we as human beings can hardly help having—which commits us to the moral life? Would the experience of being in a genuine moral community teach any rational human being who had such experience, and particularly a person who had it by way of extensive participation in such a community, that he would want to be moral and that his life as a human being would be severely impoverished if he did not strive to be a person of principle and moral integrity?

We must tread very carefully here for it is very easy, particularly if we are moral philosophers, to project our own moral images of ourselves onto humankind, imagining, for example, without good empirical evidence, that the good of self-respect is a key desideratum for every rational person. (Another pitfall is unwittingly to make it true by definition.)

Will any person, no matter how he is placed in society, or what kind of society he is in, be unhappy, or at least less happy, than he otherwise would be, if he is an unprincipled bastard? Must an immoralist, anywhere, anytime, lead a life that he would find unsatisfying or at least less satisfying than the life he would have if he were not an immoralist? Plato and Aristotle think that he would. I will skeptically query that. I shall argue that no such general answer can be given as the one that Plato and Aristotle attempt to give. Whether an immoralist will be unhappy will depend on what kind of person he is, what kind of society he lives in, what his particular situation is in that society, and what kind of a self-image he has. Happiness no more necessarily requires morality than rationality does, though it can, in certain circumstances, be compatible with retaining firm moral commitments.

## VII

We human beings, it will be said, are socialized in such a way that we inevitably will come to have a moral conscience "telling" us in specific situations what is right and wrong and nagging us, indeed not infrequently whipping us, for not doing what our conscience tells us we must do. We cannot, the claim goes, safely ignore the dictates of our conscience and remain happy. Even if we are very clever indeed at simulating moral commitment, we will, though publicly unreprobated, still pay heavily in psychic suffering if we violate the dictates of our conscience.

Suppose my conscience is bothering me because I am really acting without what I acknowledge is, morally speaking, a proper regard for others. Must I, in such a circumstance, be acting against my true interests? Must I be unhappy or less happy than I otherwise would be? Must I remain, if I don't rationalize, a person who is so bothered by his conscience? And must all rational persons in such circumstances so react?

Many people—perhaps most people—are captured by tribal taboos and tribal loyalties and are held hostage, in varying degrees, to neurotic compulsions about duties and the like. They will be, again in varying degrees, miser-

able if they do not act in accordance with what they believe morality enjoins. But people can free themselves from such superstitions and compulsions. Where they can they will not for *these* reasons by made unhappy, if
they are prudently immoral at least in terms of the morality that previously
held sway over them.

Do we, all the same, have good reason to believe that they will be less
happy than people of good will? How do we know, or do we know, that
the immoralist cannot live in such a way that he will be truly happy? (We
must beware of an unwitting intellectual cheating here, through an implicit
persuasive definition of "*truly* happy" or "*true* interests.")

It is true that an individual who rather systematically behaves in a
thoroughly unprincipled way is very likely to be found out, even when he
is clever and tolerably prudent about it. And when he is found out people
will generally turn against him—some very sharply—and it is very unlikely,
in such a circumstance, that his life will be (to put it minimally) a very happy
one. Morality—or at least behavior sufficiently like morality not to occasion
such reprobation—will, in such a circumstance, pay off.

Still this will not show that occasional quite deliberate patterns of prudent and intelligent immorality might not, on some occasions, handsomely
pay off for the perpetrator of those acts. Still, we have not yet squarely faced
questions concerning the psychological effects of the pangs of conscience. We
should ask ourselves this question. Is it not possible for those who recognize
that the dictates of conscience are not the dictates of reason, to come to
repudiate the *authority* of conscience and to come to regard their conscience
as simply their superego: an irrational or at least not-rational censor whose
authority they no longer acknowledge?

However, it will in turn be responded, that this is too rationalistic a way
of looking at the matter. We can reject the *authority* of conscience and it
can still (as reformed teetotalers know) have a hold over one. Such
conditioning—a socializing into the having of a conscience—is, under most
circumstances, humanly speaking, or sociologically speaking, inescapable, and
a rational immoralist could not wish the general conditioning circumstance
changed because he recognizes, à la Hobbes, the plain value of moral institutions for *us*. He, as we have seen, is asking "Why should *I* be moral?"
not "Why should *we* be moral?"

To this it could, in turn, be replied, that even in tolerably stable, well-
ordered societies certain individuals are not so afflicted with sharp pangs of
conscience. There is a not inconsiderable amount of unprincipled behavior
about, some of it plainly stupid and counter-productive even for its perpe-
trators, some of it more marginally stupid and counter-productive and some
of it with at least the appearance of being intelligent, controlled and plainly
advantage producing for the perpetrator of the immorality. It is a banal
falsehood that crime never pays. It surely appears at least to be the case,

that the burden of proof falls very heavily on the moralist who would maintain that deep down any such immoralist must be unhappy, must be acting
against his "true self" or at least his "true interests."

## VIII

Still, isn't he? He, being human, could not but value friendship, love,
comradeship and fraternity. But all those things would be impossible for him,
at least in their more genuine forms, if he lived the life of an immoralist.
But, in not having them, he loses a lot—loses more than he could every gain
in a tradeoff with the goods he gained by his immoralism. The very central
human goods (friendship, love, comradeship, fraternity), goods resting on a
non-calculating reciprocity, will not be available to him, it is natural to argue,
if he does not take the moral point of view. So, taking that point of view
is, after all, a necessary though not a sufficient condition for his happiness.
Not even psychoanalysis can, or will even try to, obliterate the voice of the
superego. It can at most diminish its excessive demands. Our conditioning
was too early and too pervasive for there to be any reasonable question of
turning our backs on it now. We cannot so easily cast off these ancient internalized demands.

You cannot, so the claim goes, act without regard to the dictates of morality if you really want to be happy. Yet in our societies not a few people,
some of them apparently contentedly and without evident harmful consequences
to themselves, wear their consciences very lightly indeed. Is that appearance
really deceiving? Are they all secretly miserable? Is it so clear that immorality
never pays? Do we have good grounds for believing, persuasive definitions
aside, that for us as individuals it is always in our best interests to do what
morality requires?

I am inclined to think that the belief that it is is a philosopher's myth.
A consoling story some moral philosophers tell themselves. Even if a policy
of *systematic* immoralism would make friendship, love and comradeship
impossible—things we plainly have reason to want—it need not be that to
gain these things requires any thoroughgoing moral integrity on our part.
The immoralist can be selectively and prudently immoral—and this without
a lot of rationalistic calculation. He need not be systematically or paranoidly
immoral and, like Macbeth, drive everyone from him.

Whether or not it is in your true interests to be moral depends on what
sort of person you happen to be. Beware of those moralizing moralists—
those keepers of the true faith—who read their own sentiments into all
humankind and conclude that all immoralists must be unhappy.

There is, of course, the not unreasonable worry that a person lacking
in moral integrity will face social ostracism: loss of love, contempt of family,

friends, colleagues and the like. I have suggested, in turn, that, where the person is intelligent and prudently in control of himself (as an immoralist could be), this danger is typically exaggerated by people understandably anxious to preserve the utter hegemony of morality.

## IX

There are further twists to the skein of the argument over immoralism. Even if it is the case that there are no ultimate non-question-begging grounds, in such general situations, for an individual's acting in accordance with the moral point of view rather than from a purely self-interested point of view and even if it is the case that no ultimate non-question-begging reason can be given for taking an agent-neutral perspective rather than agent-relative perspective, still these things do not show that we have vindicated an individual's having moral commitments. Rather, what we should conclude is that, in this type circumstance, justification has come to an end and that we must simply *decide* for ourselves how we should act and what sort of persons we will strive to be or to become. What all of this points to is that here at least decision is king.

If the above line of reasoning, about the incommensurability of the moral point of view and the self-interested point, is on the mark, then there can be no rational considerations showing us that we must, on pain of simply being irrational, be moral. If we are going to be through and through tough-minded and not be taken in by mythologies, we will conclude that, in the last analysis (whatever exactly that means), we must just decide to act in one way or another without having reasons sufficient to show that one course of action rather than another is *required* by reason.

## X

To reinforce the above line of argument consider the situation of what I shall call a classist amoralist in our class societies. I mean by "a classist amoralist" (a) a person who is part of the dominant elite in such a society, (b) a person who only extends his disinterested caring to his own peers and to those underlings (servants, mistresses and the like) he just happens to care about, and (c) a person who treats all other people manipulatively, deploying morality as moral ideology to keep those people in line in such a way that the interests of his class, and with that his own interests, are furthered. He has genuine moral relations with his own peers—the members of the elite class. Between such people there can be genuine love, disinterested concern, justice: the genuine reciprocities that partly constitute morality; but this is not extended, by the classist amoralists in that elite, to their relations with the vast dominated class. They, or at least most of them, are treated manipulatively. For them, our classist amoralist believes, moral ideology with its artful semblance of morality is enough. The thing to do with them, he avers, is, with the adroit use of the consciousness industry, to do a real snow job on them. But there is for the classist amoralist no question of treating them morally as equal members of a Kantian kingdom of ends. An artful disguise of morality is all that is required or desirable from the perspective of his classist amoralism.

It is not evident that such a society need be unstable or at least less stable than a society in which the moral point of view prevails. It is true that most members of ruling elites concoct comforting myths for themselves which conveniently reinforce their sense of their own class superiority. But it is not clear that all such classist amoralists must be so myth-prone. Slave societies existed in a stable manner for a long time. Is it really plausible to believe that all slave owners thought that they were somehow innately superior to their slaves? Do all Afrikaners today, who are wholehearted supporters of their system of apartheid, believe that Whites are superior to the Blacks they so cruelly exploit? It is not vastly more probable that *some* of the more intelligent and reflective slave owners or defenders of apartheid would have concluded or will conclude, as the case may be, both that there, but by the wheel of fortune go they, and that the thing to do is to continue, within reason, doing what they can to protect their own good fortune. Such persons, so reasoning, could still have the usual resources of love, trust, companionship and relatedness. A person, so reasoning and so acting, is unfair, and knows he is unfair, but, *among his peers,* he could very well be scrupulously fair, and, after all, he could say, perfectly correctly, that he didn't make the world. He just grew up in a society so structured. After all do not many of us in uncomfortable situations tell ourselves analogously comforting stories and make our little adjustments?

It looks like the burden of proof falls heavily on a moralist to prove that such a classist amoralist or immoralist need in any way be less happy, live a less self-fulfilling life, than the person of moral principle or moral integrity. Indeed in some circumstances—circumstances in which the world we live in is particularly swinish—he might even be happier or more self-fulfilled. And we have no good grounds for believing that such an immoralist in such a circumstance must be less rational or even, in a non-question begging sense, less reasonable than the person of firm and functional moral commitment.

## XI

Such a classist amoralist, note, is not as vulnerable as an immoralist who is an individual egoist. While many of us can and surely do get away with occasional thoroughly selfish and unprincipled acts, a deliberate, persistent policy of selfishness, even when it is intelligently cunning, is very likely to bring on guilt feelings, punishment, estrangement from others as well as their contempt and hostility. Classist amoralism with the reciprocity to be found in its class solidarity is far more secure than individual egoism. It is far less likely that the classist amoralist will find his sources of security, comfort, and happiness undermined. In such a society the classist amoralist (assuring he has the good fortune to belong to the dominant class) can have securely available to him, as the individual egoist cannot, things all of us, at least on reflection, want, namely companionship, love, approval, comfort, security and recognition.

Yet, even if our classist amoralist is not quite so securely placed, it still is clearly the case that sometimes for some such people, with certain personality structures, it is in their rational self-interest, even their own long-term self-interest, to do something that they recognize is clearly wrong (immoral). Where individuals are concerned, it is not the case that morality is always the best policy.

## XII

The argument in the previous section can be extended and strengthened. There is an important difference between the individual egoist's and the classist amoralist's (immoralist's) challenge to the hegemony of morality—a difference which makes the classist amoralist's position much stronger than the individual egoist's.

An individual egoist would have to stick to reasons which are ultimately self-serving. It is natural to think that the classist amoralist is pushed into the same position. But, while this may be the case for some classist amoralists, it need not be the case for all of them. They may within their class have reciprocal relationships which are not at all self-serving—let alone "ultimately self-serving." Indeed, if they did not have such non-self-interested reasons, they would suffer at least some of the vulnerabilities of egoists, for friendship and love would not, at least in their full senses, be available to them. It is an essential requirement of friendship that one desires the other's happiness and welfare regardless of self-serving purposes. But the classist amoralist can, at least within his class, have such full-fledged relationships. He is an immoralist not because he is an egoist; he is an immoralist because he is quite willing deliberately to treat members of the other classes as means only, as people to be manipulated and used to further either or both his individual interests or the interests of his class, regardless of the consequences to those people who are members of the dominated class. This is as fully immoral as the behavior of the individual egoist free-rider and, under many circumstances, the person so acting is much less vulnerable than the individual egoist and thus such actions are more attractive to rational persons as models for a way of acting than is the free-riding of the individual egoist.

My questions have been "Why believe that such a classist amoralist cannot be as rational as the person of sound moral principle?" The classist amoralist, in certain domains, is not willing to be impartial or even to try to be impartial and he does not disinterestedly care for all humankind or even have a respect for all of them as persons. He doesn't even aspire to be such a person of disinterested caring. He keeps his caring and respect within his own class and only very occasionally and selectively does he let it extend to some other people. And then it is an extension not based on moral grounds but on liking. He extends his moral concern to people he comes in close contact with and just happens to come to care for. He fully recognizes that in so acting he is being *morally* arbitrary but it does not at all follow that he is in other respects being arbitrary or that he must have made any logical or empirical mistake. In asking, if only to himself, "Why should I be moral?" he is in effect also asking why not be morally arbitrary? To say, engaging in a conventionalist's sulk, that "Being arbitrary is just something one ought not to do" is of no avail, for the classist amoralist is not arguing that in no sense is it a mistake to be arbitrary. He is only challenging, in the way I have already specified, the hegemony of morality over his life; he is asking, as a corollary of asking, "Why be moral?" why not be *morally* arbitrary, where my interests or the interests of my class are well served? To invoke a conventionalist's sulk and say "You can't ask that" is like saying "It makes no sense to ask 'Why keep my promises when it is not in my interests to do so?' " I can't, of course, ask either question, as a moral question, but the immoralist, classist or otherwise, is not asking it as a moral question, as something which might be morally legitimate to do. He knows bloody well it isn't and is still asking why he should do it. The immoralist, classist or otherwise, is asking for a proof, for a ground, which will show him why he must be impartial, have an attitude of disinterested caring or concern and why he must treat all people as ends and never as means only.

It is not evident that such a proof is available. There seems at least to be no proof or good reason for believing that, in not so responding to people, the immoralist (classist or otherwise) must have made some deductive or inductive mistakes or must have ignored, or not taken adequately into account, some empirical facts such that he must have fallen into error, so that it will be the case that immoralism must rest on a mistake. I have argued, in trying to establish the possibility of classist amoralism, that the claim that amoralism or immoralism must rest on a mistake is probably a just so story, a myth, that many moral philosophers tell themselves and many of us want to believe for perfectly evident reasons.

## XIII

From the moral point of view moral reasons plainly override prudential reasons for any other kind of self-interested or purely class based reasons. Again, trivially, from an exclusively self-interested point of view or a purely class based point of view, self-interested or class grounded reasons override moral reasons. It is natural, in reflecting on this to ask whether there is something called "the point of view of reason" which would show which kinds of reasons (form of life based reasons, if you will) are finally overrriding? Taken from this very general point of view, abstracted from moral or class commitments or prudential commitments, can we show which of these particular types of reason, from the very point of reason itself (assuming for the nonce there is such a point of view), are finally overriding? I have been concerned to argue that reason (human intelligence and understanding) without the collaboration of *moral sentiment* does not require that moral reasons be taken as overriding. They are, of course, taken as overriding from the moral point of view. But that is a different matter. *Morality requires commitment here not still further understanding.* Though this is not at all to say or to suggest that the moral commitment must be blind or without understanding. That is an entirely different thing. And it is well to remember that there are many things we reasonably do that we do not do for a reason. But it also is true that nothing has been unearthed called the 'point of view of reason' which would adjudicate matters here. We have not been able to show that reason requires the moral point of view or that all really rational persons, unhoodwinked by myth or ideology, not be individual egoists or classist amoralists. Reason doesn't decide here.

## XIV

The picture I have painted for you is not a pleasant one. Reflection on it depresses me. I detest, as much as any of you, such lack of moral integrity as one finds in immoralism. Indeed, reflecting on this picture and taking it to heart fortifies my own resolve to engage in social struggle, to do my utmost to do my bit to bring about a world in which genuine moral community will become possible and the class of immoralists, including of course classist amoralists, will wither away or at least dwindle with the social circumstances not being so conducive to their flourishing.

What then is my point of going on about the immoralist and "Why be moral?" The point is that there is an important philosophical lesson here, which perhaps also has human import. The point is this: pure practical reason, even with a good knowledge of the facts, will not take you to morality. You cannot reason or even bargain yourself into a moral commitment such that you will come clearly and correctly to acknowledge that there must have been some failing of reason on your part if you are not a person of good will, a person of genuine moral integrity. Underlying morality, for it to be what it purports to be, there must be a pervasive attitude of disinterested caring for all human life (and perhaps for all sentient creatures)—the smallest as well as the greatest of us. Morality has not always had that feature but it has come to have it. But it is not reason or the facts, either singly or in conjunction, which will logically compel us to come to favor such an attitude of disinterested concern or caring.